A GUIDE TO THE
NATIONAL PARKS
AND OTHER WILD PLACES OF
BRITAIN AND EUROPE

A GUIDE TO THE
NATIONAL PARKS
AND OTHER
WILD PLACES
OF BRITAIN AND EUROPE

BOB GIBBONS

NEW HOLLAND

First published in the UK in 1994 by
New Holland (Publishers) Ltd
37 Connaught Street, London W2 2AZ

ISBN 1 85368 237 3

Commissioning Editor: Charlotte Parry-Crooke
Project Manager: Ann Baggaley
Editor: Paul Barnett
Designer: Penny and Tony Mills
Cartography: Julian Baker, Peter McClure, Ken Smith
Index: Paul Barnett

Typeset by: Penny and Tony Mills
Reproduction by : J. Film Process (S) Pte Ltd, Singapore
Printed and bound in Malaysia by Times Offset Malaysia

/

The publishers and author gratefully acknowledge the assistance of all those
involved in the compilation of this book. All the photographs were taken by
Bob Gibbons with the exception of those listed below:

Natural Image: Paul Davies 220, 239b, 244, 246; Alec Harmer 76t; D. Westerhoff 222; Peter Wilson 114, 169, 170, 224, 225; Michael Woods 3.

Nature Photographers: Brinsley Burbidge 204, 234r; Robin Bush 38r, 121, 138, 240l, 247; Kevin Carlson 175, 178; Andrew Cleave 46b, 179; E.A. James 51r; Christopher K. Mylne 250; D. Osborn 50t; Paul Sterry xiv, 39r, 54r; J.M. Sutherland 214, 240r; Roger Tidman 14.

Picture Box/Natural History Photographic Agency: 78, 80, 83, 85l, 85r, 87.

Swan Photographic Agency Ltd: John Buckingham 4r, 17, 32, 34, 44, 51l, 54l, 173, 181, 202; Grant Demar 194; Arne K. Mala 6, 9, 41; A.N.H. Peach 7b, 160; Mike Weston 82; Don Withey 36, 45, 47.

Wildlife Pictures SC: M. Decleer 76b, R. & N. Henno 66, 73, 74, D. Hubaut 68.

The Danish Tourist Board: J. Sommer 23, Klaus Nielsen 28; The Irish Tourist Board – Bord Feilt Photo: Brian Lynch 56, 59, 64, 65, Pat O'Dea 63; Luxembourg National Tourist and Trade Office: 77; Polish Cultural Institute: 118; Swiss National Tourist Office: 142, 144, 147, 150; Eric & David Hosking: E. Hosking 2l; P.

Brough 2r; J. Luis G. Grande 187; Nicholas Turland 241, 242; Peter Wilson 24l, 191.

Jacket photographs Nature Photographers: E. A. James (front, tr), Geoff du Feu (back, br); Swan Photographic Agency Ltd: John Buckingham (front, centre, br; back, ml, br), Peter Perfect (back, tl).

(t = top; b = bottom; r = right; l = left; m = middle)

CONTENTS

Introduction   x
Scope   x
How to Use this Book   xi
Author's Note   xi

Iceland   1
  1. Northwest Peninsula   1
  2. Breidafjordur and
    Snaefellsnes Peninsula   1
  3. Thingvellir National Park   1
  4. Reykjavik Area   2
  5. Lake Myvatn   2
  6. Skaftafell National Park   2
  7. Westmann Islands   2

Norway   3
  1. Spitzbergen (Svalbard)   4
  2. Varanger Peninsula   4
  3. Stabbursdalen National
    Park   4
  4. Ånderdalen National Park   5
  5. Reisa National Park   5
  6. Øvre Anarjåkka National
    Park   6
  7. Øvre Pasvik National Park   6
  8. Øvre Dividal National Park   6
  9. Saltfjellet-Svartisen
    National Park   6
10. Børgefjell National Park   7
11. Runde Island   8
12. Dovrefjell National Park   8
13. Jotunheimen National Park   8
14. Rondane National Park   8
15. Hardangervidda National
    Park   9

Sweden   10
  1. Abisko National Park   10
  2. Sarek-Padjelanta Complex
    of National Parks   12
  3. Muddus National Park   12
  4. Pieljekaise National Park   13
  5. Skuleskogen National Park   13
  6. Sonfjället Group of
    National Parks   13
  7. Garphyttan National Park   13
  8. Stockholm Area   14
  9. Hornborgasjön   14
10. Tiveden National Park   14
11. Tåkern Lake   15
12. Store Mosse National Park   15
13. Öland   15
14. Gotland   16
15. Falsterbo   16

Finland   17
  1. Pallas-Ounastunturi
    National Park   18

  2. Lemmenjoki National
    Park   18
  3. Pyhätunturi National Park   19
  4. Oulanka National Park   19
  5. Pyhä-Häkki National Park   19
  6. Linnansaari National Park   19
  7. Petkeljärvi National Park   20
  8. Parikkala   21
  9. Southwestern Archipelago
    National Park (Saaristomeri) 21
10. Liesjärvi National Park   21

Denmark   23
  1. Skagen Peninsula   23
  2. Hantsholm Reserve   24
  3. Løgstør Bredning   24
  4. Nissum and Stadil Fjords   24
  5. Flyndersø and Stubbergard
    Sø   25
  6. Mols Bjerge Natural Park   25
  7. Ringkøbing Fjord   25
  8. Skallingen   26
  9. Gudenåens og Skjern Åens
    Kilder Natural Park   27
10. Samsø Island   27
11. Hindsholm Natural Park   27
12. Esrum Sø and Gribskov   27
13. Roskilde Fjord   27
14. Danish Wadden See   27
15. Draved Skov   28
16. Bornholm   28

Great Britain   31

Scotland   31
  1. Shetland Isles   31
  2. Orkney Isles   32
  3. Handa Island   33
  4. Invernaver   33
  5. Sutherland Flowe Country   34
  6. Inverpolly and Ben More
    Coigach   34
  7. Inchnadamph   35
  8. Uists and Benbecula   35
  9. Rhum and Eigg   35
10. Beinn Eighe and Torridon   36
11. Glen Affric   36
12. Cairngorms and Spey
    Valley   36
13. Sands of Forvie and
    Ythan Estuary   38
14. Dee Valley from Braemar
    to Dinnet   38
15. Caenlochan   38
16. Ben Lui   39
17. Ben Lawers   39
18. Loch Leven   39
19. Tentsmuir Point   40

20. Aberlady Bay and the
    Bass Rock   40
21. Solway Firth   40

Wales   41
22. Newborough Warren   41
23. Snowdonia National Park   41
24. Dyfi Estuary   42
25. Pembrokeshire Coast
    National Park   43
26. Cors Caron (Tregaron Bog)   44
27. Gower Peninsula   44
28. Brecon Beacons National
    Park   45

England   46
29. Farne Islands   46
30. Northumberland National
    Park   46
31. Lake District National Park   47
32. Silverdale Area   48
33. Yorkshire Dales National
    Park   48
34. Upper Teesdale   48
35. North York Moors
    National Park   49
36. Ribble Estuary Area   49
37. Peak District National Park   49
38. Gibraltar Point   49
39. North Norfolk Coast   50
40. Norfolk Broads   50
41. Wyre Forest   50
42. Wicken Fen   51
43. Ouse Washes   51
44. Minsmere and Dunwich   51
45. Ashridge Estate   52
46. Exmoor National Park   52
47. New Forest   52
48. Dartmoor National Park   53
49. Isle of Purbeck   54
50. The Lizard   54

Ireland   55
  1. Sheskinmore Lough   56
  2. Dunfanaghy Area   56
  3. Glenveagh National Park   56
  4. Inch Lough   57
  5. Banagher Forest   57
  6. Magilligan Point   57
  7. North Antrim Coast   57
  8. Rathlin Island   58
  9. Slievanorra and Breen
    Forest   58
10. Slieve League   58
11. The Mullet   59
12. Glenamoy Bog   59
13. Clare Island   59
14. Connemara National Park   59

CONTENTS

15. Aillebrack 60
16. Lough Carra 60
17. Ben Bulbin 60
18. Lower Lough Erne 60
19. Upper Lough Erne 60
20. Lough Neagh 61
21. Strangford Lough 61
22. Murlough Nature Reserve 61
23. Killard 62
24. The Burren 62
25. Rahasane Turlough 63
26. Shannon Estuary 63
27. Mongan's Bog 63
28. Wicklow Mountains National Park 63
29. North Bull Island 64
30. Dingle Peninsula 64
31. Skellig Islands 64
32. Killarney National Park 65
33. Wexford Wildfowl Reserve (Wexford Slobs) 65

Belgium 67
1. Westhoek 67
2. Zwin 68
3. Blankaart Lake 68
4. Molsbroek 68
5. Oude Landen 68
6. Kalmthoutse Heide 69
7. Zegge 69
8. Liereman Reserve 69
9. Hageven 70
10. Zwarte Beek 70
11. Teut and Tenhaagdoornheide 70
12. Maten 71
13. Mechelse Heide 71
14. Montagne St Pierre (De Sint Pietersberg) 71
15. Dinant Area 71
16. Seilles 72
17. Plateau des Tailles 72
18. Hautes Fagnes 73
19. Virelles Lake 73
20. Viroin 74
21. Bohan-Membre Natural Park 74
22. Lesse and Lomme Nature Reserve (Gouffre Natural Park) 74
23. Rouge Poncé Forest Reserve 75
24. Upper Semois Wetlands 75
25. Rouvroy 76

Luxembourg 77

Holland 79
1. Texel 79
2. Vlieland Island 80
3. Terschelling Island 80
4. Schiermonnikoog Island 80
5. Dollard 81
6. Lauwersmeer 81
7. Drentsche A 81
8. Zwanenwater 81
9. Boswachterij Schoorl 82
10. Wormerveer Polders 82
11. Oost-vaarders Plassen 83

12. De Weerribben and De Wieden 83
13. Dwingelderveld National Park 84
14. Kennemerduinen 84
15. Meijendel Dunes 84
16. Harderwijk Area 84
17. Kootwijker Zand 85
18. De Hoge Veluwe National Park 85
19. Veluwezoom National Park 86
20. Van Voorne Dunes 86
21. Rhine (Rhein) Delta 86
22. De Biesboch 87
23. Loonse en Drunense Duinen 88
24. Oisterwijkse Vennen 88
25. De Groote Peel 88
26. Savelsbos 88

Germany 91
1. Niedersächsisches Wattenmeer National Park 91
2. Hamburgisches Wattenmeer National Park 92
3. Schleswig-Holsteinisches Wattenmeer National Park 92
4. Selenter See and Surrounds 92
5. Vorpommersche Boddenlandschaft National Park 93
6. Jasmund National Park 93
7. Müritz National Park 93
8. Lüneburger Heide 94
9. Unteres Odertal National Park 95
10. Dümmer Naturpark 95
11. Steinhuder Meer Naturpark 96
12. Riddagshausen-Weddeler Teichgebiet 96
13. Märkische Schweiz Naturpark 96
14. Warmberg-Osterberg Area 96
15. Hoch Harz (High Harz) National Park 97
16. Spreewald 97
17. Meissner-Kaufunger Wald Naturpark 97
18. Schlierbachswald 98
19. Sächsische Schweiz National Park 98
20. Nordeifel Naturpark 99
21. Siebengebirge Naturpark 99
22. Heidenhäuschen Reserve 100
23. Thüringer Wald 100
24. Bayerischer Spessart Naturpark 100
25. Weisendorf Ponds 101
26. Fränkische Schweiz-Veldensteiner Naturpark 101
27. Schwäbische Alb (Schwaban Jura) 101
28. Altmühltal Naturpark 102
29. Bayerischer National Park 102
30. Hüfingen Orchid Woods 102
31. Federsee 103
32. Mindelsee 103
33. Bodensee (Lake Constance) 104
34. Wurzacher Ried Reserves 104
35. Pupplinger Au Reserve 104
36. German Karwendel Gebirge 104

37. Ismaninger Teichgebiet 105
38. Chiemsee 105
39. Chiemgauer Alpen Reserve 105
40. Berchtesgaden National Park 105

Czech Republic and Slovakia 106
1. Zahrádky Lakes (Czech Republic) 107
2. Jizerské Hory (Czech Republic) 107
3. Krkonose National Park (Czech Republic) 108
4. Súl'ovské Vrchy (Slovakia) 108
5. Malá Fatra (Slovakia) 108
6. Vel'ká Fatra Mountains (Slovakia) 109
7. Nízke Tatry National Park (Slovakia) 109
8. Vysoké Tatry (High Tatras) National Park (Slovakia) 109
9. Pieniny National Park (Slovakia) 110
10. Sivá Brada (Slovakia) 110
11. Vihorlat (Slovakia) 111
12. Sumava (Czech Republic) 111
13. Trebon Basin (Czech Republic) 112
14. Znojmo Area (Czech Republic) 112
15. Pálava and the Lednice Area (Czech Republic) 112
16. Danube Marshes (Slovakia) 113
17. Slovensky Kras (Slovakia) 113

Poland 115
1. Woliński National Park 115
2. Slowiński National Park 115
3. Biebrza and Augustów Marshes 116
4. Słońsk Reserve 116
5. Kampinoski National Park 116
6. Białowieza Forest 117
7. Karkonoski National Park 117
8. Milicz Ponds 117
9. Ojcowski National Park 118
10. Tatra National Parks 118
11. Bieszczadzki National Park 119

France 120
1. Les Sept-Îles 120
2. Cap Fréhel 122
3. Vauville Dunes 122
4. Cerisy Forest 122
5. Seine Valley Chalklands 123
6. Somme Estuary 123
7. Argonne Forest 123
8. Vosges du Nord Regional Natural Park 124
9. Gulf of Morbihan 124
10. Brière Regional Natural Park 124
11. Bourgneuf Bay 125
12. Grand-Lieu Lake 125
13. Brenne Area 125
14. Sologne 126
15. Fontainebleau Forest 126
16. Bois du Parc 126
17. Orient Forest Regional Natural Park 127

18. Valbois Ravine 127
19. Remoray Lake 127
20. Frasne Lake 128
21. Massacre Forest 128
22. Marais Poitevin Regional Natural Park 128
23. Arcachon Basin and the Teich Ornithological Park 129
24. Banc d'Arguin and Dune du Pilat 129
25. Causse Gramat 129
26. Lot Valley 130
27. Puy de Sancy Area 130
28. Chaine des Domes 130
29. St Flour Area 131
30. Pilat Natural Regional Park 131
31. Dombes Area 131
32. Vercors Regional Natural Park 131
33. Écrins National Park 132
34. Annecy Lake 132
35. Haute-Savoie Mountains 133
36. Vanoise National Park 133
37. Queyras Regional Natural Park 133
38. L'Étang Noir 134
39. Parc National des Pyrénées Occidentales 135
40. Forest of Grésigne 136
41. Aveyron Gorges 136
42. Millau Causses 136
43. Gorges du Tarn 136
44. Col de Montmirat Area 136
45. Cévennes National Park 136
46. Olette Reserves 137
47. Fanges Forest 137
48. La Massane Forest 137
49. Ardèche Gorges 137
50. Camargue 137
51. Crau Plain 138
52. Les Alpilles 138
53. Luberon Natural Regional Park 138
54. Port-Cros National Park 138
55. Massif des Maures 139
56. Mercantour National Park 139

Corsica (Corse) **139**
57. Désert des Agriates 139
58. Lake Biguglia 140
59. Asco Valley 140
60. Spelunca Gorge and Forest of Aitone 140
61. Scandola Nature Reserve 141
62. Vizzavona Forest and Monte d'Oro 141
63. Bonifacio Area 141

Switzerland **143**
1. Doubs Valley 143
2. Chasseral 143
3. Belchen-Passwang Region 144
4. Reuss Valley and Lake Baldegg 144
5. Lake Klingnau 144
6. Untersee 145
7. Joux Valley Area 145
8. Creux-du-Van and Areuse Gorges 145
9. Lake Neuchâtel 146

10. Hagleren-Glaubenberg Area 146
11. Lake Zug (Zugersee) 146
12. Rothenthurm Peatlands 146
13. Silberen and the Hölloch Cave 147
14. Kaltbrunner Riet Reserve 147
15. Murg Valley (Murgtal) 147
16. Rhône Delta, Lake Geneva (Lac Léman) 147
17. Vanil-Noir 147
18. La Pierreuse 148
19. Derborence 148
20. Gelten-Iffigen 148
21. Pfynwald/Finges Forest 149
22. Valais: Matterhorn (Cervin)/Monte Rosa Area 149
23. Grindelwald-Bernese Oberland Area 149
24. Binntal, Haut-Valais 150
25. Bavona Valley 150
26. Tecino (Tessin) Delta, Lake Maggiore 150
27. Piora 151
28. Monte San Giorgio 151
29. Massif de la Bernina, Haute-Engadine 152
30. The Swiss National Park 152

Austria **153**
1. Bangser Ried Nature Reserve 154
2. Rhine (Rhein) Delta, Bodensee (Lake Constance) 154
3. Karwendel Nature Reserve 155
4. Kaisergebirge (Emperor Mountains) 155
5. Otztaler Alps 155
6. Hohe Tauern National Park 156
7. Lienz Dolomites 156
8. River Inn around Braunau 157
9. Purgschachen Moor 157
10. Steinernes Meer Area 157
11. Niedere Tauern Mountains 157
12. Nockberge National Park 158
13. Karawanken Mountains 158
14. Waldviertel Area 159
15. Wildalpen-Rothwald Area 159
16. Hagensdorf Area 159
17. Lainzer Tiergarten and the Wienerwald 159
18. Marchauen Reserve 160
19. Neusiedler See 160
20. Seewinkel Area 160
21. Hohe Wand 161
22. Hundsheimer Berg 161

Hungary **162**
1. Fertö tói (Neusiedler See) 163
2. Köszeg Hills 163
3. Hanság 163
4. Gerecse Hills 163
5. Vertes Hills 164
6. Kis-Balaton Reserve 164
7. Tihanyi Peninsula and Lake Balaton 164
8. Lake Velence (Velencei-to) 164
9. Pilis and Visegrád Hills 165
10. Kiskunság National Park 165

11. Ocsa Landscape-Protection Area 166
12. Gemenc Area 166
13. Tisza Valley North of Szeged 166
14. Kardoskut Fehér-tó 167
15. Būkk National Park 167
16. Aggtelek-Karst National Park 168
17. Hortobágyi National Park 168
18. Dévaványa Bustard Reserve 169
19. Szatmár-Bereg Plain 169

Romania **170**
1. Satchinez Reserve 170
2. Retezat National Park 170
3. Eastern Carpathians 171
4. Danube Delta 171

Portugal **173**
1. Peneda-Gerês National Park 174
2. Montesinho Natural Park 175
3. Alvao Natural Park 175
4. Upper Rio Douro 175
5. Berlenga Islands 176
6. Paúl de Arzila 176
7. The Upper Rio Tejo 176
8. The Serras de Aire and Candeeiros Natural Park 176
9. Aveiro Estuary 176
10. Serra da Estrela Natural Park 177
11. Paúl do Boquilobo 177
12. Tejo Estuary 178
13. Serra de Arrábida Natural Park 178
14. Alentejo Plains 178
15. Sado Estuary 179
16. Santo André Lagoon 179
17. Serra de Monchique 179
18. Cabo de San Vicente and Ponta de Sagres 179
19. Ria Formosa Natural Park 180
20. Burgau-Lagos Area 180
21. Castro Marim Reserve 181

The Azores (Açores) **181**
22. Pico da Vara (São Miguel) 181
23. Coast of Flores 181
24. Monte Brasil (Terceira) 181
25. Montanha da Ilha do Pico 181
26. Ilhéu do Topo 181

Spain **183**
1. Los Ancares Leoneses National Reserve 183
2. Degaña and Muniellos Reserves 184
3. National Reserve of Somiedo 184
4. National Reserve of Saja 184
5. Covadonga National Park 185
6. Picos de Europa 185
7. Monte Goramakil 186
8. Sierra de Leyre 186
9. Islas Cíes Natural Park 186
10. Sierras de La Demanda and de Urbion 186

CONTENTS

11. Dehesa del Moncayo
    Natural Park 187
12. Sierra de La Peña 187
13. Mediana-Belchite Steppe
    Country 188
14. Puerto (Col) de Somport 188
15. Viñamala National
    Reserve 188
16. Ordesa National Park 188
17. Los Circos National
    Reserve 189
18. Benasque National Reserve 189
19. Val de Aran 189
20. Aigües-Tortes y Estany
    de Sant Maurici 190
21. Cadí-Moixeroi Natural Park 190
22. Volcanic Zone of Garrotxa
    Natural Park 190
23. Embalse de San Jose 190
24. Villafáfila Area 190
25. Montejo de la Vega 191
26. Arribes del Duero 191
27. Sierra de Guadarrama 191
28. Sonsaz National Reserve 192
29. Sierra de Gredos 192
30. Laguna de Gallocanta 192
31. Natural Park of Alto Tajo 192
32. National Reserve of Los
    Montes Universales 193
33. Aiguamolls de l'Emporda
    Natural Park 193
34. Sierra de Montserrat 193
35. Montseny Natural Park 193
36. Ebro Delta 194
37. Monfragüe Natural Park 194
38. Sierra de La Peña
    de Francia 195
39. Serranía de Cuenca 195
40. Trujillo Area 195
41. Tablas de Daimiel
    National Park 196
42. Natural Park of Las
    Lagunas de Ruidera 196
43. La Serena 197
44. Salinas de Santa Pola 197
45. Sierra de Cazorla y Segura 197
46. National Reserve of Sierra
    Espuña 197
47. Las Marismas del Odiel 197
48. Coto Doñana National
    Park 198
49. Córdoba Lagunas 198
50. Sierra de Grazalema Natural
    Park 199
51. Ronda Gorge 199
52. Teba Gorge 199
53. Lago de la Fuente de Piedra 199
54. Torcal de Antequera 200
55. Sierra Nevada 200
56. Tabernas Badlands 200
57. Cádiz Bay 201
58. Laguna de Medina 201
59. Punta Entinas-Sabinar and
    Roquetas de Mar 201
60. Cabo de Gata 201
61. Gibraltar 202

The Balearic Islands **202**
62. Northwest Mountains
    (Mallorca) 202

63. Puerto de Pollença Area
    (Mallorca) 202
64. Albufera Marsh Nature
    Reserve (Mallorca) 203
65. Salinas de Levante Area
    (Mallorca) 203
66. Isla de Cabrera 203
67. Menorca 203
68. Ibiza 204

The Canary Islands **204**
69. Tenerife 204
70. National Park of the
    Caldera de Taburiente (La
    Palma) 204
71. Garajonay National Park
    (Gomera) 204
72. Lanzarote 204
73. Fuerteventura 204

Andorra **205**

Italy **207**
 1. Gran Paradiso National
    Park 207
 2. Alpe Veglia 208
 3. Stelvio National Park 208
 4. Adamello-Brenta Natural
    Park 209
 5. Natural Park of Panaveggio-
    Pale di San Martino 209
 6. Cortina Dolomites 209
 7. Fusine Natural Park 210
 8. Mouth of the River
    Isonzo/Foci dell'Isonzo 210
 9. Argentera Natural Park 210
10. Mezzola Lake 211
11. Monte di Portofino
    Natural Park 211
12. Lake Superiore di Mantova 211
13. Gulf of Venice (Laguna di
    Venezia) 211
14. Po Delta 211
15. Lake Massaciuccoli and
    Surrounds 212
16. Bolgheri Wildlife Refuge 212
17. Valle del Farma 212
18. Maremma Natural Park 213
19. Orbetello and Monte
    Argentario 213
20. Vico Lake Nature Reserve 213
21. Abruzzo National Park 214
22. Lake Varano and Lake
    Lésina 214
23. Gargano Peninsula and
    Forest of Umbra 214
24. Salina di Margherita di
    Savoia 215
25. Circeo National Park 215
26. Vesuvius 215
27. Capri 216
28. Lattari Peninsula 216
29. Le Cesine 216
30. Monte Pollino Regional
    Park 217
31. Calabria National Park 217

Sardinia **217**
32. Maddalena Archipelago 217

33. Monte Albo Region 217
34. Gennargentu 218
35. Sinis Peninsula and Gulf
    of Oristano 218
36. Giara de Gésturi 219
37. San Pietro Island 219
38. Cagliari Wetlands 219

Sicily **219**
39. Stagnonie di Marsala 219
40. Zingaro 220
41. Madonie 220
42. Nebrodi Mountains 221
43. Etna 221
44. Straits of Messina, Monte
    Peloritani 221
45. Isole Eólie o Lipari 221
46. Pantani di Capo Passero 221

Yugoslavia **222**
 1. Triglav National Park
    (Slovenia) 222
 2. Postojna Caves (Slovenia) 222
 3. Risnjak National Park
    (Croatia) 222
 4. Plitvice National Park
    (Croatia) 223
 5. Fruška Gora National
    Park (Serbia) 223
 6. Djerdap National Park
    (Serbia) 223
 7. Paklenica National Park
    (Croatia) 223
 8. Kornati National Park
    (Croatia) 223
 9. Krka National Park
    (Croatia) 223
10. Mljet National Park
    (Bosnia) 223
11. Sutjeska National Park
    (Bosnia) 223
12. Durmitor National Park
    (Montenegro) 223
13. Biogradska Gora National
    Park (Montenegro) 224
14. Lovćen National
    Park (Montenegro) 224
15. Skadarsko Jezero National
    Park (Montenegro) 224
16. Mavrovo National Park
    (Macedonia) 224
17. Galičica National Park
    (Macedonia) 224
18. Pelister National Park
    (Macedonia) 224

Bulgaria **225**
 1. Rusenski Lom National
    Park 225
 2. Sreburna Reserve 225
 3. Vitosa National Park 225
 4. Rila Mountains 225
 5. Pirin (Vikhren) National
    Park 226

Albania **227**
 1. Lake Shkodra (Skadarsko
    Jezero) 227
 2. Lake Ohrid (Ohridsko
    Jezero) 227

3. Lake Prespa (Prespansko Jezero) 227
4. Thethi National Park 227
5. Lura National Park 227
6. Dajtit National Park 227
7. Divjaka National Park 227
8. Tomorri National Park 227
9. Llogara National Park 227

Greece **229**
1. Préspa National Park 230
2. Kastoría Lake and Adjacent Lakes 230
3. Aliákmon Delta 230
4. Lake Kerkini 231
5. Cholomon Mountains and Chalcidice (Khalkidhikí) 231
6. Lake Kóronia and Lake Vólvi 231
7. Lake Vistónis and Pórto Lágo 232
8. Évros Delta 232
9. Pindos (Píndhos) Mountains 1: Grammos-Smólikas Area 232
10. Pindos (Píndhos) Mountains 2: Vikos-Aóos National Park 233
11. Pindos (Píndhos) Mountains 3: Pindos National Park and Katáras Pass Area 233
12. Lake Pamvótis (Lake Ioánnina) 233
13. Metéora 234
14. Mount Olympus (Olimbos) National Park 234

15. Gulf of Árta (Amvrakikós Kólpos) 235
16. Missolonghi (Mesolóngion) Marshes 235
17. Mount Oeti National Park (Iti Óros) 236
18. Mount Parnassus (Parnassós) National Park 236
19. Delphi 236
20. Párnitha National Park 237
21. Marathón Marshes 237
22. Soúnion National Park 237
23. Kalogria Area 238
24. Mount Helmos and Panahaiko Mountains 238
25. Epidaurus (Epídhavros) 238
26. Mystra and the Taígetos (Taíyetos) Mountains 238
27. Máni Peninsula 239

The Islands **240**
28. Corfu (Kérkira) 240
29. Cephalonia (Kefallinía; Aenos) National Park 240
30. Zákinthos 240
31. Lésvos (Lesbos; Mylíni) 241
32. Rhodes (Ródhos) 241

Crete (K.rití) **241**
33. Omalós and Lévka Óri 241
34. Samaria Gorge 242
35. Phaestos (Phaistos) 242
36. Mount Jouktas 243
37. Lato and Sitía 243

Turkey **244**
1. Samsun Daği (Dilek Yarimadasi) 245
2. Manyas-Kuş Cenneti National Park 245
3. Istanbul and Surrounds 245
4. Apolyant 246
5. Uludağ 246
6. Dalyan 246

Malta **248**
1. Ghadira Nature Reserve 248
2. Dingli Cliffs 249
3. Gozo 249
4. Filfla Islet 249

Cyprus **251**
1. Akamas Peninsula 251
2. Lara 252
3. Paphos Area 252
4. Stavros Tis Psokhas 252
5. Akrotiri Salt Lake 253
6. High Troödos 253
7. Troödos Foothills 253
8. Larnaca Salt Lake 254
9. Kyrenia Mountains (Pentadhaktylos) 254
10. Karpas Peninsula 254

Selective Glossary 255
Recommended Reading 256
Index of Places 257
Index of Species 263

INTRODUCTION

Europe has a wonderful variety of scenery, habitats and wildlife, from Arctic tundra and ice to Mediterranean semi-desert. Politically, Europe is divided into about 30 nations, but no one country has a monopoly on all there is to see. The Mediterranean areas, for example, may have a superbly rich flora, far more reptiles than northern Europe, and a very different range of birds, yet there is nothing there that can quite match the spectacle of hundreds of thousands of seabirds clustered on dramatic northern rock-pinnacles, or Shags, Fulmars and Kittiwakes so tame that you can walk among them without disturbing them. And travel can introduce you not only to unfamiliar species but to new habitats and new combinations, while there is also that curious way in which having seen the floras and faunas of other countries can increase your pleasure in the familiar plants and animals of home. Aside from natural history, there is the joy of just walking among and soaking up the terrain of foreign parts – from the fjords of Scandinavia to the badlands of Spain, and from the soft rolling hills of Ireland to the spectacular peaks of the Alps.

Another good reason to travel between countries is that you can move from one season to another; for example, in March northern Europeans can leave their winter-bound homes to find masses of flowers and breeding birds in the far south, where spring is well advanced; conversely, you can escape the harsh heat and browned hills of a Mediterranean August and go northwards into the mountains of central Europe, where the flowers will be just at their best. If you include the Atlantic islands of Madeira, the Azores (Açores) and the Canaries – as this book does – you can enjoy spring or summer somewhere in Europe at almost any time of year.

In the past, largely because of political subdivisions, travel within Europe has been much more inhibited than in a comparable area of, for example, the United States. Today, though cultural and linguistic divisions remain, it has become much easier. Air transportation has reduced the 'distances' between countries to at most a few hours, and improved road networks have made almost anywhere in Europe reachable by car. Since 1992 trade and customs barriers between the member states of the ever-growing European Community have been falling, while the countries of Eastern Europe are steadily improving their facilities for visitors and clearing away most of their frustrating bureaucracy. Numerous specialist tour operators offer natural-history trips to different parts of Europe; their advertisements can be found in natural-history and birdwatching magazines.

Yet, for all this, it can be surprisingly difficult to find out much about your chosen destination in terms of where and when to see its natural history. Tourist offices hold information on National Parks, and plenty of material on castles, theme parks and hotels, but virtually nothing on where to go in the countryside to see nature. That is why this book has been written.

Scope

The geographical area covered is what is generally regarded as the whole of Europe: we include western Mediterranean Turkey, easily accessible from Europe, but exclude European 'Russia', which is not; outlying island groups that are politically part of Europe are also included.

It is a sad reflection on the great changes going on in Europe's countryside that one has to pick out specific sites to visit; 30 years ago a book like this would hardly have been needed, as wildlife was so much more prevalent and areas of nature-free agricultural land did not exist on today's gargantuan scale. Thus the number of sites selected in a country does not necessarily reflect the amount there is to be seen there. The wilder, less spoilt countries, particularly the northern Scandinavian lands and parts of the Alps, are more difficult to categorize into defined 'sites' surrounded by areas of lower interest: often there is wildlife to be seen almost everywhere. For such regions the sites chosen are often merely those that are protected in some way – though it is frequently the case that they also have a higher-than-average concentration of nature. In general, however, the sites have been selected for the breadth of their interest and the range of their habitats; a number are of especial interest to birdwatchers. Almost without exception, they are pleasant places to visit whatever your enthusiasms, and many offer magnificent scenery and walks.

The coverage is as comprehensive as possible. Political and other factors qualify this statement. Some areas are well studied; others are barely known; still others, especially in the re-forming nations of Eastern Europe, are changing even as I write. I have preferred to give partial information about a site, when that is all that is known, rather than omit the site altogether; future editions will increase the comprehensiveness of coverage as more sites are opened up to naturalists from the West.

How to Use this Book

The countries of Europe are ordered geographically, starting from the northwestern corner and moving southwards in west-east bands.

The only anomalies are the British Isles – treated geographically, as Ireland and Great Britain, rather than politically, as Eire and the United Kingdom – and the former Yugoslavia, whose fate is currently uncertain. The latter region is treated fairly summarily, and on the basis of pre-conflict knowledge. It is to be hoped – for all reasons – that the civil war will be resolved soon, and that future editions of this book can look again at a series of securely protected natural sites in this beautiful part of the world.

For each country there is an initial map to show where the sites lie, with numbers cross-referring to their text entries; this makes route-planning or the finding of a specific site a relatively quick task. In addition, for most sites there is an individual map showing boundaries, access points and other useful information; place-names are given in their language of origin – i.e., in the form that appears on local road-signs and maps. The textual discussion of the site is normally prefaced by summarized information concerning location, access and timing:

Location: Sites are located with reference to towns, roads and natural features. In fact, since very few sites are small, location is not usually a problem: the maps recommended on page 256 usually mark such things as National Parks, landscape-protection areas and even many nature reserves. To avoid potential confusion over alternative routes, distances are given as the crow flies.

Access: Under this heading are details of the roads leading to the site plus other relevant information, notably about any restrictions on travel into the area.

Timing: The best time to visit the site. The information is intended as guidance, not as an indication that there is nothing of interest for the rest of the year! That said, some sites cannot be reached at all in winter, and access to a few sites is prohibited at certain times of year. Passage times are those periods of the year when large numbers of birds are migrating through – usually March-May and September-November, depending on the species and the area. Breeding seasons for birds are normally roughly March-June, rather later further north.

The main discussion summarizes the character and habitats of the site, with an indication of its extent and a selection of species of interest. Often this has been a matter of choosing the finest pearls from among a rich treasure: the best sites may have well over 100 different breeding birds and over 1000 species of plants, and that is not to mention the insects and other groups. In such instances the descriptions can only whet the appetite and give an indication of the *type* of thing you will find there.

Species are normally identified by their common names, with taxonomic names given only for purposes of clarification or if there is in fact no well recognized common name. The separate Index of Species (see page 263) will guide you to sites where particular plants or animals of interest to you are especially prevalent. Do note, however, that – although some of the photographs may assist you in identifying species – this book is not an identification guide. A selection of such guides is given on pages 256.

SYMBOLS AND CONVENTIONS

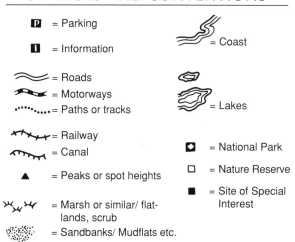

P = Parking	= Coast
i = Information	
= Roads	= Lakes
= Motorways	
= Paths or tracks	
= Railway	▣ = National Park
= Canal	▢ = Nature Reserve
▲ = Peaks or spot heights	■ = Site of Special Interest
= Marsh or similar/ flat-lands, scrub	
= Sandbanks/ Mudflats etc.	

AUTHOR'S NOTE

A book like this could not have been written in isolation. I have depended heavily on many sources and on many other people. The information given combines personal records, reports from correspondents and friends, and published accounts. I am particularly grateful to Paul Davies, not only for his invaluable contributions on Cyprus, Crete, Turkey and Sicily but also for helpful discussions on other areas and issues; and to CU Research Services for assistance with much of the original research. Bob Press kindly contributed the information on Madeira. I am grateful to the conservation and wildlife organizations in each country for their help and generosity in providing information on reserves. Any errors are, of course, entirely my responsibility.

I welcome any comments. These should be addressed to me personally, c/o the publishers.

I hope this book helps you gain as much pleasure from the wonderful natural history of Europe as I have had. Wherever you visit, please treat both the nature and the local people with respect.

Bob Gibbons, January 1994

Barents Sea

FINLAND

RUSSIA

AND

ND

VAKIA

GARY

ROMANIA

SLAVIA

BULGARIA

Black Sea

LBANIA

TURKEY

GREECE

CYPRUS

Kiriti (Crete)

Caspian Sea

| 0 | 200 | 400 | 600 | 800 | km |
| 0 | 100 | 200 | 300 | 400 | 500 | ml |

ICELAND

Well west of any major European country, and closer to Greenland than to Europe as a whole, Iceland is a large (103,000 sq km) and remote island with a population of only 250,000.

It is highly volcanic, and its scenery and, to some extent, its wildlife reflect this. Due to its isolation, it has relatively few species for its area; nor does it have many endemics, largely because of the cold climate and the recent history of complete glaciation. There are 520 species of flowering plants, most of which are found elsewhere in northern Europe, though a few—such as the lovely River Beauty—are shared instead with North America. Non-flowering plants are more abundant, and there are good lichens. Iceland is likely to prove disappointing to anyone with an interest in the more popular insect groups, as there are no regular dragonflies and the only butterflies are migrants. There are no reptiles or amphibia, and the range of mammals is limited to only 15 species, of which virtually all, including the commonly seen Reindeer and Mink, are introductions; Arctic Fox is a genuine native.

The birds are Iceland's great attraction. Although there are only just over 70 breeding species, those are abundant here and often rare elsewhere in Europe. Species like Gyrfalcon, White-tailed Eagle, Barrow's Goldeneye, Harlequin and American Wigeon are either essentially North American or, though

OPPOSITE PAGE: *Cliffs colonized by seabirds drop steeply into the huge bay of Breidafjordur.*

European, very uncommon there. Places like Myvatn, where tens of thousands of ducks of 15 different species breed, are unique in Europe.

Iceland is the prime example of the fact that it is not necessary to have a great abundance and diversity of species to make an area interesting. It is an exceptional place for the ornithologist, botanist or indeed any general naturalist to visit. Conservation is well organized. There are three National Parks and a number of nature reserves, plus many areas identified as of special interest. In addition, various individual species are protected.

As Iceland's road network is so limited, detailed location and access instructions are omitted from the text descriptions of the sites.

1. Northwest Peninsula

This large, remote piece of land includes the Hornstrandir Landscape Reserve. Beyond Isafjrdhur access is only by boat or on foot; a serious visit needs expedition planning, with food and good tents. The remoteness makes this one of the last retreats for threatened species like Gyrfalcon and White-tailed Eagle, and Arctic Fox is still relatively common. There are some superb high cliffs, where you can find most of the seabirds and other birds you would expect in wild Iceland. The rich flora is generally more visible in the more isolated areas, where there is less grazing.

2. Breidafjordur and Snaefellsnes Peninsula

The bay, a huge area of shallow sea dotted by islands, supports both Grey and Common Seals, with Hooded and Ringed Seals as visitors. Breeding birds are abundant, especially ducks (such as Eiders), waders, divers and others including Snow Bunting and terns. Some of the islands are inhabited and may be visited using locally hired boats.

The **Snaefellsnes Peninsula**, to the south of the bay, has a very substantial population of White-tailed Eagle and other wild-country birds.

3. Thingvellir National Park

This 4200ha area northwest of Reykjavik contains part of Iceland's largest lake, Thingvallavatn, with grasslands around it. Birds breeding here include various ducks, Great Northern Diver, Arctic Tern and Ptarmigan. There are Char in the lake.

4. Reykjavik Area

A good start to your trip; you may want to spend some time here. Lake Tjornin has breeding Arctic Tern and other birds, and good numbers of birds on passage. The coast near the golf course has good breeding and passage birds, plus some flowers. The botanic garden has a fine collection of labelled flowers.

5. Lake Myvatn

This exceptional place is probably the best single bird-watching area in Iceland; it comprises the island's fourth largest lake together with the River Laxa and the surrounding volcanic countryside. There are an estimated 50,000 breeding pairs of 15 duck species, including all the Icelandic rarities such as Harlequin and Long-tailed Ducks and Barrow's Goldeneye, together with other birds such as Great Northern Diver, Slavonian Grebe, Red-necked Phalarope, Gyrfalcon, Skua, Redwing and Snow Bunting. The rich flora includes many Iceland specialities, and this is a good area for coloured sulphur pools. The best starting point is the bridge over the Laxa near where it enters the lake.

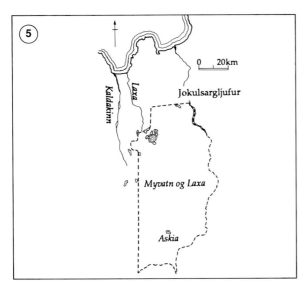

Lake Myvatn is probably the best birdwatching area in Iceland.

To the north lies **Jokulsargljufur National Park**, which includes a spectacular gorge and associated scenery. It, too, is a good area for birds and flowers.

6. Skaftafell National Park

50,000ha of wild glacial country, including the country's largest icecap and a vast sand-plain. As well as the impressive geological and landscape features, there are over 200 species of flowering plants. Breeding birds are abundant, among them Red-necked Phalarope, Red-throated Diver, Great and Arctic Skuas, Redwing, Ptarmigan and the Iceland Wren (a subspecies of Common Wren).

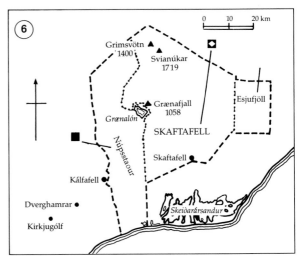

Wild glacial country in Skaftafell National Park.

7. Westmann Islands

This group, just off the mainland's southern tip, includes some of the finest seabird colonies in Europe. Heimaey, the largest and only inhabited island, is accessible by air or, from Thorlakshofn, by ferry. Also in the group is Surtsey, the volcanic island that emerged from the sea in 1963. Birds breeding here—in great abundance—include Puffin, Razorbill, three Guillemots, Gannet, Manx Shearwater, Storm and Leach's Petrels, Glaucous Gull and Great Skua.

NORWAY

Norway is a largish country, 323,900 sq km in area (excluding Spitzbergen) and covering a vast latitude range, extending far into the Arctic. Its highly convoluted coastline is very long and largely unspoilt. The low population— just over 4 million—means that pressure on land is low, and there are huge areas of unpopulated and frequently uncultivated wilderness. Much of the country is mountainous, with peaks rising to 2469m (Galdhøppiggen). The high altitudes give rise to a greatly extended area of tundra and increase the country's Arctic 'feel'.

Norway has a strong conservation policy. There are many National Parks—moves are afoot to declare several more—as well as reserves covering smaller areas. Although Norway is a marvellous country for the naturalist, the weather can be unpredictable and the summer is short; visits to northern regions after about the summer solstice are likely to be plagued by mosquitoes.

Glacier at the head of the Smeerenburg Fjord, Spitzbergen, mirrored in the still waters.

Almost anywhere in Norway has something of interest to the naturalist. Picked out below are National Parks and a few other areas of special interest; generally speaking they represent the greatest concentrations of species.

1. Spitzbergen (Svalbard)

Location: Off the far north coast of Norway, far into the Arctic.
Access: A long journey by air or, from Tromsø, by boat.
Timing: May–October.

A visit to Spitzbergen is a difficult and unpredictable business, but potentially highly rewarding. The islands of the remote archipelago offer the only real Arctic experience in Europe. They cover about 62,000 sq km, of which about half is protected within three National Parks, three nature reserves, fifteen bird sanctuaries and three plant reserves. The human population is only about 3000, so there are vast tracts of wild country. Of particular interest among the many Arctic specialities are Polar Bear, Walrus, Muskox, Reindeer, Arctic Fox and breeding birds including King Eider, Brent Goose, Phalarope, Brünnich's Guillemot, Little Auk and Ivory Gull. Although the flora is not rich, with only about 170 species, many of these are rare or unknown in the rest of Europe.

2. Varanger Peninsula

Location: The far northeastern tip of Norway (and of mainland Europe), northeast of Tana Bro.
Access: Via the E6, then the 98 and 890; or by air to Kirkenes, then by bus. Access on foot is generally unrestricted.
Timing: Late May to early August, best in June.

The Varanger Peninsula offers the closest experience to an Arctic or Siberian experience on mainland Europe. It is a thinly populated area of tundra with hills and snowfields, lakes and bogs, together with coastal cliffs. Breeding birds are abundant and varied—Phalarope, Temminck's Stint, Purple Sandpiper, Turnstone, Whimbrel, Little Stint, White-billed Diver, Steller's Eider, King Eider, Brünnich's Guillemot, Red-throated Pipit, Snow Bunting, Arctic Redpoll and many widespread northern species. The flowers are interesting, too, with plentiful Lapland Rhododendron, Diapensia, Cassiope and many other species. The mammals include Reindeer and Mountain Hare.

Altogether, this is a superb place for nature-watching— especially for birds. Note, though, that the local people are very bird-conscious and are constantly on the look-out, so you run the risk of being taken for an egg-thief! The mosquitoes become bad towards the latter part of the recommended period.

Varanger Peninsula, a superb area for birdwatchers.

3. Stabbursdalen National Park

Location: Southeast of Hammerfest, northwest of Lakselv, just west of Stabburselvbru.
Access: Via the E6 along Porsanger Fjord to Stabbursnes; here there is an information centre from which the park, 5km to the west, is accessible on foot.
Timing: May-September.

This National Park covers 9800ha of wild Arctic

The remote and austere Spitzbergen archipelago.

scenery, with some tundra, lakes, gravelly river plains and, remarkably, an area of forest—'remarkably' because the park lies north of 70°N, where trees do not normally grow. Mainly of pine with some birch, this is the most northerly forest in the world, and some of its trees are estimated to be over 500 years old. The bird-life is interesting; breeding species include Goosander, Goldeneye, Brambling and Little Bunting. Both Reindeer and Elk can be seen, and the Stabburs is a noted Salmon river. The flora is not exceptional (233 species), but includes a few rarities like the Jacob's Ladder *Polemonium acutiflorum*, a rare relative of the commoner *P. caeruleum*.

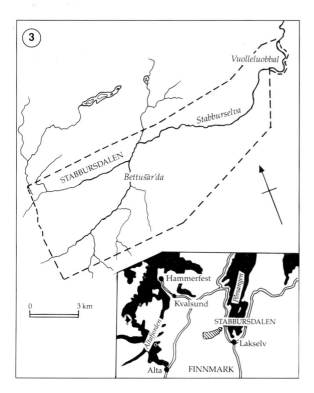

4. Ånderdalen National Park

Location: On the island of Senja, south of Tromsø, just west of Gammelsaeter.
Access: Via road 06 (E6), followed by minor roads to Storjord and Gammelsaeter; then on foot by marked trails.
Timing: May-October.

6900ha of wild mountainous scenery—there are no permanent human habitations—rising to about 700m on the park's borders. Habitats include woodland, tundra, lakes, bog and cliffs. Birds breeding here include White-tailed and Golden Eagles, Whooper Swan, Raven and Brambling; there are also Elk and herds of domesticated Reindeer. The woodlands are mainly pine and birch, and have a flora which

includes Ghost and Coral-root Orchids. Diapensia and Creeping Azalea abound on the tundra.

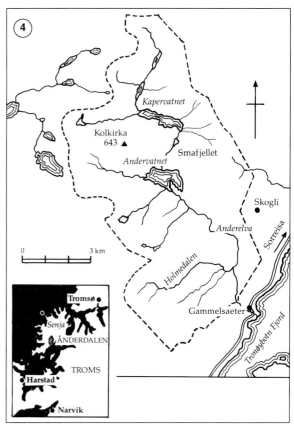

5. Reisa National Park

Location: On the Finnish border due west of Kautokeino.
Access: By minor road running inland from Storslett (on the E6), then on forestry tracks as far as Stelva, where there is access on foot or by boat.
Timing: May-October.

This National Park is a beautiful wild area of countryside covering 80,000ha; there is a further 8100ha of protected landscape immediately northeast. Mountains reach over 1350m, and there are gorges, tundra, lakes, bogs and woodland, as well as some good walking tracks. The flora is prolific—84 per cent of Scandinavia's mountain plants are recorded here. The forests are mainly of birch and Dwarf Birch, plus some pine. Some of the bogs are structurally interesting, and their rich flora includes Yellow Marsh Saxifrage and a rare Cotton-grass, *Eriophorum russeolum*. The mammals are of special interest; among them are Elk, Brown Bear, Wolverine, Arctic Fox, Lynx and Pine Marten. Breeding birds include Willow Grouse, Ptarmigan, Golden Eagle, Rough-legged Buzzard, Whooper Swan and Lesser White-fronted Goose.

6. Øvre Anarjåkka National Park

Location: Extremely remote, on the Finnish border due south of Karasjok and Karigasniemi.
Access: By minor roads southward from either of the above towns, then on foot or, if conditions permit, by boat.
Timing: May–September.

A remote, wild area (140,000ha) of undulating tundra and woodland. About half is forested; the remainder, typically of this part of Scandinavia, is pocked by hundreds of small lakes. The forest is mainly birch with some pine mixed in. The flora is not exceptional, with so far about 250 species having been recorded, but among these is the impressive Moor-king; there are also good lichens. Mammals of interest include Norway Lemming, Wolverine, Ruddy Vole, Mountain Hare, Elk, Reindeer and occasional Wolf. Rough-legged Buzzard, Hawk Owl, Capercaillie, Willow Grouse, Bewick's Swan, Jack Snipe, Spotted Redshank and others breed here.

7. Øvre Pasvik National Park

Location: At the southern end of the 'peninsula' that projects between Finland and Russia, near the end of road 885.
Access: Via road 885 to Vaggatem, then southwest along a forestry road; open on foot from there.
Timing: May–September.

This remote area of virgin forest and tundra covers 6700ha on the edge of the Siberian taiga. There is a resident population of Brown Bear; among the breeding birds are Great Grey Owl, Waxwing and Whooper Swan. The flora includes the attractive shrub Labrador Tea as well as *Ranunculus lapponicus*, *Moehringia lateriflora*, Snowy Cinquefoil and other northeastern species.

Winter vegetation transformed by sparkling ice in Øvre Pasvik National Park.

8. Øvre Dividal National Park

Location: On the Swedish border southeast of Tromsø, about 50km southeast from Overbygd.
Access: By minor road from Holt on road 87 as far as Frihetsli, then on by forest track and finally on foot via marked paths. There are some self-catering cabins.
Timing: May–September.

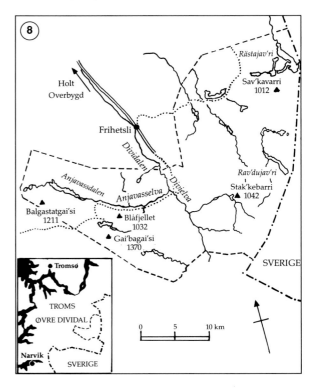

A large area (74,300ha) of wild mountainous country including peaks up to 1633m (Kistefjell) on the border. The habitats include extensive tundra—with numerous lakes, streams and bogs—and, over about 10 per cent of the area, woodland, mainly birch (*Betula odorata*) with some pine and alder. The 315 recorded flowering species include Lapland Rhododendron, Arctic Mouse-ear Chickweed, Ostrich Fern and Glacier Crowfoot. Among the breeding birds are Hawk and Tengmalm's Owls, Rough-legged Buzzard, Willow Grouse, Brambling, Redwing and many others. Reindeer, Elk, Wolf, Bear and Lynx are all in evidence.

9. Saltfjellet-Svartisen National Park

Location: Due north of Mo i Rana, stretching from road E6 to the coastal fjords.
Access: Directly from the E6, which borders the park on the east side, or via minor roads from the south. Alternatively, by boat from Holand, then on road 17 to the glacier.
Timing: May–September.

A superbly varied and unspoilt area (184,000ha)

Dwarf Cornel in fruit on a shingle beach at Saltfjellet-Svartisen.

Fox and Reindeer, with Wolf and Bear visiting occasionally. Phalarope, Bluethroat, Bean Goose, Long-tailed Duck, Rough-legged Buzzard, Osprey, Snowy Owl and many other birds breed. The flora is relatively poor: about 300 species have been recorded, but large areas are dominated by just a few; this is a good region, though, for Arctic lichens.

The **Gressåmoen National Park**, about 100km south (east of Snåsa on the E6), has spruce forest amid mountainous country. It offers a good range of mammals and birds.

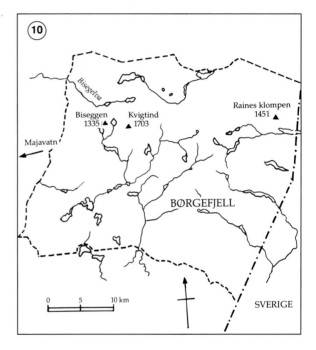

stretching from the fjords of the west coast up to peaks of over 1500m near the Swedish border, this park includes the great glacier of Svartisen (37,000ha). In the Glomdalen Valley are areas of limestone and marble with caves and swallowholes. The flora includes Mountain Avens, Lapland Rhododendron and, on the coast, Oyster Plant. There are also areas of birch with breeding Redwing, Brambling and other birds.

This is excellent walking country. There are marked trails and occasional cabins.

10. Børgefjell National Park

Location: On the Swedish border, 90km southeast of Mosjøen.
Access: No roads lead near the park. The best routes are from Majavatn on the E6, Susendal on the 804, or Simskaret at the end of a minor road. Access on foot is unrestricted; some trails are marked.
Timing: May–October.

This beautifully wild, remote area of mountains (to 1703m at Kvigtind), tundra, bogs, lakes and woodland – the latter being mainly birch with some pine – is of considerable importance to Lapps, who graze Reindeer around their summer camps here. Among the wild mammals are Wolverine, Elk, Mountain Hare, Arctic

Børgefjell National Park, on the Swedish border.

7

11. Runde Island

Location: On the west coast, 30km southwest of Åle-sund.
Access: By E69 to Ålesund, from where boats go regularly. There is limited accommodation on the island.
Timing: May–July.

This small inhabited island has superb cliffs and some of the best seabird colonies in Europe; species breeding here include Gannet, Puffin, Guillemot, Black Guillemot and Razorbill. Elsewhere there are White-tailed Eagle, Eagle Owl and Eider. A 640ha area of the island is protected as a reserve.

12. Dovrefjell National Park

Location: Either side of the E6, 130km south of Trondheim, around the village of Kongsvoll.
Access: Direct by trails from the E6, especially near Kongsvoll.
Timing: Best May–August.

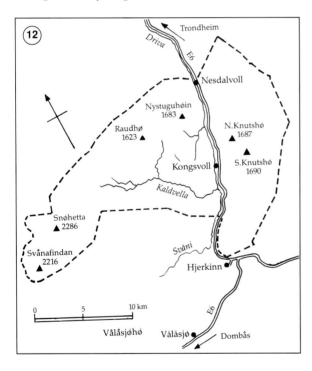

A wild area of mountainous tundra with small patches of birch and rowan woodland. There are permanent snowfields around the higher peaks (reaching 2286m) and numerous lakes and rivers, as well as some very fine areas of lichen-heath, dominated by *Cladonia* species. The park is best known for its exceptional flora, which encompasses virtually all of the Scandinavian mountain plants, notably Norwegian Mugwort, Spring Pasque-flower, Snow Buttercup, the Dovre Poppy (an endemic subspecies of *Papaver radicatum*), Small White Orchid and the tiny orchid

Chamorchis alpina, in addition to many more widespread species. Knutshø is particularly good for flowers. There is a good range of montane birds. The mammals include Europe's only Muskox population—reintroduced and now doing well—plus Northern Birch Mouse and Reindeer. At Kongsvoll are an information centre, a hotel and a small but good botanic garden containing many local rarities.

About 20km south, close to the E6, is the bird reserve of **Fokstumyra**—well worth a visit if only for its excellent variety of breeding northern birds. Permits can be obtained from the warden, based near the railway station.

13. Jotunheimen National Park

Location: In the high mountains of southern Norway, about 240km south-southwest of Trondheim, bounded by roads 15, 51 and 55.
Access: Minor roads and trails run in from all sides, and there is a summer boat service along Lake Gjende. Open access on foot.
Timing: May–September.

The 114,500ha park includes Norway's highest mountain, Galdhøppiggen (2469m), as well as numerous lakes and large areas of tundra, bog and woodland. The prolific flora includes Cassiope species, the orchid *Chamorchis alpina*, Norwegian Wintergreen, Spring Pasque-flower, *Draba fladnizensis* and many others. There are both wild and domestic Reindeer, and a good high-altitude bird fauna.

14. Rondane National Park

Location: About 20km southeast of Dombås (on the E6).

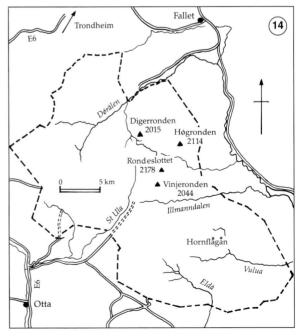

Access: Minor roads run eastwards from the E6 to the park; open access on foot from there.
Timing: May–September.

Norway's first National Park, established in 1962 to protect 58,000ha of fine mountain country, has habitats mainly of montane tundra, with bogs, lakes, snowfields, gorges and cliffs and about 1000ha of mainly birch-dominated woodland. You can find wild Reindeer (no domestic ones) as well as Elk and Otter. Breeding birds include Rough-legged Buzzard, Gyrfalcon, Ptarmigan, Red-necked Phalarope, Dotterel, Golden Plover, Snow Bunting and Bluethroat. This is fine walking country and interesting for its archaeological relics.

15. Hardangervidda National Park

Location: 160km west of Oslo, bounded by roads 7, 8, 37 and E76.
Access: Easy access via the above roads, then by trail or boat.
Timing: May–October.

Norway's largest National Park (342,000ha) covers what could be described as North Europe's greatest mountain plateau; it reaches 1719m at Sandflot. The flora (450 species recorded) has relatively few rarities but a good number of widespread species, often in great abundance; the southernmost outposts of many Arctic species are within the park. Golden Eagle, Osprey, Tengmalm's and Pygmy Owls, Dotterel, Purple Sandpiper, Temminck's Stint, Bluethroat and

Brambling are among over 50 birds breeding here. The 21 recorded mammals include Europe's largest herd of wild Reindeer.

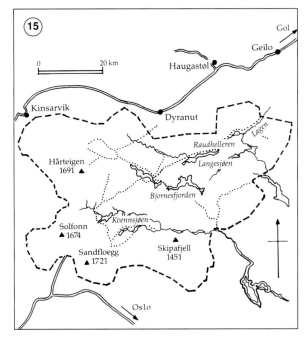

This is a very popular walking and nature-watching area, and there are many marked trails and a good number of manned and unmanned overnight huts. In some years snow lies (or even falls) well into the early summer.

Hardangervidda, Norway's largest National Park.

SWEDEN

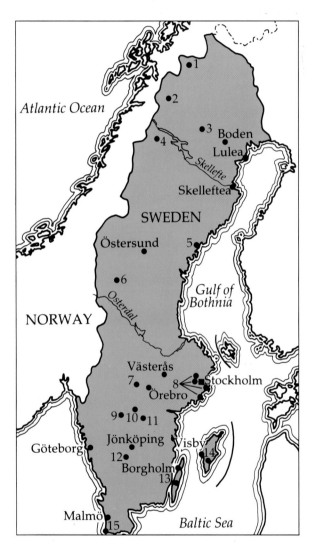

With an area of 450,000 sq km, Sweden is one of Europe's largest countries, yet has a population of just over 8 million, most living in a few large towns. Consequently there are vast areas of wild and uncultivated country, especially in the north where the population density is lowest. About 56 per cent of the area is forest-covered and a further 10 per cent consists of lakes; only 9 per cent is agricultural land. The landscape was scraped bare during the last ice age, which left a legacy of water-filled hollows and morainic debris. This was colonized by a predomi-

nantly coniferous forest, though in the higher mountains and regions of the centre and north there is a greater proportion of bare tundra.

Sweden is fascinating to visit, although the severe winters not only strongly influence the composition of the fauna and flora but also mean that the visiting season for naturalists rarely extends outside April– October. The flora and fauna are not exceptionally rich in species, but there tend to be very large numbers of what does occur, so that you have a much better chance of seeing features of interest. Moreover, many of the species that occur here—e.g., Rough-legged Buzzard, Common Crane and Calypso Orchid—are extremely rare elsewhere in Europe.

Nature conservation in Sweden is well organized and far-reaching. There are 20 National Parks, over 1000 nature reserves and a number of other sites or areas where nature has some protection.

1. Abisko National Park

Location: In the far north, 85km northwest of Kiruna alongside road 98.
Access: Via road 98 or by rail (station by the park HQ); on foot or by cablecar into the park from Abisko, where there is accommodation and an excellent information centre.
Timing: May–September.

The 7700ha park is noted as one of Scandinavia's finest botanical localities; it includes mountainous country with tundra, a large area of northern birch forest, and lakes and rivers. The flora really is exceptional, with many rarities as well as more widespread Arctic and Alpine species—One-leaved Butterfly Orchid, Arctic Rhododendron, Arctic Bellflower, Arctic Campion, Ghost Orchid, *Chamorchis alpina* in abundance, both Cassiope species, Norwegian Wintergreen and many others of note. The breeding birds are also of interest; they include Arctic Warbler, Rough-legged Buzzard, Snow and Lapland Buntings and Bluethroat. The delta at Abiskojokk is a bird sanctuary, with restrictions during the breeding season. Reindeer, Lemming and Elk are residents, while Arctic Fox and Wolverine pass through.

Northwest of Abisko, west of Lake Torneträsk towards the Norwegian border, the **Vadvetjåkka National**

OPPOSITE PAGE: *Gorge below Abisko National Park in the far north of Sweden.*

10

Stone stripes, left by glaciation, in Abisko.

Park covers 2630ha of mountainous country. Access is difficult and there are no facilities.

2. Sarek-Padjelanta Complex of National Parks

Location: On the Norwegian border southwest of Kiruna, about 120km south of Narvik.
Access: A very remote area; Vietas, by minor road from road 88, gives reasonable access to Stora Sjöfallet; other areas on foot only.
Timing: May–September.

The three contiguous National Parks of Stora Sjöfallet, Sarek and Padjelanta, together with Norway's smaller Rago Park, protect the largest wilderness area in Europe (well over 500,000 ha). This is a remote, wild, uninhabited terrain of mountains, glaciers, lakes, bogs, tundra, grasslands and some woodland, mainly birch. It sports most of what inland Arctic Europe has to offer, though spread over a wide area. The mammals include Elk, Wolverine, Lynx, Lemming, Arctic Fox and Mountain Hare. Rough-legged Buzzard, Bluethroat, Lesser White-fronted Goose, Gyrfalcon, Dotterel, Purple Sandpiper and Temminck's Stint breed here, and birds like Snowy and Hawk Owls occur in numbers varying according to the numbers of Lemming. The flora is rich, especially on the limestones and serpentine of the Padjelanta Park,

and includes three species found nowhere else in Sweden: *Gentianella aurea*, *Arenaria humifusa* and *Potentilla hyparctica*.

3. Muddus National Park

Location: Between Jokkmokk and Gällivare on road 88.
Access: By gravel road alongside the Stora Lule River, running eastwards from road 88; access on foot from the terminal parking area.
Timing: May–September.

The park covers 49,300ha of wild forest, bog and tundra in largely unexploited form; there are good walking trails, with overnight cabins for longer excursions. About half the park is coniferous forest (mainly Norway Spruce and pine) with some mixed forest and a huge area of bog—a characteristic northern Scandinavian mixture, here at its best. There are also lakes, threaded through with eskers and drumlins. The park is a refuge for many mammals, including Bear, Lynx, Wolverine, Elk and Otter. Among over 100 breeding birds are many uncommon species like Whooper Swan, Bean Goose, Broad-billed Sandpiper, Jack Snipe, Osprey, Ural and Eagle Owls and abundant Siberian Jays. The overall flora is not especially prolific, but there are fine displays of woodland species like Twinflower and several sites for the rare and beautiful Calypso Orchid, plus Ghost Orchid and the full spectrum of acid-bog species.

4. Pieljekaise National Park

Location: Just south of road 95, about 60km east of the Norwegian border, south of Jäckvick and Sädvaluspen.
Access: On foot via the Kungsleden trail, south from Jäckvick or north from Adolfström.
Timing: May–September.

This 15,340ha tract of wooded mountainous country includes one of the world's finest remaining areas of virgin birch forest—about 10,000ha of Mountain Birch – as well as a mixture of bog, open water and bare mountain/tundra habitats. Northern Wolfsbane, *Lactuca alpina*, Globeflower, Moor-king, Twinflower, Purple Saxifrage and Fragrant Orchid are among the plants of interest, while breeding birds include Scoter, Goosander, Black-throated Diver and the occasional Gyrfalcon. Among the mammals are Elk, Bear and Wolverine as well as, during the summer, regular herds of Reindeer—the area lies within the Lapp grazing grounds.

5. Skuleskogen National Park

Location: On the coast, east of the E4 near Näske, 40km south of Örnsköldsvik.
Access: By minor roads from the E4 to Näske or Käl; thereafter on foot-trails.
Timing: April–October.

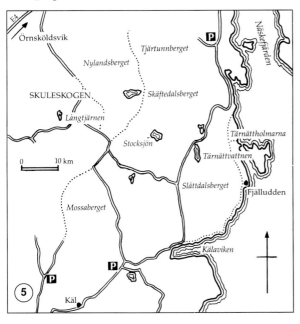

This park, 3000ha of undisturbed forested hilly country on the coast, is notable as an area in which southern species approach their northern limits. The forest trees include Field Maple, Large-leaved Lime and hazel as well as the more usual spruce and pine. Mezereon, Alpine Sow-thistle, Baneberry and Lesser Butterfly, Bog and Early Marsh Orchids are among the flowers, and there are good lichens; here you can find one of the few sites for the impressive Old Man's Beard

(*Usnea longissima*). The breeding birds are dominated by forest species like Three-toed and Grey-headed Woodpeckers, Siberian Jay and Willow Grouse. You can also find Lynx, Otter and Elk.

6. Sonfjället Group of National Parks

Location: Sonfjället lies about 15km south of Hede, northwest of Sve. Töfsingdalen is west of here, close to the Norwegian border; Hamra lies to the southeast, 5km east of road 81.
Access: Minor roads south from Hede and Hedeviken lead to parking areas and information centres; thereafter on foot via marked trails.
Timing: May–October.

Sonfjället National Park covers 2622ha, and is the largest of the three National Parks in this part of the central Swedish mountains. About half of it is coniferous forest; there is also some birch forest, plus patches of tundra and bog. The area is particularly known for its substantial resident population of Brown Bear; there are also Elk, Lynx and Otter. The two other parks in the group have broadly similar countryside; Hamra is noted for its insect life, which includes over 450 beetle species in an area of only 28ha.

7. Garphyttan National Park

Location: 15km west of Örebro, on the E3.
Access: Via minor road off the E18 to Garphyttan.
Timing: April–October.

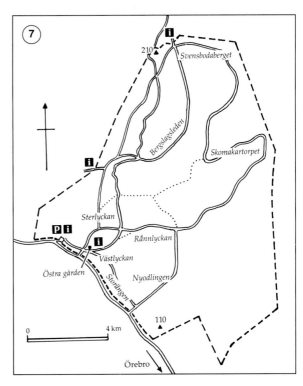

This is more of a nature reserve than a National Park, comprising 111ha of land that was once partly cultivated; today it has a mixture of forest—both coniferous and deciduous—and meadows. Its flora is particularly prolific, totalling about 300 species, including many lime-loving, more southern plants like Hepatica, Mezereon, Cowslip, Lily-of-the-Valley, Toothwort and Columbine. Dormouse and Northern Birch Mouse are found, and this is a good area for woodpeckers (several species breeding) and other woodland birds, such as Hawfinch. The flowery meadows and woodland edges are good for butterflies, notably Fritillaries.

8. Stockholm Area

Location: Around Stockholm.
Access: Various.
Timing: April–October.

Stockholm is within easy striking distance of some surprisingly fine reserves and places of interest. **Hjälstaviken Bird Reserve** lies just north of the E18, about 45km to the northwest; it has a good mixture of wetland breeding birds, including Slavonian Grebe, Bittern and Marsh Harrier, and at passage periods there are good waders and wildfowl. Due east of Stockholm, accessible via Stavsnäs, the **Bullerö and Långskär Reserve** covers a cluster of uninhabited islands in the archipelago; there is an excellent range of breeding birds—e.g., Black Guillemot, Eider, Velvet Scoter, Long-tailed Duck and Goosander—and Bullerö has a field centre and nature trails. In the northern part of the archipelago, accessible from Vättershaga by boat, is the idyllic **Ängsö National Park**, 73ha of formerly cultivated landscape, with meadows, woods, beautiful displays of flowers in May–June and good birds.

In Uppsala, about 60km north of Stockholm on the E4, two excellent botanic gardens associated with the work of Linnaeus show a very wide and clearly labelled range of Scandinavian and other flowers.

9. Hornborgasjön

Location: About 10km southeast of Skara, on the E3 about 120km northeast of Göteborg.
Access: On the 184 south from Skara to Bjurum, thence into the reserve on marked trails.
Timing: April–October.

A partly drained lake that has become an important bird reserve, with reedbeds, carr and open water. In April several thousand Common Crane stop here and begin displaying before moving north. Among the 100 or so species of birds known to breed here are Slavonian and Black-necked Grebes, Garganey, Bittern, Marsh Harrier and Wood Sandpiper, and others pass through on autumn migration. On the east side, close to open water, is an observation tower.

Boardwalk to the visitor centre at Hornsborgasjön.

10. Tiveden National Park

Location: 110km due north of Jönköping, just west of Lake Vättern, near Tived.

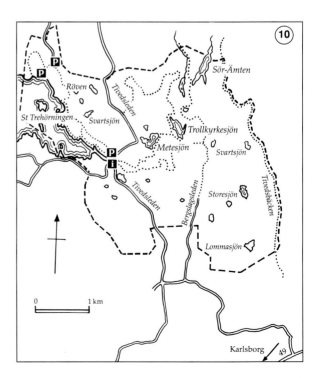

Acidic lake in the midst of Tiveden National Park.

Access: A minor road signed from road 49 near Bölet, north of Karlsborg, leads into the park; access on foot via marked trails.
Timing: May–October.

1353ha of hilly coniferous forest with scattered lakes and bogs. The forest has been, for southern Sweden, relatively unexploited, and many old trees remain. Breeding birds include Tengmalm's and Pygmy Owls, Three-toed Woodpecker, Willow Grouse, Black-throated Diver and Goldeneye. The flora includes many bog species, woodland species like Twinflower, and the Pale Pasque-flower. Among the lakes and bogs you can find a good selection of the commoner dragonflies.

11. Tåkern Lake

Location: Between the E4 and Lake Vättern, about 70km north of Jönköping.
Access: Road 50 runs from the E4 past the lake's west shore, and a minor road through Väderstad runs up its east shore; in the breeding season access on foot is restricted to trails and hides.
Timing: April–October.

This huge, partly drained freshwater lake covers over 5000ha, of which about one-third is currently reedbeds. The clean water sustains a good aquatic flora of pondweeds, stoneworts, Water-milfoil and water-lilies, and there is a fine range of breeding birds, including all five European grebes, Bittern, Black Tern, Great Reed Warbler, Bearded Tit and 10 duck species. Swans and geese moult here, and in autumn the lake is visited by huge numbers of Bean Goose— up to 40,000—as well as smaller numbers of other species. The spring passage periods, while interesting, are less spectacular.

12. Store Mosse National Park

Location: 50km south of Jönköping, between Värnamo and Hillerstorp.
Access: Road 151 from Värnamo (on the E4) to Hillerstorp passes through the reserve; access from here to hides and trails.
Timing: April–July.

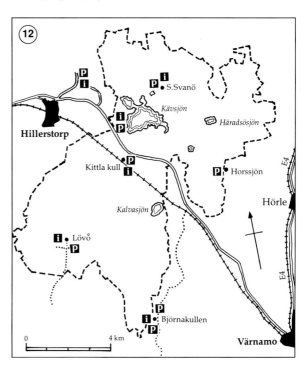

About 90 per cent of this 7750ha area of low-lying land is dominated by huge boggy tracts, with open water and coniferous forest. The superb range of breeding birds predominantly comprises northern species: there is a large colony of Common Crane together with, among others, divers, Whooper Swan, grebes, Long-tailed Duck, Marsh Harrier, Dunlin, Jack Snipe, Golden Plover, Wood Sandpiper and Three-toed Woodpecker. East of the road, near Lake Kävsjön, there is a good tower hide.

13. Öland

Location: An island just off Sweden's south coast, opposite Kalmar.
Access: The E66 crosses by road-bridge from Kalmar to the island; roads radiate from there.

Timing: All year; best April–October. Very busy at weekends and in high summer.

Öland is an attractive and historic island, well worth a week's holiday, especially in late May or June. It is long and narrow—135km by (at widest) about 15km—and has a wonderful range of habitats. The western shore has extensive limestone cliffs, the centre has low hills, with the characteristic limestone pavement and grassland areas known as *alvar*, and the east slopes gradually into the sea, with a range of 'soft' coastal habitats. At the northern tip is an attractive enclosed lagoon surrounded by forest and saltmarsh.

The flora is exceptional in both variety and abundance. Many species are at the north of their range here; others are exclusive to Öland. Among them are Shrubby Cinquefoil (in abundance), *Globularia vulgaris*, a Rock-rose (*Helianthemum oelandicum*), 29 orchids—including both colour-forms of Elder-flowered Orchid—Spiked Speedwell, Yellow Pheasant's Eye, Hepatica and Pasque-flower. The limestone *alvar* areas, marked on many maps, are noteworthy.

Öland's range of breeding birds is good, too, particularly in the woodlands: Corncrake, Avocet, Ruff, Red-backed Shrike, Icterine and Barred Warblers, Red-breasted Flycatcher, Thrush Nightingale and others. At both spring and autumn passage periods huge numbers of some species—such as Eider and a good selection of other waders and wildfowl—make their appearance. Butterflies abound, notably on quieter *alvar* areas, and there are breeding dragonflies and damselflies in sheltered areas of the Baltic.

14. Gotland

Location: A large island in the Baltic, east of Öland.

Access: By air from Stockholm, or by ferry (minimum four hours) from Västervik or Oskarshamn.
Timing: April–October.

Gotland is a large, attractive island. Much broader than Öland (site 13) and therefore not quite so maritime in character, it is nevertheless very similar in many ways; it is a major holiday destination and has much of general interest. It has a very rich flora, especially on limestone areas, sharing many species with Öland and having a few of its own, such as an endemic subspecies of Pasque-flower, *Pulsatilla vulgaris gotlandica*. The range of habitats is similar, but there are more areas of wetland, including marshes and lakes. The breeding birds are good, much like those on Öland; there are seabird colonies on the Karlsö islands off the west coast, and the marshes have species like Crane, Caspian Tern, Little Gull, Ruff, Avocet and Marsh Warbler.

15. Falsterbo

Location: At the extreme southwestern tip of Sweden, about 25km south of Malmö.
Access: Via the E6 and then a minor road; generally open on foot.
Timing: Best in April–July and September–October.

Although the whole area has good habitats, with interesting breeding birds, the peninsula that ends at Falsterbo is noteworthy as one of Europe's best spots for watching migrating birds. In the autumn migration huge numbers converge from a vast area of Scandinavia and western Russia to cross towards Denmark. Raptors, especially Honey and Rough-legged Buzzards, Osprey, Red Kite and a few eagle species pass through in their thousands between early September and mid–October, with Honey Buzzard peaking near the start of this period.

FINLAND

Finland is one of Europe's larger countries—337,000 sq km—but also one of the least known. The low population—about 5 million—means that colossal areas are uncultivated and relatively unspoilt. The country is dominated by lakes and forests: there are over 60,000 lakes, from tiny to very large, and some 65 per cent of the land surface is forested. Geologically Finland is not very varied, so there tend to be great tracts of similar habitat. Species which require large areas often do well here, but only at low densities—Brown Bear, Elk, Lynx, Crane, White-tailed Eagle and many waders and wildfowl have substantial but scattered breeding populations. Managed regions may offer greater varieties of species, but these are mainly common and widespread ones that have come in at the expense of the more demanding ones.

The forests are mainly coniferous, and a surprisingly high proportion is managed and often replanted. Indeed, there are very few areas of genuinely virgin forest, especially in the lowlands, but many National Parks seek to protect or recreate fragments of it.

Conservation is well organized and large expanses are protected, often under state ownership. There are 27 National Parks, 19 strict state nature reserves and 173 peatland reserves, plus a wealth of private and other reserves. Many National Parks offer information leaflets in languages other than Finnish, notably English.

Much of Oulanka National Park is dominated by water.

The heavily forested Pallas-Ounastunturi National Park.

1. Pallas-Ounastunturi National Park

Location: Northern Finland, close to the Swedish border, between Enontekio and Muonio.
Access: Road 21 passes close by, and minor roads lead into the park from several directions; open on foot, with marked trails.
Timing: May–September.

50,000ha of upland plateau and taiga, with lakes, tundra, gorges and vast areas of coniferous forest—dominated by pine with some spruce—plus, at higher levels, birch forests. Norway Spruce reaches its northernmost limits here, and the trees tend to be stunted, with many glades. Breeding birds include Crane, Whooper Swan, Great Grey Owl, Rough-legged Buzzard, Golden and White-tailed Eagles, Snow and Lapland Buntings, Ptarmigan and Bluethroat. Gyrfalcons breed not far away to the northwest, and visit the park area. There is a good flora—Globeflower, Melancholy Thistle, Ostrich Fern, Lapland Buttercup, the rare *Polemonium acutiflorum*, Diapensia, Polar Willow, Arctic Saxifrage and others. Bear, Elk, Wolverine, Wolf and Lemming are found.

2. Lemmenjoki National Park

Location: In the far north, on the Norwegian border about 60km southwest of Inari.
Access: Via the Inari-Pokka road, then by a minor road to Lisma.
Timing: May–September.

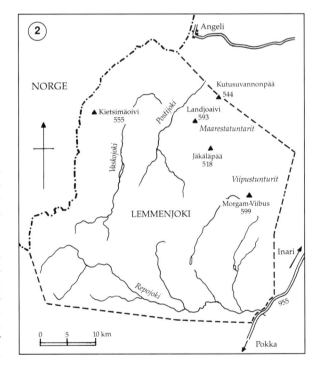

Finland's largest National Park (280,000ha) is a vast and genuine wilderness of bog, forest, mountain and lake. Towards the east the mountains rise to 600m at Morgam-Viibus, while in the centre there are bands of huge *aapa* bogs; these bog areas are especially good. Rough-legged Buzzard, Hawk Owl, Ptarmigan, Willow Grouse, Golden Plover, Whimbrel, Waxwing, Shore Lark, Bluethroat, Whooper Swan and others breed here. Brown Bear and Wolf are still present in small numbers, and domestic Reindeer graze the area. The flora has a good cross-section of northern bog and forest species.

3. Pyhätunturi National Park

Location: 50km north of Kemijärvi, west of the road to Pelkosenniemi.
Access: Trails and a chairlift go off from the information centre by the road.
Timing: May–September.

The park covers 4200ha around the southernmost of Finland's main mountains, Pyhätunturi, which rises to 540m in a chain of similar peaks. The habitats include pine and spruce forests, with extensive *aapa* bogs and high-level tundra. The flora and fauna are strongly Russian in flavour, with a number of taiga species. Breeding birds include Rough-legged Buzzard, Phalarope, Redwing, Siberian Jay and Siberian Tit. The flora is rich in bog and tundra species, and there are numerous lichens; special flowers include Baneberry and Large Marsh Saxifrage. Lynx, Bear and Wolverine all appear, as does the occasional Wolf. The whole area is good walking country.

4. Oulanka National Park

Location: About 45km north of Kuusamo, on the Russian border.
Access: Road 5 north from Kuusamo, then by a minor road towards Hautajärvi; access on foot unrestricted.
Timing: May–September.

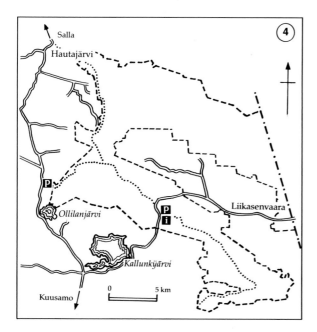

27,000ha of varied and extremely beautiful countryside, with bogs, tundra, coniferous forest, gorges,

broad rivers—with rapids and falls—lakes and meadows. The northern part has extensive wet bogs; the southern part is hillier and more varied. There are fine flowery meadows, and the park's overall flora includes Lady's Slipper Orchid, Yellow Marsh Saxifrage, Arctic Saxifrage, Mountain Avens and many others. Over 120 species of breeding birds have been recorded, including divers, Whooper Swan, Goldeneye, Wood Sandpiper, Siberian Tit and Brambling, with Red-flanked Bluetail occurring in the gorge of the Oulankajoki River. The 29 mammals include Wolf, Bear, Wolverine and Rat-headed and Grey-sided Voles. There is a good information centre towards the south of the park, and a number of trails with huts.

5. Pyhä-Häkki National Park

Location: 30km northeast of Saarijärvi (north of Jyväskyla), around Lake Iso Kotajärvi.
Access: A minor road north from Saarijärvi runs through the park.
Timing: May–September.
This 1200ha park has been protected since 1912, and the forests which cover half of it have gradually become more natural; some of the trees, notably the Scots Pines, approach 400 years in age. Because of the old timber, there are especially good numbers of beetles – e.g., the Bark Beetle *Ips longicollis* and numerous longhorn beetles—as well as other wood-boring insects. Besides the forest there are extensive bogs. Breeding birds include Waxwing, Siberian Jay, Tengmalm's Owl and Red-breasted and Pied Flycatchers, and this is also a good area for butterflies and moths.

6. Linnansaari National Park

Location: About 80km northeast of Mikkeli, just east of Rantasalmi on the edge of Haukivesi Lake.

Amphibious Bistort blanketing one of Finland's many lakes.

Access: By boat from Rantasalmi or from Oravi on the opposite shore.
Timing: May–October.

An unusual National Park made up largely of water with scattered wooded islands; there are plans to increase its current 2200ha to 3800ha. The park itself occupies only a small part of the huge lake, but is important as a breeding area for the rare Saimaa Ringed Seal (*Phoca hispida saimensis*), believed to have adapted to freshwater life here in the aftermath of the last ice age. The woodlands are mainly coniferous, but include areas of birch, alder and lime. An interesting bird fauna is scattered through the islands, including breeding Osprey, Goosander, Black-throated Diver, Greenish Warbler, Golden Oriole and many common woodland species.

7. Petkeljärvi National Park

Location: On the Russian border, east of Joensuu and about 20km southeast of Ilomantsi.
Access: A minor road leads from the Ilomantsi-Möhkö road into the park.
Timing: May–October.

A beautiful area of typical Finnish lakeland scenery, with a fine mixture of lakes—about half the park's 630ha—bogs, moorland and woodland; there are good examples of eskers. The woods are mainly Scots Pine, open in character, with birch and juniper here

Finland's larger mammals include Reindeer.

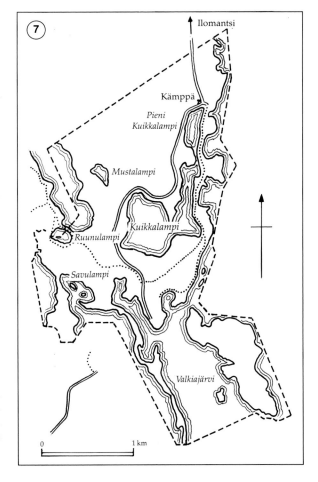

and there. Breeding birds include occasional Common Crane, Greenshank, Siberian and Crested Tits, Three-toed Woodpecker and Parrot Crossbill. Lynx can still be seen, and Pine Marten, Red Squirrel and Mountain Hare are widespread.

8. Parikkala

Location: On road 6, close to the Russian border, southeast of Savonlinna.
Access: From road 6. The good areas are by the lake just west of the road.
Timing: April–July.

Parikkala lies on a large lake in an area that is more water than land. Part of the eastern shore is managed as a WWF nature reserve; there are good reedbeds, scrub and open water. A particular attraction is breeding Blyth's Reed Warbler, at the western edge of its range; there are also River Warbler, Osprey, Red-necked and Slavonian Grebes, Spotted Crake, Thrush Nightingale, Scarlet Rosefinch and others. This is probably the easiest place to see and appreciate many of these essentially Russian species.

9. Southwestern Archipelago National Park (Saaristomeri)

Location: About 50km southwest of Turku (Åbo).
Access: By boat, either by arrangement or on one of the regular services from Turku or Kastnäs. Nötö has some facilities.
Timing: May–September.

This National Park covers the islands scattered across 3000ha of water and displays an interesting mixture of natural and previously cultivated habitats, together supporting a rich mixture of flowers, insects and birds. Breeding birds include Razorbill, Nutcracker and White-tailed Eagle, and there are Grey Seal around the islands.

10. Liesjärvi National Park

Location: Just northeast of the main Helsinki-Pori road (road 2), 25km southeast of Forssa.
Access: A minor road, signed to the Korteniemi information shelter, runs off road 2; from here access on foot is open.
Timing: May–September.

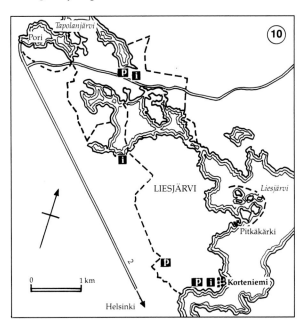

630ha of lakes, forests (mainly spruce, some planted), bog and previously cultivated land. The fauna is particularly prolific, with abundant Elk, White-tailed Deer and Pine Marten; breeding birds include Black and Three-toed Woodpeckers, Pied Flycatcher, several gulls and terns, Red-breasted Merganser, Goosander, Goldeneye, Black-throated Diver and Wryneck. The whole area is an attractive blend of habitats, and is popular for walking; there is also a small, old, traditionally managed farmstead.

DENMARK

Denmark, with an area of only 43,000 sq km, is composed of a large peninsula (Jutland or Jylland) plus a number of islands of varying size. Though low-lying, reaching only 173m at its highest point (Ejer Bavnehog) Denmark is rarely flat: it has an undulating glacial landscape of hills and hollows. It is relatively populous and cultivated, over 70 per cent of its land area being agricultural. Forests cover about 10 per cent, though many are coniferous plantations with a poor natural history. The large areas of peatlands and heathlands that once were here have now been largely drained or ploughed and hold little of interest; but some have been left unimproved, and most of these are today reserves of one sort or another.

Although the flora and fauna are not especially rich, Denmark is without a doubt an excellent place to see birds. The complex, low-lying and largely unspoilt coastline offers a superb range of habitats, many of which lie on main migration routes. Breeding birds and autumn passage numbers are especially good.

Nature conservation in Denmark is well organized, and the natural history is well recorded. There are no National Parks, but instead a number of Natural Parks and many state and private reserves.

OPPOSITE PAGE: *Lakeside in the lovely valley of Gudenåens og Skjern Åens Kilder.*

1. Skagen Peninsula

Location: The extreme northeast tip of Jutland.
Access: Road 40 runs to the point; generally open on foot.
Timing: April–June.

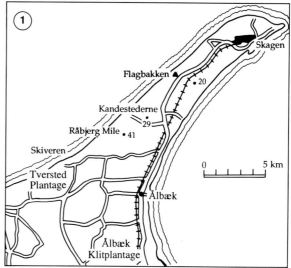

The mobile Råbjerg Mile dune on the Skagen Peninsula.

Much of this sandy peninsula is a 4300ha nature reserve. It includes a superb variety of all types of dune formation, including the mobile Råbjerg Mile dune, which is large enough to be marked on most maps. There is a good dune flora, but the area is best known as a place for watching migrant birds— especially in spring, when large quantities of birds of prey and passerines arrive. Honey Buzzard and Buzzard are the most frequent, but rarities often turn up with them. April–May is best; among the finest vantage points is the Flagbakken Hill, west of Skagen.

2. Hantsholm Reserve

Location: At the northwest corner of Jutland, south of Hanstholm.

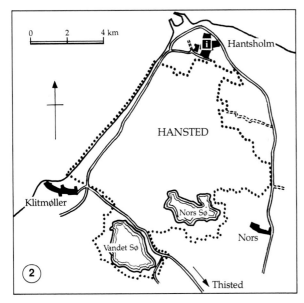

Dunes at Hantsholm, with Autumn Hawkbit (foreground).

24

Access: Off road 181; access into the reserve is restricted during the bird–breeding season.
Timing: March–October.

A large area of dunes (over 3000ha) with heathland, woods and lakes, this site is most important for birds. Small numbers of Common Crane, Golden Plover, Wood Sandpiper and others breed, and migrants include Greylag, Pink-footed and Bean Geese, Whooper and Bewick's Swans and various ducks, plus further cranes. The dune flora is modest, perhaps because the sand is too acid.

3. Løgstør Bredning

Location: The central part of the huge channel (the Limfjorden) that almost separates the tip of Jutland from the remainder, between the towns of Løgstør and Thisted.
Access: Roads 11 and 581 give reasonable access and views.
Timing: April–October.

This vast shallow sea inlet is a fine area for birds, though it is easier to see them in the smaller lakes and marshes to the north of the main road, around Temmerby. Birds breeding here include Bittern, Red-necked and Black-necked Grebes, Marsh Harrier, Black-tailed Godwit, Ruff, Avocet, Dunlin, Little Gull and Gull-billed Tern. At passage times there are good waders and wildfowl, together with other birds.

Mute Swans in winter on the Løgstør Bredning.

4. Nissum and Stadil Fjords

Location: On the coast west of Holstebro.
Access: Road 181 runs along the coastal edge of the sites; access on foot is largely open.

Timing: April–October.

Nissum Fjord is a large lagoon with a small exit to the sea through the dunes; to the south is a series of lakes or saline lagoons—collectively of great interest—together with reedbeds and grazing marshes. The many breeding birds include Avocet, Ruff, Black-tailed Godwit, Marsh Harriers and Arctic, Little and Sandwich Terns. Late summer and autumn bring large numbers of wildfowl including swans and waders. The flora has a good range of dune and saltmarsh species.

5. Flynderso and Stubbergard So

Location: 30km west of Viborg, just southwest of Skive; the site lies just west of road 34.
Access: Footpaths from road 34 and minor roads.
Timing: May–September.

A landscape-protection area (16,000ha) comprising two large and several small lakes in a steep-sided valley, with heaths and woods. The valley has good examples of several glacial features, notably the series of kettle holes (left when blocks of ice melted) that form the lakes. The flora includes Chickweed Wintergreen, Twinflower, Bearberry, Crowberry, various bur-reeds, lots of sedges and many others. Among the birds breeding here are a few Wood Sandpiper, and after the breeding season the larger lake has gatherings of Goosander, with regular Osprey at passage times.

6. Mols Bjerge Natural Park

Location: On the east side of the Helgenaes Peninsula, just northeast of Århus.
Access: By minor roads from Lyngsbaek; generally unrestricted on foot.
Timing: May–November.

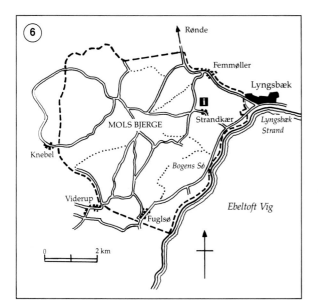

An attractive protected area (almost 3000ha) made up of a mosaic of heath, woodland and grassland, with scattered marshy areas and open water. The rich flora (about 600 species recorded) has bog and heathland specialities. Sand Lizard and Adder are among the reptiles, and the invertebrates are of interest, especially the spiders—including the rare and spectacular Ladybird Spider.

The adjacent **Ebeltoft Vig**, a shallow bay, is important for birds, with breeding Avocet and Sandwich and Arctic Terns, and large numbers of moulting duck in late summer and autumn. Along the Fuglsoø-Lyngsbaek road are good information centres giving details of wildlife and walking.

7. Ringkøbing Fjord

Location: On the west coast 45km north of Esbjerg.
Access: Good views and access from road 181, which runs along the fjord's seaward side; restrictions in some reserve areas.
Timing: April–November; parts are busy during summer holidays.

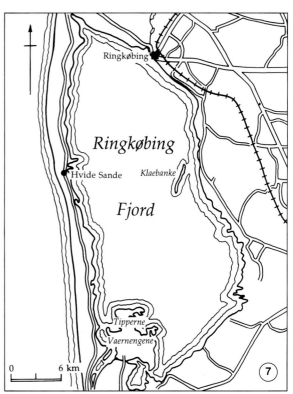

Separated from the sea only by a line of dunes, this is one of the largest of the west Jutland fjords and probably the best for birds. Habitats include dunes, saltmarshes, shallow brackish water, grazing marshes, hay meadows and reedbeds, with a few areas of coniferous forest. Breeding birds include Avocet, Black-tailed Godwit, Ruff, Marsh Harrier, Sandwich and Gull-billed Tern. At passage times, and especially in autumn, vast

Fishing nets spread at Ringkøbing.

numbers of wildfowl—including geese and swans—and waders come here. The low-lying peninsula at the fjord's southern end is a major nature reserve, with a good flora and important breeding birds. South of Nymindegab are further reserves, with dunes and woodland. The fjord and the coast to its south are excellent for bird-watching and general natural history.

8. Skallingen

Location: Projecting westwards across the Ho Bugt from Esbjerg.
Access: By minor roads southwards from Ho or Oksby; unrestricted on foot.
Timing: April–November.

Skallingen is a long sandy peninsula, about 3km broad and of area about 2300ha, with dunes along the seaward side and grazing marshes and saltmarshes on the Ho Bugt side. There is a large area of unspoilt dune vegetation, with Sea Bindweed, Sea Holly, Marram, Lime Grass and other species. On the inland side vast numbers of birds visit in spring and autumn,

particularly geese, ducks and waders; thousands of Eider come in autumn.

To the northwest is the **Kallesmaesks Hede**, a moorland area with lakes; here Wood Sandpiper breed, with Black Grouse in the woods. The point at **Blåvandshuk** is a good migration-watching point.

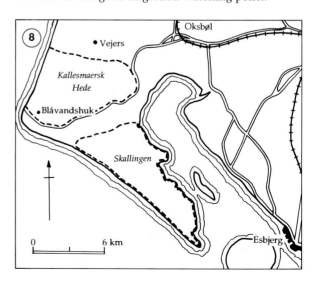

9. Gudenåens og Skjern Åens Kilder Natural Park

Location: Just northwest of Tørring, 15km north of Vejle.
Access: Minor roads off road 13; access on foot is unrestricted.
Timing: May–October.

A lovely valley with numerous springs and several lakes amid a complex mixture of marshes, grassland and woodland, plus a large area of oak scrub. Two of Denmark's main rivers, the Gudenå and Skjern Å, flow outwards from the ends of the wettest area. The rich and varied flora has many bog and marsh species like Lesser Bur-reed, sundews, numerous sedges and Marsh Orchids. The springs feeding the lakes and marshes have an unusual aquatic invertebrate fauna, thought to be survivors from soon after the ice age; there are also interesting insects in the rest of the site, such as the Northern Damselfly and other damselflies and dragonflies. Breeding birds include Marsh Harrier, Corncrake and Wood Sandpiper.

10. Samsø Island

Location: Southeast of Århus.
Access: By ferry from Hov (on Jutland) or Kalundborg (on Zealand); footpaths within the reserve area.
Timing: April–October.

The northern part of Samsø is protected as a nature reserve. Habitats include dry grassland, heathland and woodland, coastal saltmarshes, mudflats and offshore islands and spits. Birds breeding in the coastal area include hosts of Eider plus Avocet, Arctic Tern and various gulls. In late summer and autumn there are large numbers of waders and wildfowl in Stavns Fjord, in particular copious Eider. The good flora in the dry grassland areas contains a surprising number of southern and eastern species.

11. Hindsholm Natural Park

Location: The northeastern end of the large island of Fyn, at the tip of the peninsula north of Kerteminde.

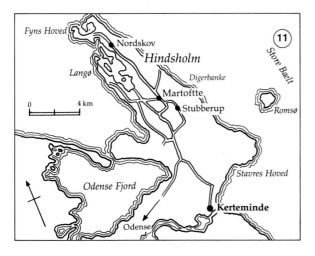

Access: Minor roads from Odense or Kerteminde; open on foot.
Timing: April–July.

The peninsula is a pleasantly varied piece of rural countryside, much of it lying within the Natural Park. Habitats include old grassland and ancient deciduous woodland. At the northern tip, the **Fyns Hoved Reserve** has steep cliffs with colonies of breeding seabirds, including Black Guillemot. This is a good migration-watching point.

12. Esrum Sø and Gribskov

Location: North of Copenhagen (København), 12km west of Helsingør.
Access: Road 227 runs north in the forest along the edge of the lake; generally open on foot.
Timing: Best April–November.

A combination of one of Denmark's largest freshwater lakes, Esrum Sø, and one of the country's largest forests, Gribskov. The woodland mixes beech and spruce with some oak, limes and ash; the breeding birds—many of which are rare in Denmark—include Black Woodpecker, Honey Buzzard, Green Sandpiper, Nightjar and Thrush Nightingale. The lake supports copious aquatic life, both plant and animal, and attracts reasonable numbers of wildfowl.

The northern point of Zealand, **Gilbjerg Hoved**, is a noted spot for watching spring migrations (April–May): large numbers of raptors and passerines can be seen on a good day.

13. Roskilde Fjord

Location: About 25km west of Copenhagen (København), just west of Roskilde.
Access: Via minor roads north from road 155; access restricted to footpaths.
Timing: Some interest all year.

The southern shore of the fjord is a convoluted hilly area with low peninsulas and islands projecting into the lake, plus scattered smaller lakes. Habitats include meadows, beech and oak woodlands, marshes and open water; further north, the fjord becomes more coastal in character. Breeding birds include Avocet, Marsh Harrier, terns, Honey Buzzard and Great-crested Grebe; outside the breeding season there are large numbers of swans, geese, ducks, Goosander and Coot, plus White-tailed Eagle and other predators.

14. Danish Wadden See

Location: On the west coast of Jutland, from the island of Rømø southwards to the German border.
Access: Road 75 runs from Skaerbaek on to Rømø; minor roads (e.g., the 419) give access to the mainland coast.
Timing: April–November.

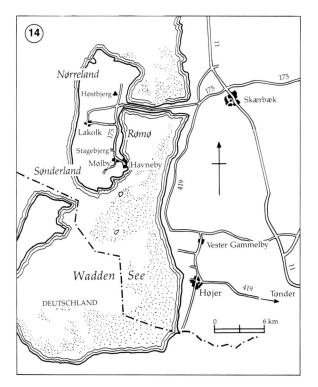

The Wadden See, running northwards from the Dutch coast through Germany and into Denmark, is one of Europe's great wetlands and a superb bird-watching area. The interest here is essentially the same as for the areas further south (see Wadden See and Wattenmeer in the index), with huge numbers of waders and wildfowl, especially in autumn; the causeway to Rømø is particularly noted for the large flocks of Avocet gathering nearby in autumn.

Rømø itself is a Natural Park, and has superb dunes, meadows, marshes and reedbeds with breeding Marsh Harrier, Avocet, Ruff, Black-tailed Godwit, Red-necked Grebe and Kentish Plover, among others. Its dunes have a good flora.

15. Draved Skov

Location: 9km northeast of Tønder, towards Løgumkloster.
Access: Minor roads off road 25; access on footpaths.
Timing: May–August.

An area of old woodland and the remnant of a formerly huge raised bog, Kongens Mose. The woodland is deciduous, with Small-leaved Lime, oak, ash, elm, etc., and a rich ground flora. The remnant of Kongens Mose covers several hundred hectares and has breeding Black Tern, Marsh and Montagu's Harriers, Wood Sandpiper and Short-eared Owl, plus a good bog flora.

16. Bornholm

Location: An isolated island well east of most of Denmark, in the Baltic close to Sweden.

Rocky coastline at Helligdommen on the isolated island of Bornholm.

Access: By ferry from Ystad (Sweden) and Køb to Rønne; access by road from there; mainly unrestricted on foot.
Timing: May–September.

Ecologically, Bornholm has more in common with Sweden than with Denmark. The northern part is a Natural Park where old woods and areas of heathland, with a rich flora, overlie acid granite and gneiss. In the centre of the island the extensive (over 5000ha) part-deciduous **Forest of Almindingen** has a good selection of breeding woodland birds, including Honey Buzzard, Black Woodpecker and Nightjar. Bornholm is a good place for a general holiday and has interesting historic and prehistoric sites.

GREAT BRITAIN

Britain (Ireland, north and south, is treated elsewhere: see pages 55–65) – is long and thin, spanning a wide latitude range, the climate also varies markedly from south to north. Thus the total climatic variation is extremely great.

The British Isles are biologically rather poorer than adjacent parts of mainland Europe, since many species failed to colonize after the last ice age. To an extent this is compensated for by the abundance of some species that are otherwise rare in Europe; for example, Britain's seabird colonies are of international importance, and in particular the Scottish colonies contain high proportions of the European populations of a number of species. Grey and Common Seals are particularly abundant around Britain thanks to the long coastline, the isolated islands and the productive seas.

Nature conservation here is a strong movement with a long history. There are National Parks in England and Wales, together with a network of state-run National Nature Reserves, including large ones like Cairngorm and Beinn Eighe in Scotland, which serve almost as National Parks. In addition there are many nature reserves run by voluntary organizations like the county conservation trusts, the Royal Society for the Protection of Birds (RSPB) and the National Trust (NT); recent changes in the state conservation organization, formerly the Nature Conservancy Council, have highlighted the need for these. Many of the reserves have hides, visitor centres and/or facilities that give excellent opportunities for viewing and photography.

The United Kingdom, which occupies most of the British Isles, has a total area of 244,100 sq km and a population of about 56 million. Although not an especially large country, it has a very diverse landscape, thanks to the extraordinarily varied geology and land use. The weather is dominated by Atlantic depressions, which strongly affect the western parts of the country for much of the year, though their influence fades to the east. Because the main part – Great

OPPOSITE PAGE: *Derwentwater in the Lake District, with Skiddaw rising in the distance.*

SCOTLAND

1. Shetland Isles

Location: About 160km north of John o' Groats.
Access: By boat from Aberdeen; by air from Aberdeen or Edinburgh; generally open access to unenclosed land.
Timing: May–October.
The Shetlands, Britain's northernmost outpost, are at

Hermaness, northernmost point of the Shetland Isles.

the same latitude as Bergen. They provide a very different experience from the rest of Britain; although the range of species is limited, their abundance more than compensates for this. Most parts are of some interest, and there are birds everywhere, while Otter roam widely along the shores. A good deal of time is required to do these islands justice; the sites discussed here probably provide the most concentrated amounts of wildlife.

Fetlar, an island to the east of Yell, has a large (700ha) RSPB reserve with breeding Red-throated Diver, Red-necked Phalarope, Whimbrel, Golden Plover, Dunlin and Arctic and Great Skuas as well as reasonable numbers of seabird colonies. Both Grey and Common Seals breed, and there are Otter around the coast. There is a reasonable flora, especially on the serpentine rock, which is base-rich; it includes Northern Marsh Orchid and Northern Rock-cress. There is a rich intertidal life, as in most of the Shetlands.

Foula, a remote 1380ha island well west of Lerwick, has spectacular scenery and vast colonies of seabirds on its high cliffs and grassy slopes. The main species are Great and Arctic Skuas, Puffin, Guillemot, Black Guillemot, Razorbill and Storm Petrel.

Unst is the most northerly island of the group. At Hermaness, Britain's northernmost point, there are superb seabird colonies including Skua, Gannet, most of the commoner seabirds, breeding waders and Red-throated Diver. Otter and both seals thrive around the coast. The island's botanic interest centres on northern species like Lovage and Moss Campion, as well as

a more specialized flora on the Keen of Hamar, on the east coast.

Noss is an uninhabited island off Bressay, just east of Lerwick. Part of it is a National Nature Reserve, with some of the finest seabird colonies in Britain (over 100,000 pairs of various species). Otter and both seals are found around the coast. The flora is attractive, especially on the cliffs in May–June.

Fair Isle, about 40km south of the main Shetland group, halfway to the Orkneys (site 2), has reasonable seabird colonies as well as seals, Otter and a good coastal flora, but is best known for the marvellous array of migrant birds – over 300 species recorded – that make a landfall here in spring and autumn. There is a famous observatory (with hostel) where many thousands of birds have been ringed.

2. Orkney Isles

Location: Just northeast of John o' Groats.
Access: By car ferry from Scrabster or Aberdeen; by passenger ferry from John o' Groats; by air from Aberdeen and elsewhere. Access on foot to unenclosed areas generally open.
Timing: May–October.

The Orkneys, like the Shetlands, though somewhat less extreme in climate and with more agricultural land, offer something a little different from the rest of the British Isles. Birds are the main attraction, but there are rare plants such as Scottish Primrose and Oyster Plant as well as, around the coast, good mammals.

Mainland Orkney has some good seabird colonies and protected areas of moorland where Hen Harrier, Merlin and Short-eared Owl breed. The reserves at Dale of Cottasgarth, Hobbister and Marwick Head are worth visiting. Otter and seals frequent the coast.

Papa Westray, at the north of the group and partly a reserve, has a huge Arctic Tern colony, many Skua and good cliff colonies of seabirds. There are also breeding waders, like Dunlin and Oystercatcher, and scattered Eider. The flora includes Scottish Primrose and Spring Squill.

North Ronaldsay, to the northeast, has limited seabird colonies but a good range of breeding birds like waders, Corncrake, Eider and Twite. Also of interest are the Ronaldsay Sheep, confined to the coastal areas by a perimeter wall.

Noup Head, at the northwest tip of **Westray**, is an exceptional seabird cliff colony, with vast numbers of birds, especially Guillemot.

Copinsay, off the mainland's southeastern tip and an RSPB reserve, has large colonies of cliff-nesting birds and terns, plus Oyster Plant on the shore.

3. Handa Island

Location: Off the northwest Highland coast, just north of Scourie.
Access: Via the A894, then minor road to Tarbert; regular boats in spring–summer.
Timing: Best April to late July.

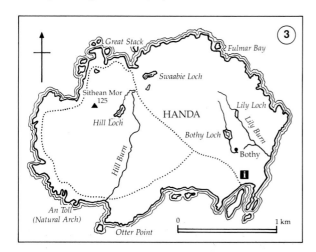

The habitats of this impressive 310ha island include moorland, grassland, bog, sandy beaches and high cliffs, together with small freshwater lochans – superb Highland scenery. It is known best for its dramatic western and northern cliffs, where huge numbers of seabirds breed, especially Guillemot, Razorbill, Kittiwake, Black Guillemot and Puffin. On the moorland areas are Great and Arctic Skuas, Eider, Golden

Handa Island, best known for its vast seabird colonies.

Plover and others. The interesting flora includes masses of Roseroot and Lovage, Royal Fern, Pale Butterwort and Northern Marsh Orchid. Grey Seal, Dolphin and Porpoise may be seen around the shore.

4. Invernaver

Location: In the centre of the north coast, around the village of Bettyhill on the A836.
Access: From Bettyhill and the A836; generally open on foot.
Timing: May–September.

A lovely combination of northern and coastal habitats, partly (552ha) within a reserve. Habitats include seashore, dunes, blown-sand machair, moorland and lochans. The area is noted for its rich flora, a mixture of mountain, Arctic and coastal species like Mountain Avens, Purple and Yellow Saxifrages, Alpine Bistort, Scottish Primrose, Purple Oxytropis, Dark Red Helleborine and Dwarf Juniper. There are also good lichens and bryophytes; this is the only British locality for the moss *Brachythecium erythrorrhizon*. Birds breeding here include Greenshank, Snipe and Eider.

The prolific flora at **Strathy Point and Bay**, about 14km east of Bettyhill, features Scottish Primrose.

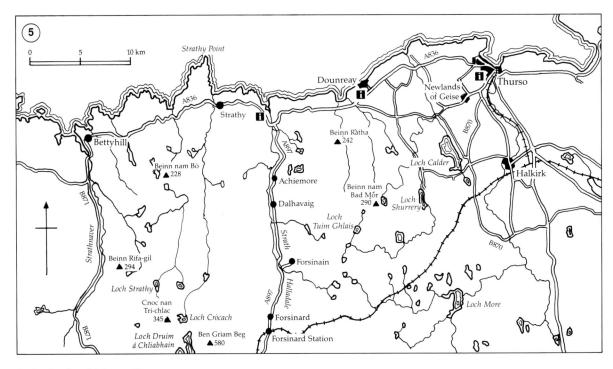

5. Sutherland Flowe Country

Location: The area of northeast Scotland between Bettyhill and Thurso.
Access: The B871 and A897 cross the area; access on foot is generally unrestricted but difficult.
Timing: May–October.

The Flowe country is a vast peatland wilderness, mainly in Sutherland but partly in Caithness. There are no concentrated areas of interest, but overall it supports a high proportion of Britain's breeding upland and northern birds as well as prolific moorland and bog flowers and insects. It is of particular importance as a place where Red-throated Diver, Greylag Goose, Scoter, Hen Harrier, Greenshank, Golden Plover, Dunlin and a few Whimbrel breed.

Any exploration of the region requires preparation, since the terrain is difficult and isolated – you can walk for days without seeing anyone. Large tracts have been planted with conifers, and the forest tracks give some access to wilder areas.

6. Inverpolly and Ben More Coigach

Location: About 15km north of Ullapool, west of the A835.
Access: Via the A835; direct access from Knockan and surrounds, or by minor roads running west into the area; some restrictions on access during September–October.
Timing: Interesting all year, but best May–August.

These two important reserves cover a huge area (17,000ha) of almost continuous wild mountain country and some coast. Habitats include upland birch woodlands, moorland, grassland, high-mountain areas (up to 743m at Ben More Coigach), cliffs, bogs and scattered lochans. Ptarmigan, Red-throated Diver, Red-breasted Merganser, Greenshank, Golden Plover, Twite and Ring Ouzel are among the many birds breeding here, and there are large numbers of Red Deer, plus Wildcat, Otter, Pine Marten and Badger.

The site is botanically quite rich, with a good range of bog and mountain species and, wherever the limestones outcrop, lime-loving species. Altogether about 400 species have been recorded, including Mountain Avens, Pale Butterwort, Lesser and Intermediate Bladderworts, Trailing Azalea and Northern Buckler

Inverpolly lies amid some of Scotland's wildest country.

Fern. The insect life has not yet been fully studied, but includes a wide range of moths as well as northern dragonflies like Highland Darter and Azure Hawker.

This is good walking country if you are well prepared, but many areas are very remote. It is also interesting geologically, with ancient rocks overlying younger ones. Information by the trail at Knockan tells how explaining this situation led to clearer ideas about movement within the Earth's crust.

7. Inchnadamph

Location: To the east of the A837 at the eastern end of Loch Assynt, about 15km east of Lochinver.
Access: On foot from the A837 at or south of Inchnadamph. Access is restricted July 15–October 15.
Timing: Best May–July.

This 1300ha area of limestone uplands has some fine karst features: caves, swallowholes, underground streams, etc. The rich upland-limestone flora contains species like Mountain Avens, Purple Saxifrage, Alpine Meadow-rue, Norwegian Sandwort, Globeflower, Dark Red Helleborine, Small White Orchid and uncommon sedges like *Carex rupestris* and *C. capillaris*. Breeding birds on the moorland areas include Golden Plover, Red Grouse and Ring Ouzel. The bones of Brown Bear, Arctic Fox, Reindeer and Lemming, all now extinct in the wild in Scotland, have been found in the Allt nan Uamh Valley, at the south of the reserve.

8. Uists and Benbecula

Location: In the southern part of the Outer Hebrides, opposite Skye.
Access: By ferry from Oban or Skye; causeways link the islands. Access is generally open on foot, although the reserves impose some restrictions during the bird-breeding season.
Timing: April–September; best May–June.

Between them, North and South Uist and the linking island of Benbecula hold much of what is best in the Outer Hebrides. The whole area is of great interest: there are several reserves, and other parts have good machair, bogs and lakes. Otter and seals occur all around the shores, and the range of seashore life is good. **Balranald Reserve**, near the northwest tip of North Uist, has some superb machair habitat, with high densities of breeding waders like Dunlin and Redshank and beautiful displays of flowers in May–June. There are also Corncrake, and lochans with breeding divers. **Benbecula** has good machair habitats and excellent coastal mud and sand; Little Tern breed here and there. The large **Loch Druidibeg Reserve** lies towards the northern end of South Uist, where the B890 joins the A865. The loch has an interesting flora, including Water Lobelia, as well as breeding Greylag

Goose, Red-breasted Merganser and Eider. West of the main road lies an area of machair and dunes with a rich flora and good breeding waders and terns. There is an observation tower at Loch Druidibeg. The whole area is good for walking and merits several days' stay.

9. Rhum and Eigg

Location: Islands off the southwest tip of Skye.
Access: By boat from Mallaig or Arisaig; permits are needed for parts of Eigg. There is limited accommodation on both islands.
Timing: April–June best; midges are a plague in July–August.

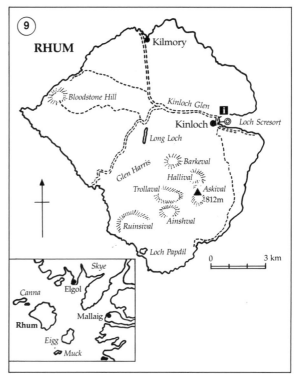

The boat journey to either of these dramatic islands is marvellous in good weather, with seabirds (including Shearwater), seals and Common Dolphin, not to mention spectacular scenery. Rhum is a National Nature Reserve, the first area set aside for a White-tailed Eagle reintroduction programme; it also has breeding Golden Eagle, Peregrine, Manx Shearwater (in huge numbers), Golden Plover and Red Grouse, and mammals including a good population of Red Deer, Otter and both seal species, together with feral goats. The flora has species like Pyramidal Bugle, Wilson's Filmy Fern, Mountain Avens, Northern Rock-cress and Scottish Asphodel in a variety of habitats. The surprisingly varied insects include Dark Green and Small Pearl-bordered Fritillaries, Fox Moth, Northern Eggar and Poplar Hawkmoth.

Eigg, smaller and partly covered by nature reserves, has a good flora, breeding birds and, as with all this area, superb views.

10. Beinn Eighe and Torridon

Location: Between Loch Torridon and Loch Maree, enclosed by the A896 and the A832.
Access: On foot from the main roads; access restricted in autumn.
Timing: May–September.

These two large reserves form part of the much larger Gairloch Conservation Unit and encompass some of the finest mountain scenery in Scotland, rising to 1063m at Liathach; this is excellent walking country. There are examples of most mountain habitats, including grassland, moorland, cliffs, glacial lakes and woodland, notably some fine remnants of Caledonian forest along the shore of Loch Maree. Among the birds breeding here are Golden Eagle, Peregrine, Merlin, Red-throated Diver, Greenshank and Redwing. Resident mammals include Red and Roe Deer, Wildcat, Pine Marten, Otter and Red Squirrel. The flora is rich in places, especially in the pinewoods and among the limestone outcrops; there are Creeping Lady's Tresses, Pyramidal Bugle, wintergreens, saxifrages and many others. Mosses, liverworts and lichens are all good, with species like Lungwort very abundant. Among the insects are surprising abundances of Azure Hawker, White-faced Darter, Large Heath Butterfly and Emperor Moth. There are visitor centres at Anacaun (for Beinn Eighe) and Torridon.

Beinn Eighe nature reserve offers excellent walking.

11. Glen Affric

Location: About 40km southwest of Inverness.
Access: A minor road runs into the area from Cannich, on the A831; access on foot is via trails.
Timing: Beautiful all year; best May–July and October.

One of the most attractive valleys in Scotland; about 1300ha lies in a reserve with remnants of native Caledonian Pine forest – other trees besides Scots Pine are birches, rowan, aspen and juniper. The flora has pinewood specialities like Creeping Lady's Tresses, and the autumn fungi are excellent. Breeding birds include Capercaillie, Crested Tit, Black Grouse and Common Sandpiper. Red Squirrel is common. With the wild high mountains all around, Glen Affric offers magnificent walking.

12. Cairngorms and Spey Valley

Location: Southeast of Inverness, around Aviemore, and extending south towards Braemar.
Access: The A9 gives best access; a minor road (with skilift) from Coylumbridge gives good access to higher areas.
Timing: Interesting all year; best May–August.

One of Britain's finest areas for the naturalist, with a marvellous concentration of habitats and species.

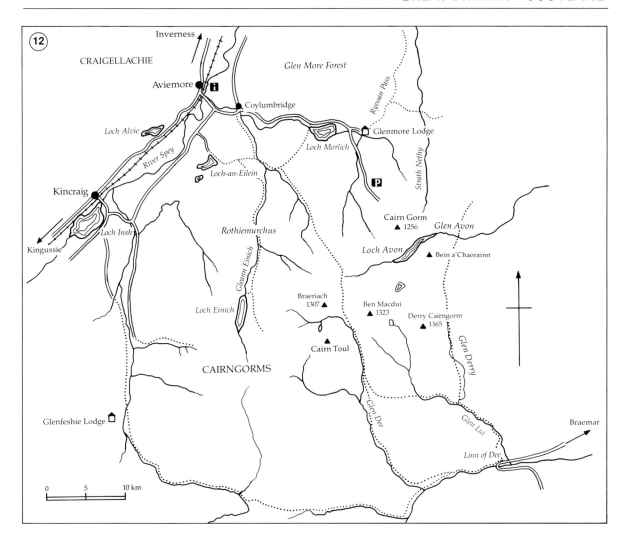

Between Kingussie and Grantown-on-Spey the Spey Valley has a superb series of reserves which between them offer ancient pinewoods and birchwoods, marshes, lakes, heathland, grassland and other habitats. The Cairngorms, rising to 1309m at Ben Macdui, form a high windswept plateau that is climatically like northern Iceland, with deeply cut valleys and glacial lakes. Here there are breeding Ptarmigan, Dotterel, Golden Plover and Golden Eagle, along with Mountain Hare, a herd of Reindeer (introduced, but doing well) and a good flora. In the valley are numerous breeding birds of interest, including Osprey, Peregrine Falcon, Wood Sandpiper and Crested Tit. The pinewoods have all the expected specialities, like Twinflower, and good autumn fungi. The insects are very prolific, too; among them are various northern dragonfly species, moths like Kentish Glory and Rannoch Sprawler, and beetles including several old-forest longhorns and the attractive Bee-chafer.

There is also a Wildlife Park near Kingussie, infor-

Tranquil Loch An Eileann in the Spey Valley.

mation centres at Aviemore, Loch Garten, Abernethy Reserve and elsewhere, and numerous general tourist facilities. This area merits a good deal of your time.

13. Sands of Forvie and Ythan Estuary

Location: About 20km north of Aberdeen, just beyond Newburgh.
Access: From the A975 or the B9003; access restricted to paths and hides.
Timing: April–July for all aspects; good winter birds.

Covering over 1000ha of estuary, dunes and moorland on the north side of the River Ythan, this is noted as Britain's best breeding site for Eider Duck, with over 2000 pairs – a marvellous sight and sound. It is also good for breeding Shelduck and Sandwich, Common, Arctic and Little Terns. In autumn and winter there are good numbers of waders and wildfowl, including some resident Eider. The dunes have a reasonable flora and, on more stable areas, some good lichen-heath.

14. Dee Valley from Braemar to Dinnet

Location: Along the River Dee, west of Aberdeen.
Access: The A93 runs right through the area; generally good access on foot to the best areas.
Timing: Best for most groups May–August; good views of deer and other mammals in winter.

the landscape must have looked like soon after the last ice age. **Glen Muick**, running south from Ballater, is good for Red Deer and Mountain Hare. The mountain of Lochnagar, at its head, has a superb Arctic-Alpine flora on the high corrie cliffs. The **Coyles of Muick** – serpentine peaks on the valley's west side – have an unusual flora. Just northwest of Dinnet, the **Muir of Dinnet Reserve** has two lakes with intervening moorland and woodland and a curious glacial hollow, Burn o' Vat, on the stream nearby; there are good breeding and wintering birds, rare insects like Kentish Glory Moth, and a good flora.

15. Caenlochan

Location: East of the A93, where Grampian and Tayside meet, as far as the head of Glen Clova.
Access: Via the A93 or B955.
Timing: April–August; some restrictions in the latter part of this period.

This large mountainous tract is one of Scotland's finest regions for Arctic-Alpine flowers. The best parts tend to be the high cliff areas with base-rich rock – notably Glas Maol and Glen Doll/Coire Fee – though these can be hard to reach. Among the many plants of interest are Purple Saxifrage, Alpine Saw-wort, Alpine Saxifrage, Rock Speedwell and Alpine Meadow-rue. This is also a good area for montane birds like Golden Eagle, Ptarmigan, Golden Plover, Dunlin and Ring Ouzel, and there are Red Deer and Mountain Hare.

The River Dee, flowing through Ballochbuie Forest. Mount Lochnagar rises at its head.

Coire Fee, in the mountainous region of Caenlochan.

This beautiful stretch of valley has a number of areas of great interest scattered along it. At the upper end, just southwest of Braemar, **Morrone Birkwood**, comprising open birch and juniper woodland on base-rich soil and with a rich flora, gives a good idea of what

16. Ben Lui

Location: Southwest of Tyndrum, on the A82.
Access: On foot only, from the A82 or from the Forestry Commission Car Park on the A85.
Timing: May–August.

Ben Lui (1140m) has a rich collection of Arctic-Alpine flowers on its base-rich mica schists and limestones, especially on the north-facing cliffs and crags. This is a remote and difficult area, and you should make good preparations for any expedition into the higher parts. Species of interest include Alpine Bartsia, Mountain Avens, Purple, Yellow and Starry Saxifrages, Alpine Saw-wort, Round-leaved Wintergreen and Mountain Bladder-fern.

17. Ben Lawers

Location: On the north side of Loch Tay, northeast of Killin.
Access: Via a minor road north from the A827 to the visitor centre; marked footpaths thereafter.
Timing: May–August; April for Purple Saxifrage.

Ben Lawers (1214m), Britain's best known mountain for flowers, supports an exceptional range of species, often in great abundance. There are numerous outcrops of eroding mica-schist, especially in the higher parts, and it is here that the floral displays are at their best, with species like Alpine Forget-me-not, Snow Gentian, Drooping Saxifrage, Rock Speedwell, Alpine Cinquefoil, Alpine Saw-wort and various rare sedges and rushes, as well as good lichens, mosses and club-mosses. There are also Mountain Hare, Raven and interesting insects like Small Mountain Ringlet and Northern Eggar.

Most of the mountains in the Breadalbane Range are good for flowers wherever there are outcrops of mica-schist, and this is good walking country. Away from Ben Lawers you will have it much to yourself.

18. Loch Leven

Location: Just east of Kinross, on the M90 between Dunfermline and Perth.
Access: Roads encircle the lake, and there are several marked access points; access into the reserve is restricted.
Timing: April–July and October–March.

A large freshwater lake and fringing wetlands covering about 1600ha, with an additional reserve nearby at Vane Farm. From autumn through winter large numbers of Pink-footed Goose arrive, followed by Greylag Goose, Whooper Swan, numerous ducks, other geese in small numbers and waders. In spring and summer considerable numbers of Great-crested Grebe, Tufted Duck, Gadwall, Wigeon, Shoveler and Shelduck breed here. Plentiful interesting freshwater fishes, of numerous species, are found in the lake.

Ben Lawers supports an exceptional flora.

Vane Farm RSPB reserve at Loch Leven.

19. Tentsmuir Point

Location: About 5km southeast of Tayport.
Access: By minor road from Leuchars, then on foot from the parking area.
Timing: All year.

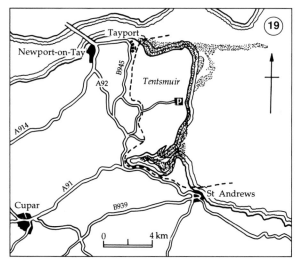

A large headland of accreting sand; a reserve covers over 500ha. Habitats include large expanses of sandy and muddy foreshore, dunes and scrub. From autumn through spring large numbers of waders – including Sanderling, Dunlin, Grey Plover, Oystercatcher and even Little Stint – feed and roost. Hosts of ducks gather off Tentsmuir in autumn and winter, including thousands of Eider, Scoter, Scaup . The dunes are botanically rich – over 400 species recorded – with Grass-of-Parnassus, Coral-root Orchid, Purple Milk Vetch, Seaside Centaury and many others making fine displays. Grayling and Dark Green Fritillary are everywhere.

20. Aberlady Bay and the Bass Rock

Location: Aberlady Bay is about 15km northeast of Edinburgh; the Bass Rock is about 5km northeast of North Berwick.
Access: Via the A198 for Aberlady; for the Bass Rock boats and landing permission can be obtained at North Berwick.
Timing: April–July for flowers, insects and breeding birds; autumn-winter for birds.

The extensive mudflats, sand, saltmarshes, dunes and stable grassland of Aberlady Bay are partly protected by a 582ha local nature reserve. Of the well over 200 bird species recorded, many – including Eider, Shelduck and Ringed Plover – breed here, while in winter there are large numbers of geese, ducks, grebes and waders, with hosts of waders at passage periods. The rich flora has a mixture of saltmarsh and dune species, and all three eelgrass species are present on the mudflats; there are also 15 sedge species, various orchids, Moonwort, Grass-of-Parnassus and many others.

The Bass Rock supports a huge gannetry – one of the most accessible in Britain – and you can also see other seabirds and seals.

The entire coastline between these two sites is of interest.

21. Solway Firth

Location: To the south of Dumfries.
Access: The B725 and minor roads off it give access to the best areas.
Timing: Best late autumn to spring for birds; early summer for Natterjack Toad.

Although the whole Solway Firth area is of interest,

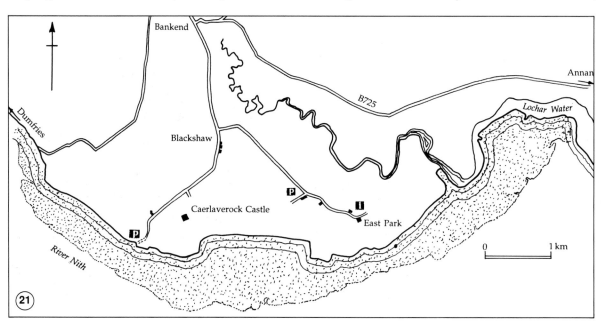

the area with the best facilities and the most birds is around Caerlaverock, where there are two linked reserves. Birds start to arrive in quantity from autumn onwards, notably tens of thousands of Barnacle Goose (virtually all of Spitzbergen's breeding population), Pinkfoot Goose and Whooper and Bewick's Swans; there are also many waders and ducks and smaller numbers of raptors. Viewing facilities are excellent, with warm hides from which you can watch feeding areas and tower hides that look out over the grazing marshes. In summer you can see breeding waders like Redshank and Oystercatcher. Natterjack Toad breed in the pools at the upper edge of the saltmarsh.

WALES

22. Newborough Warren

Location: At Anglesey's southern tip.
Access: Off the A4080 to a car park, then on foot via marked tracks.
Timing: April–October.

Mostly protected by a large nature reserve, this is one of Britain's finest dune systems. The lime-rich sand supports an extremely rich flora (over 560 species); aside from widespread dune plants like Sea Spurge and Sea Holly there are many less common species,

Glaciated valley at Nant Ffrancon in Snowdonia National Park.

including Meadow Saxifrage, Grass-of-Parnassus, Round-leaved Wintergreen, Yellow Bird's Nest, Early Marsh Orchid and Dune Helleborine. The reserve also has areas of saltmarsh and a rocky headland, and there is a large plantation nearby. Among the reserve's insects are Green Tiger Beetle and numerous butterflies, including Dark Green Fritillary. The coast has a good range of birds all year round.

Elsewhere on Anglesey, the southern side of **Holyhead Island** (partly a nature reserve, at South Stack) has marvellous seabird colonies, flowery clifftops and meadows, breeding Chough and other features of interest.

23. Snowdonia National Park

Location: Southeast of Bangor, stretching south to beyond Dolgellau.
Access: Numerous roads including the A5 and A4086.
Timing: Interesting all year; best May–August.

Well over 200,000ha of superb mountain country, including the highest mountains in England or Wales, numerous natural lakes, moorland, grassland, cliffs and deciduous woodlands. The whole area is excellent walking country, though large tracts are rather bereft of species. Good areas include the Cwm Idwal/Llyn Idwal area, Snowdon itself, the great dune system at Morfa Harlech and the isolated peak of Cader Idris, near the south of the park. The Alpine flora is reasonably rich, and includes Purple, Tufted and Mossy Saxifrages, Alpine Cinquefoil, Alpine Sawwort and the famous Snowdon Lily, confined in Britain to a few nearby mountains. Other plants of interest are Water Lobelia, in stony upland lakes, and

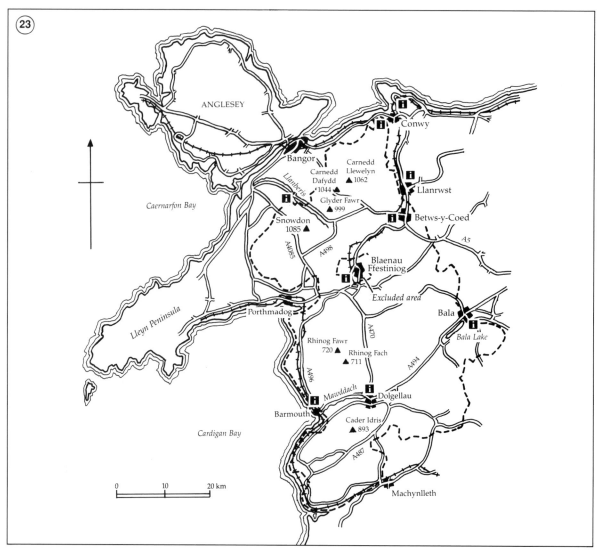

(23)

ANGLESEY

Conwy

Bangor

Carnedd Llewelyn ▲ 1062

Carnedd Dafydd ▲ 1044

Llanberis

Caernarfon Bay

Glyder Fawr ▲ 999

Llanrwst

Snowdon 1085 ▲

Betws-y-Coed

A5

Blaenau Ffestiniog

Excluded area

Lleyn Peninsula

Porthmadog

A498

A4085

A470

Bala

Bala Lake

A494

Rhinog Fawr 720 ▲

Rhinog Fach ▲ 711

A496

Mawddach

Dolgellau

Barmouth

Cardigan Bay

Cader Idris ▲ 893

A487

Machynlleth

0   10   20 km

good dune species on the coastal sites. The breeding birds are limited but include a number of uncommon species like Peregrine Falcon, Chough, Raven, Buzzard, Pied Flycatcher and Ring Ouzel. The insects are scant, though some groups, like Fritillaries and old-woodland beetles, do well.

Snowdonia needs a long visit – preferably several at different times of year – if you are really to appreciate its remarkable scenery and natural history.

24. Dyfi Estuary

Location: Southwest of Machynlleth, north of Aberystwyth.
Access: The A487 and B4353 lead into the area; marked paths for access on foot.
Timing: All year.

The attractive Dyfi Estuary area is worth visiting all year round for birdwatching.

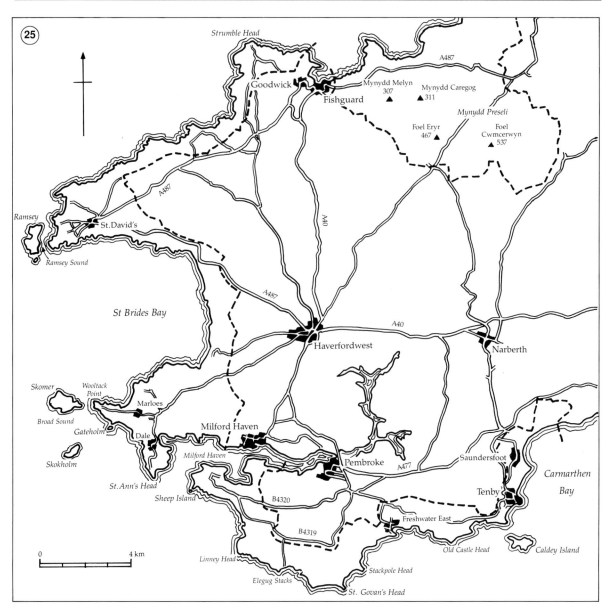

The south side of this attractive estuary has a fine range of habitats, partly protected by three important reserves. **Ynis-hir**, at the eastern end, includes some fine old Sessile Oak woodlands together with alluvial grasslands, open water, saltmarsh and mudflats. It has an information centre (where day permits can be obtained) and a series of hides, and is good for birds all year, with 67 breeding species and large numbers of wintering wildfowl and waders. The flora is ample, and there are over 30 butterfly species. **Ynyslas**, at the mouth, is made up mainly of dunes; these have a rich flora – including fine displays of Marsh Orchids in early summer – and a good range of insects. Offshore there is a fine example of a submerged forest. **Cors Fochno**, south of the B4353, is a fine raised bog accessible by permit only (apply at Ynyslas centre, at the dunes car park).

25. Pembrokeshire Coast National Park

Location: The Dyfed coast from Cardigan to just beyond Tenby.
Access: Numerous roads run into the area; access on foot is generally open.
Timing: All year; best April–July.

Established mainly to include 270km of wild Welsh coastline but including also some inland hills and heaths, the park covers 58,000ha of rocky shores, cliffs, islands, saltmarshes, moorland and heathland, open water and other associated habitats, all with spectacular scenery. Its main interests include the seabird colonies on the islands of Skokholm, Skomer, Grassholm and Ramsey. Skomer is the most accessible – from Martinshaven by regular boats – and has Skomer Vole, resident Grey Seal and impressive early-summer flowers

Whitesands Bay on the beautiful Pembrokeshire coast.

as well as the excellent bird colonies. Grassholm is a spectacular gannetry; getting there requires a longer boat-trip, available only after mid-June. Skokholm is most easily visited on week-long courses or on day-trips (Mondays). Dowrog Common and other commons near St David's have a rich flora, with heath and bog species, and good insects, like the damselfly *Coenagrion mercuriale* and Small Red Damselfly. The Bosherston estate, south of Pembroke, has a marvellous mixture of lakes (with exceptional White Water-lily displays and Otter), grassland, dunes, limestone cliffs, heathland, and excellent seashore life. Many of the cliffs and coastal headlands of the park have spectacular displays of flowers during April–June.

The whole park is walking country *par excellence*, and a long-distance path runs right around the coast. Most areas have a terrific range of seashore life, and the Study Centre at Dale specializes in it.

26. Cors Caron (Tregaron Bog)

Location: Just north of Tregaron (northeast of Lampeter), to the west of the B4343.
Access: From the B4343; access is limited to marked walks.
Timing: Best May–September.

One of the best remaining examples of a raised mire in England and Wales. At 800ha the reserve is large enough to allow the ecosystem to work properly, and so to show a whole spectrum of mire development. The flora includes most bog species – e.g., all three sundew species, Bog Rosemary, Bog Asphodel and Cranberry, plus good sedges and *Sphagnum* species. Over 40 bird species breed, and many more visit in autumn or winter; Red Kite hunt regularly from nearby breeding grounds. Otter and Polecat are present, and the good insect fauna includes dragonflies, damselflies and butterflies like Green Hairstreak.

27. Gower Peninsula

Location: To the southwest of Swansea.
Access: Via the A4118 and minor roads; generally access on foot to unenclosed land is open.
Timing: April–September.

A superbly varied and historic area, despite its nearness to Swansea and its popularity as a holiday destination. Habitats include saltmarsh, dunes, ancient woodlands, limestone cliffs and beaches, moorland and grassland. The northern coast has superb saltmarshes, culminating in the dunes at **Whiteford Point**, which have a good flora. The estuary to the north attracts many birds in winter and at passage times. The southern limestone hills and cliffs, from Rhossili eastwards, have a rich flora with rarities like Hoary Rock-rose, Yellow Whitlow-grass and Goldilocks Aster.

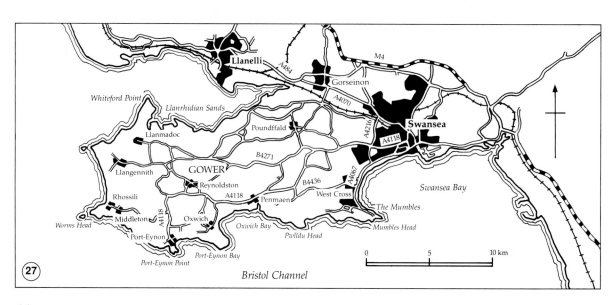

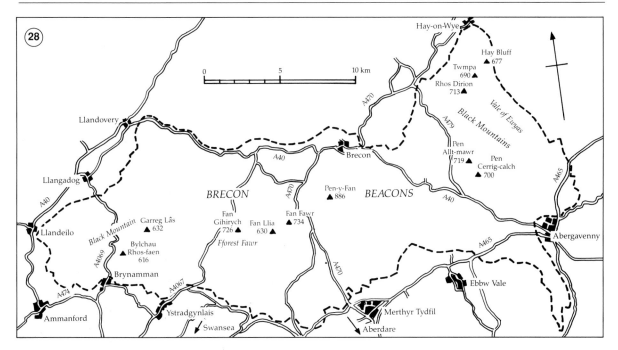

A large reserve at **Oxwich Bay** protects some species-rich dunes together with wetland and woodland. Some of the small inland valleys, particularly on National Trust land, have good fringing ancient woodland and wet meadows.

The whole southern coastline is excellent for seashore life, particularly Oxwich Bay and the Mumbles. The Gower is a great place for walking; you need several days fully to appreciate it.

Pen-y-Fan, the highest point in the Brecon Mountains.

28. Brecon Beacons National Park

Location: Between Merthyr Tydfil and Brecon.
Access: The A470, A4067, A4069 and various minor roads run through the park; access on foot is generally open, and there are many paths.
Timing: May–October.

The 134 sq km park is dominated by the Brecon Mountains, which rise to over 800m at Pen-y-Fan. The rounded southern slopes are clothed mainly with sheep-grazed grassland, but the northern slopes are steep and in places heavily glaciated. Other habitats include ancient woodlands, open waters and limestone

pavements and grasslands. The upland grasslands tend to lack interesting species; the good bits include the northern cliffs, especially at Craig Cerrig Gleisiag, east of Pen-y-Fan. Craig-y-Cilau, about 10km west of Abergavenny, is a fine limestone valley with old woodland, scrub, grassland, cliffs and bogs and a particularly rich flora that mixes montane, limestone, woodland and bog species, among them many rarities. Birds here include Peregrine Falcon, Ring Ouzel and Dipper, and the bats in the caves include Lesser Horseshoe. **Ogof-ffynnon-ddu Reserve**, northwest of Ystradfellte, contains one of the longest cave systems in Britain as well as some fine limestone pavement and grassland, capped by Millstone Grit; it has a rich flora.

There are some fine waterfalls and caves around the southern part of the park, and the whole area is heartily recommended for walking.

ENGLAND

29. Farne Islands

Location: Northeast of Seahouses, about 25km southeast of Berwick-upon-Tweed.
Access: Regular boats from Seahouses to selected islands in late spring–summer; non-members of the National Trust must pay landing fees.
Timing: Late April to early July.

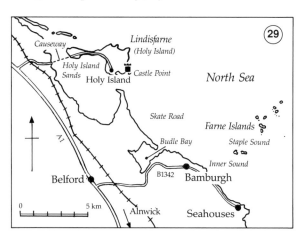

These rocky dolerite islands off the Northumberland coast are best known for their superb colonies of seabirds, especially Puffin, Guillemot, Razorbill, Kittiwake, Arctic and Common Terns, Fulmar and gulls, together with Eider Duck and smaller numbers of other species. Although access is controlled and you can go only as part of a large group, the birds are so tame and abundant that the experience is not to be missed. Take a hat to avoid damage from Arctic Tern on Inner Farne! There are also Grey Seal, and good displays of common coastal flowers like Thrift and Sea Campion and the introduced *Amsinckia intermedia*.

Kittiwakes and Shags breeding on Staple Island in the Farne group.

Not far north, **Lindisfarne** (Holy Island), accessible by road causeway when the tide is low, has fine dunes with good flowers and large areas of mudflats which attract numerous waders and wildfowl. Shelduck and Eider Duck breed in quantity.

30. Northumberland National Park

Location: Much of the inland uplands of Northumberland.
Access: The A68, A696 and many minor roads run through the park.
Timing: Best April–October.

Foxgloves colonizing a shingle bank beside Harthorpe Burn, Northumberland National Park.

The broad tracts of grassy moors, with their low density of species, can be relatively disappointing in this vast area (113,000ha) of upland country, rising to over 800m in the high Cheviots. The best parts tend to be the bogs and flushes, where there are plants like sundews and Bog Orchid, and the craggy areas like Harbottle Crags, west of Rothbury, while the ancient valley-side woodlands tend to have good bryophytes and lichens and a range of flowering plants. At the south of the park, in the area around Housesteads, is one of the finest stretches of Hadrian's Wall, with an impressive Roman fort. Around here you can find a good mixture of natural lakes (loughs) with fringing marsh or bog, some good Whin Sill cliffs, and, south of the B6318, base-rich grasslands and quarry areas on limestone.

Nearby **Kielder Forest** – a huge planted area with only fragments of original vegetation, together with a large reservoir – is of some interest. It has good trails and information points.

31. Lake District National Park

Location: Most of south-central Cumbria.
Access: Numerous roads; access on foot is excellent, with huge numbers of footpaths.
Timing: All year; best April–November.

Coniston Water, popular with visitors to the Lake District.

With its wonderful mountain and lakeland scenery, this National Park is popular at all times of year. Although not a mecca for naturalists, perhaps because of the lack of good high-Alpine flowers and uncommon breeding birds when compared to Scotland, it has much of interest and is so colossal (224,000ha) that there is always something new to discover. The ancient oakwoods (with birch and rowan) in areas like Borrowdale have good lichens and bryophytes and flowers such as Alpine Enchanter's Nightshade and Touch-me-not Balsam. Roudsea Wood, northeast of Ulverston, has a mixture of basic and acid soils and a rich flora to match. The many bogs and fens where

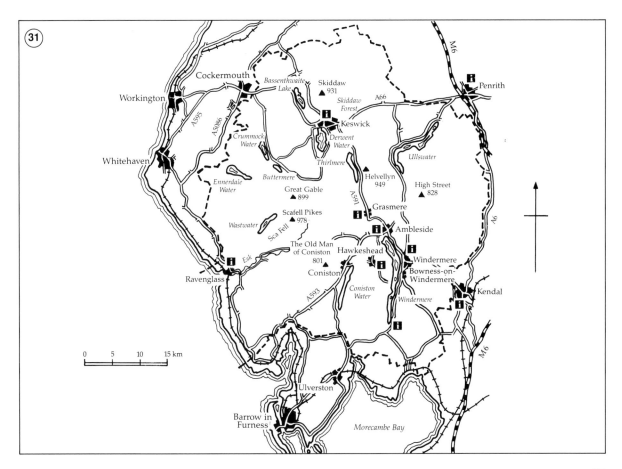

lakes have gradually filled in with peat – as at Esthwaite Water and Buttermere – often have a good flora. At Ravenglass there are good dunes, a very rich flora and all six species of native amphibians as residents. The park's main display and information centre is at Brockhole, just south of Windermere, where there are also good lakeside birds.

Outside the park, **Walney Island**, south of Barrow-in-Furness, has a fine mixture of coastal habitats, especially dunes, shingle and saltmarsh, with a good flora and, at the southern tip, a bird hide.

32. Silverdale Area

Location: Around Silverdale and Arnside, on Morecambe Bay.
Access: The B5282 and minor roads lead into the area; variable access on foot.
Timing: All year.

This is a marvellous and varied array of high-quality sites, all within quite a small area. Most of it is underlain by limestone: there are particularly good hills and limestone-pavement areas at Arnside Knott and Gaitbarrows, whose very rich floras include rarities like Teesdale Violet in a white form, Bearberry and Dark Red Helleborine, along with abundant butterflies like Dark Green, High Brown, Pearl-bordered and Duke of Burgundy Fritillaries. Just south of Gaitbarrows are lakes with marginal fen as well as ancient woodland. **Leighton Moss**, a bird reserve with many breeding wetland species, also has Otter and a good flora. **Morecambe Bay** is a top site for wintering waders and some wildfowl.

33. Yorkshire Dales National Park

Location: Northwest North Yorkshire, just extending into Cumbria, between Skipton, Kirby Lonsdale and Richmond.
Access: Numerous roads thread through the area; access to unenclosed land is generally open.
Timing: Some interest all year; best May–July.

A marvellous area (176,000ha) of upland countryside, dominated by Carboniferous limestone. The park includes upland base-rich grasslands, limestone pavements, mountains, lakes, waterfalls, hay meadows and deciduous woodlands amid a historic and attractive landscape. Malham is a good centre, with nearby limestone pavement, dramatic cliffs at Malham Cove (and rare plants like Jacob's Ladder) and the large natural lake at Malham Tarn (with fringing bog and fen, and good plants and insects). Wharfedale, Swaledale, Littondale and Ribblesdale have some fine hay meadows (though many have been agriculturally improved) with flowers like Wood Cranesbill, Melancholy Thistle and Cowslip. There are a few good, flora-rich woods, such as at Grassington. This is excellent walking country, and there are fascinating caves and swallowholes.

Thornton Force, near Ingleton in the Yorkshire Dales.

34. Upper Teesdale

Location: In the upper Tees Valley, above Middleton-in-Teesdale.
Access: The B6277 runs into the area; access via footpaths.
Timing: April–August.

This remarkable upland area, noted for its assemblage of rare plants, is covered by the Upper Teesdale Nature Reserve and, further west on the high watershed, the Moor House Reserve. Outcrops of metamorphosed limestone (sugar limestone) on Widdybank and Cronkley Fells and in a few other places support Spring Gentian, Teesdale Violet, Teesdale Milkwort, Teesdale Sandwort, Hoary Rock-rose and many other rare or local plant species, including mosses and liverworts. Other good areas include the valley hay meadows, the banks of the Tees, flushed pastures and Whin Sill basalt cliffs. There is an extensive juniper wood near High Force. Breeding birds are abundant – Black and Red Grouse, Dunlin, Golden Plover, Common Sandpiper, Redshank, Ring Ouzel, etc. Insects are not much in evidence, but there are some interesting northern and upland species.

The higher hills to the south have similar flowers plus more markedly Alpine species like Alpine Forget-me-not. The whole area provides superb walking, with fine views and dramatic waterfalls, and really needs several days for thorough exploration.

35. North York Moors National Park

Location: North of York, just north of Pickering.
Access: The A169, A171 and many minor roads lead through the park; access to unenclosed areas is generally open.
Timing: April–September.

A hilly upland area (138,000ha) without significant peaks but including Britain's largest area of heather moorland – in August vast sweeps of the hillsides are purple. Several long-distance paths cross this magnificent walking terrain. Some areas are particularly species-rich, such as the limestone around Rievaulx and Sutton Bank, where there are good woods, grasslands and fen areas. The moorlands support breeding birds such as Red Grouse, Merlin, Dunlin and Golden Plover. The displays of Wild Daffodil in the fields and woods along the upper reaches of the River Dove in Farndale are famous. At the Bridestones, 15km west of Scarborough, there are impressive sandstone tors plus good flowers, insects and birds in a mixed woodland and moorland reserve. The coastline is spectacular in parts, especially around Whitby and Robin Hood's Bay; the latter offers particularly good seashore life.

Southeast of the park, on the coast south of Filey, the **Bempton Cliffs Reserve** has superb seabird colonies on high chalk cliffs, including mainland Britain's only Gannet breeding site.

36. Ribble Estuary Area

Location: West of Preston.
Access: Via the A565 on to minor roads and seawall.
Timing: All year.

Together with the area just south, the Ribble Estuary comprises a fine range of important coastal and associated habitats. The extensive saltmarshes, sandbanks and mudflats of the estuary itself attract enormous numbers of waders, ducks and geese – e.g., Pink-footed Goose – in late autumn and winter. **Martin Mere**, just east of Southport, is an important wildfowl reserve, drawing hosts of wildfowl and waders from autumn through spring; it also has good collections of pinioned wildfowl as well as hides and viewing areas. **Ainsdale dunes**, south of Southport, sport many plant species, including rarities like Dune and Green-flowered Helleborines, plus a population of Sand Lizard (at the species' northern limits in Britain) and a large colony of Natterjack Toad. Red Squirrel is common in the pines. North of the Ribble, just northwest of Lytham St Anne's, is a small area of flowery dunes.

37. Peak District National Park

Location: Between Sheffield and Manchester.
Access: The A57, A6 and numerous other roads lead into the park. Access on foot to unenclosed areas is

Monsal Dale, Peak District, seen from Monsal Head.

generally unrestricted, and there are numerous footpaths.
Timing: All year; best May–July.

The 140,000ha 'Peak Park' falls roughly into two sections. The northern Dark Peak area has mainly high peaty moors, where the exceptionally acid soil supports very few species; Dunlin, Red Grouse and Curlew breed. Further south lies the White Peak area, with exposed Carboniferous limestone (many caves) and lovely valleys with scrub and grassland, occasional woods and clear streams. The very rich flora includes such uncommon species as Jacob's Ladder, Mezereon, Mossy Saxifrage, Bloody Cranesbill and Spring Cinquefoil. Among the interesting butterfly population are Blues, Duke of Burgundy and Brown Argus. The streams sustain a diversity of fish and abundant caddis-flies, alderflies and stoneflies. Particularly good areas are Lathkilldale, Dovedale, Monk Dale and Cressbrookdale.

38. Gibraltar Point

Location: About 5km south of Skegness, on the Lincolnshire coast.
Access: Via minor road south from Skegness; access on foot via marked paths.
Timing: All year.

Almost 500ha of dunes in parallel ridges with saltmarsh between, plus mudflats, open water and various minor habitats. Pyramidal Orchid, Cowslip, Field Mouse-ear, Small Bugloss, Henbane and many other species thrive on the dunes, while the saltmarsh supports fine displays of Sea Milkwort, Sea Wormwood and Sea Lavender. Little Tern and Ringed Plover nest on the sandy point; at passage times and through the winter large numbers of waders, together with Grey Heron, Short-eared Owl, ducks and many other birds flock here. Common Seal swim just offshore. There are also a good visitor centre and field station at the end of the road, a hide overlooking a lagoon, and a bird-ringing area.

Saltfleetby, some 25km north, has good dunes with more wet slack areas than has Gibraltar Point; it is noted for its spectacular displays of Marsh Orchid in June and for resident Natterjack Toad. **Donna Nook**, just beyond that, has good flowers and birds and regular Common and Grey Seals.

39. North Norfolk Coast

Location: From Hunstanton to Sheringham.
Access: The A149 runs all along the coast; minor roads, paths and boats give access from there.
Timing: All year.

This 45km stretch of almost entirely low-lying Norfolk coast has a wonderful array of coastal habitats, greatly enhanced by large numbers of visiting birds – indeed, birds are always in evidence here. Most of the stretch is protected by a series of reserves and designations of importance. There are dunes, shingle, mudflats and lagoons, with some classic coastal features like the curved spit of Scolt Head. Avocet, Bittern, Marsh Harrier, Sandwich Tern, Little Tern, Bearded Tit and other coastal and wetland birds breed here, and passage periods see large numbers of birds of many different species, including rare vagrants, while throughout the winter there are thousands of waders and wildfowl. The rich flora of the dunes, salt-marsh and shingle areas includes most of the specialities of such habitats.

Some particularly good areas include Titchwell, Holme Dunes, Holkham Meals and the whole area around Blakeney and Cley. There are many hides and other facilities in the reserves, and a visitor centre just east of Cley, where day-permits for some of the hides can be obtained. The sandbanks at **Blakeney Point** are a good place to see some of the area's many Common Seal.

Common Seals basking on a sandbank, North Norfolk coast.

Hickling, one of the best nature sites in the Broads.

40. Norfolk Broads

Location: From the Norfolk coast to just northeast of Norwich.
Access: The A1062 and minor roads give best access; access on foot is variable.
Timing: Best May–October.

This is a large area of wetland habitats punctuated by open waters (broads) that were formed by medieval peat-digging. Sadly, serious eutrophication has in recent years led to the dramatic decline of much of the aquatic life, but there are still good isolated broads and large areas of fine wetland habitats, and great efforts are being made to restore the water quality. Breeding birds of interest include Bittern, Marsh Harrier, Savi's Warbler and Bearded Tit, and the abundant flowers include Water Soldier, Water Violet, Fen Orchid and Holly-leaved Naiad. Insects are plentiful and varied, with such rarities as the Norfolk Hawker Dragonfly and the Swallowtail Butterfly. Among the best sites are Hickling Broad, Strumpshaw Fen (east of Norwich) and the Bure Marshes, in which lies the Broadland Conservation Centre, with trails and exhibitions.

Winterton dunes, on the coast north of Winterton, have reasonable flowers and breeding Natterjack Toad.

41. Wyre Forest

Location: West of Kidderminster, just west of Bewdley.
Access: Via the A456 or B4194; car parks and tracks give access on foot.
Timing: May–October.
A fine area of ancient forest, covering hundreds of

hectares, partly protected within reserves. The forest is mainly of Common and Sessile Oaks, though there are also Wild Service Tree, Small-leaved Lime and others. Many old-woodland species adorn the flora: Lily-of-the-Valley, Meadow Saffron, Mountain Melick, Columbine, Wood Cranesbill, etc. The scattered meadows have anthills and a different range of flowers. Breeding birds include all three native woodpeckers, Redstart, Pied Flycatcher, Wood Warbler, Dipper and many more. The insect population is abundant and diverse, with good butterflies like Silver-washed Fritillary and White Admiral and many stream insects – rare caddis-flies, dragonflies and others. Club-tailed Dragonfly comes in from the nearby River Severn. The mammals include Dormouse.

42. Wicken Fen

Location: About 15km northeast of Cambridge, southwest of Wicken.
Access: Signposted from the A1123; access on foot is by trails (with hides) after you have checked in at the visitor centre.
Timing: All year; best May–August.

One of the best relics of the great fenland that once covered much of eastern England. Despite its considerable size, Wicken Fen is partly maintained by 'water-proofing' against the surrounding drained land. There are areas of Saw-sedge still cut traditionally, reedbeds, open water and woodland. The prolific flora includes rare species like Marsh Pea and Milk Parsley. The bird fauna is good, both at breeding time and in autumn–winter, and there is a rich insect fauna – the site was known first as an entomological location – particularly for lesser-known groups like flies and beetles.

Wicken Fen, an outstanding relic of ancient fenland.

43. Ouse Washes

Location: Around Welney, about 15km north of Ely.
Access: The A1101 and B1411 give access; there are signposted parking and access areas at several points.
Timing: All year; can be spectacular in a cold winter.

Two great parallel drains running northeastward across the Bedford Levels are used to allow the area between them to flood, creating a large sheet of water in winter and rich, flowery alluvial meadows with breeding waders in spring and summer. Winter brings vast numbers of wildfowl, especially all three swan species (in particular thousands of Bewick's) and up to 30,000 Wigeon. Ruff, Black-tailed Godwit, Snipe and other waders breed here in spring, and there is a good range of wetland flowers. The main observation areas are at the Ouse Washes Reserve, southwards through Purl's Bridge, with numerous hides; and at Welney Wildfowl Refuge, where there is supplementary feeding in winter.

44. Minsmere and Dunwich

Location: On the Suffolk coast between Aldeburgh and Walberswick.
Access: Via minor roads from the B1125; numerous signed car parks; access into reserves is variable. At Minsmere non-members of the RSPB must pay a fee.
Timing: All year.

Virtually the whole stretch between Walberswick and Sizewell is protected in one way or another as an important, attractive and still relatively quiet and unspoilt assemblage of coastal habitats – heathland, reedbeds, open water, brackish water, grazing marsh and saltmarsh. Minsmere is a famous bird site, with breeding Avocet, Marsh Harrier, Bearded Tit and Bittern, and numerous passage and winter birds. Walberswick has many breeding wetland birds, and is noted for wintering waders and birds of prey. The heathland areas, as at Dunwich, support a fine array of heathland flowers together with insects like spider-hunting Wasps, Tiger Beetle and Green Hairstreak Butterfly.

Heathland flora at Dunwich on the Suffolk coast.

South of Aldeburgh, there are further good sites at **Orford Ness** and **Havergate**. There is easy access from Shingle Street to a shingle bar with excellent flowers.

45. Ashridge Estate

Location: 5km north of Berkhamsted, astride the B4506.
Access: Numerous footpaths off minor roads; generally open access on foot, except to enclosed farmland.
Timing: April–November.

A large (2000ha) National Trust estate including a variety of typical Chiltern habitats like chalk downland, beech woodland, mixed deciduous woodland, scrub and heathland. The chalk grassland, particularly on Ivinghoe Beacon, has a rich flora and fauna, with Pasque-flower, Rock-rose, Felwort, Horseshoe Vetch, Squinancy Wort and Adders' Tongue Fern. Butterflies include Duke of Burgundy and Chalkhill and Small Blues. The beechwoods, too, have interesting flowers, including a number of orchids, and offer fine displays of autumn colour. Among the mammals are Muntjac, Chinese Water Deer, Fat Dormouse and several bat species.

To the north, **Dunstable and Whipsnade Downs** and **Totternhoe Knolls** all have good chalk downland areas.

46. Exmoor National Park

Location: On the Somerset-Devon coast between Minehead and Ilfracombe.
Access: The A39, B3223 and many minor roads run into the area; open access on foot to unenclosed land.
Timing: All year; best May–July.

One of England's smallest National Parks, covering just under 70,000ha of uplands (rising to 519m at Dunkery Beacon), with a dramatic north-facing stretch of coastline. The best habitats are ancient woods in deep valleys and high heather moorland, in a beautiful mixture. Breeding birds include Merlin, Black and Red Grouse (in small numbers), Pied Flycatcher, Redstart, Ring Ouzel and Dipper. There is a substantial population of Red Deer, and many semi-wild Exmoor ponies, the least altered of British pony breeds. The flora includes northern or upland species like Parsley Fern and Lesser Twayblade, as well as southwestern species like Irish Spurge. The lichens and bryophytes of the old woods are especially good, with many old-woodland and pollution-intolerant species. Insects include Heath Fritillary and Northern Eggar Moth. Among the best areas are the combes running up from Horner, the woods just east of Lynton and Lynmouth, the woods along the Barle near Tarr Steps, and the high moorland around Dunkery. The whole coastline is superb, and it too has some good woods.

47. New Forest

Location: Between Southampton and Bournemouth.
Access: Via the A35, B3078 and other roads. Access on foot is virtually unrestricted; numerous car parks.
Timing: All year.

This marvellously varied and unexpected area, covering almost 40,000ha in the heart of developed southern England, can seem disappointing at first, because it lacks the intense variety of chalk downs or ancient coppice woods, but your persistence will be rewarded: the whole area needs many days to appreciate fully.

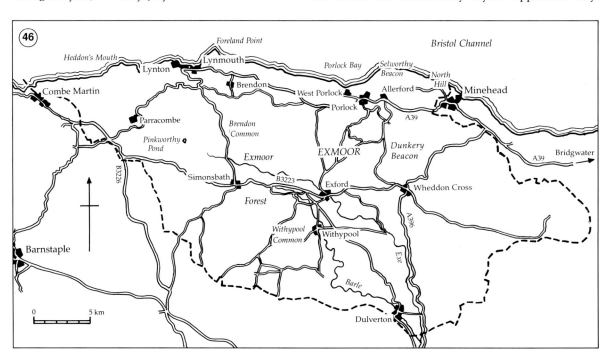

The habitats include beech and oak woodland, heathland, bog, open water, grasslands and a small section of coast. Much of the forest is unenclosed, and the habitats grade naturally into each other. It contains the best and largest examples of many habitat types in lowland Britain and supports a great range of unusual species. Among the many birds breeding here are Honey Buzzard, Buzzard, Hobby, Dartford Warbler, Stonechat, Nightjar and Woodlark. There are Smooth Snake and a few Sand Lizard. The flowers are of especial interest – many bog, grassland and heathland species, including rarities like Wild Gladiolus, Pillwort, Narrow-leaved Lungwort, Coral Necklace and Hampshire Purslane – as are the lichens, particularly in the old woods. There is an enormous range of invertebrates, the area being particularly good for dragonflies, damselflies (the best area in Britain, with around 30 species) and old-woodland species of beetles and flies; there is also the only British site for a Cicada. Five deer species and most British species of bat can be found here. The coast around Beaulieu has good birds and a further range of flowers.

Lush vegetation at Lydford Gorge, Dartmoor.

48. Dartmoor National Park

Location: Between Exeter and Tavistock.
Access: The B3212 runs through the centre of the park, and many other roads give access. Access on foot to unenclosed areas is generally open.

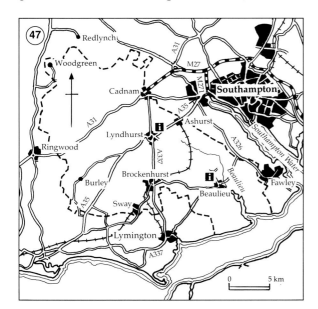

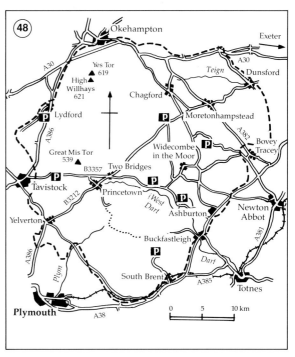

Autumn birches on Sharpen Hill, near Burley, in the New Forest.

Timing: Best May–September.

This 95,000ha park consists mainly of heather- and grassland-clad granite uplands, often topped by tors. It is a wild and wet area, like Exmoor (site 46) in many respects but higher and larger, and lacking any coastal region. The breeding birds are similar to those of Exmoor; in addition, Dunlin and Golden Plover – northern species at the southern edge of their range – have occasionally been recorded. The slopes of many of the deep valleys, like those of the Dart and Teign, are clothed in fine woodlands, and there are good high-altitude woods at Wistman's Wood and Black Tor Copse, where gnarled lichen-rich oaks survive among granite boulders. In August the displays of heather and Western Gorse, often dressed with Dodder, are spectacular, but otherwise the flora is unremarkable except for scattered rarities like Flax-leaved St John's Wort and Irish Lady's Tresses, and superb displays of Wild Daffodil at Steps Bridge (on the Teign). Dartmoor ponies can be seen throughout the open moor; other mammals include Roe and Fallow Deer.

49. Isle of Purbeck

Location: On the coast just southwest of Poole.
Access: Via the A351, or by ferry from near Poole; access on foot mostly unrestricted.
Timing: All year.

In fact a peninsula, jutting eastwards from Lulworth, the 'isle' has a marvellous variety of unspoilt habitats despite being near large towns and popular as a holiday area. Here are superb examples of heathland, chalk and limestone grassland, old commonland, bog, woodland, dunes, saltmarsh and mudflats; there are several reserves and other protected areas. The flora

and fauna are too numerous to detail, but this is a particularly good place for heathland birds, Sand Lizard, bog, heath and grassland flowers – with specialities like Early Spider Orchid, Marsh Gentian and Dorset Heath – butterflies, dragonflies, grasshoppers, crickets and many other insects. Among the best areas are Studland dunes, the downs at Ballard Point, the south-facing coastal limestone grasslands south and east of Worth Matravers, Corfe Common, and most of the heath and bog of the northern part of the peninsula. There are small seabird breeding colonies just west of Durlston Head.

Poole Harbour has fine wintering waders and wildfowl. **Brownsea Island** has Red Squirrel and Sika Deer.

50. The Lizard

Location: On the coast south of Helston, Cornwall.
Access: Via the A3083 and B3293 from Helston; access on foot to key areas is generally good.
Timing: April–September.

This large, geologically mixed rocky peninsula, jutting out into the Atlantic, is best known to naturalists for its assemblage of rare and uncommon plants, engendered by a combination of mild climate, unspoilt countryside and serpentine rock; specialities are Cornish Heath, Smooth Rupturewort, Hairy Greenweed, Crimson and Upright Clovers, Sea Asparagus, Prostrate Broom, Thyme Broomrape, Spotted Cat'sear, Sand Quillwort and Slender Yellow Gentian, and there are many other, more widespread, coastal and heath species. The best areas are down the west side, especially at Kynance Cove, Mullion and Predannack.

Loe Pool, just off the Lizard to the west, is an interesting lake with fringing woods and a shingle bar.

Worbarrow Bay, Isle of Purbeck.

Kynance Cove on the rocky Lizard Peninsula.

IRELAND

The island of Ireland has an area of 84,421 sq km; of this, just over 70,000 sq km is the Republic of Ireland, Eire, the remainder, Northern Ireland, being part of the UK. Despite this political division, the island is a single ecological unit, and is treated here accordingly. Travel across the border is reasonably unhindered, and so it is practicable to cover the whole island in a single visit.

It is dominated by its mild Atlantic climate. The west in particular has a very strongly oceanic climate, so that the difference between summer and winter is not very pronounced; for example, Clare has a summer that equates with that in northern Finland and a winter that equates with that in the South of France.

Ireland has rather poor flora and fauna. After the last ice age the island was recolonized from the continent largely via mainland Britain, from which it was fairly early cut off by rising seas; this is why it is very poor in reptiles and lacks many mammals, invertebrates and flowers. For the naturalist this is to some

Fair Head and Murlough Bay on the North Antrim coast.

extent compensated for by the fact that different species have become commoner here than in mainland Britain – e.g., Hairy Hawker Dragonfly, Pine Marten and Wood White Butterfly. There is, in addition, a strong 'Lusitanian' element, particularly in the flora, with survivors from before the ice age – e.g., Strawberry Tree, Great Butterwort and Kerry Slug – being much more like the species of Spain and Portugal. Ireland is also very rewarding to visit because of its relatively unspoilt countryside, its lovely west coast and its lack of hordes of other tourists.

Eire has National Parks, National Nature Reserves and reserves privately owned or managed by organizations like the Irish Wildbird Conservancy and An Taisce, the Irish National Trust. Northern Ireland has no National Parks but 45 National Nature Reserves, private reserves run by the Ulster Trust for Nature Conservation (UTNC) and reserves run by UK-based organizations like the National Trust (NT) and the Royal Society for the Protection of Birds (RSPB).

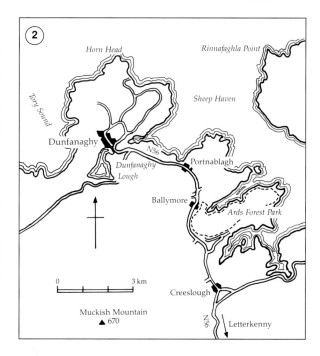

1. Sheskinmore Lough

Location: On the west coast, south of Naran, on Dunmore Head, due west of Strabane.
Access: Via the R261 north from Ardara, then west on a minor road, and finally on footpaths.
Timing: All year.

Run by the Irish Wildbird Conservancy, this nature reserve (about 150ha) comprises a lake, reedbeds and damp grassland. In winter there are good numbers of Barnacle and Greenland White-fronted Geese, among other wildfowl. Breeding birds include Dunlin, Redshank, Lapwing, Chough and Corncrake. The damp calcareous grassland makes this a fine place for flowers, including orchids.

2. Dunfanaghy Area

Location: On the north coast, northwest of Letterkenny.
Access: The N56 runs through the area, and minor roads lead north and east from it; unrestricted on foot.
Timing: Best April–July.

A rich mixture of habitats covering hundreds of hectares around the village of Dunfanaghy. Between Dunfanaghy and Ards Country Park to the south lie dunes, saltmarshes, open water and woodlands. Creeslough Wood, near the village of the same name, is deciduous and has a good range of breeding birds. At Horn Head, north of Dunfanaghy, there are fine cliffs where Puffin, Razorbill, Kittiwake, Redstart, Chough and others breed. In winter there are good numbers of wildfowl, notably Whooper Swan, on the lakes. Flowers of interest include Field Gentian and Lesser Clubmoss.

3. Glenveagh National Park

Location: Northwest of Letterkenny, roughly bounded by the R251 and R254.
Access: Roads R251 and R254 go around the area; the L77 leads to the visitor centre on Lough Veagh.
Timing: Some interest all year; best April–July.

9700ha of hilly country with upland grassland and moorland, deciduous woodland, lakes and bogs, this is a good area for mammals, with a large herd of Red Deer plus Badger, Fox and Stoat. Breeding birds include Raven, Peregrine Falcon, Merlin, Red Grouse,

Glenveagh Castle in County Donegal.

Redstart and Wood Warbler. The humid unpolluted atmosphere in remnants of ancient oak-birch woodland – now rare in Ireland – fosters luxuriant ferns (including Filmy Ferns), mosses, liverworts and lichens. The upland flora includes good displays of Bog Asphodel.

The excellent garden of nearby **Glenveagh Castle** has a fine range of plants, and a few kilometres west of the park, at the eastern end of **Lough Nacung**, there is a good bog with rare western flowers such as Mackay's Heath and Blue-eyed Grass.

4. Inch Lough

Location: 10km northwest of Londonderry, around Inch Island in Lough Swilly.
Access: Via minor road off the R238 near Burnfoot.
Timing: Some interest all year; best April–June, December–February.

Inch Lough, just southeast of Inch Island, is barely separated from the sea. From late autumn onwards its highly productive waters attract large numbers (up to 1500) of Whooper Swan plus other wintering wildfowl, such as Greenland Whitefront and Pale-breasted Brent Goose. Birds breeding nearby include Sandwich Tern, Redshank and Snipe.

A few kilometres to the southwest, north of Newtown Cunningham, **Blanket Nook**, a small lake with marshland, has good wintering and breeding birds and a rich fen flora.

5. Banagher Forest

Location: In the Sperrin Mountains, 30km southeast of Londonderry, alongside the B40 due south of Dungiven.
Access: Via the B40; unrestricted on foot.
Timing: April–August.

An area of forest and surrounding moorland, partly within a National Nature Reserve. Hen Harrier, Merlin and Raven breed on the moorland, the woods have Crossbill and Redstart as well as lots of Red Squirrel, and there is a good range of Lepidoptera, including Silver-washed Fritillary, Wood White and Poplar Hawkmoth.

Just northwest of Claudy, signed from the A6 road, lies **Ness Wood**, which has a fine river, a spectacular waterfall, and resident Otter.

6. Magilligan Point

Location: At the mouth of Lough Foyle, 20km west of Coleraine.
Access: Via the A2 and the B202 on to the point. Parts of the area are unrestricted; for others you need a permit from the Department of the Environment in Belfast.
Timing: All year.

A fine National Nature Reserve, being mainly a series of dunes, varying from unstable to stabilized, plus mudflats to seaward. This is a good place for seashore shells, and the calcium-rich sand of the dunes sustains a rich flora. Among the birds breeding here is Little Tern, at its only Northern Irish site.

Just to the southeast is another dune reserve, the **Umbra**, which has a good flora and interesting butterflies; entry requires a permit from UTNC. Lough Foyle as a whole is an excellent area for birds, especially geese, swans, ducks and waders, with peak numbers usually in late autumn. Another National Nature Reserve, the **Roe Estuary**, midway along the eastern shore, has good passage and wintering birds.

7. North Antrim Coast

Location: From Portrush to Fair Head, the northeastern point of Ireland.
Access: The A2 runs close to the coast, and many minor roads lead off it; access on foot is generally

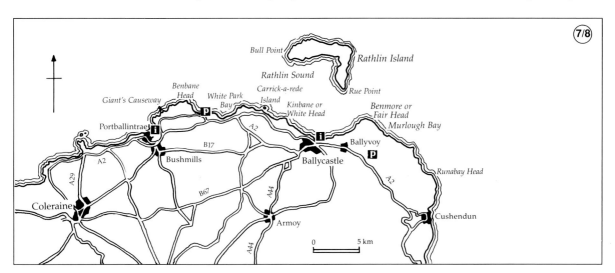

open. You have to pay to visit the Giant's Causeway.
Timing: All year; best April–July.

This stretch of coast has a spectacular variety of unspoilt scenery, with wildlife to match. Particular highlights include the Giant's Causeway – a basaltic lava flow with hexagonal columns (designated a World Heritage Site) – Benbane Head, White Park Bay – good dunes, grassland and scrub, and fine chalk cliffs just to the east – and Fair Head, where there are dramatic cliffs, old woodland, and clifftop heath and bog. Breeding birds include Chough, Rock-dove, Rock Pipit, Raven and a few seabirds. There are fine views of Gannet, Manx Shearwater, Eider and other birds feeding offshore, and in summer you have a good chance of seeing Porpoises and Dolphins. Prime areas for flowers include White Park Bay and Fair Head/Murlough, where unusual mixed natural deciduous woods thrive on base-rich soils. This is excellent walking country, and the rockier parts of the shore make for good rock-pool searching.

The spectacular Giant's Causeway, North Antrim.

8. Rathlin Island

Location: Off the north Antrim coast, 8km north of Ballycastle.
Access: By boat (daily from Ballycastle), with open access on foot.
Timing: Late April–July is best.

A wild and dramatic island, about 7km long, with fine cliffs, maritime grassland, heath, bog and lakes. The impressive seabird colonies are best on the cliffs at the western end (where there is a National Nature Reserve): Puffin, Kittiwake, Black Guillemot, Guillemot, Manx Shearwater, Chough and Peregrine Falcon are among the species on view; the island's lakes and sandy shores support other breeding birds of interest. Grassy areas of the island sustain an interesting flora, including Lesser Butterfly, Heath-spotted and Fragrant Orchids, Spring Squill and Thrift. You may encounter Grayling and Dark Green Fritillary butterflies. Thanks to the clear unpolluted waters of this coast, the seashore life is very rich.

9. Slievanorra and Breen Forest

Location: About 10km south of Ballycastle.
Access: Via minor roads south from Ballycastle or west from Cushendun; access on foot is unrestricted.
Timing: Interesting all year; best April–July.

An extensive area of mixed woodland and moorland, falling within several neighbouring reserves or other protected areas. Breen Forest, at the north end, is a fine example of an ancient oak wood (rare in Northern Ireland). Plants of interest include Lesser Twayblade Orchid, Cranberry, Lesser Clubmoss and Wilson's Filmy Fern. Merlin, Hen Harrier and Red Grouse breed on the moorland and Wood Warbler, Redstart and Buzzard in the woods. Insects of interest include Silver-washed Fritillary and the attractive ground-beetle *Carabus nitens*.

10. Slieve League

Location: On the northern side of Donegal Bay, just southwest of Carrick (An Charraig).
Access: By a minor road south from Carrick to Teelin, then on foot.
Timing: May–August.

A dramatic quartzite mountain, with almost sheer southern cliffs – Ireland's highest – dropping to the sea and a northern face that is nearly as steep, this is one of the best Irish areas for Arctic-Alpine flowers. There are no great rarities, but the range of commoner species – Mountain Avens, Dwarf Juniper, Least Willow, Alpine Saw-wort, Purple Saxifrage, Alpine Meadow-rue, sedges like *Carex bigelowii* and ferns like Holly Fern – is impressive.

West of Slieve League, **Rathlin O'Birne**, off Malin

Beg, has a substantial British Storm Petrel colony, and Leach's Petrel may breed here.

11. The Mullet

Location: On the northwest coast of Mayo, attached to the mainland at Belmullet (Béal an Mhuirhead).
Access: By the R313 from Bangor Erris.
Timing: All year.

A windswept peninsula, virtually an island, with lakes, moorland and calcareous grassland. Termoncarragh Lake, just south of Corclogh, is excellent for breeding waders like Redshank, Dunlin, Snipe and Lapwing, with small numbers of Red-necked Phalarope; large numbers of wildfowl are here in winter and Corncrake breed in the grasslands. The flora in the marshy areas and grassland nearby is rich in wetland species. Around the cliffs of the peninsula are seabird colonies; and there are further good colonies of seabirds, including terns, on islands off the Mullet's west coast.

12. Glenamoy Bog

Location: North of the village of Glenamoy (on the R314).
Access: From a minor road running north from Glenamoy; access on foot is unrestricted, but take care.
Timing: Best May–September.

An excellent example of a lowland bog with a prolific flora including Cranberry, Marsh Andromeda, Bogbean and Bog Asphodel, plus many sedges, cottongrasses, etc. The numerous bog pools sustain species like Bladderwort. Irish Hare is to be found in good numbers, and Snipe and Curlew are among the breeding birds.

13. Clare Island

Location: Off the western coast of Mayo, near Roonah Quay, 25km west of Westport.
Access: By regular boat from Roonah Quay; open access on foot.
Timing: May–August.

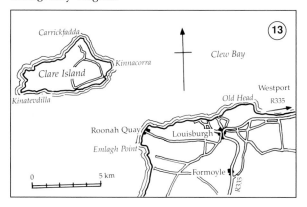

Harbour at Clare Island, off the western coast of Mayo.

This rocky island, about 6km long, has cliffs, grassland, moorland and bog. Seabirds in colonies on the cliffs include Razorbill, Guillemot, Kittiwake, Fulmar and Puffin, plus Gannet (off the island's southern tip) and scattered Chough; other breeding birds include Corncrake and Corn Bunting. The flora is interesting, though no more than that, and there is a good range of seashore life.

14. Connemara National Park

Location: In Connemara, alongside the N59 a few kilometres northeast of Clifden.
Access: Open from Letterfrack on foot.
Timing: Best April–September.

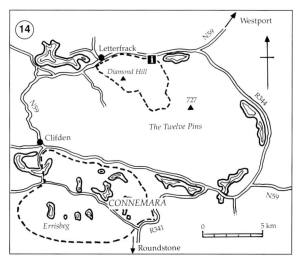

A small National Park (2000ha) comprising characteristically moist western Irish mountain habitats, with bog, moorland, mountain grassland and woodlands. On the heathland you can find St Dabeoc's Heath as well as more widespread plants, while higher on the mountains are species like Purple Saxifrage, Alpine Meadow-rue and Holly Fern plus, in a few loughs, the rare and curious Pipewort. Breeding birds include Merlin, Peregrine and Stonechat; mammals include Red Deer (an introduced herd), pure-bred Connemara ponies and a good range of bats. The visitor centre at the park entrance provides more detailed information.

South of the N59, between Clifden and Roundstone, lies the huge (over 4000ha) **Errisbeg/Roundstone bog complex**, which has a rich flora, including the rarer Irish heathers like Mackay's and Irish. It is an important feeding area for Greenland White-fronted Goose, and Merlin are regular visitors.

15. Aillebrack

Location: In the far west of Galway, just southwest of Ballyconneely at the end of a minor road off the R341.
Access: Take the minor road towards Slyne Head; unrestricted on foot.
Timing: May–July.

A fine area of machair grassland and dunes, with small patches of saltmarsh. The flora includes many widespread dune species plus lime-loving species like Dense-flowered Orchid, Irish Eyebright and Lady's Tresses. As with most machair areas, this is good for breeding waders – e.g., Ringed Plover, Dunlin, Redshank and Lapwing – and terns breed nearby. Recommended also for beachcombing.

16. Lough Carra

Location: Alongside the N84 between Castlebar and Headford.
Access: Minor roads almost encircle the lake; parking on the east.
Timing: Best May–July.

A large shallow marl lake – one of the best in the British Isles – surrounded by limestone, with associated fens, ash/hazel woodland, grassland and limestone pavement. Spring Gentian and Early Purple and Dense-flowered Orchids are among the plentiful flowers. The lake is good for breeding wildfowl, and reasonable numbers of birds winter on it; it also supports characteristic aquatic plants like Stonewort.

17. Ben Bulbin

Location: About 12km north of Sligo.
Access: A minor road off the N15 leads to a mine at the top.
Timing: March (for Purple Saxifrage) to September; best May–July.

This extensive area of limestone mountain (reaching 525m), with steep cliffs and moorland, has a very rich Arctic-Alpine flora containing numerous species that are absent or rare elsewhere in Ireland. The best areas are the cliffs, especially at Glenade, to the northeast, and at Annacoona, near Gleniff. Among the interesting plants are four saxifrages – including the rare Alpine Saxifrage – Mountain Avens, Northern Rock-cress, Irish Sandwort, Alpine Meadow-rue and Moss Campion, as well as, among the ferns, the limestone-loving Holly Fern and Green Spleenwort. Nearby **Glenade Lough** has a good aquatic and marginal flora.

18. Lower Lough Erne

Location: To the northwest of Enniskillen.
Access: The A46, A47 and other roads encircle the lake; good foot access generally.
Timing: Some interest all year; best April–August.

This large freshwater lough has a very convoluted shoreline and numerous islands; sections of the coast are unspoilt, with marshes, fens, reedbeds, woodlands and unimproved grasslands. As a whole, Lough Erne is important for breeding birds, notably Common Scoter, Dunlin, Snipe, Curlew, Redshank and Sandwich Tern, and there are also reasonable numbers of wintering wildfowl, including geese. There are resident Otter and many insects of interest, like Hairy Hawker and Ruddy and Common Darter. The aquatic and marginal floras have been somewhat depleted by eutrophication in recent years, but are still good, and the limestone areas of the shore (e.g., around the western end) offer further species.

South of the lough, centred on **Lough Navar Forest** and **Ross Lough**, is a superb complex of habitats including small lakes, fen, reedbeds, deciduous woodland, bog and cliffs protected by a series of reserves.

19. Upper Lough Erne

Location: To the southeast of Enniskillen.
Access: Major roads (A509, B514) almost encircle the lough, and the B127 runs across it; access on foot is variable. Non-members of the National Trust are charged a parking fee at Castle Crom.
Timing: Some interest all year; best May–September.

An extraordinarily convoluted wetland area with an extensive stretch of open water broken by numerous drumlins to produce a great range of habitats and some surprisingly remote areas. The whole area has been affected by lowering water-levels and eutrophication. Many birds breed here, among them Great-crested Grebe, Water Rail, Redshank, Curlew, Corncrake and Snipe, and there are rich fen and aquatic floras – most of the widespread species plus rarities like Marsh Pea. The range of dragonflies is good: Hairy Hawker, Brown Hawker and many others. Otter are still relatively common, along with Water Vole and other semi-aquatic species.

The **Crom Castle estate**, to the west of Newtown

Upper Lough Erne on the Castle Crom estate.

Butler, has an information centre and offers good access to a cross-section of the area's habitats.

20. Lough Neagh

Location: West of Belfast.
Access: Minor roads run down to the shore at various places; access on foot is variable.
Timing: All year.

Ireland's largest freshwater lough has a total area of almost 40,000ha. It and its associated marginal habitats sustain many breeding birds, including large numbers of Great-crested Grebe, Shelduck, Teal, Shoveler, Curlew, Redshank and Snipe. The numbers of wintering birds – grebes, swans, geese and ducks, etc. – can likewise be high, with additional species at passage times. The meadows, reedbeds and woodland of Oxford Island (actually a peninsula), just northwest of Lurgan, are home to many birds, and there are hides for observation; also to be found here are Otter and Irish Hare. Just west of Antrim, at the northeast corner of the lake, are several reserves with a good flora and a hide for watching birds, notably courting grebes.

At the southwest corner of the lake, close to Junction 13 of the M1, the **Peatlands Country Park** offers an interesting insight into the workings of bog country (some good bog areas are protected as reserves). The rare Large Heath butterfly is among a wide spectrum of bog species to be seen.

21. Strangford Lough

Location: Southeast of Belfast, south of Newtownards.
Access: Major roads (A22, A25) encircle the lough; access on foot is permitted in places.

Timing: All year.

This huge sea lough (almost 14,000ha) is landlocked except for its narrow exit at Strangford; at low tide great areas of mudflats are exposed. The lough sustains a very diverse wildlife. Four tern species (including scattered colonies of Roseate Tern), Cormorant, Redshank, Great-crested Grebe, Shelduck and many commoner species breed here, and passage periods and winter bring tens of thousands of waders and wildfowl, with especially large numbers of Pale-bellied Brent Goose. The marine and seashore life is extremely rich, though difficult to see much of; the best areas are probably along the sides of the narrow exit channel, south of Strangford. Otter and Common Seal are found, and Porpoise and Dolphin occasionally enter the lough. The best shoreline areas are, clockwise from Strangford, Castle Ward, Quoile Pondage reserve (southwest corner), Castle Espie (near the northwest corner, with good hides) and many parts of the eastern shore, where the road runs along the loughside.

22. Murlough Nature Reserve

Location: On the eastern coast just north of Newcastle, towards Dundrum.
Access: Direct off the A2; marked paths are open all year. Some parts are occasionally restricted.
Timing: April–July.

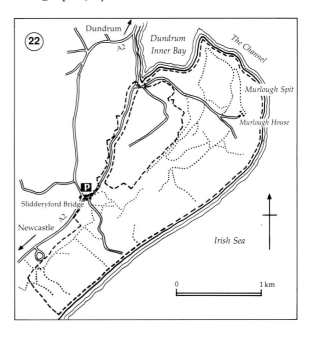

A large (400ha) area of dunes and associated habitats on a peninsula jutting northwards into Dundrum Bay, with spectacular views southwards to the Mourne Mountains. Some of the dunes are very high, and their historical development is well known. The sand is mainly lime-rich, and the flora is correspondingly rich, with hundreds of plant species, including some

Dunes at Murlough Nature Reserve, the Mourne Mountains glimpsed beyond.

that are rare in Ireland, though some areas have developed heathland on leached soils; the dunes also support good lichens. The insect population has been well recorded: over 1100 species are known, including 21 butterflies. About 60 bird species have bred on the reserve, and it is a good area for migrants and for watching birds like terns and Gannet feeding offshore. Also viewable offshore are Common Seal.

Dundrum Inner Bay, just west of the dunes, always has birds and is especially good at passage periods and in winter; among others, all three swan species can be seen. The granitic **Mourne Mountains**, just south of Newcastle, are high enough to support a mountain flora and fauna, though not an exceptionally rich one.

23. Killard

Location: On the coast east of Downpatrick, just south of Kilclief.
Access: The A2 passes by the site; access on foot unrestricted.
Timing: All year; best April–June and November–March.

A small but varied coastal site with mobile dunes, stable grassland, scrub, heath, low cliffs and rocky foreshore. The dunes and grassland are calcareous, and their rich flora has many orchids – e.g., Bee, Frog, Pyramidal and Northern Marsh – and Spring Squill. Breeding birds include Common, Arctic and Sandwich Terns and Shelduck. In winter there good numbers of ducks (including Long-tailed) and waders on the shore and nearby. Irish Hare is found on the grasslands and Common Seal pass offshore.

24. The Burren

Location: On the west coast of Clare, around Lisdoonvarna and Kilfenora, bisected by the N67.
Access: Via the N67 and many minor roads; generally open on foot.
Timing: Interesting all year; best April–July.

One of Europe's outstanding botanical areas, but with many other features of interest, the Burren covers thousands of hectares; it takes many days to appreciate it fully. There is an information centre at Kilfenora and there are (contentious) plans to build another at Mullagh Mor.

The Burren is primarily a Carboniferous limestone upland, with extensive limestone pavement and other features, but there are also turloughs, fens, woods, dunes, shingle and other habitats. The flora is exceptional, with spectacular displays of rare flowers in a unique mixture of Arctic, Alpine, Mediterranean and coastal species: Spring Gentian, Dense-flowered Orchid, Hoary Rock-rose, Fen Violet, Shrubby Cinquefoil and many more. Birds of interest include Chough and resident mammals include Polecat. Butterflies and moths are abundant, among them Pearl-bordered and Marsh Fritillaries, Wood White and a pale form of Grayling. The area is also fascinating archaeologically, with hundreds of prehistoric sites.

Nearby sites of interest include the dramatic cliffs of **Moher**, southwest of Lisdoonvarna, where there are good seabird colonies and flowers like Roseroot. There are fine dunes at **Lehinch**, west of Ennistimon. The **Aran Isles**, immediately west of the Burren, are geologically similar, and have many of the same flowers. Remarkably unspoilt, they have much of historic and archaeological interest as well as areas of machair,

Limestone pavement at the Burren.

breeding Chough, terns and other seabirds, and resident Otter foraging around the shoreline. The rockpools and shores have superb wildlife. Access is from Galway or from Doolin, a small port west of Lisdoonvarna (for Inisheer).

25. Rahasane Turlough

Location: On the River Dunkellin, just west of Craughwell, southeast of Galway on the N6.
Access: On a minor road running west from the N6 just north of Craughwell; open on foot, but respect farming activities.
Timing: All year, but bird numbers vary with water-levels.

This turlough, unusual in being on the course of a river, is surrounded by damp grassland extending up towards limestone outcrops and scrubby woodlands, which have some of the same interesting flowers as the Burren (site 24) plus butterflies like Wood White and Marsh Fritillary. This is an important site for winter and passage birds with, at times, large numbers of Whooper and Bewick's Swans, White-fronted Goose, various ducks and thousands of waders. However, numbers are heavily dependent on water-levels, which are difficult to predict.

26. Shannon Estuary

Location: West of Limerick.
Access: Numerous roads, especially the N69, approach the estuary; ease of access on foot varies.
Timing: Best October–April for birds.

The Shannon is the longest river in the British Isles. Its narrow estuary covers 34,000ha, including tributaries. Habitats include saltmarshes, wet meadows and extensive mudflats. This is one of the most important Irish estuaries for birds, attracting huge numbers of wildfowl and waders from autumn through spring, including Shelduck, Wigeon, Shoveler, Golden Plover, Dunlin, Knot and Black-tailed Godwit.

27. Mongan's Bog

Location: At Clonmacnoise, just west of the Shannon, 11km south of Athlone.
Access: Via minor roads off the N62; access open on foot.
Timing: Best May–July; the winter birds are interesting.

Owned and managed by An Taisce, this beautiful raised bog, with a well developed pool-and-hummock system on the surface, is one of the best left in Ireland. Among the plants of interest are Cranberry, Bog Rosemary, Bog Asphodel, sundews, Lesser Bladderwort and many sedges and cotton-grasses; the butterflies include Green Hairstreak. In winter small flocks of Greenland White-fronted Goose spend time here. It is worth making a detour to see the nearby monastic settlement of Clonmacnoise.

About 24km to the east, 2km south of Clara around the road to Rahan, **Clara Bog** has a similar flora and fauna.

28. Wicklow Mountains National Park

Location: To the west of Wicklow.
Access: Roads R755, R756 and minor roads lead into the area; generally open access on foot.
Timing: May–August.

This extensive area of partly wooded mountains, rising to 926m at Lugnaquilla, with upland moorland and grassland, supports good populations of Peregrine Falcon, Hen Harrier, Merlin, Ring Ouzel, Redstart and Wood Warbler; 3700ha of the best habitat is protected within the National Park. The Glendalough Valley and nearby Rathdrum woods, just south, make a good centre, with ancient oak and birch woods, heather moor, a lake and marginal wetlands. Flowers of interest include sedges and rushes, Marsh Pennywort, Marsh St John's Wort, Marsh Violet, pondweeds and Yellow Pimpernel. Butterflies are plentiful in woodland clearings, and this area is also good for deer. There is an information centre at Glendalough Upper Lake and displays at the monastic settlement at Glendalough, where there is also a famous tower.

The area known as **the Murrough**, on the coast just north of Wicklow and stretching northwards towards Greystones, has a lovely mixture of unspoilt coastal habitats, including dunes, shingle, lakes and marshes, with good birds and flowers.

Wicklow Mountains near Glendalough.

29. North Bull Island

Location: On the north side of Dublin Bay, stretching towards the Howth Peninsula.
Access: Via the causeway from the coast road.
Timing: All year.

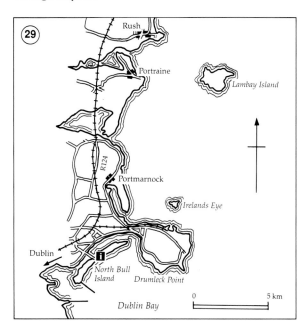

A narrow, 5km-long island built up largely of sand against a harbour wall, with dunes, grassland, salt-marshes and mudflats. Little Tern and others breed here, and from autumn to spring there are huge numbers of waders and wildfowl – up to 37,000 – including Pale-bellied Brent Goose, Shoveler, Shelduck, Wigeon, Oystercatcher, Dunlin, Redshank and Curlew. It is relatively easy to get good views of the birds from the causeway and elsewhere. The flowers are also noteworthy, especially on the dunes and in damp hollows, and there is a visitor centre for further information.

30. Dingle Peninsula

Location: To the west of Tralee.
Access: The R559 and R561 run on to the peninsula; generally open on foot except where the land is enclosed.
Timing: All year; best May–July.

A beautiful, wild and varied peninsula with a superb unspoilt coastline and mountains rising to 962m (Mount Brandon). Habitats include dunes, cliffs, rocky shores, lakes, marshes and bogs, moorland, grassland and offshore islands. The Castle Gregory peninsula, on the north side, is particularly good; Lough Gill supports large numbers of wintering wildfowl, and there is a colony of the rare Natterjack Toad; the dunes to the north have a rich flora; and the Magharee islands, just offshore, have breeding Shag, Cormorant and three tern species. Mount Brandon's rather poor flora has a few Alpine species, and birds such as Ring Ouzel breed there. The **Blasket Islands**, off the peninsula's tip, have fine breeding-bird colonies, especially of British Storm Petrel, Manx Shearwater, Puffin and Chough. The **Inch Spit**, jutting southwards from Inch, has a good dune flora and resident Natterjack Toad, and abundant waders and wildfowl winter on the nearby saltmarsh and mudflats.

31. Skellig Islands

Location: Off the tip of the Kerry Peninsula.
Access: Hired boat from Portmagee or other nearby ports; no landing on Little Skellig without permit.
Timing: April-August.

This group of dramatic islands, including both the main Skelligs and others scattered around, supports just about all the British Isles' breeding seabird species, usually in large numbers. Great Skellig is especially important for British Storm Petrel, along with Manx Shearwater, Puffin, Guillemot, Razorbill, Kittiwake and others. Also of interest on the island are the monastic ruins of Skellig Michael. The birds on Little Skellig, an Irish Wildbird Conservancy reserve, include a colony of Gannets (estimated 22,000 pairs).

Other good islands nearby are **Puffin Island** and **Scarrif Island**. On the mainland, just south of Caherdaniel, **Lamb's Head** (and its offshore islands) has a good heath flora, including the rare Kerry Lily, as does the adjacent **Derrynane National Historic Park**.

The Skellig Islands support large numbers of breeding seabirds.

32. Killarney National Park

Location: To the south and west of Killarney.
Access: The N71 and minor roads pass through the park; access on foot is generally open.
Timing: Interesting all year; best May–October.

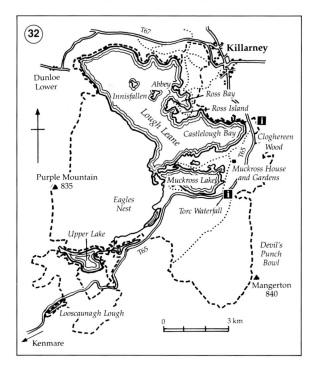

Over 10,000ha of the special southwest Ireland landscape and its rich flora. Within the park are extensive areas of ancient woodlands, mainly Sessile Oak but with yew on limestone areas, like the Muckross Peninsula, and scattered Strawberry Tree (its only native locality in the British Isles). There are also many lakes, with fringing wetland, moorland, bog and mountain habitats, reaching 840m (Mangerton). The prolific flora includes St Patrick's Cabbage (actually a saxifrage), Greater Butterwort, Blue-eyed Grass, Irish Spurge and Pipewort; the whole area is good for ferns, bryophytes and lichens. Red Deer have their only native population here, supplemented by introduced animals, and good numbers of Sika Deer are present – as are Irish Hare, Red Squirrel and Pine Marten. The invertebrate life is of interest: Hairy Hawker dragonflies are abundant, and there are Marsh Fritillaries, Wood White and Large Heath butterflies. The impressively large Kerry Slug occurs locally. There is a visitor centre at Muckross House.

MacGillycuddy's Reeks, just to the west, are Ireland's highest mountains; they are largely covered by bog and moorland, and have a rather poor flora and fauna. **Glengarriff Wood** (near Glengarriff, due south of Killarney) and **Uragh Wood** (by Inchiquin Lough) are areas of old deciduous woodland with good flowers, ferns, mosses and lichens.

33. Wexford Wildfowl Reserve (Wexford Slobs)

Location: The north side of Wexford Harbour, out to Raven Point.
Access: Off the R741; partly open on foot. Observation tower.
Timing: All year; best May–July and winter.

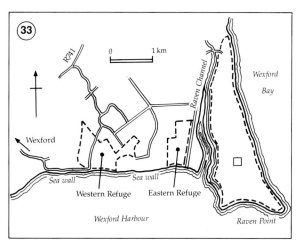

One of Ireland's premier wildlife areas, combining a wildfowl reserve and the Raven Nature Reserve. Habitats include grassland, saltmarsh, mudflats, woodland, reedbeds and dunes. The latter form much of the southern boundary of the site, and have a rich flora with rarities like Wild Asparagus, Lesser Centaury, Round-leaved Wintergreen and Yellow Birdsnest. Birds breeding here include Little Tern, plus other terns in variable numbers. The site assumes its greatest ornithological interest from autumn onwards: about half the world population of Greenland Whitefront Goose winters here, along with Brent and smaller numbers of several other geese, and it is also good for ducks and waders. Various transatlantic rarities turn up regularly, especially at passage periods, and smaller numbers of raptors pass through or winter here.

Tacumshin Lake, due south of Wexford, is a coastal lagoon with good birds and coastal flowers.

Wexford is one of Ireland's premier wildlife areas.

BELGIUM

With a surface area of only 30,521 sq km, Belgium is one of the smallest countries in Europe. Although often perceived as being without much countryside of interest, it actually has a considerable variety of landscapes and some high-quality protected habitats. Despite great losses during this century, there are still numerous bogs and heaths of interest, and the higher hills along the east and south borders have some excellent areas of woodland and moorland. The Ardennes is a particularly rewarding region – much more so, indeed, than the relatively small protected areas.

Belgium has no true endemic species. However, its flora and fauna are reasonably rich for the country's size, and are made up of an interesting mixture of southern, central and northern elements. A number of species – e.g., Downy Oak – reach their northernmost limits on Belgium's warm limestones.

There are no National Parks, but there are a number of State Nature Reserves and Natural Parks as well as a wide range of private reserves. The foremost voluntary conservation organization is the RNOB (Association of Nature and Bird Reserves of Belgium).

1. Westhoek

Location: On the coast immediately west of De Panne, by the French border.
Access: Roads run close to the site, but access is on foot only, on five paths that lead in from the corners.
Timing: April–September.

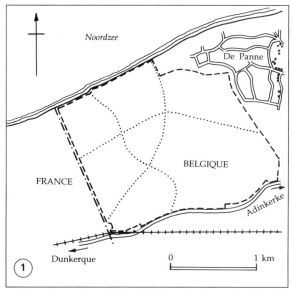

A 340ha area of unspoilt dunes on an otherwise built-up stretch of coastline; habitats include mobile colonizing dunes, dune slacks and stabler dunes with scrub in places. The area is botanically rich, with a range of dune species – e.g., Sea Bindweed, Sea Spurge, Sand Catstail, two Storksbills and Burnet Rose – growing in mildly calcareous sand; in the slacks are Grass-of-Parnassus, the tiny Chaffweed, Variegated Horsetail, Fen Orchid and Marsh Helleborine. There are also interesting lichens and mosses, including abundances of *Tortula ruraliformis* and *Camptothecium lutescens*. Breeding birds include Whitethroat, Nightingale and Kentish Plover. Natterjack Toad is resident and Common Lizard frequent.

About 20km to the northeast, at Middelkerke, the small but rich dune reserve **Les Warandeduinen** is worth a detour from the N34.

2. Zwin

Location: On the coast east of Zeebrugge, by the Dutch border.
Access: By minor road east from Knokke-Heist. Part of the reserve is open daily; some parts are restricted. From Easter to October there are guided walks on Sundays and Tuesdays.
Timing: Some interest all year; best April–July.

The main part of this important coastal wetland reserve – 125ha in Belgium plus 25ha in Holland – is a series of lakes, partly connected to the sea, with intervening saltmarsh, reedbeds and other coastal habitats. Breeding birds include Redshank, Shelduck, Avocet, Oystercatcher, terns and Short-eared Owl; White Stork has been especially encouraged, and there is now a small colony – the only one in Belgium. These birds can be readily seen in the reserve's ornithological park. There are large numbers of passage birds and in winter good numbers of wildfowl, waders and birds of prey. The flowers are limited, but there are fine displays of Common Sea Lavender together with other saltmarsh and coastal species.

At Zeebrugge, just towards Blankenberge, a small reserve, **Les Fonteintjes**, has a species-rich dune-slack area with open water.

The important reserve of Zwin consists of lakes, saltmarsh and other coastal habitats.

3. Blankaart Lake

Location: About 8km south of Diksmuide, just west of the N369.
Access: Off the N369; access around the reserve on marked footpaths, with occasional guided walks.
Timing: April–July for flowers and birds; winter for birds.

An 82ha wetland reserve consisting of a large lake with surrounding reedbeds, marshland and woodland, together with an old duck decoy, still used for bird-ringing. This is an important site for breeding wetland birds like Marsh Harriers, Grey Herons (a large heron-

ry), Ruff, Great-crested Grebe and Cetti's, Savi's, Reed and Sedge Warblers. Passage birds include Bittern and Little Bittern, Osprey, Spotted Crake and numerous waders, while wintering numbers of wildfowl are very high, especially of Mallard. Flowers of interest are Purple Loosestrife, Meadow-rue, Marsh Valerian, Marsh Pea, Greater Spearwort and Yellow Flag.

4. Molsbroek

Location: About 24km northeast of Gent, just east of Lokeren on the River Durme.
Access: By minor road from Lokeren; restricted to paths within the reserve.
Timing: May–August; good wintering birds.

An 80ha area of wetland habitats including open water, reedbeds, marshes and carr in the Durme Valley. Breeding birds include Shoveler, Mallard, Pochard, Tufted Duck, Long-eared Owl and Sedge Warbler; flowers include Flowering Rush, Purple Loosestrife, Gipsywort and other widespread species. This is also a good area for dragonflies and damselflies.

A series of small wetland reserves runs along the Durme downstream as far as the confluence with the Escaut. All are good for birds and flowers.

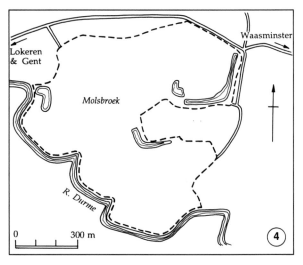

5. Oude Landen

Location: Just west of the A12 motorway immediately northwest of Antwerp (Anvers).
Access: Via footpaths. There are nature trails and regular guided walks.
Timing: May–July.

A surprising reserve (90ha), very close to Antwerp and hemmed in by roads, yet rich in species and relatively peaceful, encompassing grasslands, marshy areas, scrub and woodland. Its generous flora includes several orchids – e.g., Bee and Spotted – plus several Marsh Orchids, Adder's Tongue Fern and Creeping Bellflower. Savi's, Grasshopper and Reed Warblers are among the birds breeding here, and Alpine Newt and Edible Frog are found.

6. Kalmthoutse Heide

Location: On the Dutch border, about 15km due north of Antwerp (Anvers), just west of Kalmthout.
Access: Minor roads from Kalmthout; access on foot mostly unrestricted.
Timing: April–September.

An extensive (861ha) and important area of heathland with surrounding buffer zones. The habitats include dry and wet heath, bog, open water and woodland, together with some unstable inland dunes. The sheep on the heathland were introduced from Lüneburger Heide in Germany (see page 94). Over 100 species of breeding birds have been recorded, including 10 birds of prey (e.g., Hobby), wetland species (e.g., Black-necked Grebe, Black Tern) and heathland species (e.g., Woodlark, Nightjar). The combination of bogs and open water is excellent for dragonflies, and 90 per cent of Belgian species are found here. The rich flora has Bog Orchid, Marsh Gentian, Bladderwort, sundews, Marsh Clubmoss, Royal Fern and other heath and bog species. Smooth Snake are found, and this is a good area for solitary bees and wasps, spiders and other heathland invertebrates.

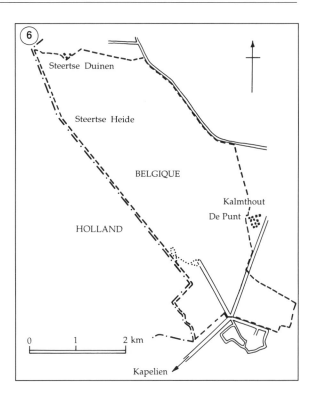

Marsh Gentian, one example of the rich flora of Kalmthoutse Heide.

7. Zegge

Location: About 35km east of Antwerp (Anvers), just north of the Campine Canal near Geel.
Access: By minor roads from Lichtaart, on the N123; access into the reserve by arrangement with the Warden, Groene Wandeling 9, 2232 Gravenwezel.
Timing: April–July.

A private peatland reserve (87ha) with open water, bog and scrub-woodland. The prolific flora features several locally uncommon species, like Bog Arum, Ivy-leaved Bellflower, Lesser Butterfly Orchid and Royal Fern. Breeding birds include Bluethroat (very rare in Belgium), Spotted Crake, Golden Oriole and numerous warblers. Grass Snake are common.

Just north of nearby Herentals is another wetland reserve (20ha), **Snepkensvijver**. Access is only through the Warden, Kattenhagenstraat 32, 2451 Lichtaart.

8. Liereman Reserve

Location: About 8km northeast of Turnhout, next to the canal.
Access: By minor roads from Schuurhovenberg, then on footpaths.
Timing: May–August.

The reserve covers 167ha of an extensive area of acid heathland and bog. Plants include Water Violet, Cranberry, Heath Spotted Orchid, Marsh Clubmoss, Bog Myrtle and Marsh Violet; Curlew, Black Grouse and Black-tailed Godwit are among the birds breeding here. This is a good place for dragonflies.

69

To the southeast, along the Turnhout-Hasselt canal, are several small wetland reserves of interest.

9. Hageven

Location: About 3km north of Neerpelt, close to the Dutch border.
Access: A minor road runs through the reserve; access is on footpaths.
Timing: May–September.

135ha of sheep-grazed heathland and associated habitats – wet and dry heaths, bogs, lakes, reeds and woodland. For such a small area there is a good list of breeding birds: Hobby, Sparrow-hawk, Marsh Harrier, Bittern, Water Rail, Kingfisher and Nightjar, among others; until quite recently there was also Montagu's Harrier, but this has now disappeared. There is a rich bog-heath flora and a good range of insects, from dragonflies to sand wasps. The main mammals are Fox, Roe Deer and Muskrat.

10. Zwarte Beek

Location: About 20km north of Hasselt, between Koersel and the N73.
Access: Minor roads from Koersel cross the area; access on foot is variable, some parts being restricted for military or conservation reasons.
Timing: May–September.

An extensive tract of heathland colonized by pine

Edible Frog, found in the species-rich site of Zwarte Beek.

forests and with bogs, grassland and inland dunes; the reserve itself covers 160ha, but a much larger area is partly managed for conservation. This is a very species-rich site. Over 500 species of plants have been recorded – a third of the total Belgian flora. The breeding birds vary, with over 110 species being represented, including Stonechat, Grasshopper Warbler, Red-backed Shrike, Ortolan Bunting and Black Woodpecker. Common and Alpine Newts, Edible and Common Frogs and the rare Smooth Snake are found. The clean water supports a good fish fauna, including Brook Lamprey, Spined Loach and Bullhead. Access permitting, this whole area is worth exploring.

11. Teut and Tenhaagdoornheide

Location: About 12km northeast of Hasselt beside the E314/A2 motorway north of Zonhoven.

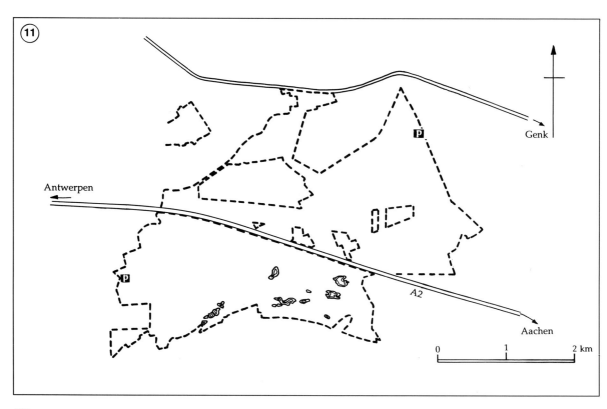

Access: Minor roads from Junction 29; open access on footpaths.
Timing: May–September.

Two separate reserves, one each side of the motorway, but close enough to be part of the same heathland system. Together they protect just over 400ha of heathland, scrub, lakes and bogs. The prolific flora includes Petty Whin, Marsh Clubmoss, White-beaked Sedge, Cranberry, Marsh Gentian and Marsh Andromeda. There are breeding Nightjar, Woodlark, Stonechat, Ortolan Bunting and Red-backed Shrike, to mention but a few. Butterflies of interest include Alcon and Silver-studded Blues and Grayling; Red Squirrel and Roe Deer are among the resident mammals.

Just to the south, about 3km east of Zonhoven, the reserve of **Slangebeekbron** protects another fragment of heath and bog with, among other things, Western Spadefoot Toad.

12. Maten

Location: About 3km west of Genk, between the N75 and the Albert Canal.
Access: Via minor roads from Genk. The western part is open all year; the eastern part closes during the nesting season.
Timing: May–August.

An interesting and varied 164ha area of heathland, scrub and wetlands, with about 35 scattered old fishing-lakes. The flora and fauna are very rich for such a small area. The numerous wetland flowers include Yellow and White Water-lilies, Arrowhead, Lesser Water Plantain, Awlwort and Six-stamened Waterwort. Black Tern, Great-crested and Black-necked Grebes, Kingfisher, Bittern, Water Rail and others breed here. Moor Frog, Common Frog, Natterjack Toad and Common Toad are found around the lakes, as are several newts. The whole area is excellent for dragonflies and damselflies.

13. Mechelse Heide

Location: About 15km north of Maastricht, just west of Maasmechelen.
Access: Via minor road northwest from Maasmechelen; limited to footpaths within the reserve.
Timing: May–September.

About 400ha of heath and bog with additional areas of interest nearby. The rich flora has Cranberry, Marsh Andromeda, Marsh St John's Wort, Bog Orchid and many sedges characteristic of acid habitats, like *Carex limosa* and *C. canescens*. The good range of lichens includes *Cetraria islandica*. Nightjar, Stonechat and other heathland birds breed here; Edible and Moor Frogs and Smooth Snake are also found.

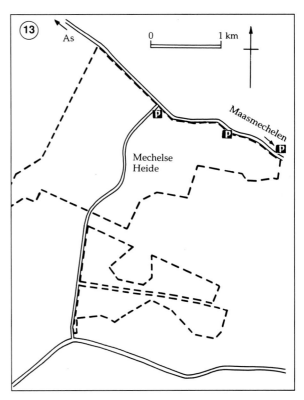

A nearby reserve of interest is the **Ziepbeek Valley**, just west of Rekem.

14. Montagne St Pierre (De Sint Pietersberg)

Location: On the west bank of the Meuse, about 17km north of Liège, close to Lanaye.
Access: Minor roads run to the reserve from east and west; except for one small area, open access by footpaths.
Timing: April–September.

A narrow riverbank strip of limestone grassland and scrub, plus a small detached area, Eben-Emael, open only by permit. The grassland flora is very rich, with 24 orchid species recorded as well as Cut-leaved Germander, Swallow-wort, Field Gentian, Barberry and Grass-of-Parnassus. The old stone workings house an extremely important bat roost: over the years, 15 species (out of Belgium's total of 17) have been recorded here, though not all are currently present. The good insect fauna includes butterflies, solitary wasps, spider-hunting wasps and grasshoppers, all in good numbers.

15. Dinant Area

Location: In the Meuse Valley above and below Dinant.
Access: Off the N92 and N96 roads. Access is open via footpaths. An entry fee is payable at Furfooz Natural Park.

Timing: March–September.

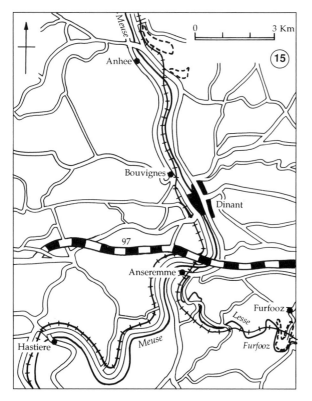

A series of four protected areas, totalling just over 200ha, on limestone hills along the valleys of the Meuse and its tributary the Lesse. **Champalle** and **Poilvache** lie on the east side of the Meuse Valley, just south of Yvoir (north of Dinant); the **Dinant Reserve** lies just north of Dinant; **Waulsort** lies about 8km southwest of Dinant near Hastière; and the **Furfooz Natural Park** lies in the Lesse Valley some 5km southeast of Dinant.

On hard limestone, the sites include cliffs, grassland, scrub and woodland, together with caves, ancient castles and superb views. Flowers of interest include Yellow Whitlow-grass, Tassel Hyacinth, Mossy Saxifrage, Bloody Cranesbill and woody species like Box, Juniper and Downy Oak. Although the primary interest is botanical, this is a good place for butterflies, moths, lizards and snakes, and is also fine walking country, especially Furfooz Natural Park.

16. Seilles

Location: In the Meuse Valley between Namur and Huy, just north of Andenne.
Access: From a minor road on the north side of the valley; access on footpaths.
Timing: April–August.

An interesting area once exploited for heavy metal ores and now possessing a specialized flora. Most notable are the Pansy *Viola calaminaria*, a variety of the Penny-cress – *Thlaspi caerulescens calaminare* – a variety of Thrift – *Armeria maritima* var *halleri* – and varieties of Spring Sandwort and White Campion.

17. Plateau des Tailles

Location: About 50km southeast of Liège, around Baraque de Fraiture at Junction 50 on the E25/A26.
Access: Via the old main road; access on foot via marked paths.
Timing: May–October.

360ha of bog, heath and woodland in a reserve divided into several parts, of which the most significant is the Grande Fagne. This is an important area for moorland and bog plants like Bog Asphodel, sundews, Crowberry, Cranberry, cotton-grasses and numerous

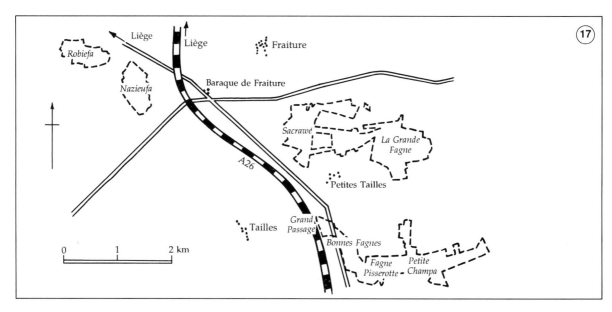

sedges. Upland dragonflies – e.g., White-faced Darter and Four-spotted Chaser – proliferate, and there are northern or Arctic representatives among other insect groups. Breeding birds of interest include Black and Hazel Grouse, Honey Buzzard, Black Woodpecker and Tengmalm's Owl; Common Crane stop over on passage.

18. Hautes Fagnes

Location: South of Aachen, east of Verviers, on the German border.
Access: The N68 runs through the area; access is on foot by marked paths.
Timing: Interesting all year; best May–August.

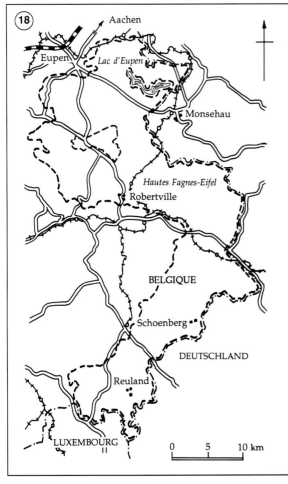

Hautes Fagnes, Belgium's largest reserve area, in the grip of winter.

The largest reserve area in Belgium, an unspoilt high plateau (500–700m) of which about 4000ha is protected within nature reserves, much of the remainder lying within a Natural Park. Habitats include bogs, pools, moorland and coniferous and beech woodland. The flora is a rich mixture of many bog, moorland and mountain species, including Baldmoney, Chickweed Wintergreen, Rampion, May-lily, sundews, cotton-grasses and numerous sedges. Among the many birds that breed here are Honey Buzzard, Red Kite, Black Grouse, Tengmalm's Owl, several woodpeckers and Red-backed Shrike. Red and Roe Deer, Wild Boar and Wildcat are among the mammals, and the invertebrate fauna is of great interest, including Moorland Clouded Yellow, White-faced Darter Dragonfly, Musk Beetle and many other woodland and moorland specialities.

The area is excellent for walking, with numerous marked paths and nature trails. There is an information centre at Botranges.

19. Virelles Lake

Location: Due south of Charleroi, about 15km from the French border, just northeast of Chimay.
Access: Via minor road from Chimay; access is to the south side of the lake only.
Timing: All year.

A large, attractive freshwater lake, partly surrounded by reedbeds and woodland, within a private reserve covering 120ha; there is an observation hide at the edge of the water. Breeding birds include Bittern, Little Bittern,

BELGIUM

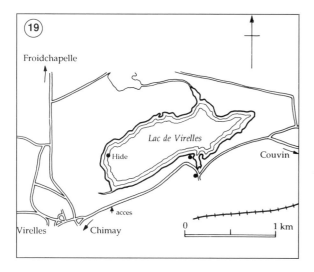

20. Viroin

Location: About 18km southeast of Philippeville (south of Charleroi), immediately north of the N99 east of Couvin.
Access: Via footpaths off the N99 and minor roads.
Timing: April–September.

An area of hills on calcareous schists; about 500ha is protected as a reserve. The area is botanically very rich, with Man, Burnt-tip, Lady, Bee, Fly and Late Spider Orchids – even Violet Limodore at the northern edge of its range – plus Pasque-flower, Bloody Cranesbill, Burnet Rose, Spring Cinquefoil, Box and Downy Oak. The insects have been less fully studied but are probably equally interesting, with 'New Forest' Cicada and numerous butterflies and beetles. Breeding birds include Woodlark; Honey Buzzard and Red Kite are in the area.

Reed, Sedge and Savi's Warblers, Water Rail, Kingfisher and other wetland species; there are good numbers of wintering wildfowl and a wide variety of passage species. Most of the usual wetland plants occur, plus the diminutive Slender Gentian, *Cicendia filiformis*.

Yellow Water-lilies spread across the peaceful lake of Virelles.

21. Bohan-Membre Natural Park

Location: On the French border about 20km northeast of Charleville-Mézières, around a loop of the River Semois.

Access: Via minor roads north from Bohan and Membre; access on foot unrestricted.

Timing: Mainly April–October.

177ha in an attractive area of hilly Ardennes countryside, with some superb ancient forest, mainly beech. There are fine trees of all ages and a wide range of old-woodland species, including lichens (e.g., *Lobaria pulmonaria*), numerous mosses and liverworts, and an excellent fungus flora. Polecat, Otter, Red Squirrel, Roe Deer, Badger, Fox and a good spectrum of woodland birds are found. The insect fauna includes several longhorn beetles.

22. Lesse and Lomme Nature Reserve (Gouffre Natural Park)

Location: 25km southeast of Dinant, immediately south of Rochefort.

Access: A minor road south from Rochefort enters the area; access is open on marked paths.

Timing: April–September.

A very attractive area of limestone and schist hills, partially wooded, with 836ha protected as a reserve (sometimes called Gouffre Natural Park), this is one of the best botanical localities in Belgium, with over 680 flowering species occurring in the dry grasslands, woodlands and scrub. The many trees and shrubs of interest include Downy Oak, Cornelian Cherry, Beech, Juniper, Large-leaved Lime and Wild Service Tree. Among the many flowers are orchids, Angular Solomon's Seal, Pasque-flower, Mezereon, Wild

Daffodil and, notably, flowers with a southerly distribution that are here at their northern limits. The breeding birds are also of interest: Honey Buzzard, Red Kite, Nightjar, Black Woodpecker, Middle Spotted Woodpecker and Red-backed Shrike. Most of Belgium's lizard and snake species are to be found here, and butterflies abound.

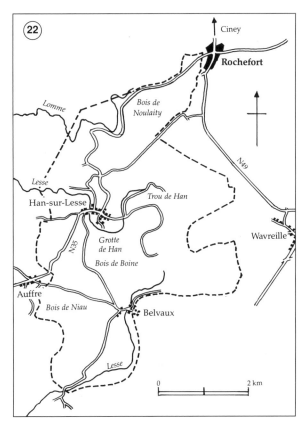

This is good walking country, and especially at Han the caves are very popular tourist attractions. The Lesse disappears underground for about 1km.

23. Rouge Poncé Forest Reserve

Location: On the Ardennes Plateau southwest of La Roche-en-Ardenne, by the village of Tenneville.

Access: On marked paths and via minor roads from Tenneville.

Timing: Interesting all year; best April–June.

Within the Saint-Hubert Forest, lying on an acid plateau at an altitude of 500–700m, are a number of old peat bogs, including the 37ha Rouge Poncé Reserve. This has a typical bog flora, with cotton-grasses, sundews, sedges, several bog-moss *Sphagnum* species, Cranberry and others, together with more northern or montane species like Chickweed Wintergreen. The combination of the bog area with the surrounding forest yields a rich breeding-bird community, including Honey Buzzard, Red Kite,

Angular Solomon's Seal in the botanically outstanding Lesse and Lomme Nature Reserve.

Purple Emperor, Rouge Poncé Forest Reserve.

Hazel Grouse, Black and Middle-spotted Woodpeckers and Red-backed Shrike. Among the butterflies of note are Large Heath and Purple Emperor.

The 48ha moorland reserve of **Anciennes Troufferies** is about 20km to the southwest, by the village of Libin.

24. Upper Semois Wetlands

Location: Along the upper Semois River, west of Arlon, especially between Vance and Chantomelle and around Tintigny.
Access: The N83 passes close to the sites. Access on

Interesting sites abound along the upper reaches of the Semois River.

foot is variable, in some places being only by permit.
Timing: May–September.

The Semois winds its way across southern Belgium from Arlon, eventually joining the Meuse. In its upper reaches is an extremely interesting series of marshes and oxbow lakes; some parts have an intriguing land-use history, showing traces of ancient peat-cutting. The flora includes many fen species, particularly sedges, plus a broad range of aquatics, and this is a good place for amphibians and dragonflies. The Forests of Anlier (north of Habay-la-Neuve) and Chiny (south of Neufchâteau) are especially good areas. The largest reserve lies south of Vance; its Warden can be contacted at N. Perin, Rue Netzer, 34, 6700 Arlon.

25. Rouvroy

Location: At the southernmost point of Belgium, just above the village of Rouvroy.
Access: By footpaths.
Timing: April–October.

This small reserve has a rich insect fauna and a flora more in keeping with regions further south. The calcareous rock supports numerous orchids, such as Late Spider and Military, plus many more widespread plants. Among the insects are several Blue butterflies, New Forest Cicada, Praying Mantis and the blue-flashing grasshopper *Oedipoda caerulescens*.

LUXEMBOURG

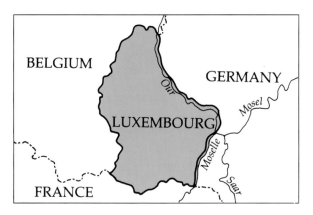

Tiny Luxembourg has an area of only 2586 sq km. Its most important habitats for the naturalist are the woodlands, together with small areas of bog, mainly in the Ardennes, where Luxembourg borders Belgium and France.

The main area of interest, although also a very popular recreation area, is the Luxembourg Natural Park, which encompasses much of the north of the country along the border with Germany. This heavily wooded area, with deep valleys and unpolluted streams, has a rich flora and fauna including, among much else, 36 orchid species and breeding Honey Buzzard, Black Stork, Black Woodpecker and Red-backed Shrike.

In the extreme south of the country there are scattered areas of interest and small nature reserves.

Though tiny, Luxembourg contains some superb areas of natural interest. Its wooded valleys and clear streams are rich in bird and wild flower species.

HOLLAND

Despite its small size (37,300 sq km) and high population density (over 400 per sq km), Holland (The Netherlands) is an attractive country for the naturalist, especially the ornithologist. It occupies much of the eastern coast of the North Sea, and virtually the whole of that coastline has some importance for birds; the Waddenzee, in particular, is an internationally important area with a marvellous array of species.

Holland's reputation for flatness is well deserved. Much of the western part of the country has been reclaimed from the sea as a series of polders, which have gradually matured. With more recent reclamations, parts have sometimes been set aside as nature reserves while the remainder has been cultivated. Away from these reclaimed areas, many of which are below sea-level, the rest of the country is flat or rolling, much of it on recent coastal or glacial deposits. Some of the artificial habitats, especially the wet grasslands, have proved highly attractive to otherwise uncommon breeding birds; for example, Holland supports substan-

OPPOSITE PAGE: *De Groote Peel (the Great Marshes), a wonderfully unspoilt area of woodland, wetlands and heath.*

tial populations of Black-tailed Godwit and Ruff. Holland's flora is less important, but has a good mixture of northern, southern and coastal elements.

Conservation is well advanced, as reflected by the many reserves spread through the country, some surprisingly large for so populous a nation – including both state and private reserves (involving various different organizations), they cover over 5 per cent of the land surface. Most are readily accessible, and a number are being upgraded to National Park status.

Holland is certainly worth more than just a cursory look on the way to somewhere else.

1. Texel

Location: The southernmost and largest of the Waddenzee islands off Holland's northern coast.
Access: By ferry from Den Helder; generally open on foot, though in places restricted to paths. The Tourist Information Office in Den Burg can help with permits.
Timing: All year for birds; April–June for everything else.

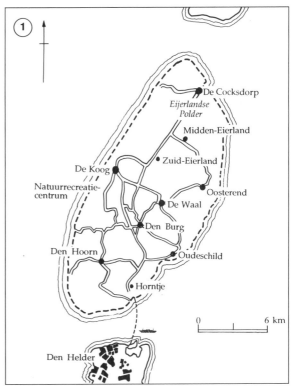

Texel is one of northern Europe's most important areas for breeding birds.

Texel is just under 20km long, and its habitats include dunes, saltmarshes, lagoons, freshwater lakes, marshes and scrub, with reserves scattered throughout. The whole island is of great interest as one of the finest bird-watching areas in north Europe, meriting a visit of several days, if not longer. It is particularly important for breeding birds, with Spoonbill, Avocet, Black-tailed Godwit, Curlew, Redshank, Ruff, several terns, Yellow Wagtail and many others, is extremely good for passage waders and wildfowl, and plays host to large numbers of wintering birds – e.g., over 20,000 Bar-tailed Godwits. The flora is rich, especially on the dunes and dune heaths along the island's west side and in the meadow and marshland areas. Guided walks can be arranged from the excellent information centre south of De Koog.

The bay to the east of Den Helder has extensive saltmarshes and mudflats, with good breeding and visiting birds.

2. Vlieland Island

Location: Just north of Texel.

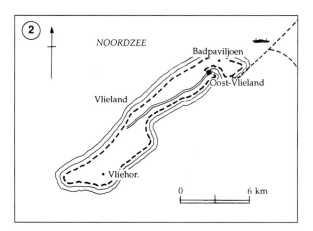

Access: By ferry from Harlingen; buses cover part of the island; access on foot is variable, restricted to paths in places, with no access to the southern one-third of the island.
Timing: All year for birds.

The important parts of the island, about 1300ha in all, are mostly protected within nature reserves. Habitats include dunes, saltmarshes, lagoons, grassland and woodland. This is a fine area for breeding birds – large numbers of Spoonbill, Avocet, Redshank, Curlew and Marsh Harrier, among others – and an important site for passage and wintering wildfowl and waders. There is a good dune and saltmarsh flora, especially along the west coast.

3. Terschelling Island

Location: An island north of Vlieland and northwest of Leeuwarden.
Access: By ferry from Harlingen to West-Terschelling; minor roads at the west end of the island; access on foot unrestricted except in military area (western end) and in parts of reserves during breeding season.
Timing: All year for birds.

About two-thirds of Terschelling's 12,000ha are still in an unspoilt state and mostly covered by several nature reserves; there is a good information centre at West-Terschelling. The whole of the eastern end falls within the uninhabited 4400ha Boschplaat Reserve. Habitats include dunes with grassland and slacks, saltmarshes, lagoons, woodland and freshwater areas. This is an important place for breeding birds – Spoonbill, Marsh and Hen Harriers, Spotted Crake, Avocet, Black-tailed Godwit, Curlew, Redshank and numerous gulls and terns – and for passage and wintering waders and wildfowl, with very large numbers at peak times; e.g., almost 20,000 Brent Goose in late winter. The island has a rich and varied flora, particularly on the dune systems, with fine displays of Marsh Orchid plus Grass-of-Parnassus, Dyer's Greenweed, Rest-Harrow, Marsh Gentian, Chickweed Wintergreeen and Sea Holly.

Ameland, the next island eastward, likewise has a fine range of unspoilt coastal habitats with good breeding and visiting birds and a rich flora. It is accessible from Holwerd.

4. Schiermonnikoog Island

Location: The most northeasterly large Dutch Waddenzee island.
Access: By ferry from Lauwersoog; minor roads radiate from Schiermonnikoog village, but there is no normal motor traffic; access on foot is unrestricted, except into the main reserve area during April 15–July 15.
Timing: All year for birds; April–July for flowers.

5400ha of Schiermonnikoog has been a National Park since 1989. It encompasses a superb range of coastal

Common Seals on Schiermonnikoog Island.

habitats, particularly dunes and saltmarshes. West of the main village, the area of Westpunt has a rich wetland and dune flora with, among other things, numerous orchids. The vast stretch of uninhabited sandy land to the east has a good flora and a fine array of breeding birds, including several hundred pairs of Eider and many waders, harriers, gulls and terns, and is a superb site for wintering and passage waders, wildfowl and raptors. The island is a breeding ground for Common Seal, though numbers have been reduced by the recent virus disease. This is an excellent place for walking, cycling and peaceful beach recreation.

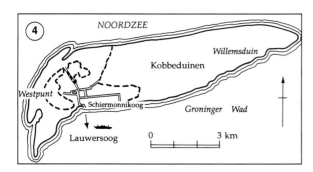

5. Dollard

Location: In far northeastern Holland, on the Ems Estuary.
Access: Minor roads lead into the area from Delfzijl and Winschoten; access into the reserve is limited to the sea-wall and the visitor centre; guided walks arrangeable at the latter (outside breeding season).
Timing: All year.

A large (4372ha) basin within the upper Ems Estuary, with habitats including mudflats, saltmarsh and reedbeds; they are characterized by the variable salinity of the water, itself governed by the relative states of the tide and river. This is an important bird area; some 5 per cent of Europe's Avocet population nest here, and about 80 per cent pass through or feed here. Among the many other breeding birds are Redshank, Oystercatcher and Bearded Tit, and there are substantial numbers of wintering birds. The area has a regular population of about 30 Common Seal, and its varied saltmarsh flora includes Sea Aster growing to over 2m!

6. Lauwersmeer

Location: On the north coast, about 30km northwest of Groningen.
Access: The N361 runs along the seaward side, and minor roads lead southwards; some areas are restricted by the military.
Timing: All year.

This large (10,000ha) dammed estuary, now mainly freshwater with remnant saltmarsh, is important for birds, with good numbers of breeding birds – Marsh Harrier, Shelduck, Gadwall, Garganey, Avocet, etc. – and abundant passage and wintering geese, swans, ducks and waders, plus some raptors (e.g., Rough-legged Buzzard). The main road and the minor roads to the northeastern shore give the best views and access.

The adjacent Waddenzee coast is relatively unspoilt, especially eastwards, and has good birds and flowers.

7. Drentsche A

Location: 6km northeast of Assen, between Oudemolen and Gasteren.
Access: Minor roads to Oudemolen; on foot from there.
Timing: April–September.

1000ha of mixed wet habitats, including heath, bog, wet woodland, grassland and drier pine forests, with a rich variety of birds, mammals, flowers and insects. Breeding birds include Corncrake, Whinchat and Black Grouse. The plants are mainly acid species like sundews, Cranberry, Marsh Gentian and Marsh Cinquefoil. Otter, Polecat and Roe Deer are among the mammals.

Zuidlardermeer, a few kilometres northeast, is an interesting freshwater mere with surrounding wet grasslands. About 6km west of Assen, **Esmeer** and the area to its west comprise a species-rich complex of wet peaty habitats with good birds, flowers and insects, partly protected in nature reserves.

8. Zwanenwater

Location: On the coast between Alkmaar and Den Helder, immediately west of Stolpen.
Access: By minor road south from Callantsoog; access into the reserve via marked paths.

Timing: April–September; very busy in holiday periods.

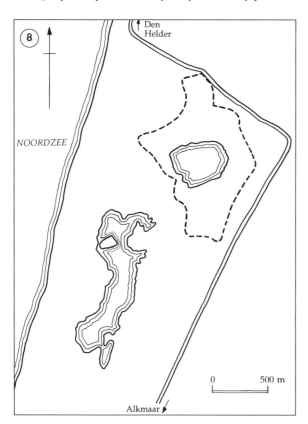

A 573ha nature reserve based on dunes and made up of stable dunes and dune slacks, freshwater lakes, marshy areas, scrub and woodland. There are over 100 breeding birds, including Spoonbill, Bittern, Water Rail, Kentish Plover, Curlew and Spotted Crake. The flora, too, is lavish, with Marsh and Fen Orchids, Tufted Loosestrife, Grass-of-Parnassus, wintergreens and many widespread dune and wetland species, and there is a good butterfly fauna.

De Putten nature reserve, Zwanenwater.

9. Boswachterij Schoorl

Location: West of Bergen, just northwest of Alkmaar.
Access: Minor roads encircle the landward side; access is on foot from Schoorl or Camperduin.
Timing: Some interest all year; best April–July.

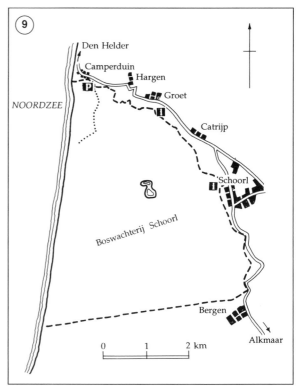

1000ha of dune habitats, with open dunes, planted pine forests, heathland on stable dunes, dune slacks, grassland and open water. Overall the area has a rich flora, with a mixture of dry-dune and damp-slack species, plus moorland species like Crowberry. It is also good for bird-watching, with Red-backed Shrike, Shelduck, Crake and many others.

To the south is another extensive, though fragmented, area of dunes covered by the Noordhollands Duinreservaat. It has some of the highest dunes in Holland.

10. Wormerveer Polders

Location: Northwest of Wormerveer, about 15km north of Amsterdam, in an area bounded by the A9, N8 and N244.
Access: Minor roads thread the area; some access on foot is permitted.
Timing: All year.

Largely protected by nature reserves, an extensive tract (about 10,000ha) of polders, made up of wet grassland, ditches, canals, reedbeds and open water, notably the Alkmaardermeer. Breeding birds include

Bittern, Marsh Harrier, Shoveler, Lapwing, Ruff, Black-tailed Godwit and Black Tern. Spoonbills feed here throughout the year, and in winter there are large numbers of wildfowl.

11. Oost-vaarders Plassen

Location: About 25km northeast of Amsterdam, on the coast of Markerwaard between Almerestad and Lelystad.
Access: Roads encircle the site; access into the reserve is mainly restricted, but there are good views from the roads and an observation tower; in particular, the minor road running south from just west of Lelystadhaven gives good views and access to the hide.
Timing: All year.

A very large area (5600ha) of recently reclaimed polder set aside as a nature-protection area, with habitats including wet meadows, reedbeds and open water. It is excellent for birds, with breeding Cormorant, Bittern, Purple Heron, Spoonbill, Marsh and Hen Harriers, Avocet, Bearded Tit and many others. Passage periods and winter bring vast numbers of wildfowl and waders, plus White-tailed Eagle and other birds of prey.

Harderbroek marsh area, just west of the N302 where it enters Flevoland, is another good area – indeed, the whole of Flevoland is of some interest.

Low-lying De Weerribben is rich in wetland plant species.

12. De Weerribben and De Wieden

Location: About 20km north of Zwolle, between Zwartsluis and Steenwijk.
Access: The N334 and N333 pass through; marked trails; boat trips possible.
Timing: All year; best April–July.

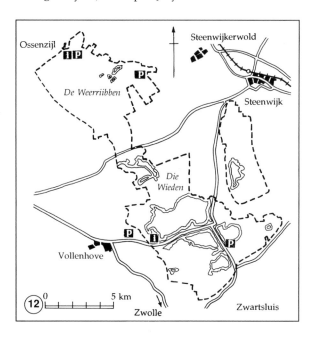

A good place for canoeing and cycling, as well as for

natural history, this 7000ha area of low-lying wetland is protected by two reserves, one of which – De Weerribben – is a proposed National Park. Reeds are still cultivated here for harvesting. The natural habitats include marsh, bog, open water, colonizing and mature woodland, and reedbeds, largely on an area of cut-over peat deposits. The flora is very rich, with excellent displays of most widespread wetland species as well as less common plants like Water Soldier, Fen Orchid, Slender Cotton-grass and the rare sedge *Carex buxbaumii*. The fine array of breeding birds includes Bittern, Purple Heron, Marsh Harrier, Spotted Crake, Curlew, Black Tern and marshland Warblers such as Savi's and Grasshopper, and this is a good area for wintering wildfowl. Otter are found, and the insects include numerous dragonflies and a strong colony of Large Copper Butterfly.

13. Dwingelderveld National Park

Location: Between Hoogeveen and Assen, flanked by the E232/A28 and N371.
Access: Minor roads from Dwingeloo; largely unrestricted access on foot.
Timing: May–September.

This extensive area (3600ha) of heathland, fen and woodland, with numerous small water bodies, is a proposed National Park. The heathland is superb: large tracts of virtually unbroken heather, scattered with juniper, are grazed by flocks of sheep. Breeding birds include Black-necked Grebe, Marsh Harrier, Black Tern and Red-backed Shrike, and there are good numbers of wintering wildfowl on the waters. Along with a wide range of heathland flowers and insects are reptiles like Smooth Snake and Sand Lizard. A good place for walking and cycling.

14. Kennemerduinen

Location: On the coast immediately northwest of Haarlem.
Access: Minor roads out of Haarlem; open on foot.
Timing: Best April–August; very busy in holiday periods.

About 2000ha of dunelands is protected here, partly as an old National Park, not yet redeclared under the new system. Habitats include open and stabilized dunes, pine plantations, freshwater and wet areas. The original dune slacks have dried out as the water table has dropped, and wet areas have been re-created by excavation. The dunes support a wide spectrum of characteristic flowers, birds and mammals, though the latter are disturbed by the large numbers of visitors.

A few kilometres south, just south of Zandvoort, lies another important protected dune area, the **Amsterdamse Waterleidingduinen**. Managed as a water-reserve, it too has a rich flora and fauna, including Polecat. As in other dune areas along this coast, its water table is declining, causing slack areas to dry out.

15. Meijendel Dunes

Location: On the coast immediately north of The Hague (Den Haag).
Access: By minor road from Wassenaar; open on foot.
Timing: Best April–June; very busy during holidays and weekends, though large enough to accommodate this.

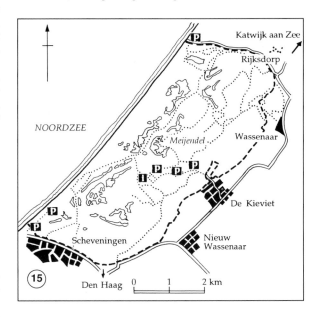

A substantial protected area (over 1000ha) of dunes, used also as a water-catchment and purification region, this comprises a mixture of duneland habitats with woodland and many stretches of open water and associated marshland. The flora and fauna are typical of the slightly acid dunes found all along the Dutch coast. At the end of the access road is a good visitor centre where you can select nature trails and guided walks.

16. Harderwijk Area

Location: Just southeast of Harderwijk.
Access: The N302 and minor roads enter the area; access on foot is mainly unrestricted.
Timing: Best April–September.

An attractive and varied area (about 1800ha) protected within several nature reserves based on old estates; these are known as **Leuvenumse Bos**, **Leuvenhorst** and **Hulshorsterzand**. The habitats include heathland, mixed woodland, mobile dunes, flowing water and conifer plantations. Most of the many flowering species represented are commonplace. Breeding birds of interest are Honey Buzzard, Goshawk and Red-backed Shrike, and there are also Wild Boar and Pine Marten. The Hierdense Beek, flowing through the area, has a good fish fauna, several amphibians and a range of dragonflies, including agrions – indeed, the whole area has an excellent insect fauna, thanks to the mosaic of semi-natural habitats.

Harderwijk is a good centre from which to explore Flevoland (site 11).

17. Kootwijker Zand

Location: Southeast of Kootwijk, about 15km west of Apeldoorn.
Access: Direct from Kootwijk; mostly unrestricted on foot.
Timing: All year; best May–September.

An interesting area (about 600ha) of unstable dunes and dune heath. Some dunes remain surprisingly bare for an inland site, while other parts have extensive lichen-heath, dominated by *Cladonia* species. The flora, though rather poor, contains species rare in Holland like Viper-grass and Arnica. The reptiles include Sand Lizard and Smooth Snake.

The **Harskampse Zand** area, to the southeast, is also of interest, though mostly restricted by the military.

Shifting dunes characterize the interesting Kootwijker region.

18. De Hoge Veluwe National Park

Location: About 6km north of Arnhem and about 15km southwest of Apeldoorn.
Access: Via the N304 and minor roads off it; access on foot is largely open.
Timing: Interesting all year; best April–October.

One of the old Dutch National Parks, founded 1935, this covers 5400ha and has a great variety of habitats, though all on rather acid sandy soil – heathlands, dunes, conifer plantations, mixed woodland (both old and new), fens and wet heath. There are introduced or maintained populations of Red and Roe Deer and Mouflon; also found are Wild Boar, Polecat, Pine

Marten and Red Squirrel. Honey Buzzard, Hobby, Nightjar, Red-backed Shrike, Golden Oriole and others breed here. This is a good place for heathland reptiles like Sand Lizard. There is an information centre in the northern part of the park, along with a national museum and a mammal observation area.

Immediately to the east, more or less linking this with site 19, is the **Deelerwoud Reserve**, covering 1150ha of similar heathland and woodland.

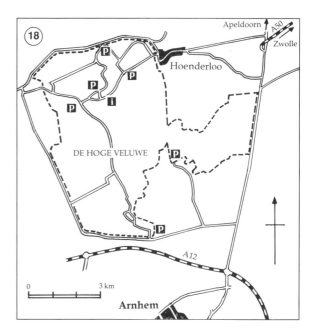

Veluwe, one of Holland's old-established National Parks, has a great variety of habitats, all based on sandy soil.

19. Veluwezoom National Park

Location: Just east of site 18, northeast of Arnhem.
Access: Many minor roads enter the area, particularly from the N48; access on foot is mainly unrestricted.
Timing: Best April–October.

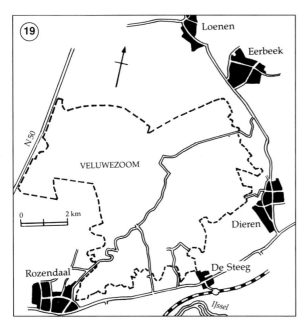

An early National Park (originally declared 1930), this covers 4800ha of heathland with mixed deciduous and coniferous woodland. Although relatively flat, the landscape is attractive and shows a range of glacial features like moraines. Red and Roe Deer, Wild Boar, Fox, Badger and Pine Marten are among the mammals, and the breeding birds include Hobby, Honey Buzzard, Common Buzzard, Goshawk and Great Grey Shrike. There is a good invertebrate fauna, especially of grasshoppers, crickets (e.g., Wart-biter), spiders and solitary bees and wasps.

20. Van Voorne Dunes

Location: On the coast due west of Rotterdam, just southwest of Oostvoorne.
Access: Direct from Oostvoorne and Rockanje; access is open in parts, with some areas restricted to members of managing organizations or to people with day permits (from the Oostvoorne information centre).
Timing: April–July.

A large duneland reserve (about 900ha) in an arc stretching southwards from Oostvoorne to Hellevoetsluis, beyond the N57. Habitats represented are dunes, foreshore, woodland, marshland and open water in the form of two lakes. The dunes are chalkier than many further north, and have a richer flora – over 700 species, many rare in Holland. Well over 100

bird species breed here regularly, including Marsh Harrier, Bittern, Little Bittern, Hobby and Bearded Tit.

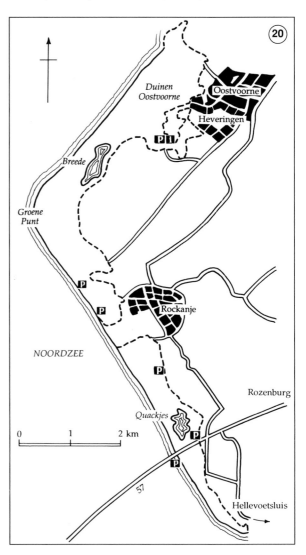

21. Rhine (Rhein) Delta

Location: To the southwest of Rotterdam.
Access: Numerous major roads (N57, N59, N256, etc.) and a maze of minor roads enter the area; many areas are open on foot.
Timing: All year.

A vast and complex area, covering hundreds of square kilometres. The damming of the estuary's main exit channels has created a series of areas of water of differing salinities, relatively little influenced by the sea, but the whole area is extremely good for birds at all seasons, especially autumn through spring. Some parts are designated reserves. Especially good areas include that around **Stellendam**, on the north side of the island of Goeree, where the N57 crosses to Voorne; **Grevelingen Lake**, towards the north of the site, readily viewed from the main roads; the south coast of **Schouwen Island**, especially west of Zierikzee; and **Veerse Meer**, in the south of the area, just north of Middelburg and not far from the port of Vlissingen. Breeding birds include Bittern, Little Bittern, Marsh Harrier, Avocet, Black-tailed Godwit, Kentish Plover, terns and Bluethroat. In winter the numbers of birds can be very high; this is an especially good place for grebes, divers, ducks, geese, various waders and several raptors.

Part of the Belgian reserve of Zwin (see page 68), on the southern edge of the site, lies within The Netherlands.

22. De Biesboch

Location: Southeast of Dordrecht, between the Waal and Bergse-Maas branches of the Rhine (Rhein).
Access: Minor roads run into the area; access on foot is limited by the terrain; the best way is by boat from waterfront villages.
Timing: All year.

A vast and complex wetland area, about 18,000ha in all, made up of several separate reserves and intervening land or water, comprising the upper part of the Rhine (Rhein) Estuary channels, here – because of damming – freshwater and little subject to tidal fluctuations. Changes are still going on as the area settles into the new freshwater regime, but birds currently

breeding here include Cormorant, Marsh and Hen Harriers, Spotted Crake, Avocet, Black-tailed Godwit and a surprisingly high density of Bluethroat. There are also good numbers of wintering wildfowl and some waders.

Guided walks are sometimes available in the northernmost reserve, **Sliedrechtse Biesboch**. The area as a whole is a proposed National Park.

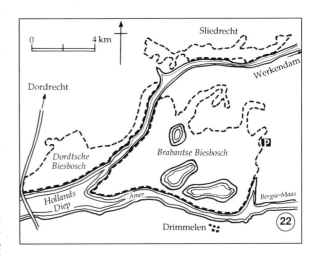

De Biesboch contains a vast and complex wetland system.

23. Loonse en Drunense Duinen

Location: About 8km northeast of Tilburg, just south of Waalwijk.
Access: At various points from minor roads, especially between Loon op Zand and Waalwijk; access on foot is mostly unrestricted.
Timing: April–September.

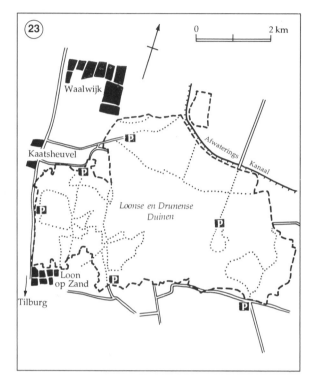

An area of sandy heathland in a nature reserve (about 3000ha). The habitats include dry heath, coniferous plantations, oak woodland and invading birch woodland. The flora and fauna are typical of other Dutch heaths, with specialities like Hobby, Red-backed Shrike, Nightjar, Woodlark, Stonechat and Smooth Snake.

24. Oisterwijkse Vennen

Location: About 12km east of Tilburg, northwest of Eindhoven, immediately southeast of Oisterwijk.
Access: Minor roads run south from Oisterwijk; mostly open on foot, but some areas are closed in breeding season; the Kampina Reserve requires a permit.
Timing: April–September.

Two adjacent reserves, the Vennen and Kampina, contain about 1400ha of mixed heathland, woodland, bog and open water. The western part, the Vennen, has a particularly fine array of small ponds bearing an interesting flora that includes species like White Water-lily, Pillwort, Quillwort and several of the insectivorous Bladderworts; these areas also have a rich dragonfly fauna, with many breeding species.

Birds of interest include most of the heathland species and a few wetland ones like Kingfisher, Black Tern and grebes.

To leave the road to enter the Kampina Reserve you need to have permission from or be a member of the Natuurmonumenten society.

White Water-lilies, Oisterwijkse Vennen.

25. De Groote Peel

Location: About 30km east of Eindhoven, north of Weert, astride the state boundary.
Access: Minor roads lead from Meijel, just east of the site; access on foot is by marked paths.
Timing: May–September.

Jewel-coloured Kingfisher, De Groote Peel.

De Groote Peel (Great Marshes) is a remnant of a former peat bog that once covered a huge area; the reserve itself – a proposed National Park – covers 1320ha of unspoilt heath, bog, marsh, open water and woodland, all kept wet by careful management. This is a superb place for most forms of nature. The many breeding birds include Black-necked and Red-necked Grebes, Bittern, Marsh Harrier, Black Tern, Kingfisher and Nightjar, and among the good range of birds on passage are a few hundred Common Crane. There is a broad spectrum of heath and bog flowers and an excellent selection of dragonflies. This is also a good place for amphibians.

About 6km to the northeast, accessible from minor roads running west from Horst, is the reserve of **Mariapeel/Marienveen**, which has a similar flora and fauna but not nearly as much open water.

26. Savelsbos

Location: About 12km south of Maastricht, close to the Belgian border, on the edges of the Meuse floodplain.
Access: Unrestricted on foot; visitor centre and nature trail.
Timing: April–October.

This area is well known for its Neolithic flint-mines, with their deep shafts and radiating galleries. The 176ha reserve is made up of grassland and woodland

Pasque-flower, one of hundreds of attractive species occurring in Savelsbos.

on one of the few Dutch outcrops of calcareous rock. The flora and fauna are very similar to those of Montagne St Pierre (see page 71), just over the border in Belgium. There are numerous orchids and hundreds of calcareous specialities – including Pasque-flower, Horseshoe Vetch and Common Lungwort – many of them rare in Holland. There are plentiful butterfly species, both in the woodland and on the open grassland. Breeding birds include Firecrest, Hawfinch and Golden Oriole.

GERMANY

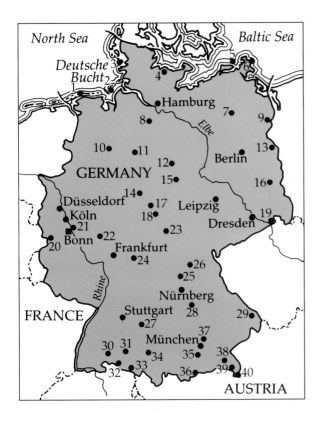

Reunited Germany, with an area of 357,000 sq km, has a dominant and central position in mainland Europe. Ecologically, it is not a distinct unit, bordering on nine other countries; it therefore has few endemic species in a rich flora and fauna that shows influences from all quarters.

Germany is an essentially lowland country, with vast areas of rolling, moderately hilly country, punctuated by lakes – the legacies of the retreat of the ice-sheets. There is a long northern coastline on the North and Baltic Seas, but otherwise Germany is mainly land-locked. Southwards are scattered hilly and low moun-tain areas, such as the Harz and Thüringer Wald areas, but substantial mountains are confined to the far south, where Germany shares a narrow strip of the northern Alps with Switzerland and Austria.

OPPOSITE PAGE: *Siberian Iris in a grassy meadow amid the slopes of Chiemgauer Alpen Reserve.*

For the naturalist, Germany is of enormous interest. The northern coastline and the southern parts of Bayern and Baden-Württemberg are especially rich, with marvellous mosaics of unspoilt habitats, often protected as reserves. The conservation movement is very strong, although until quite recently there were only two National Parks. However, several more were declared in West Germany in the 1980s, and a further six after reunification. Besides these National Parks, six of which lie adjacent to protected areas in other coun-tries, there are numerous large Natural Parks (*Naturparks*; this translates as 'Nature Parks', but 'Natural Parks' gives a clearer impression of their pur-pose), which give a degree of protection to landscape and wildlife but do not necessarily have anything of special interest to the naturalist. In addition there are literally thousands of reserves of one sort or another, protecting all types of habitat and the associated wildlife; these may be run by the state or by any of a number of private organizations. Only the larger, more species-rich or better known of these reserves can be included here. Most of the sites discussed below have a broad range of habitats and features of interest.

1. Niedersächsisches Wattenmeer National Park

Location: Along the Wattenmeer/North Sea coast, from the Dutch border to Wilhelmshaven.
Access: Several main roads (e.g., 70, 461) run into the area; the offshore islands can be reached by public transport from nearby ports, though cars are generally banned.
Timing: All year.

240,000ha of beautiful, unspoilt coastal scenery, com-prising the long chain of East Friesian islands and a vast area of mudflats and saltmarsh stretching across to the mainland. Together with sites 2 and 3, this links with protected areas in Holland and Denmark to form a huge and vitally important conservation area. All the islands pursue a very ecologically sound man-agement policy, are at least partly covered by nature reserves, and are well worth visiting. The area is espe-cially important for birds, with breeding Little and other terns, Ringed and Kentish Plovers, Redshank, Avocet and others. On migration, and through the winter, huge numbers of waders and wildfowl feed and roost here. Common Seal breed and feed in rea-sonable numbers.

The **Dollart Reserve**, just south of Emden on the

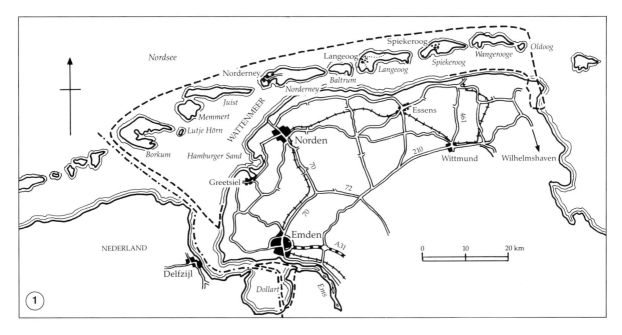

Ems Estuary is a smaller continuation of Holland's equivalent Dollard Reserve (see page 81).

Wattenmeer, a huge and important conservation area.

2. Hamburgisches Wattenmeer National Park

Location: Immediately north of site 1, west of Cuxhaven and Sahlenburg at the mouth of the Elbe.
Access: The Park touches the coast just south of Sahlenburg. There is a path from here, but access is generally difficult.
Timing: Good all year.

A small National Park, covering 11,700ha, made up largely of mudflats and saltmarsh, with two main islands – Scharhörn and Neuwerk. It shares the general characteristics of sites 1 and 3, and adjacent areas of Holland and Germany. Hamburgisches Wattenmeer is especially important for breeding seabirds on its isolated uninhabited islands, with over 10,000 terns such as Common and Sandwich, and many others. It is a wild and beautifully unspoilt area.

3. Schleswig-Holsteinisches Wattenmeer National Park

Location: On the west coast of Schleswig-Holstein, from the Elbe Estuary to the Danish border.
Access: Numerous roads run into the area; there are boat or rail links to the islands.
Timing: All year.
This protects an area of habitats similar to those of site 1, and is likewise of immense importance for birds, with over a million wildfowl and probably as many waders spending part of their year here. All parts are good; a visit to the eastern coast of Sylt is particularly recommended.

4. Selenter See and Surrounds

Location: About 15km east of Kiel.
Access: Road 202 runs south of the lake; access on foot is mainly by marked footpaths.
Timing: All year.

The Selenter See forms part of an extensive area of lakes and woods that is very good for birds. Habitats include reedbeds, bog and mixed deciduous woodland as well as open water. Breeding birds here and on the small lakes nearby or the Binnensee to the east

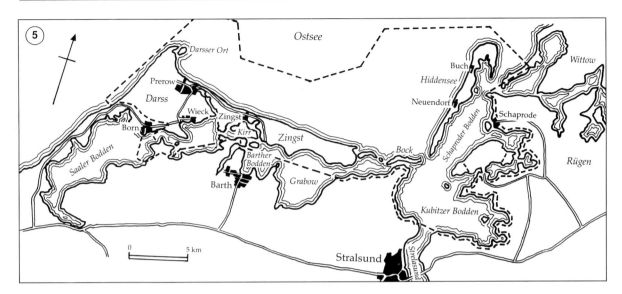

include Bittern, Black-necked Grebe, Goosander, Marsh Harrier, Avocet, White-tailed Eagle and Savi's and Great Reed Warblers. This is an important moulting area for several wildfowl.

5. Vorpommersche Boddenlandschaft National Park

Location: On the Baltic coast, about 50km northeast of Rostock, between the Darb-Zingst Peninsula and the island of Rügen.
Access: Via numerous minor roads; generally unrestricted on foot.
Timing: All year.

One of Germany's new National Parks, this is best described as an 'amphibious landscape'; it has great beauty, with low-lying islands and peninsulas set amid mudflats and saltmarshes. Other habitats include dunes (up to 13m, the tallest unforested dunes in Germany), dune heaths, lagoons, freshwater, mixed oak and birch woodlands and pine plantations. Among the many breeding birds are a few Common Crane, Marsh Harrier, Black Woodpecker, Red-breasted Flycatcher, Bluethroat, Little Tern and Avocet. The area is also of great importance for birds on passage, especially cranes and wildfowl; waders have decreased in recent years as a consequence of saltmarsh reclamation. The lagoons are particularly good for fish – over 40 species recorded – and the dunes have a good flora. Amber is regularly found. Altogether, this is a fascinating area, little visited by non-Germans.

6. Jasmund National Park

Location: On the northeast coast of Rügen, north of Sassnitz.
Access: Road 96 leads into the area; access on foot is generally unrestricted.
Timing: Best May–November.

Although small (3000ha), this new National Park is very varied and beautiful. Chalky cliffs, topped with beechwoods and up to 100m sheer in places, run for 8km. Other habitats include lakes and ponds (some of which are turning into bogs) and large areas of woodland, dominated by beech but also with yew and Wild Service Tree. Among the breeding birds are Raven, Honey Buzzard, Red-breasted Flycatcher (common) and, on the cliffs, House Martin, while Wild Boar frequent the woods. The woodland flora is very rich – in places over 60 different species may be represented per 100sq m; it includes Lady's Slipper, Short-spurred Fragrant and Lady Orchids. Drier areas support plants more characteristic of the steppe country further east. Other species of interest include Smooth Snake and Agile Frog.

The whole of Rügen is of great interest and scattered with reserves of all sorts, including offshore islands that have good seabird colonies. The southeast part of the island is a biosphere reserve.

7. Müritz National Park

Location: On the east side of the Müritz See, 180km due east of Hamburg, extending eastwards as far as Neustrelitz, with a small detached area yet further east.
Access: Roads 198 and 96 lead into the area; minor roads from there. Good access on foot, in places by boat.
Timing: Best April–November.

A remarkable and relatively unknown 31,000ha area made up mainly of lakes and woodland, with bog, heathland, reedbeds, marshland and pasture, including a small part of the Müritz See and many other scattered lakes. The principal woodland trees are beech, oak, birch and pine. The many breeding birds include Common Crane (in good numbers), White-tailed Eagle (several pairs), Lesser Spotted Eagle, Black Stork,

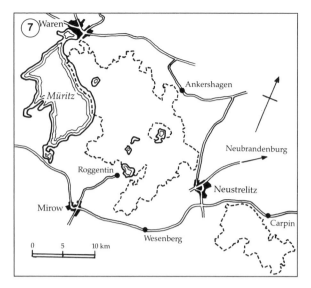

Bittern, Spotted Crake, Kingfisher and Barred Warbler; numerous birds like cranes and geese can be seen on autumn passage. The flora is very rich – over 700 species have been recorded, including many orchids

Lakes and woodland characterize Müritz National Park.

(special orchid areas are set aside), Baltic Field Gentian, Lungwort, Long-leaved Sundew and the Pink *Dianthus superbus*. Otter are plentiful, and there are excellent dragonflies as well as over 800 recorded butterfly and moth species.

8. Lüneburger Heide

Location: A few tens of kilometres due south of Hamburg, just west of the A7.
Access: Minor roads run through the park area; access on foot, mainly restricted to paths.
Timing: Best April–October; busy at weekends and during holidays.

A large area (about 2000ha) of heathland and associated habitats protected within a Natural Park and several nature reserves. The heathland is grazed by a special sheep breed, Heide Schnucken, not unlike Mouflon. The distinctive landscape is characterized by columnar juniper scattered through the heath. Among the breeding birds are Black Stork (now doing well), Crane and many heathland birds like Nightjar and Stonechat. The best places for flowers are in the boggy areas and wet heaths, where Cranberry, Marsh Andromeda and many others are found. The insects are of interest, especially the dragonflies (e.g., White-faced Darter), grasshoppers and crickets (e.g., Wartbiter). Sand Lizard are frequent.

This is a popular walking area, and there are good information centres at Döhle, Niederhaverbeck and Undeloh.

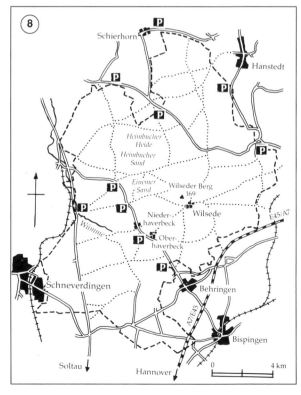

Dark junipers dot the distinctive Lüneburger Heide.

9. Unteres Odertal National Park

Location: Along the Oder, on the Polish border from Szczecin (in Poland) south to Hohensaaten.
Access: Road 2 passes through the area and minor roads into it; access on foot is difficult in places.
Timing: All year; best April–June and September–November.

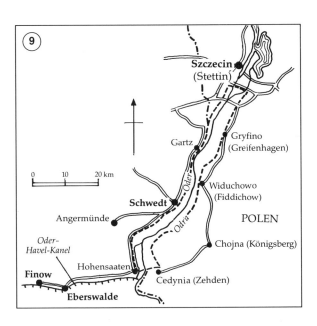

A cross-border National Park, with 22,384ha in Germany and 10,500ha in Poland, this large area of floodplain habitat has a fine mixture of marshland, open water, reedbeds and grazing marshes, subject to flooding at times. Breeding birds are abundant: Bittern, Little Bittern, White Stork, Red Kite, White-tailed Eagle, Marsh, Hen and Montagu's Harriers, cranes, Aquatic and Barred Warblers, Bluethroat, etc. Large numbers of birds pass through at migration times; wintering species include Rough-legged Buzzard and White-tailed Eagle. The flora, less important, has eastern species like Yellow Adonis. This is also a good area for dragonflies and amphibians – and mosquitoes!

10. Dümmer Naturpark

Location: 40km northeast of Osnabrück and 10km south of Diepholz.
Access: Road 51 passes through; minor roads and paths give access.
Timing: All year.

A large semi-protected area, based on the sizeable freshwater Dümmer See but extending around it to include areas of wet pasture, moorland and woodland. About 140 birds breed here at some time or another; they include Bittern, Little Bittern, White Stork, Marsh Harrier, Black Tern, Short-eared Owl and Bearded Tit. Among the passage birds are Osprey, and good numbers of ducks, together with cranes and Hen Harrier, appear in winter. There are good peatland flowers. The dragonflies include Hawkers, White-faced Darter and northern species like Northern Damselfly.

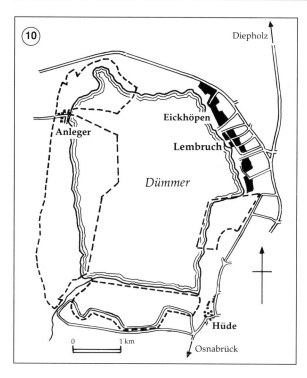

Access: Via roads 6 or 441 from Hannover; access on foot is generally unrestricted or, in the reserve on the east and southwest banks of the lake, by marked paths.
Timing: All year.

Within the park's 3200ha lies the large freshwater Steinhuder Meer, one of northern Germany largest lakes. Despite limited drainage into it, this has a stable water-level, being largely spring-fed. The east and southwest sides of the lake are reserves with open water, reedbeds, wet grassland and bog. Breeding birds include Bittern, Greylag Goose, Garganey, Marsh Harrier, Spotted and Little Crakes, Corncrake and Barred Warbler. Passage and wintering birds are good, too, with over 10,000 wintering wildfowl. The area is of botanic interest, with good aquatics in the relatively unpolluted water and bog and marsh plants nearby.

12. Riddagshausen-Weddeler Teichgebiet

Location: Immediately east of Braunschweig, near Riddagshausen and Weddel.
Access: Roads 1 and 248 run near the area, and minor roads enter it; access on foot is variable, and within the reserve area is confined to marked paths.
Timing: April–October.

A landscape-protection area covering 1800ha, including a 650ha nature reserve. The main habitats are a series of ancient fishponds surrounded by reedbeds, wet pastures, heaths and carr. Breeding birds include Red-necked Grebe, Bittern, Marsh Harrier, Little Crake and Black Woodpecker. Moderate numbers of wildfowl appear at passage periods, and a few stay on through the winter. This is a good area for amphibians: among the 12 recorded species are Agile, Moor, Marsh, Edible and Common Frogs.

To the east the moorland is virtually contiguous with the protected area of **Diepholzer Moorniederung**, around the small town of Wagenfeld; the flora and fauna are broadly similar. The southern race of Golden Plover breeds here in reasonable numbers, and this is another good place to observe migrating cranes.

11. Steinhuder Meer Naturpark

Location: About 18km west of Hannover.

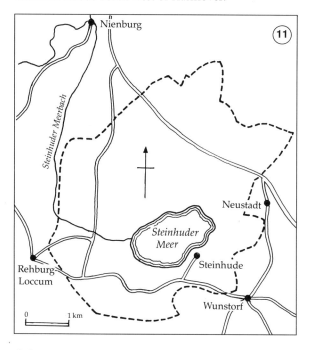

13. Märkische Schweiz Naturpark

Location: About 50km east of Berlin, just north of Müncheberg.
Access: Via road 1 and minor roads; access on foot is unrestricted except to enclosed farmland.
Timing: April–July.

The park encompasses an attractive glacial landscape of small lakes, coniferous and deciduous forests on low hills, and patches of heath and bog. Black-necked Grebe is among the breeding birds, and the flora is very rich – over 800 recorded species. There are Small-leaved and Large-leaved Lime in the woods; some notable trees are over 35m high.

Just to the west, the **Schermützelsee Nature Reserve** has good breeding birds.

14. Warmberg-Osterberg Area

Location: 22km northwest of Kassel, south of Liebenau, along the Warme Valley.

Access: By a minor road south from Liebenau; unrestricted on foot.
Timing: April–July.

This area of limestone hills, with open dry grassland and areas of deciduous woodland, together with some coniferous plantations, is noted for its rich flora, especially its orchids: Military, Toothed, Lady, Lady's Slipper, Musk, Bee and Fly Orchids and Dark Red, White and Red Helleborines are among those recorded here. The rest of the flora is rich, with many other lime-loving species like Large Self-heal, at the northern limit of its range. The generous butterfly fauna includes several Blues and Fritillaries.

15. Hoch Harz (High Harz) National Park

Location: In the Harz Mountains northeast of Göttingen.
Access: Numerous roads (e.g., 241, 242, 496) pass through the area; access on foot is good.
Timing: Interesting all year; best May–October; very busy in holiday periods (lower areas tend to be quieter).

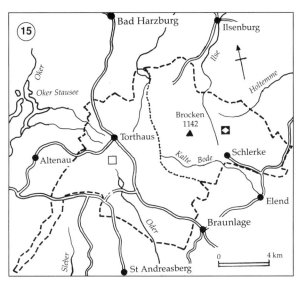

The National Park covers 5868ha of the High Harz Mountains, although the area of interest extends much more widely to include peripheral nature reserves and nature parks; the region has suffered very badly from acid rain. The mountains are mainly granite, rising to 1142m at the Brocken, the highest point in northern Germany, and are well wooded, with a large area of spruce forest and some beechwoods. There are extensive areas of moorland and bog, and some open water. The hills are too acid to sustain a very rich flora; among a mixture of northern species and a few Alpines are Brocken Anemone, Alpine Milk Vetch, Arnica and an endemic Bedstraw, and there are good lichens in more sheltered areas. Tengmalm's Owl, Peregrine Falcon, Ring Ouzel and Crossbill breed here, while the mammals include Red and Roe Deer,

The Harz Mountains are well wooded, though lacking a particularly varied flora.

Wild Boar and Mouflon. This is good walking country.

16. Spreewald

Location: Along the Spree Valley, southeast of Berlin, from north of Lübben to Cottbus.
Access: Roads 115, 320 and many minor roads give access; access on foot is limited by the terrain, but there are good marked trails; some access by boat.
Timing: Some interest all year; best April–June.

Thousands of hectares of attractively unspoilt low-lying wetland landscape in the Spree's floodplain. Canals, channels, lakes, ponds, woodlands and marshes make up an internationally important wetland. Among the breeding birds are Black and White Storks, Great-crested and Black-necked Grebes, Pochard, Marsh Harrier, Kite and Heron; migration times bring many other species, including White-tailed Eagle, Crane and Osprey. The plant-life is likewise varied and rich, particularly aquatics and marshland plants, with fine displays of Yellow and White Water-lilies, Bog Arum and many others. There are numerous dragonflies (some rare) and amphibians, and some Otter.

The ponds just south of Peitz are particularly good for birds, and this is a pleasant area for a water holiday, especially from villages like Lehde – known locally as 'Little Venice'. Boating opens up good opportunities for observing wildlife.

17. Meissner-Kaufunger Wald Naturpark

Location: East of Kassel; the core nature reserve lies about 4km northwest of Meissner.
Access: Roads 451 and 7, then minor roads; numerous marked footpaths.
Timing: April–October.

This Naturpark encompasses several thousand hectares of hilly country, about half wooded, plus many areas of farmland and orchards; it is a noted area for spring fruit blossom. The best part lies within the Meissner Nature Reserve, with spruce and beechwoods on acid soil, lakes, bog, moorland, flowery grassland and an area of limestone with scrub, woodland and grassland. The flora is rich, with species like May–lily, Lily-of-the-Valley, Whorled Solomon's Seal, Arnica, Spiked Rampion and White Woodruff in the acid areas and Lady's Slipper Orchid and Martagon Lily on the limestone. The plateau bog areas have impressive displays of cotton-grasses, and there are good moths and butterflies everywhere. The mammals include Red Deer, Wildcat, just surviving, and introduced Mouflon. Black Woodpecker, Honey Buzzard and Tengmalm's Owl breed here.

Fine display of Cotton-grass in Meissner Nature Reserve.

18. Schlierbachswald

Location: The hilly region south of Eschwege (25km southeast of Kassel), especially around Weissenborn.
Access: Minor roads from Eschwege, then tracks and marked paths.
Timing: April–July for most things.

An attractive, unspoilt area of limestone hills, rising to about 500m, with extensive areas of beech forests and open limestone grassland; other trees include Whitebeam, Oak, Wild Service Tree and Large-leaved Lime. The extremely rich flora includes an unusual association of species; among the many hundreds of flowers are Lady's Slipper, Red and Dark Red Helleborines (and many other orchids), Martagon Lily, Broomrapes, the beautiful violet-and-yellow Wood Cow-wheat and a number of rare Whitebeam species and hybrids. Insects and invertebrates – e.g., spiders – do well, the abundant butterflies including Wood White, Duke of Burgundy, and many Blues and

Limestone forest and grassland in Schlierbachswald.

Fritillaries. Buzzard, Dark and Red Kite and Wood Warbler are among the breeding birds.

19. Sächsische Schweiz National Park

Location: On the Czech border southeast of Dresden, along the Elbe.
Access: Road 172 from Dresden, then minor roads; access on foot is good, mainly via marked paths.
Timing: Interesting all year; best April–October. Very busy during summer holidays.

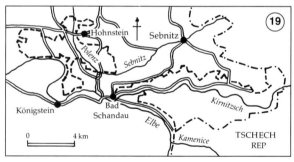

This new National Park covers 9300ha of bizarre landscape: extensive woodland laps around the lower slopes of more than 1000 assorted rock towers, separated by deep gorges and valleys. Areas of basalt, such as on the Grosse Winterberg, have a rich mixed deciduous woodland, with beech and lime, while the sandstone regions are largely covered by forests of Norway Spruce. The deep valleys often have an unusual flora, with a curious mixture of Alpine, northern and western species; plants of note are Labrador Tea, Yellow Wood Violet, *Aruncus sylvestris*, Crowberry, Cranberry and numerous ferns, mosses, liverworts and lichens. Breeding birds include Black Stork, Tengmalm's Owl, Black Woodpecker, Stock Dove, Dipper and Kingfisher. Otter can still be found, and there is a small population of Lynx; bats are frequent. The clear streams sustain a rich invertebrate and fish fauna.

Bizarre sandstone formations at Sächsische Schweiz.

The adjacent part of the Czech Republic has a rather similar landscape, fauna and flora.

20. Nordeifel Naturpark

Location: On the Belgian border just south of Aachen (Aix-la-Chapelle).
Access: Numerous roads run through the area, which is very well served with footpaths.
Timing: Interesting all year; best May–August.

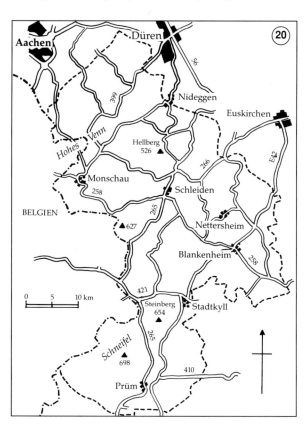

This huge park (almost 175,000ha) links with the Hautes-Fagnes area in Belgium (see page 73) and has a similar landscape, with wooded hills, mostly around 500m, separated by deep gorges and valleys. About 40 per cent of the woodland is deciduous, including beech, sycamore, oak and ash. There is a rich flora, especially on the dry limestone grasslands and in deciduous woods on limestone. The mammals include Red and Roe Deer and introduced Mouflon, and the breeding birds include Black Woodpecker, Black Grouse, Crossbills and many widespread woodland species.

The **Südeifel Naturpark**, just south and linking with the Luxembourg Naturpark (see page 77), has large expanses of woodland, moorland and gorges, with superb walking country rising to 698m at the Schwarzer Mann. An interesting reserve at **Kasselburg** includes captive rare animals. **Hillesheim** has a geological trail and good flowers on its limestone.

21. Siebengebirge Naturpark

Location: A few kilometres southeast of Bonn, between the A3/E35 and road 42 in the Rhine (Rhein) Valley.
Access: Minor roads through the park, with ample parking; access on foot is unrestricted.
Timing: April–October.

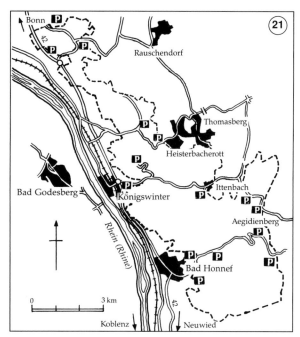

This exceptionally varied area (4200ha) of hilly wooded land, remarkably unspoilt considering how near it is to Bonn, has been protected since 1830. The park has a very varied geology; its numerous peaks are of volcanic origin. The forests are mixed, with oak, beech, hornbeam and Wild Service Tree, and the rich flora has both northern and southern elements, with Blue Gromwell, Alpine Squill, Field Wormwood and Loose-flowered Sedge. The mammals include Fallow and Roe Deer and Wild Boar, and there is a series of enclosures where species can be seen at close quarters. Among the birds breeding here are Honey Buzzard, Red Kite, Wryneck and eight woodpecker species. The area is excellent for walking and general natural history. There are numerous good trails, with refuges in higher areas.

22. Heidenhäuschen Reserve

Location: 4km northeast of Hadamar, 40km northwest of Frankfurt-am-Main.
Access: Off road 54 and minor roads; unrestricted on foot.
Timing: Best April–June.

A ridge, rising to 398m, wooded by beech plus horn-beam, Pedunculate and Sessile Oaks, Large-leaved Lime and Field Maple. The slightly basic basalt rock supports a rich flora that includes numerous orchids – e.g., Long-leaved Helleborine, Bird's Nest and Lesser Butterfly – as well as Coral-root, Columbine and Lily-of-the-Valley.

23. Thüringer Wald

Location: In the south of Thüringen Länd, northwest from Ilmenau and Saalfeld.
Access: Numerous roads and tracks; many marked footpaths.
Timing: May–October.

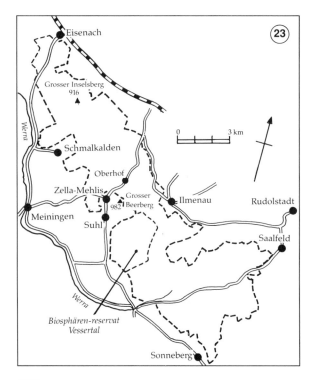

Thüringer Wald is a huge area of hilly forest, lying mainly on sandstones and rising to 982m at Grosser Beerberg. The woods are very varied – beech, spruce, pine, Silver Fir, sycamore, yew, birch and others – and there are flowery meadows and areas of high moorland and bog. Among the breeding birds are Eagle Owl (rare), Tengmalm's Owl, Grey-headed and Black Woodpeckers, Red-breasted Flycatcher, Honey Buzzard, Red Kite, Black Grouse, Capercaillie and Woodlark. The reasonable flora includes a wide range of woodland species such as Umbellate Wintergreen, May-lily and One-flowered Wintergreen. Other species of interest are Fire Salamander and Alpine Newt.

The **Vessertal**, southeast of Suhl, is a biosphere reserve.

24. Bayerischer Spessart Naturpark

Location: About 30km east of Frankfurt-am-Main, running as far east as Lohr-am-Main.
Access: Road 26 and numerous others enter the park; excellent access on foot.
Timing: Some interest all year; best April–August.

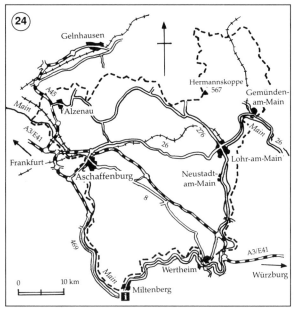

A huge area of wooded hilly land which, with the adjoining **Hessischer Spessart Naturpark** to the north, makes up a vast protected area. The park has large areas of both semi-natural deciduous woodland and planted conifers. Breeding birds include Capercaillie, Black Grouse, Honey Buzzard and several wood-peckers; mammals include Red Deer, Pine Marten and Wild Boar. The flora is rich but patchy, and sparse in some acid coniferous areas. The best areas for plants are on lime-rich rocks, particularly in the adjacent Hessischer park, where good orchids, including Lady's Slipper, and other uncommon species occur. The boggy areas found in many of the valleys likewise have a good flora as well as abundant insects, such as several species of Darter Dragonflies, Swallowtails and Musk Beetles – indeed, overall the Spessart has a very rich insect fauna, with particularly good old-forest species and abundant butterflies like European Map. The information centre at Miltenberg gives details about the many reserves and areas of special interest in the forest.

The vast Bayerischer Spessart Naturpark.

25. Weisendorf Ponds

Location: About 20km northwest of Nürnberg (Nuremberg), between Höchstadt and Erlangen.
Access: Numerous minor roads radiate from Weisendorf; access on foot by paths in places.
Timing: Best April–July.

Around the village of Weisendorf, in an area covering many thousands of hectares, there are about 2000 small lakes and ponds in a marshy and wooded landscape, with pine woodland in drier parts. This region – partly protected within a landscape reserve – is especially important for breeding wetland birds like Black-necked Grebe, Garganey, Bittern, Little Bittern, Purple Heron, White Stork, Marsh Harrier, Kingfisher and Bluethroat. There are good amphibians and dragonflies.

26. Fränkische Schweiz-Veldensteiner Naturpark

Location: North of Nürnberg (Nuremberg) as far as Kulmbach and Lichtenfels.
Access: Numerous roads (e.g., 2, 22, 470) run through the park; access is generally unrestricted.
Timing: April–October.

About 250,000ha of attractive, 'peaky' Jurassic and dolomitic limestone landscape, with a clear distinction between the two. Karst features include caves and collapsed underground water-courses (dolines). About one-quarter of the park is forested, mainly with beech and spruce though also with lime, ash, whitebeam and many others. The flora is very rich, as you might expect

in such a large limestone area; there are numerous orchids together with gentians, Columbine, Martagon Lily and hundreds of others. The grassy and rocky areas support rich butterfly and grasshopper faunas. The caves are well worth visiting – the Teufelshöhle has the largest cave entrance in Germany. This is also great walking country, with over 4000km of waymarked trails.

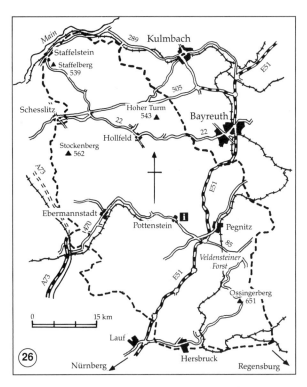

27. Schwäbische Alb (Schwabian Jura)

Location: East of Stuttgart, ringed by Schwäbisch Gmünd, Geislingen, Ulm and Aalen.
Access: Via roads 19, 466 and others, with access on foot generally good.
Timing: April–July.

A broad ridge of Jurassic limestone hills rising to nearly 1000m in places, with dramatic ridges and deep valleys, extensive grasslands and rocky slopes, and some wooded parts. The region is renowned for its extremely rich flora, which mixes southern, central and eastern European elements. Over 50 orchid species are known – a high proportion of Germany's total – including attractive plants like Red Helleborine and Military and Lady Orchids as well as more obscure ones like *Epipactis muelleri* and *E. microphylla*. There are scattered nature reserves, as at Volkmarsberg and southwest of Heubach.

North of the Schwäbische Alb, the **Schwäbisch-Frankischer Wald** is a similar but less dramatic area, again with a good flora. A large Naturpark covers the area, which offers excellent walking and cycling.

28. Altmühltal Naturpark

Location: North of the Danube, from Oettingen east almost to Regensburg.
Access: The A9 bisects the park area, and major roads (e.g., 13, 299) run through it; foot access is generally unrestricted.
Timing: Best April–July.

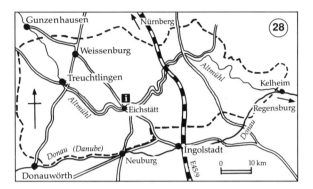

Much of this huge (almost 300,000ha) park is managed farmland. Large parts overlie Jurassic limestone, where there are fine woods with beech, ash, yew, limes and hornbeam and a rich flora that includes Martagon Lily and many orchids. To the west the soils are more acid and over sandstone, and there is a poorer flora with a different range of species, including Arnica and May-lily. The breeding birds include Honey Buzzard, Red Kite, Sparrow Hawk, Eagle Owl (rare), Redstart and several woodpeckers. At the western edge of the park, just southwest of Kelheim, at Weltenburger Enge, where the Danube cuts a spectacular gorge in the Jurassic limestone, there is a fine nature reserve with a rich flora and fauna. There are good facilities throughout the park, and an excellent nature centre in a former monastery at Eichstätt.

South of the park, along the Danube, especially between Donauwörth and Ingolstadt, several wetland reserves protect the floodplain habitats and the birds dwelling there.

29. Bayerischer National Park

Location: On the Czech border, north of Passau, northeast of Deggendorf.
Access: Via numerous minor roads; excellent walking facilities.
Timing: Some interest all year; best May–August. Very busy during summer holidays.

13,000ha of mountainous granite and gneiss country, almost all wooded. Although little of the forest is virgin, the present management policy of allowing it to develop naturally means that it is gradually acquiring the characteristics of virgin forest. The dominant trees are Norway Spruce, beech and Silver Fir, though elms, limes, Bird Cherry and others can be found. The flora,

though less rich than in equivalent limestone areas elsewhere, has much of interest, including Mountain Tassel-flower (a Snowbell relative), May-lily, Chickweed Wintergreen, Hungarian Gentian, Austrian Leopard's Bane, numerous unusual hawkweeds, Monkshood, Alpine Sow-thistle and many other woodland and bog plants. Honey Buzzard, Goshawk, Black Grouse, Hazelhen, Red-breasted Flycatcher, Black and White-backed Woodpeckers and Tengmalm's Owl breed. Red and Roe Deer are both common, alongside Wild Boar, Red Squirrel, Pine Marten and Badger. Various species known to have resided here in the past are now being reintroduced.

There is an excellent information and display centre, with a small botanic garden, at Neuschönau. Across the road from it is a large reservation where many representatives of the park's present and past animals are kept in semi-natural conditions, so that you can get excellent views of Bison, Otter, Lynx, Wild Boar and others, together with a selection of birds.

The protected area extends northwards, with much of the same type of countryside, into the larger **Bayerischer Wald Naturpark**. Over the Czech border the Sumava Forest (see page 111) extends the area still further, so that collectively it probably represents the largest forest in central Europe. The whole region is excellent walking country, with numerous facilities and marked trails.

Sunlit clearing in the wooded hills of Bayerischer National Park.

30. Hüfingen Orchid Woods

Location: Southwest of Hüfingen, either side of road 31 southwest of Donaueschingen.
Access: Via road 31; on foot into the reserves on marked trails.
Timing: April–July.

Many of the woods in this area lie on base-rich soil, which supports a very rich flora. Two of these woods are reserves, with special orchid trails, allowing you to see superb displays of, among others, Lady's Slipper, Coral-root, Ghost Orchid, helleborines and Spotted,

A haven for butterflies in the spruce woods of Hüfingen.

Marsh Cranesbill is abundant in the fens of Mindelsee.

Fly and Butterfly Orchids, together with a good range of woodland flowers like Martagon Lily, May-lily, Mezereon, Serrated Wintergreen and *Galium rotundifolium*. Kite, Crossbill and Red Squirrel are resident, and the woodland-butterfly fauna includes attractive species such as Silver-washed Fritillary and White Admiral.

31. Federsee

Location: About 8km west of Biberach, south of Ulm.
Access: Via minor roads to Bad-Buchau; access on foot from there.
Timing: Good all year; best April–June.

This 1400ha nature reserve, containing the lake and its surrounding reedbeds and wet meadows, is excellent for breeding birds, including Purple Heron, Bittern, Little Bittern, White Stork, Marsh Harrier, Bluethroat, Savi's Warbler and Bearded Tit. Wildfowl, waders, terns and raptors stop here on migration, and some overwinter; Red and Black Kites regularly hunt overhead. The area is excellent for dragonflies and amphibians, and there is a good wetland flora, with species like Greater Spearwort, Marsh Cinquefoil, Yellow and Purple Loosestrife, Water-lily and Great Water Dock.

Bad-Buchau has a good visitor centre and a raised walkway to hides (small fee). Boats can be hired locally for better views of the lake.

32. Mindelsee

Location: Near the western end of Lake Constance (Bodensee), south of Stockach.
Access: Via road 33, then minor roads to Möggingen; thereafter on foot.
Timing: Some interest all year; best May–September.

An attractive natural lake with surrounding reedbeds, wet meadows and pastures, fens and woodland – about 400ha in all. There are breeding Little Bittern, Common Tern, Buzzard, Dark Kite, Kingfisher and a range of wetland warblers. The flora is rich and varied, especially in the wet meadow areas – Marsh Cranesbill is abundant, along with Purple and Yellow Loosestrife, Marsh Orchid, numerous sedges, Siberian Iris and many others. There are good dragonflies, notably Brilliant and Downy Emerald, Ruddy Darter; Swallowtails, Brimstones and other butterflies are plentiful, and crickets and grasshoppers are everywhere. The amphibians include abundant Edible Frog.

The site combines strong nature protection and management with good access for walking and cycling, plus limited bathing and fishing.

33. Bodensee (Lake Constance)

Location: On the Swiss and Austrian borders.
Access: Major roads around the lakeside; access into reserve areas is variable, and usually by marked footpaths.
Timing: All year.

Shared with Austria and Switzerland, this huge lake is extremely important for wildfowl. Around the shores is a series of wetland reserves, with reedbeds and fen, supporting good breeding birds and often with a rich flora and invertebrate fauna. Among the breeding birds are Red-crested Pochard, Great-crested Grebe, Marsh Harrier, Common Tern, Whinchat and numerous wetland warblers, while passage and wintering species include Pochard, Tufted Duck, Coot, swans and various other wildfowl, often in huge numbers. The wetland-reserves flora has Siberian Iris, Marsh Gladiolus, Bird's-eye Primrose and Bug, Fen and Marsh Orchids, together with occasional *Microstylis monophyllos* (a rare orchid). There are good dragonflies, especially Hawkers and Darters, and varied amphibians such as Marsh and Moor Frogs.

Some important reserve areas lie around the Untersee, particularly the **Mettnau Peninsula** west of Radolfzell, the shore south of Radolfzell, and the **Wollmatinger Ried Reserve** around the Reichenau Peninsula (see page 143 for Swiss sites). On the main lake there are good areas just southeast of Überlingen and at **Eriskircher Ried**, southeast of Friedrichsaven.

34. Wurzacher Ried Reserves

Location: Just north of Bad Wurzach, about 15km northwest of Leutkirch.
Access: Road 465 runs through the reserves; numerous tracks and cycleways give closer access.
Timing: May–September.

This substantial tract of peatland (about 1300ha), with habitats including raised bog, fen, reedbeds, damp meadows, open water and woodland, is beautifully unspoilt and rich in wildlife. Over 500 flowering species have been recorded, with bog specialities like Cranberry, Rannoch Rush, sundews, Bog and Early Marsh Orchids and many others, along with a rich lichen and bryophyte flora. Breeding birds include Curlew, Snipe, Spotted Crake and many others in the surrounding spruce woodlands. Insects abound: the site is particularly good for butterflies, with not only specialist bog species but also more widespread ones, like Heath Fritillary, around the edge. Grasshoppers, crickets and dragonflies are all prolifically represented.

There are many reserves, mostly based on small lakes or peaty areas where lakes have vegetated over, often with associated woodlands. Examples include the **Rohrsee**, the **Gründlen Ried** (north of Kisslegg), **Fetzachmoos** (south of Leutkirch) and the lakes and fens around Vorsee, on road 32 northwest of Ravensburg.

One of the many small lakes of Wurzacher Ried.

35. Pupplinger Au Reserve

Location: About 25km south of Munich (München), just north of Wolfratshausen, where the rivers Loisach and Isar join.
Access: Minor roads east of Wolfratshausen; on foot via marked paths.
Timing: May–September.

This unusual reserve, combining the braided course of the Isar with the woods and grasslands to its east, is particularly noted because many Alpine plants, washed down in the rivers, survive – and even thrive – at low altitudes on the river shingle; they include Mountain Avens, Alpine Gypsophila, Hutchinsia and Myricaria. This is also an excellent place for orchids, notably a very large colony of Lady's Slipper Orchids and some huge Fragrant Orchids.

36. German Karwendel Gebirge

Location: Due south of Munich (München), bounded by roads 2, 13 and 307 and the Austrian border.
Access: Via the 307 and minor toll roads; on foot via marked paths.
Timing: May–October.

Austria's Karwendel Gebirge is a major reserve of limestone mountains (see page 155); this smaller – but still large – reserve on the German side of the border comprises the rest of the mountain area, reaching north as far as the Isar headwaters. As well as the broad, gravelly river floodplain there are extensive spruce and beech forests and areas of grassland on mountains reaching over 2250m. The flora is rich, with Alpines like Mountain Avens and the tamarisk-like Myricaria growing in the river valley at low levels. Elsewhere there are good orchids, including Marsh, Dark Red and Broad-leaved Helleborines and Fragrant, Small White and, higher up, Globe and Black Vanilla Orchids. Chamois and Red Deer are resident, and there are good woodland and mountain birds – e.g.,

Golden Eagle, Hazel Grouse, Tengmalm's, Pygmy and Eagle Owls, numerous woodpeckers and Bonelli's Warbler.

37. Ismaninger Teichgebiet

Location: About 5km northeast of Munich (München) along the Mittlerer-Isar Canal.
Access: Via minor roads from Ismaning; open on foot.
Timing: All year.

Reservoir, canal, fishpond and associated wetland habitats cover 900ha in all. Despite being so near Munich, this is a fine area for bird-watching, with breeding birds including good numbers of Black-necked Grebe, Night Heron, -Red-crested Pochard, Little Bittern, Water Rail, Common Tern and Penduline Tit. In autumn large numbers of moulting wildfowl come, followed by hosts of wintering wildfowl.

38. Chiemsee

Location: About 15km east of Rosenheim, just north of the A8/E52.
Access: Minor roads around the lake; access is open to most areas, limited in the reserve area.
Timing: Best April–August; some winter birds.

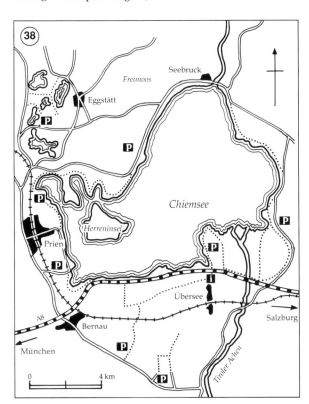

A large, deep lake, mainly used for recreation. However, there are good areas around the south side,

especially at the southeast corner, where the **Tiroler Ache Reserve**, just west of Grabenstätt, protects a large area of reedbed, grassland, woodland and lake. Notable breeding birds include Black-necked Grebe, Kingfisher, Bluethroat, Whinchat and River, Savi's and Great Reed Warblers, and this is also an important place for passage and wintering wildfowl. The flora of the fen and grassland areas is of interest; it includes Siberian Iris, Fen Ragwort and Marsh Orchids.

39. Chiemgauer Alpen Reserve

Location: 20km southwest of Salzburg, either side of road 305, and including the Mittersee and Lödensee.
Access: Off road 305; good access on foot via numerous paths.
Timing: May–September.

A lovely area of the lower Alpine slopes, rising to nearly 2000m along the Austrian border, with lakes surrounded by fens and many grassy stretches among spruce and pine woods. The lavish flora includes Red Helleborine, Lesser Butterfly and other orchids, Blue-eyed Grass, Siberian Iris (in abundance by the lakes), the Fleabane-like *Inula brittannica*, Bladder Gentian and Bird's-eye Primrose. Honey Buzzard, Eagle Owl, Tengmalm's Owl, Ptarmigan, woodpeckers and Bonelli's Warbler breed.

40. Berchtesgaden National Park

Location: To the south of Salzburg, in an enclave almost surrounded by Austria.
Access: Roads 20 and 305 run to the edge of the park; access is on foot or by boat only from there.
Timing: Beautiful all year; best May–September. Very busy at weekends and during holiday periods.

A superb Alpine area (21,000ha), rising to 2713m at Watzmann. Among the habitats, rich in flora and fauna, are a range of woodlands, including beech-lime, Norway Spruce, larch and Mountain Pine, together with Alpine pastures, lakes, cliffs, small glaciers and bare rock. The many breeding birds include Golden Eagle, Honey Buzzard, Ptarmigan, Eagle, Tengmalm's and Pygmy Owls, Grey-headed, Black, Three-toed and White-backed Woodpeckers and Alpine Chough. The flora has a marvellous mixture of Alpine and woodland species: gentians, Dragonmouth, Primula species, Rock Jasmine, Martagon Lily, Snowbell, Alpine Poppy, saxifrages, crocuses, orchids, Edelweiss, wintergreens and many others. There are Marmots, Ibex, Chamois, Mountain Hare, Snow Vole and Red Deer, and Alpine Salamander occurs throughout. The butterflies include Apollo, Fritillaries and numerous Blues. There are information centres at Königssee and Berchtesgaden; boats run the length of the lake from Königssee, stopping at various points. Further access is on foot: you will not regret the walk.

THE CZECH REPUBLIC
and
SLOVAKIA

At the time of writing, the former Czechoslovakia has just split into two separate countries. This may affect travel between the two countries, and their separate attitudes to nature conservation may alter, but it is hoped relatively little will change. Here they are treated together for convenience, and as a reasonably coherent ecological unit. They have a joint area of 130,000 sq km, and are intermediate in character between eastern and western Europe, having boundaries with Germany, Austria, Hungary, the former

The wooded hills of Sumava, where the Czech Republic borders on Germany.

USSR and Poland. Essentially, Slovakia occupies the eastern half of the former country, from the river Morave eastwards.

Although they have no coast, there is a wide range of other habitats. Almost all the northern border is mountainous, with a series of protected areas culminating in the High Tatras National Park (site 8). These areas, generally forested – particularly with conifers – are among the worst-affected by acid-rain damage in Europe, with a consequent impairment of their wildlife, although there are still genuine wildernesses where Bear, Lynx and Wolf roam. There are mountainous areas in the southwest, along the German border, and through the eastern half of the area. The complex geology, with limestone, gneiss, granite and volcanic mountains, contributes to a rich, varied flora.

Wetlands are an important habitat. Many have been drained, but an important area survives in the Danube (Dunaj) Valley, and there are thousands of artificial lakes, large and small, scattered throughout the two countries, mostly for fishing; where they occur in high concentrations (e.g., around Trebon) they assume considerable importance for wetland species. Here and there in the warmer southeastern parts of Slovakia a few remnants of steppe grassland survive, but they are declining and fragmented. Steppe species like Great Bustard are found there.

For its size, the area has a very rich flora and fauna, with a number of endemic plants and insects centred on the Tatra area. Conservation is well organized, and there are four National Parks (three in Slovakia, one in The Czech Republic) plus numerous reserves and protected landscapes. Some protected areas seem to be suffering from loss of status or lack of enforcement.

1. Zahrádky Lakes (The Czech Republic)

Location: About 60km due north of Prague (Praha), just south of Česka Lípa, around the village of Zahrádky.
Access: Road 9 runs through the area and minor roads enter it; access on foot to some areas.
Timing: April–October.

A collection of fishponds extending over about 12km and including the reserve at Novozámecky Rybnik, the easternmost pond. There are reedbeds around the ponds and hay meadows and woods between them. This is a good – though deteriorating – area for breeding birds, among them Bittern, Little Bittern, Marsh Harrier, Crake and various marshland warblers; passage birds include White-tailed Eagle and Osprey. The dragonflies are good, though eutrophication is taking its toll of the number of species.

A little northwards is an attractive area of pine woods on sandstone, with heathland and woodland flowers and Red-backed Shrike.

2. Jizerské Hory (The Czech Republic)

Location: To the northeast of Liberec, near the Polish border.
Access: Roads 14, 35 and 10 run around the site and minor roads enter it; largely unrestricted on foot.
Timing: May–October.

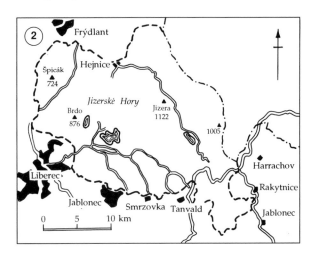

An area of rounded wooded mountains (the Iser Mountains) on granite and basalt, rising to just over 1000m. There are fine beech woods, some very ancient, and Norway Spruce. The higher areas have extensive, partly wooded blanket bog with numerous ponds and plants like cotton-grasses, various sedges, Chickweed Wintergreen, Dwarf Birch and Bistort. Flowers in the woodland areas include Plane-leaved Buttercup, Alpine Sow-thistle, May-lily and *Senecio nemorensis*. Black Grouse, Honey Buzzard, Corncrake and others breed. The higher areas have suffered severe acid-rain damage, and there are large areas of dead, dying or cleared conifers.

Typical bog pool in the high moorlands of Jizerské Hory.

3. Krkonose National Park (The Czech Republic)

Location: About 100km northeast of Prague (Praha), on the Polish border just north of Vrchlabí.
Access: Roads 295 and 296 run into the park; checkpoints for nonresidents; access on foot generally open.
Timing: May–October; very busy at weekends and in holiday periods.

38,500ha within an impressive area of wooded mountains, rising to over 1600m. There are large areas of beech and spruce forests, together with Alpine pastures, meadows, bogs and small lakes and granite cliffs. Some parts are protected as strict reserves; others are subject to normal agriculture. Though the mainly acid soils limit species numbers, there is a reasonably rich flora, including many widespread woodland and montane plants and a number of endemic species or subspecies. The prolific breeding-bird community includes Black Stork, Hen Harrier, Capercaillie, Tengmalm's and Eagle Owls and Bluethroat. Among the butterflies is Clouded Apollo. In the upper parts acid rain is seriously affecting woodland communities. This is excellent walking country, with chairlifts to the higher areas.

4. Súl'ovské Vrchy (Slovakia)

Location: South of Bytca and Zilina.
Access: Minor roads run into the area from road 61; access on foot is by numerous paths.
Timing: Best April–July; busy at peak periods.

Limestone peaks in the Súl'ovské Vrchy area.

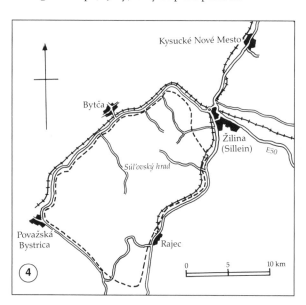

An attractive area (about 3000ha) of limestone mountains, popular with walkers. There are especially good parts around Súl'ovské Skály, with limestone crags, pinnacles and gorges. The ample flora includes many widespread limestone species, like Military Orchid,

Spring Cinquefoil, Herb Paris, Swallow-wort, Bastard Toadflax and White Rock-rose, alongside more specialized plants like the rare Pink *Dianthus nitidus* and the House-leek *Sempervivum hirtum glabrescens*. Green and Wall Lizards and Red Squirrel are found, and among the abundant butterflies are Scarce and Common Swallowtails, Apollo and Dark Green Fritillary.

5. Malá Fatra (Slovakia)

Location: 15km east of Zilina, northwest of Ruzomberok.
Access: Off the 18/E50, or off the minor road (with cablelifts) running south from Terchová; access on foot is unrestricted.
Timing: April–October; busy at peak periods.

A beautiful area (about 20,000ha) of limestone mountains, rising to over 1700m, featuring some fine peaks and cliffs, mountain pastures and beech, spruce and yew forests, with Mountain Pine higher up; excellent walking country, with numerous paths and lifts. The lavish flora includes rarities and endemics; the grasslands are especially good, with masses of Round-headed, Early Purple and Military Orchids, Clustered

Lavish grassland flora in the beautiful Malá Fatra.

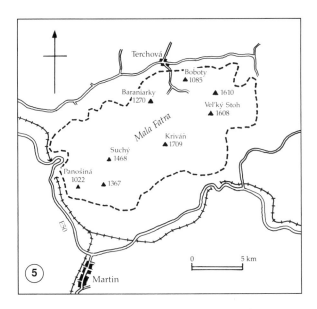

Bellflower, Sainfoin and Yellow Scabious, plus rarities like Carpathian Snowbell, *Dianthus nitidus*, *D. praecox* and Slavonian Pasque-flower. Golden Eagle, Peregrine Falcon, Hazel Grouse, Eagle Owl and various wood-

peckers breed. Bear are still found, as are Lynx and Red Deer. The amphibians include Alpine Newt and Fire Salamander. Butterflies abound, especially in the flowery grasslands; they include Apollo, Scotch Argus and Water Ringlet.

6. Vel'ká Fatra Mountains (Slovakia)

Location: From just north of Banská Bystrica as far as road 18/E50.
Access: Roads 18, 59 and 65 encircle the area and a few minor roads lead into it; access on foot is unrestricted.
Timing: Best April–August.

A large, wild and unspoilt mountainous limestone region (60,000ha), rising to over 1500m. There are extensive forests (virgin in places) of beech, spruce, fir and Scots and Mountain Pines, and some fine karst landscapes. The lavish flora is much like that of site 5, with many Carpathian endemic species and sub-species. The area is very important for breeding birds: Black Stork, Honey Buzzard, Lesser Spotted and Golden Eagles, Tengmalm's and Eagle Owls, Rock Thrush, numerous woodpeckers, etc.

This is fine walking country, although parts are very remote; there are a few cablelifts and scattered refuges.

7. Nízke Tatry National Park (Slovakia)

Location: 20km northeast of Banská Bystrica; 10km northwest of Brezno.
Access: Main roads encircle the park, road 72 bisects it, and minor roads enter it, the most useful being the one (with cablelifts) running south from Liptovská Mikulás; access on foot is unrestricted.
Timing: Best April–July; busy at weekends and during holiday periods.

An enormous area of mountainous terrain (81,000ha), excellent for walking, rising to 2043m at Dumbier. The geology is very varied, with acid crystalline rock and dolomitic limestones. Among the habitats are extensive beech, spruce, fir and pine woods, pastures, small lakes and bogs. The rich flora includes two bell-flowers (*Campanula carpatica* and *C. bohemica*), *Jovibarba arenaria* (a Houseleek-relative) and *Gladiolus imbricatus*. The mammals are particularly important: Lynx, Wolf, Bear, Otter and Wildcat. Golden and Lesser Spotted Eagles, Black Stork, Honey Buzzard, Eagle Owl, Barred Warbler and Collared and Red-breasted Flycatchers breed, while the butterflies, Longhorn Beetles and moths are also of interest.

8. Vysoké Tatry (High Tatras) National Park (Slovakia)

Location: Along the Polish border, north of Liptovská Hrádok and Poprad.

Access: Road 537 runs along the park's south side and minor roads enter it; cablecars and paths go to higher areas; access on foot is unrestricted.
Timing: May–October; exceptionally busy during main holiday period.

A large and spectacular mountainous area, rising to 2633m at Gerlachovsky Stít, very attractive and superb for walking, covering 50,000ha plus additional buffer zones. Although a tourist mecca, the park is extremely important for its natural history as an isolated and well protected high-mountain area. There are extensive forests, particularly coniferous – spruce, Silver Fir, larch and several pines – with some areas of beech, plus numerous lakes, grassland areas, bogs, high cliffs, waterfalls and other minor habitats. The rock is mainly granite, though there are some limestone areas. The flora is extremely rich, with over 1200 recorded species including at least 25 endemics; among local rarities are the Snowbells *Soldanella hungarica* and *S. carpatica* and the Milk Vetch *Oxytropis carpatica*. More than 700 lichen species and 500 bryophytes have been recorded.

The mammals are of special interest: Bear, Wolf, Wildcat, Chamois, Lynx, Marmot, Wild Boar, Marten, Red and Roe Deer and Otter. Among the many breeding birds are Golden and Lesser Spotted Eagles, Eagle Owl, Capercaillie, Hazel Grouse, Three-toed and other woodpeckers and Wall Creeper. The invertebrate fauna is extensive, particularly butterflies, moths and beetles, including endemics like the ground-beetle *Nebria tatrica* and *Deltomerus tatricus*.

9. Pieniny National Park (Slovakia)

Location: About 25km northeast of the High Tatras, on the Polish border northwest of Stará L'Ubovna.
Access: Road 543 from just west of Stará leads into the park; unrestricted on foot.
Timing: May–October.

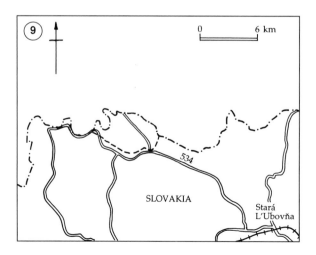

A small (2115ha) but important park area adjoining Poland's Pieninski National Park (see page 119) and made up mainly of limestone mountains with impressive pinnacles, cliffs and gorges clad in beech, spruce and fir forests. The very rich flora contains various endemic species or subspecies like *Chrysanthemum zawadskii*, the Self-heal *Prunella pieninica*, the Rock-cress *Arabis pieninica* and a subspecies of Columbine, *Aquilegia vulgaris ullepitschii*. Lesser Spotted Eagle, Hazel Grouse, Eagle Owl, Three-toed Woodpecker, Nutcracker, Red-backed Shrike and Ring Ouzel breed here. Apollo Butterfly, endemic beetles and other insects are found, as are Montandon's and Alpine Newts.

10. Sivá Brada (Slovakia)

Location: On the south side of the 18/E50, about 12km east of Levoca.
Access: Open on foot direct from the main road.
Timing: April–July.

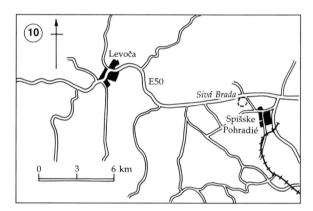

This small but very rich reserve consists mainly of a limestone hill crowned by an old chapel and with a tufa spring. The flora is lavish, with an interesting mixture of salt-tolerant and limestone flowers; among the many of interest are several orchids, Horseshoe Vetch, Northern Bedstraw, Arrow-grass, the attractive lily-like *Anthericum ramosum* and Field Fleawort. There is a rich downland butterfly fauna. Stonechat and Quail breed.

11. Vihorlat (Slovakia)

Location: The extreme east of Slovakia, close to the Russian border, about 25km northeast of Michalovce.
Access: A minor road from Michalovce runs into the park; open access on foot from there.
Timing: May–July.

A remote area (about 5000ha) of wooded volcanic hills rising to just over 1000m. The woods are deciduous, mainly beech but also oak, sycamore and hornbeam. This is an important place for breeding birds, including Golden, Lesser Spotted, Short-toed and Booted Eagles, Honey Buzzard, Kite, Saker, Eagle and Ural Owls, Red-breasted Flycatcher and at least seven woodpeckers. Noteworthy flowers are May-lily, Downy Woundwort and Black Broom. Snakes are common, and the large stonefly *Dinocras cephalotes* very abundant.

The western end of the artificial Lake Michalovce, in the centre of the protected area, is a holiday area, but retains interesting parts. There is a woodland reserve just to its northeast.

12. Sumava (The Czech Republic)

Location: Along the border with Germany (partly adjacent to the Bayerischer Wald National Park – see page 102), west of České Budějovice.
Access: Roads 4 and 141 and many minor roads enter the area; access to uncultivated areas is open.
Timing: April–October.

A vast area (163,000ha) of partly protected wooded hills, rising to 1378m (Plöckenstein). The forests are mainly spruce with some Silver Fir and beech, especially lower down. There are lakes, streams, cirques, peat bogs, moors and other habitats, mostly on rather acid gneiss and granite. There are several more strictly protected reserves, including **Boubínsky Prales**, which protects an area of virgin beech-fir forest. Overall the flora is rich, with five gentians (Bavarian, Fringed, Cross, Brown and Marsh), 17 orchids, many unusual hawkweeds and a wide range of acid-neutral soil species. Among the many birds breeding here are Black and White Storks, several eagles, Harrier, Hazel Hen, Corncrake, Tengmalm's and Eagle Owls and Bluethroat. Butterflies, including Large Blues and

Gentle landscape in Sumava. Jacob's Ladder flowers in the foreground.

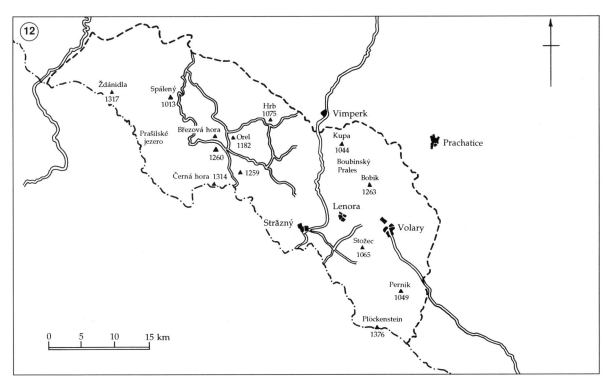

Apollos, abound. The whole area is excellent for walking, though some parts are very remote.

13. Trebon Basin (The Czech Republic)

Location: All around Trebon, on the E49/34, east of České Budějovice.
Access: Roads E49, E551, 150 and minor roads run through the area and offer good views; access on foot is variable.
Timing: Some interest all year; best April–July.

A vast tract of low-lying land (70,000ha) with at least 500 bodies of water; other habitats include reedbeds, marshes, meadows, coniferous woodland and deciduous floodplain woods with lime, maple and oak. This is a very important region for breeding wetland birds, some in large numbers; among them are Purple and Night Herons, Black and White Storks, Bittern, Little Bittern, Marsh Harrier, Kingfisher, Icterine, River and Savi's Warblers and Penduline Tit. Not surprisingly, this is also a rich area for amphibians, dragonflies and damselflies. Particularly good are Velky and Maly Tisy and, at the northern end of the area, the Horusicky Rybník lake with its associated bogs and marshes.

Lake in the wetlands of the Trebon Basin.

14. Znojmo Area (The Czech Republic)

Location: South and west from Znojmo to the Austrian border.
Access: Minor roads; mainly unrestricted on foot.
Timing: Best April–June.

This protected landscape area, locally called a National Park though not listed as such, has extensive oak, beech and spruce woods among stretches of flowery grassland. Parts are good for breeding steppe birds – one of the few such places in Czechoslovakia – and there is a small population of Great Bustard, plus Stone Curlew, Tawny Pipit and Lesser Grey Shrike.

15. Pálava and the Lednice Area (The Czech Republic)

Location: On the Austrian border around Mikulov, 20km northeast of Břeclav.
Access: Road 52/E461 runs down the west of the area, and numerous minor roads enter it.
Timing: Best April–September; good in winter and at passage times.

A very varied area of great interest, comprising three parts. The Pálava Hills, just northeast of Mikulov, are of craggy limestone and support a very rich flora, with a lovely mixture of widespread and local lime-loving

Limestone rock garden in the Pálava Hills.

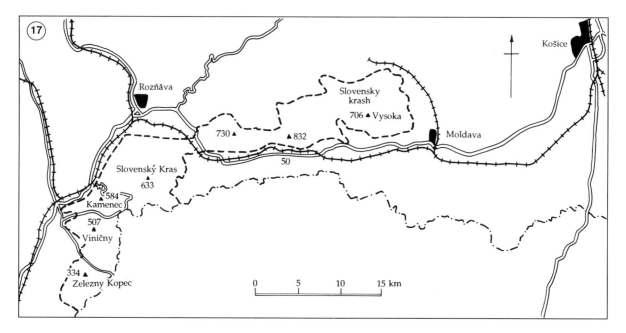

species, including a range of orchids, bellflowers like *Campanula macrostachya*, the little yellow *Alyssum montanum montanum*, Wall and Mountain Germanders, flaxes and *Inula ensifolia*. Rock Thrush breed. Butterflies abound, especially Blues, Hairstreaks and Fritillaries, and there are good grassland grasshoppers. The saxicolous lichens on the limestone outcrops are also of interest.

Better known are the lakes around Lednice. These have an excellent range of breeding wetland birds: Black-necked Grebe, Red-crested Pochard, Black and White Storks, Bittern, Little Bittern, Purple and Night Herons and Marsh and Montagu's Harriers. There are interesting birds at migration times and reasonable wintering wildfowl.

To the southeast of Břeclav, where the Dyje and Morava meet, lies a vast tract of floodplain wetlands and woodland, rich in breeding birds and invertebrates. Collared Flycatcher are particularly abundant in this somewhat inaccessible area.

16. Danube Marshes (Slovakia)

Location: Southeast from Bratislava as far as Komárno, along the main course of the Danube (Dunaj).
Access: Roads 63 and 506 and many minor roads give general access. Some areas are inaccessible without a boat.
Timing: Best April–July; also good in winter and at passage times.

An enormous area (about 150 sq km) of floodplain and river habitats, mainly along the Danube but also along the Little Danube (Maly Dunaj), which flows to the north. Though fragmented by agriculture, the whole region is of great interest, parts of special note lying just southwest of Gabcikovo, west of Samorín

and in the Bustard reserve at **Zlatná na Ostrove**, about 12km west of Komárno. The area is particularly important for its breeding birds – Black and White Storks, Purple and Night Herons, Marsh and Montagu's Harriers, Bluethroat, Penduline Tit, Moustached Warbler, Great Bustard, etc. – and for its large numbers of wintering wildfowl.

17. Slovensky Kras (Slovakia)

Location: By the Hungarian border, south of Roznava.
Access: Road 50/E571 runs through the area, and minor roads lead off it; mostly unrestricted on foot.
Timing: April–September.

A superb area (36,000ha) of craggy karst country adjacent to Hungary's similar Aggtelek region (see page 168), with gorges (especially that at Zádielska, a protected reserve), limestone pavements, caves and some fine deciduous forest of ash, Manna Ash, beech, oak and hornbeam. The flora is exceptionally rich (over 1000 species); besides numerous orchids and widespread limestone species there are specialities like the Pink *Dianthus praecox*, the Hare's-ear *Bupleurum affine*, Dogtooth Violet, the Mallow-relative *Lavatera thuringiaca*, Bladder-nut, the Maple *Acer tataricum* and Black Broom. Breeding birds include Imperial, Lesser Spotted and Short-toed Eagles, Eagle and Ural Owls, Roller, Woodlark and Red-backed Shrike. Common, Wall and Green Lizards are found. The butterflies are particularly abundant, among them Southern White Admiral, Large Tortoiseshell, Camberwell Beauty, numerous Fritillaries – large and small – Hairstreaks and Blues.

This is magnificent walking country and delightfully quiet away from tourist sites like the gorges; the obverse of this is that many areas are remote and lack facilities.

POLAND

Poland has an area of 312,000 sq km and a population of about 37 million. Though rarely flat, it is mainly low-lying, with significant mountains only along its southern borders. Especially in the north, there are numerous lakes, mostly natural; open water covers over 2 per cent of Poland's area, and there are estimated to be over 1000 lakes above 1ha. Forests cover about 28 per cent, though many are coniferous plantations or highly managed.

Poland has a long eastern border with Russia, Lithuania, Belorussia and Ukraine, and its natural history is strongly influenced by these eastward links, though it also shares species with the countries on its other borders. Despite the population density, there are many wildernesses and areas of virgin forest; the Biebrza marshes (site 3), the Białowieza Forest (site 6) and the High Tatra area (site 10) are good examples. Overall, Poland is probably most attractive to the birdwatcher, though other aspects of natural history are certainly not lacking.

There are 14 National Parks, with more under implementation, plus a good network of reserves,

mainly run by the state. Voluntary and international conservation organizations as yet play a relatively small part.

1. Woliński National Park

Location: On Wolin, in far northwest Poland, by the Baltic coast and German border.
Access: The E65 and minor roads run into the park; open access on foot.
Timing: April–October; can be busy during holiday periods.

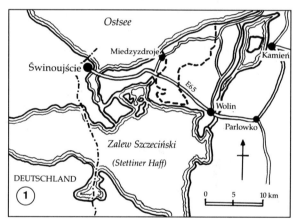

Covering almost 5000ha of the island's northern and western parts, the park has a varied landscape of woodland – including some ancient forest – lakes, bog, seacliffs, saltmarshes and dunes. There is a rich coastal flora, and breeding birds include White-tailed and Spotted Eagles and Eagle Owl. The coastal wetlands on either side of the park are of international importance for breeding wetland birds and as migration staging-posts for wildfowl and waders. The whole region is of great interest.

2. Slowiński National Park

Location: On the Baltic coast northwest of Gdansk and northeast of Słupsk.
Access: Via minor roads north from the E28/6; open on foot.
Timing: April–July.

18,000ha of unspoilt coastal land around two large lakes, Łebsko and Gardno. Habitats include coniferous

OPPOSITE PAGE: *Peaks reach to well over 2000m in the Tatras Mountains, a superb area for naturalists.*

115

woods, high mobile dunes (up to 40m), bogs, marsh-land and open water. Many birds breed here – e.g., Cormorant, Bittern, Black and White Storks, White-tailed Eagle, Marsh Harrier, Crane, Eagle Owl and Black Tern – and this is an important stopover area for migrant wildfowl and waders, especially in autumn. The dune flora is rich and varied.

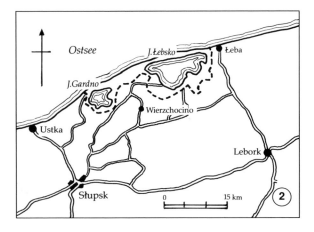

Black Stork – one of the many breeding birds found in Slowiñski National Park.

3. Biebrza and Augustów Marshes

Location: Along the River Biebrza, between Augustów and Łomzo, northeast of Warsaw.
Access: Roads 61 and 669 pass through the area; minor roads and tracks lead off them. The whole area is very wet.
Timing: April–July.

One of the best and best known sites for birds in Poland, with a marvellous range of breeding species. The floodplain is broad and marshy with vast areas of fen, grazed marshes, reedbeds, carr and open water. Bittern, Little Bittern, Black and White Storks, Marsh

Harrier, White-tailed and Lesser Spotted Eagles, Crake, Ruff, Black-tailed Godwit, Great and Jack Snipes, Black and White-winged Black Terns and numerous ducks, warblers and other birds breed. There is a major Great Snipe lek near the village of Budy. The lakes and marshes north of Augustów are also of great interest. The whole area is superb, though difficult to work; much still awaits discovery. There are observation hides on the east side of the valley, north of Gugny.

4. Słoñsk Reserve

Location: On the German border southwest of Gorzów, where the Odra (Oder) and Warta rivers meet.
Access: Roads 22 and 133, running east from Kostrzyn, skirt the area; access deep into the reserve is by permit only.
Timing: April–October.

A large area of marshy floodplain, of which 3000ha is partly and a further 1100ha strictly protected. The habitats include meadows, pastures, reedbeds, open water and carr, and many areas are flooded for over half the year. Breeding birds are of especial importance here – Red-necked and Black-necked Grebes, Bittern, White-tailed Eagle, Marsh Harrier, Corncrake, Ruff, Black-tailed Godwit, River Warbler, Penduline Tit, etc. Hosts of wildfowl congregate here in spring and autumn, and rather lower numbers winter here.

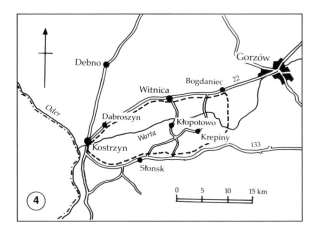

5. Kampinoski National Park

Location: A few kilometres northwest of Warsaw, south of the River Wisła.
Access: By minor roads north from the E30; open on foot.
Timing: May–October.

22,000ha of varied landscape: inland dunes, pine forests, deciduous woodland, bogs, marshy areas, grassland and flowing water. The site is very close to Warsaw and suffers some despoliation as well as flocks of visitors. Birds breeding here include Black and White Storks, Marsh Harrier, Lesser Spotted Eagle, Corncrake, Crane, Black and other woodpeckers, Ortolan Bunting and many more. Elk have been reintroduced from the former USSR. The deciduous forests contain oak, hornbeam, lime, birch and alder.

6. Białowieza Forest

Location: On the Russian border east of Warsaw, southeast of Białystok.
Access: By minor road east from Bielsk to Białowieza village, then on paths and tracks; permits obtainable locally.
Timing: Interesting all year; best April–July.

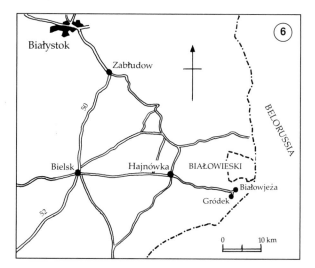

One of Europe's most famous forests; about 5000ha is protected here in Poland and a large part extends over the border into Belorussia. The area is best known as a relic of virgin temperate mixed forest, with pine, Silver Fir, oak, lime, birch, hornbeam, Norway Maple, rowan, ash and many others. It also holds one of the last remaining European populations of Bison, reintroduced earlier this century; the herd is genuinely wild and thus difficult to observe, but there are captive animals near the park centre. There is much else of interest: other mammals include Beaver, Lynx, Elk, Red Deer and visiting Wolf, and over 200 birds breed, including many rarities and eastern species and a wealth of commoner forest species. The area is botanically rich: 26 orchid species are known, plus many other ancient-woodland flowers, both widespread and rare, and about 1000 fungi. There are also good butterflies.

This superb region is quite unlike anywhere else in Europe, and requires plenty of time if you are to see it properly. Some travel companies offer winter visits with better opportunities for seeing the rare mammals, often from sleds.

7. Karkonoski National Park

Location: On the Czech border southwest of Wrocław, just south of Jelenia Góra.
Access: Via minor roads south from Jelenia to Karpacz; open on foot from there.
Timing: May–September.

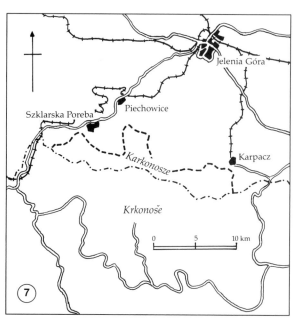

Part of the same mountain system as in The Czech Republic's Krkonose National Park (see page 108), this has essentially the same habitats and wildlife and suffers the same acid-rain problems. At its highest point, Sniezka (1603m), there are good mountain flowers, birds and butterflies, as well as Mouflon.

8. Milicz Ponds

Location: Northeast of Wrocław, west of Ostrów, along the Barycz Valley.
Access: Minor roads radiate from Milicz; there are good views from these.
Timing: April–October.

A huge marshy area (about 8000ha) between Zmigród and Odolanow, scattered with artificial fishponds and natural wetlands. This is a superb place for dragonflies, amphibians and other wetland groups, and breeding birds – e.g., Red-necked and Black-necked Grebes, Bittern, Little Bittern, Purple Heron, Ferruginous Duck, Black and White Storks, Greylag Goose, Kite, Bluethroat, River and Great Reed Warblers, Red-breasted Flycatcher and Golden Oriole. The wildfowl can be good at autumn passage periods. There is an ornithological centre in Milicz.

9. Ojcowski National Park

Location: About 15km northwest of Kraków, in the Pradnik Valley.
Access: By minor roads off the E40; open on foot.
Timing: May–September; busy at weekends.

An attractive and interesting area, 1590ha of unusual hilly landscape, with some striking pinnacle rock formations. In places there are fragments of ancient Silver Fir/beech, sycamore, hornbeam and oak woods, together with the form of Silver Birch known as Ojców Birch. The rich flora includes Lady's Slipper Orchid and the Steppe Feather-grass *Stipa pannonica*. At least 12 bat species populate the caves and hollow trees, and there is a good range of breeding birds.

10. Tatra National Parks

Location: In the mountains along the Slovak border, south of Kraków.
Access: Road 95 to Nowy Targ; minor roads from there into the various parks.
Timing: May–October.

The border with Slovakia runs along the ridge of the mountains made up of the Tatras, the Beskids and other ranges. There are several National Parks on the Slovak side (see page 110) and four on the Polish side, two of which form cross-border areas. From the west the parks

Snow-covered Mount Miedriene in the Tatras.

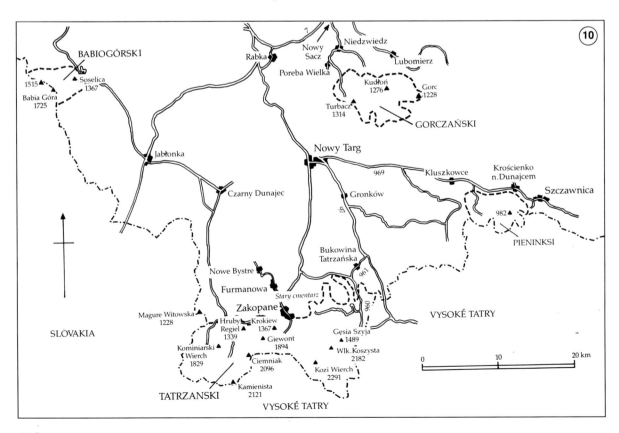

are Babiogórski, Tatrzanski, Gorczanski and Pieninski. All have superb scenery and good flora and fauna.

Tatrzanski (21,400ha) covers the High Tatras south of Zakopane, where fine snowy peaks reach to well above 2000m, with cirques, lakes, high pastures and extensive forests. The rich wildlife includes abundant Chamois, Lynx, Marmot, Wildcat and other mammals; Golden Eagle, Eagle and Ural Owls, Hazel Grouse, Three-toed Woodpecker, Alpine Chough and many other birds breed. This is a superb area for the botanist: the flora mixes endemics with widespread species – all told, well over 1000 – like the Snowbell *Soldanella carpatica*, Swertia, *Pedicularis exaltata*, *Gentiana pannonica* and *Campanula carpatica*.

Babiogórski (1720ha) has peaks reaching 1725m (Babia Góra), fine forests and plenty of animals and plants. **Gorczanski** (6000ha) has mountains up to 1300m and a very rich flora, including specialities like *Alchemilla gircensis*, *Crocus scepusensis* and the Moonwort *Botrychium lanceolatum*. **Pieninski** (2330ha), adjacent to the equivalent Slovak National Park (see page 110), has a good flora and Butterflies like Apollo and Clouded Apollo.

The whole region, including the parts between the parks and, of course, the Slovak side, is of enormous interest and should be accorded a long stay rather than a fleeting visit.

11. Bieszczadzki National Park

Location: In the far southeast, where Poland meets Slovakia and Ukraine.
Access: Road 98 from Sanok, then southeastward on minor roads.
Timing: May–September.

In one of the most remote parts of Poland, but well worth the trip, this superb park covers 6000ha of the eastern part of the Carpathians. The mountains reach over 1300m and are largely forested with Silver Fir, spruce and beech. The mammals are especially fine – Wolf, Brown Bear, Lynx, Wildcat and free-roaming Bison – and there is a broad range of forest and mountain birds, including Spotted Eagle, Eagle Owl and Hazelhen. The flora contains many species rare or absent elsewhere in Europe, like the Pink *Dianthus compactus*, the Knapweed *Centaurea kotschyana* and the Violet *Viola dacica*.

FRANCE

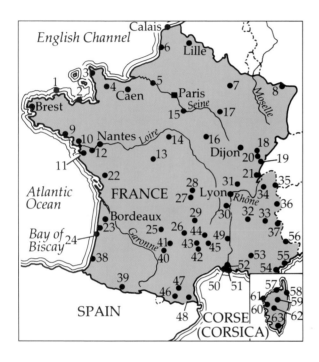

France is the largest (547,000 sq km) and arguably the most varied country in Europe, with an enormously long coastline on two quite separate seas and extensive mountains reaching up to the highest point in Europe, Mont Blanc (4807m). It has a wonderful variety of scenery and a very rich flora and fauna.

Until 20 years ago, virtually everywhere in France held natural history of interest. However, there have been far-reaching and continuing changes in the French countryside, affecting particularly the north but noticeable also elsewhere, even in the rocky hills of the south, where the impact of tourism has been dramatic. It is now much harder to find sites of note, and vast areas have been rendered virtually devoid of wildlife interest.

Nevertheless, France is a wonderful country in which to travel and explore, with a good climate, a low population density – many areas have been little affected by habitation or agriculture – and easy access to the countryside. At least in the mountains and over much of the south it is still reasonably accurate to say that anywhere is of interest, and few visitors will be disappointed. The sites selected for description here are the best and/or most easily accessible – the list is certainly not exhaustive.

As in most western countries, the organization of nature conservation is complex. Six National Parks, offering varying degrees of protection, cover 0.7 per cent of the land surface, mainly in mountain areas. An extensive system of 26 Regional Natural Parks covers about 7 per cent of the land surface; they vary enormously, from useless to superb, and the rules governing their protection are very lax. There are also numerous nature reserves, which may be statutory, national or local, or run by any of a number of voluntary organizations like the LPO (national Bird Protection Organization), SEPNB (Brittany Nature Conservation Society) and ONF (National Forest Organization). The reserves and parks are not necessarily the most rewarding areas to visit (though many are), so the list includes some non-reserve sites.

Corsica (Corse) Although politically part of France, Corsica (see page 139) – 160km south of Provence, yet only 12km from Sardinia and 80km from Italy – is ecologically quite distinct. Almost everywhere on this mountainous and remarkably unspoilt island is of some interest. The boundaries of the substantial Natural Regional Park in the mountains are difficult to appreciate on the ground, and so I have covered the area without reference to them.

1. Les Sept-Îles

Location: Off the north Brittany coast, near Lannion.
Access: By boat from Perros-Guirec, from June through the summer.

Gannets soar above Les Sept-Îles, France's best seabird colony.

OPPOSITE PAGE: *Gorges de la Jonte in the* causses *region.*

120

Timing: Best in June; interest decreases as summer progresses.

This group of granite islands forms France's best seabird colony. Substantial numbers of Puffin, Gannet, Storm Petrel, Razorbill, Guillemot, Fulmar, Shag, Sandwich Tern and Kittiwake breed, plus a few Raven. Grey Seal are resident. You can land on Île aux Moines, but others can be viewed only from the boat.

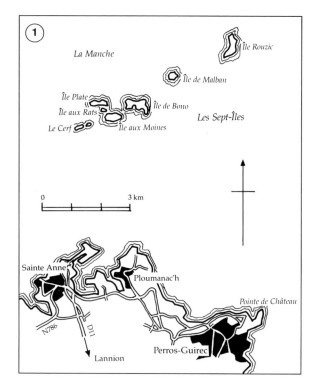

2. Cap Fréhel

Location: North Brittany coast, about 20km west of St Malo.

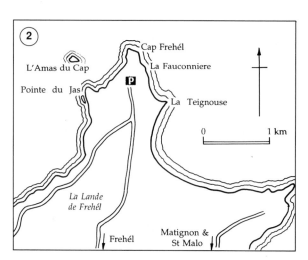

Access: Two minor roads lead into the site; access is generally open.
Timing: Best May–August.

An impressive headland with fine heathland, coastal grassland and cliffs, partly run as a reserve by the SEPNB. The flora includes most heathland species plus uncommon western specialities like Kerry Lily, the tiny gentian-like *Exaculum pusillum*, Autumn Squill and the rare fern *Ophioglossum azoricum*. The insects include the spectacular Large Marsh Grasshopper. Fulmar, Shag, Guillemot, Razorbill and Raven breed on the cliffs and Cetti's Warbler in the scrub.

3. Vauville Dunes

Location: On the coast about 12km west of Cherbourg, near Biville and Vauville.
Access: Minor roads run close to the site; thereafter footpaths. Some parts are limited by firing-range requirements.
Timing: Best May–September.

A mixed coastal site, with high dunes (to 80m), dune slacks, open water and marshland. The flora is especially rich, with rarities like Water Germander, Spiked Speedwell, Penny Royal, Wild Asparagus and Mudwort. The amphibians are particularly good for a northern site: Common Tree-frog, Natterjack Toad, Midwife Toad, Marbled Newt and others. Among the breeding birds are Bearded Reedling and Water Rail. The insects, too, are of interest: they include over 30 dragonfly species and a rare coastal tiger beetle.

4. Cerisy Forest

Location: 15km southwest of Bayeux along the D572 to St Lô.
Access: Unrestricted on foot from the D572.
Timing: Late spring to early autumn.

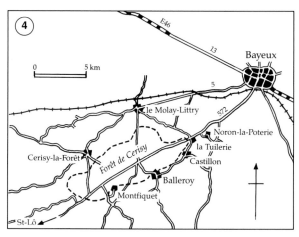

Predominantly beech and mixed woodland, this site (about 3000ha) is noted for its rich insect fauna, and is thus partly a reserve. Among the good selection of butterflies are Lesser Purple Emperor, White-letter Hairstreak and Camberwell Beauty, plus moths like Clifden Nonpareil and Lobster Moth. Other insect groups, like longhorn beetles, are also well represented. The woodland flowers and breeding birds are reasonable.

5. Seine Valley Chalklands

Location: Both sides of the Seine for about 40km upstream from Rouen.
Access: Open access on foot from riverside roads like the N15.
Timing: April–September.

The Seine cuts deeply through the chalk uplands here to produce some fine downland and wooded scarps. The flora is very rich, with abundant orchids – Monkey, Military, Lady and others – plus uncommon plants like Hepatica, Bastard Balm, White Rock-rose and the endemic Rouen Pansy. Butterflies abound – Duke of Burgundy, Wood White, Scarce Swallowtail, Adonis Blue, etc. – along with other insects, notably Field Cricket. Interesting sites can easily be found by driving along the riverside roads. Especially good parts include the **Roches d'Orival**, just upstream from Rouen, and the downland near **Les Andelys**.

Horseshoe Vetch and Meadow Clary in the flower-rich chalklands of the Seine Valley.

6. Somme Estuary

Location: On the coast northwest of Abbeville.
Access: The D940 and D3 encircle the estuary; access to the shore on foot.
Timing: Winter for birds; summer is good for the breeding birds, flowers and ornithological park.

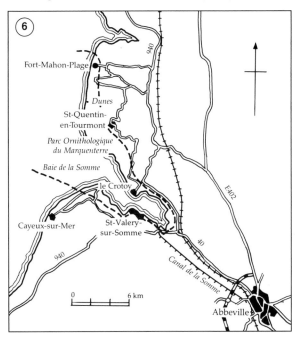

This sizeable estuary and bay, with a large area of mudflats at low tide, is noted especially for its winter birds, including large numbers of waders and wildfowl as well as unusual species like Snow Bunting and Shore Lark; the birds are also good at migration times. Kentish Plover, Fan-tailed Warbler and Shelduck are among those breeding here. The Ornithological Park and Reserve at Marquenterre (open April–November) offers closer views of many species.

Scattered areas of dunes, like those north of **Le Crotoy** and on towards **Fort-Mahon-Plage**, have good floras.

7. Argonne Forest

Location: 70km east of Reims, north of Bar-le-Duc.
Access: The A4 and many other roads pass through the area. Access to the woods is generally open; that to the lakes and marshes is more limited.
Timing: Best late spring and summer.

This extensive forested ridge standing out from the low-lying Champagne country, with an area of marshland and water to the south, is particularly noted for its birds. The fine range of uncommon breeding birds includes Red and Black Kites, Honey Buzzard, all three harriers, Hobby, Golden Oriole, Grey-headed Woodpecker and Wryneck. The flowers and insects are reasonably rich.

8. Vosges du Nord Regional Natural Park

Location: To the north of Strasbourg.
Access: Largely unrestricted via numerous tracks, paths and roads.

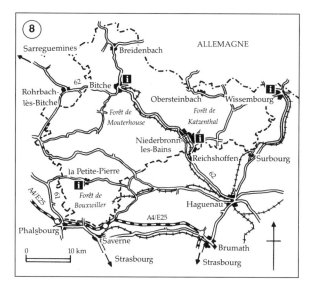

Mountain Pansy in various colour forms in the Vosges du Nord.

Timing: Interesting all year; best May–September.

This 1175 sq km park includes a great diversity of hilly scenery with extensive woods – natural spruce and beech – bogs and fens, upland grassland and lime-stone-grassland areas. Except for the intensively farmed sections, all areas are of interest, and generally good for walking. Over 150 birds are found, including Hazelhen, Capercaillie and Honey Buzzard. There are Red and Roe Deer, Wild Boar and introduced Chamois and Lynx. Butterflies include Cardinals, Purple Emperor, Map, Large Tortoiseshell, Scarce and Common Swallowtails – the insect fauna as a whole is rich and varied. The calcareous areas are best for flowers, especially orchids, though all the other habitats have something of interest – e.g., May-lily and One-flowered Wintergreen in the spruce woods.

9. Gulf of Morbihan

Location: Immediately south of Vannes.
Access: Good roads with many viewpoints encircle the bay; boat trips from Locmariaquer.
Timing: All year; winter and passage times are especially good.

A huge shallow tidal basin, over 20km across, emptying at low tide to reveal vast areas of mud and a scatter of islands. It is good all winter for Brent Goose and large numbers of ducks and waders; Common and Sandwich Terns breed on Er Lannic, and Shelduck are common everywhere. There is an ornithological reserve north of Sarzeau, while the Étang (Lagoon) de Noyalo, on the east side, has some fine viewpoints. The flora, unremarkable except at **Grand Mont Point**, just south of the gulf, includes many shingle, sand and saltmarsh species.

10. Brière Regional Natural Park

Location: Immediately north of St Nazaire.
Access: Numerous roads encircle and cross the area; boats can be hired from Fédrun, and there is access on foot into the marsh.
Timing: All year; best May–July for most things.

Within the park's 40,000ha lies the superb Grand Brière marsh (about 7000ha), composed of open water, reedbeds, marsh, fen and woodland. Its lavish flora includes numerous wetland plants like Water Violet, Flowering Rush, Lax-flowered Orchid and lots of aquatics. Of special interest are the many breeding birds – Marsh and Montagu's Harriers, Spotted Crake, Purple Heron, Black Tern, Bluethroat, etc. – and there are good numbers of wildfowl in winter. Mammals of note include Muskrat, Otter, Water Vole, Wild Boar and Brown Hare. Dragonflies are especially numerous, and other insects of interest include Musk Beetle, associated with the old willows. There is a park office and display at Île de Fédrun.

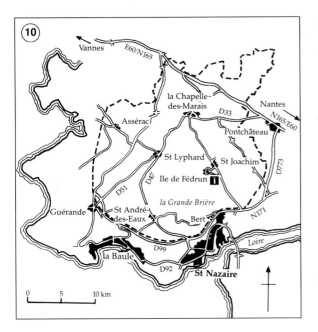

similarly good range of reedbed warblers, and Bluethroat breed on the marshland. The amphibian fauna is rich, and Coypu, Genet, Otter and Pine Marten are among the mammals. The flora is reasonable, with fine displays of Yellow, White and Fringed Water-lilies and the rarer Water Chestnut. Dragonflies abound.

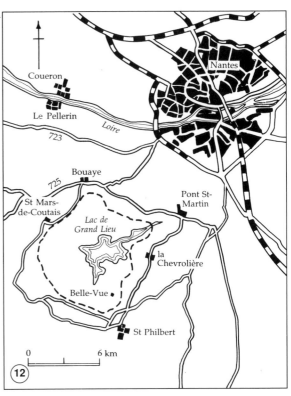

11. Bourgneuf Bay

Location: About 35km southwest of Nantes.
Access: Roads encircle the bay; access is largely open.
Timing: Best in winter or during bird-breeding season.

This very large bay, partially enclosed by the Île de Noirmoutier peninsula, with extensive areas of intertidal land, is particularly worth visiting in winter for its large numbers of wildfowl and waders – Brent Goose, Grey Plover, etc. – along with Merlin and other raptors. Birds breeding here include Marsh Harrier, Black-winged Stilt, Short-toed Lark, Kentish Plover, Avocet and Hoopoe. The remaining grazing marshes to the east have good dragonflies like Norfolk and Hairy Hawker.

The **Pays de Monts Forest**, just south, has breeding Hoopoe and some remnants of dune flowers.

12. Grand-Lieu Lake

Location: About 15km southwest of Nantes, at the mouth of the Loire.
Access: Road access to the site is easy, via the D65, but ways into it are very limited; best from Passay, where boats may be hired.
Timing: All year for birds; April–July for everything.

This large freshwater lake (4000ha–5600ha, depending on conditions) is surrounded by extensive reedbeds and willow/alder carr. The grazing marshes of **La Marzelle** lie to the south and west. The site features a broad range of wetland birds, with numerous breeding Marsh Harriers, a large mixed heronry, Black-winged Stilt and Black-tailed Godwit, the latter two being respectively near the north and south of their ranges. There is a

13. Brenne Area

Location: Midway between Châteauroux and Châtellerault.
Access: Various roads thread through the area; access into the wilder areas is variable, and some parts are private.
Timing: Best April–July.

The site consists of a large area of low-lying land (about 500 sq km) studded with hundreds of lakes and marshes; Mézières-en-Brenne and La Gabrière make good centres for the extended visit the area merits. The whole region has plentiful breeding birds – e.g., Purple Heron, Bittern, Little Bittern, all three harriers, Spotted, Baillon's and Little Crakes, Black and Whiskered Terns and Black-necked Grebe. The dragonflies and damselflies are exceptional, with 57 recorded species including rarities like the Orange-spotted Emerald. Among the amphibians and reptiles are four newts, Spadefoot Toad and Pond Terrapin, while the mammals include a recently rediscovered outpost of European Mink. The flowers are interesting, with a long list of marsh and aquatic species and some fine displays of White Water-lily.

14. Sologne

Location: South of Orléans.
Access: The N20, D922 and many other roads pass through the area; access on foot is open in some parts, but others are shooting preserves.
Timing: Late spring and summer.

This area of heathy wooded land, dotted with numerous lakes, is too colossal to be fully described here; take it as read that all parts are worth visiting—in general, the north is heathier and the south more wooded. The many birds breeding here include Purple and Night Herons, all three harriers, Black-necked Grebe and Baillon's Crake among the wetland species and Red-backed Shrike and Nightjar among those on the heathland. Amphibians in the wet areas include Edible and Agile Frogs and Spadefoot and Midwife Toads; among the reptiles are Green, Sand and Wall Lizards and Smooth and Western Whip Snakes. The insect life is particularly noteworthy, with numerous dragonflies – about 40 species – and the heathy areas are especially fine for grasshoppers, robber flies, sand wasps and other predatory Hymenoptera like the striking *Bembix rostrata*. You can see native mammals at Chambord Park, a National Hunting Reserve 10km east of Blois.

15. Fontainebleau Forest

Location: About 60km south of Paris. (IGN 1:25000 map no 401 covers the area exactly.)
Access: Numerous roads, including the N6 and N7, enter the area; foot access is almost all open.
Timing: Best April–August; very busy at weekends and holidays.

A varied and important area. The forest covers about 170 sq km, within which are substantial areas of oak,

Beech woodland within Fontainebleau Forest.

beech and mixed woodland, open rocky areas, heath, bog and limestone grassland. Numerous trippers come here, sometimes in hordes; a few areas are maintained as no-access reserves.

The forest is rich in birds, with breeding populations of six woodpecker species, Wryneck, Short-toed Treecreeper, Honey Buzzard, Golden Oriole, Redstart, Nightjar and many more. The plants are varied and abundant, with numerous woodland, grassland and 'breckland' species, including many orchids, Pasque-flower, Swallow-wort, Spring Speedwell, Blue Bugle, Cypress Spurge and hundreds more. Among the insects are numerous old-woodland specialities like Longhorn and Stag Beetles, Goat Moth and many butterflies, including Camberwell Beauty. Wild Boar are locally common, and the attractive Green Lizard can be found this far north.

Particularly noteworthy areas are **Rocher Cuvier Chatillon**, the **Gorge et Platières de Apremont**, the **Gorges de Franchard** and the **Vallée du Jauberton**.

16. Bois du Parc

Location: 25km south of Auxerre, opposite Mailly-le-Château, in the Yonne Valley.
Access: Paths run into the wood from the (unnumbered) riverside road.
Timing: Spring–summer.

An attractive and botanically rich area of valley-side woodlands, cliffs and grassland on limestone, with numerous caves. The dry grassland supports many southern plant species. Flowers include Snowdrop Windflower, Crown Vetch, Alpine Squill, the lovely pink Bindweed *Convolvulus cantabrica*, Asarabacca and many others, and among the insects are 'New Forest' Cicada, Praying Mantis and many butterflies. Aesculapian Snake and Asp Viper are found, especially by the Short-toed Eagle, which visits regularly to feed on them

About 10km to the east, at **Voutenay-sur-Cure**, is a superb ancient woodland on limestone, with numerous flowers.

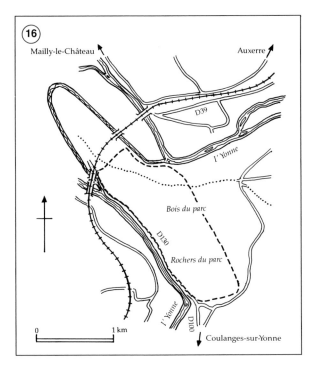

17. Orient Forest Regional Natural Park

Location: About 20km east of Troyes.
Access: The N19 runs through the site, and minor roads lead around it; access from there is generally open, except in reserve areas.
Timing: Good at all times for birds; late spring and summer for flowers, insects and amphibians.

At the park's centre is a huge lake (2300ha) surrounded by forest. This is a noted bird site, especially in winter, when there are hosts of wildfowl and spe-

The enormous lake in the centre of Orient Forest is an important bird site.

cialities like White-tailed Eagle and Common Crane; Marsh Harrier, Great-crested Grebe and many warblers breed. The woodlands, especially to the east, have a good old-woodland flora and numerous butterflies along the rides. Also on the east side is a reserve (with hide), and this section is good for amphibians like Edible Frog and Common Toad.

About 30km northeast the even larger lake of **Der-Chantecoq** is likewise well known for wintering birds, especially cranes.

18. Valbois Ravine

Location: 20km southeast of Besançon.
Access: The D241, running south from Ornans, passes the site; paths into most of the site; part is private.
Timing: Best April–September.

A beautiful hidden Jurassic limestone gorge with cliffs, scrub, woodland and grassland. The very rich flora includes Mountain Kidney Vetch, Hoary Rock-rose, Moon Carrot and Baldmoney. Peregrine Falcon, Hazelhen, Raven and numerous warblers and others breed, and the insect fauna is lavish, with over 700 butterflies and moths recorded, including Apollo, a rare Burnet Moth (*Zygaena fausta*) and Europe's largest Tiger Moth (*Pericallia matronula*).

19. Remoray Lake

Location: About 20km south of Pontarlier.
Access: From the D437 on to paths around the reserve.
Timing: Spring and summer for flowers and birds; winter for some birds.

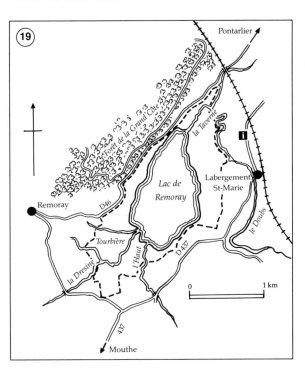

A natural lake surrounded by extensive bog, with woodland nearby. The bog flora is of interest, with Rannoch Rush, Grass-of-Parnassus, Bog Rosemary, Cranberry and others. Among the birds breeding here are Tufted Duck, both kites and Fieldfare. Moderate numbers of duck use the area in winter.

20. Frasne Lake

Location: In the Jura between Pontarlier and Champagnole.
Access: Marked paths off the D49.
Timing: Migration times and May–August.

This extensive area of marsh and open water with bogs is good for birds, especially at passage time, when species like Black Stork, numerous waders, Osprey and many others can turn up. Both kites, Common Sandpiper, Hobby and other species breed.

Lac de Bouverans, a breeding site for Fieldfare, Curlew, Spotted Crake, Great Grey Shrike and others, lies 3.5km southwest.

21. Massacre Forest

Location: 14km south of Morez (40km northwest of Geneva on the N5).
Access: Via the D25, then on minor roads and paths; access on foot is open.
Timing: Best April–September.

A beautiful high-level forest with a mixture of woodland and pastures on the limestones of the Jura. The site is botanically lush – it remains flowery right through the summer – with Martagon Lily, Alpine Sow-thistle, Yellow Gentian, Globeflower and numerous orchids in the shadier areas; the pastures' flora is sub-alpine, with Snowbell, White and Purple Crocuses, Spring Gentian and Yellow Anemone, among many others. The abundant butterflies include High Brown, Dark Green and Silver-washed Fritillaries, with Apollo in the higher areas.

The **Gorge du Flumen**, just southeast of St Claude, is another botanically rich area.

22. Marais Poitevin Regional Natural Park

Location: Westwards from Niort as far as the coast just north of La Rochelle.
Access: Numerous roads and a few tracks and paths pass through; boats can be hired from Coulon and La Garette to explore the canals.
Timing: April–September.

There is an excellent range of breeding birds in this huge area of low-lying grazing marshes, seamed with ditches and canals, often lined with poplar or tamarisk; they include Black-winged Stilt, Ruff, Black and Whiskered Terns, Golden Oriole, Bluethroat and Marsh and Montagu's Harriers. Marsh and water plants abound, with Butterfly Iris, Star-fruit, the Centaury *Centaurium spicatum* and Reversed Clover

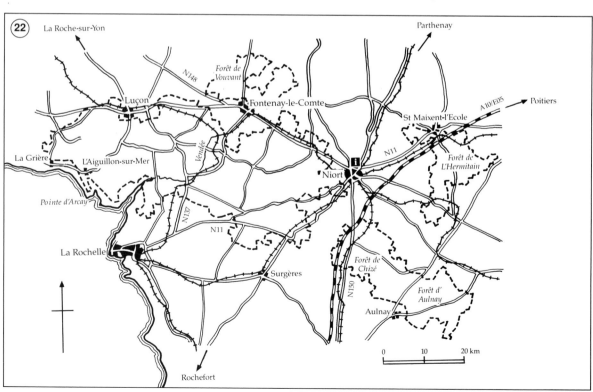

among the many rarities. Dragonflies are particularly widespread and varied, including unusual species like Norfolk Hawker, Orange-spotted Emerald, Brilliant Emerald, Downy Emerald and the orange damselfly *Platycnemis acutipennis*. There are frequent Pond Terrapin and resident Otter.

23. Arcachon Basin and Teich Ornithological Park

Location: On the coast about 35km southwest of Bordeaux.
Access: Roads encircle the bay; minor roads to the shore in places.
Timing: Winter and passage times for the bay; spring–summer for the park.

A major feature of this section of coast, the basin empties at low tide to reveal large areas of mudflats. It is particularly good for wintering waders and wildfowl, with many further interesting birds at passage times. The ornithological park includes numerous tame or semi-wild native birds. The large mixed heronry in the nearby reserve has mainly Grey Heron plus a few Night Heron and Egret, all readily viewed from hides. White Stork nest here sometimes.

24. Banc d'Arguin and Dune du Pilat

Location: On the coast immediately south of site 23.
Access: Open access on foot to the dunes; the bank can be viewed from boats out of Cap Ferret and Pyla-sur-Mer.
Timing: May–August.

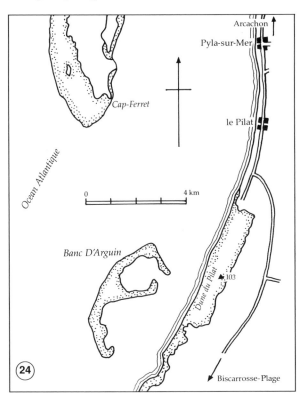

Sunset over the sandbanks of Banc d'Arguin.

This site consists of two separate elements. The Pilat dune is claimed to be the highest in Europe; it probably is not – several dunes in Spain at least equal it – but at 103m it is certainly impressive. The good dune flora has, in addition to widespread species, Spotted Rock-rose and the local Toadflax (*Linaria thymifolia*). Red Squirrel and Crested Tit are common in the pine woods.

The Banc d'Arguin is a reserve comprising offshore sandbanks with breeding colonies of Sandwich Tern, Kentish Plover, Tawny Pipit and Oystercatcher; it is good in winter for waders and wildfowl.

25. Causse Gramat

Location: North of Cahors, between the N20 and N140 south of Rocamadour.

Lizard Orchids and Viper's Bugloss crowd a roadside in the Causse Gramat region.

Access: Generally open from numerous minor roads.
Timing: Best April–July.

The *causses* of the southern Massif Central are broad dissected limestone plateaux. Their limestone soils and rock support a rich flora, especially orchids – e.g., Red Helleborine and Lizard, Military, Monkey and Lady Orchids – often in great abundance. The gorges tend to be best for birds, with Crag Martin, Alpine Swift, Peregrine, Hobby and Bonelli's and Short-toed Eagles among the breeding species. Butterflies, including Provence and Short-tailed Blues, Swallowtails and many others, are abundant and varied, especially in sheltered places; among the other insects are a fine array of grasshoppers and crickets, including both red- and blue-flashing *Oedipoda* species.

26. Lot Valley

Location: The Espalion-Entraygues area, some 20-30km north of Rodez.
Access: The D920 runs the length of the site; open access on foot to unenclosed country.
Timing: Best May–July.

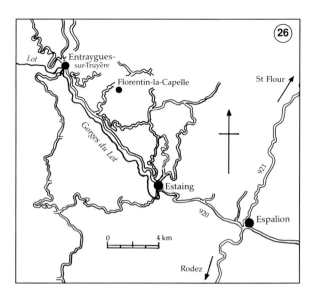

Water Crowfoot on the broad waters of the River Lot.

The rocks into which the River Lot cuts down here are volcanic, but the region all around is beautiful wild limestone country, largely uninhabited, and particularly good for flowers like Military, Lady, Lizard and Woodcock Orchids and Pheasant's Eye Narcissus; even the cornfields have plentiful poppies and cornflowers as weeds. The river itself is rich in aquatics like Water Crowfoot and excellent for large-river dragonflies like *Gomphus* relatives. The whole area is of interest.

27. Puy de Sancy Area

Location: About 25km southwest of Clermont-Ferrand.
Access: The D983 leads into the site; access on foot is open.
Timing: Interesting all year (but snowy in winter); best May–August.

Puy de Sancy (1885m) and Puy Ferrand (1816m), just to its south, offer marvellous displays of mountain flowers, including several daffodil species and hybrids, Alpine Pasque-flower, Narcissus-flowered Anemone, Rock Jasmine and Snowbell. Birds breeding hereabouts include Crag Martin, Rock Thrush, Ring Ouzel and Alpine Accentor, and this is a good area for raptors.

Most of the Auvergne is of great interest to the naturalist. The **Puy-Mary/Plomb du Cantal** area, further south, is excellent.

28. Chaîne des Dômes

Location: Immediately west of Clermont-Ferrand.
Access: The D941 and D941A pass through the area; access is generally open, but limited by snow in winter.
Timing: All year; best April–August.

A beautiful area of old volcanic mountains, reaching 1465m at Puy de Dôme. The varied bird fauna includes Tengmalm's Owl, Short-toed Eagle, Red Kite, Goshawk, Hen Harrier, Black Woodpecker, Crossbill and many others. The rich flora has species similar to those of site 27. The butterflies are abundant and varied, with Apollo and occasionally Clouded Apollo, Fritillaries and two Swallowtail species, amongst others.

The **Montagne de Serre**, just south of Clermont, is another excellent area for flowers and birds – especially for watching autumn migrations.

29. St Flour Area

Location: About 70km south of Clermont-Ferrand.
Access: Generally open.
Timing: Best April–August.

The high wild country south of the attractive town of St Flour is very flowery, with great drifts of Narcissus and of various colour forms of Elder-flowered Orchid, together with Globeflower and the red Cévennes Pasque-flower. The bird life is likewise rich, with Red-backed and Woodchat Shrikes, Short-toed Treecreeper, Crested Tit, Booted Eagle and other large raptors. The mammals include abundant Red Squirrel.

30. Pilat Natural Regional Park

Location: 10km southeast of St Étienne.
Access: Unrestricted, though with two 'zones of silence'.
Timing: Best summer-autumn.

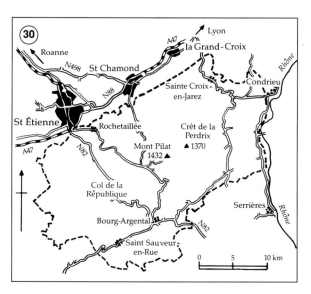

The park's 600 sq km includes much agricultural land along with extensive woodlands and moorlands rising to Mont Pilat (1432m). Numerous woodland birds breed here, including Red Kite, various woodpeckers, owls, Golden Oriole and Hoopoe. From the Rhône Valley end you can see a spectacular southwards bird migration in autumn. The mammals include Red and Roe Deer, Red Squirrel and Wild Boar. The predominant acidity of the rocks inhibits the flora, but species like Arnica and May-lily occur.

31. Dombes Area

Location: Northeast of Lyon, either side of the N83, centring on Villars-les-Dombes.
Access: Numerous roads through the area; access off them is variable.
Timing: Best spring–summer, though not bad at other times.

This extraordinary area of flat land between the Rhône and Saone valleys, holding literally hundreds of lakes and ponds, often with associated wetlands, is best known for its breeding wetland birds – Black-necked Grebe, Purple, Night and Squacco Herons, Little Egret, Little Bittern, Red-crested Pochard, Whiskered and Black Terns, harriers and numerous warblers. The area is also of interest for its fishes, amphibians and dragonflies. Near Villars-les-Dombes is an ornithological park/display; open all year, this allows good views of many of the local species, and White Stork breed.

32. Vercors Regional Natural Park

Location: To the southwest of Grenoble.
Access: Generally open from numerous tracks and roads, notably the D531.
Timing: Interesting all year; best April–September for most things.

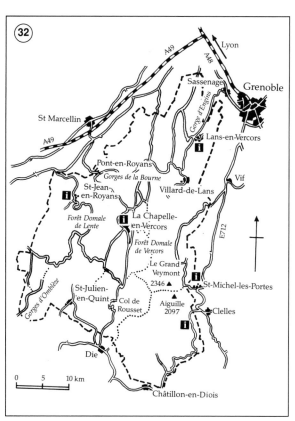

Scarlet carpet of poppies, Vercors Regional Natural Park.

This beautiful mountainous subalpine limestone area, excellent for walking, is little known outside France. It has superb scenery and wildlife, with numerous peaks, cliffs and gorges; the highest point is Grand Veymont (2341m). Part of the park is a nature reserve – at 16,662ha the largest in France. The flowers include numerous orchids and low-altitude limestone species along with higher-altitude gentians, primulas, bellflowers, Rock Jasmines and many more. Among the birds breeding here are Golden, Bonelli's and Short-toed Eagles, Eagle Owl, Pygmy Owl, Nutcracker, Wall Creeper and Ptarmigan. Mammals are scarcer, and the Alpine species have disappeared, although there are plans to reintroduce Lynx. The insects include numerous butterflies, ascalaphids, grasshoppers and crickets, with an interesting blend of lowland, highland, southern and northern species.

33. Écrins National Park

Location: About 40km southeast of Grenoble.
Access: Open, limited only by snow and altitude.
Timing: Best April–September.

Though less well known than the Vanoise (site 36),

this is the largest National Park in France, covering 1080 sq km and containing one-third of France's permanent glaciers. The central mountains – the Dauphine Alps – reach 4102m (Barre des Écrins), and there is some superb high-altitude scenery, including peaks, cliffs and glacial lakes. The park is geologically and climatically varied and consequently has a rich flora and fauna, much like that of the Vanoise. Birds include Golden Eagle, Ptarmigan, Tengmalm's Owl, Snow Finch and both choughs; mammals include Mountain Hare. Flower species are too numerous to mention, though Lady's Slipper Orchid and Orange Lily are worth noting; the Alpine botanic garden near the Lautaret Pass (1829m) is well worth a visit.

The **Col du Galibier** (2545m), just north of the park on the D902, has good flowers and Alpine insects.

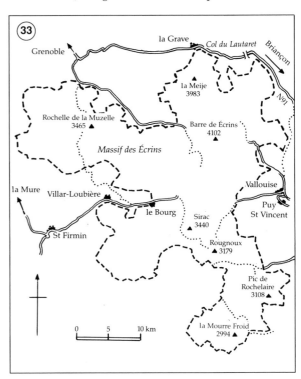

34. Annecy Lake

Location: Southeast of Annecy.
Access: Roads encircle the lake; paths lead into the interesting areas.
Timing: All year.

The whole lake is extremely beautiful, and has good populations of wintering waterfowl. Two shore areas are outstanding. The marsh at the southern end has a rich fen flora, and wetland birds like Reed Warbler and Little Bittern breed. Just north of Talloires, on the east coast, the Roc de Chère, a headland with woodland and grassland, has a lavish flora curiously mixing acid and lime-loving, Mediterranean and montane species. Peregrine breed; interesting reptiles include Green Lizard and Aesculapian Snake.

Alps rising to the north of Écrins National Park.

35. Haute-Savoie Mountains

Location: Around Chamonix.
Access: Generally open, with roads, skilifts and paths into higher areas.
Timing: Late spring and summer.

Some of the highest and finest peaks in Europe, these are largely unprotected from ski-resort and other developments, and the scattered reserves are not particularly the best places to see things. Geologically varied, the area has a correspondingly rich flora of predominantly acid-loving species: gentians, Primula species, Queen-of-the-Alps, Alpine Columbine and numerous orchids vie with many others. Birds include high-altitude specialists like Ptarmigan, Rock Partridge, Black Grouse, Ring Ouzel and Pygmy Owl. Alpine Salamander is found; among the insects, the butterflies and grasshoppers are particularly fine. The whole area is good – parts of it, like the Aiguilles Rouge, the Aiguille du Midi and the slopes of Mont Blanc, particularly so. This is superb walking country.

36. Vanoise National Park

Location: South of Bourg-St-Maurice.
Access: Open from the minor roads entering the park; the Col de L'Iseran (2270m) on the D902 gives good access to high areas.
Timing: Interesting all year; best and easiest in summer.

529 sq km of largely unspoilt mountain scenery, reaching 3852m (La Grande Cassé) and containing a superb mixture of high-altitude habitats. The wildlife is too prolific and diverse to be detailed here; the following are merely notes. The superb flora contains lime-loving *and* acid-loving species in abundance; birds include both choughs, Wall Creeper, Alpine

Arnica in bloom on rock-strewn slopes in Vanoise National Park.

Accentor and Snow Finch; mammals include good populations of Ibex, Chamois and Alpine Marmot; and insects include Cynthia's Fritillary, Mountain Clouded Yellow, Peak White and Scarce Copper. Although busy near roads and around key areas, this is excellent walking country.

37. Queyras Regional Natural Park

Location: South of Briançon towards the Italian border.
Access: The D947 is the best entry road; generally open access on foot.
Timing: May–August.

This glorious yet little known part of the French Alps, half enfolded by Italy, lacks the very high peaks of some other parts of the Alps but has a fine range of scenery and habitats. Botanically it is extremely rich, with at least 2000 Alpine, Mediterranean and

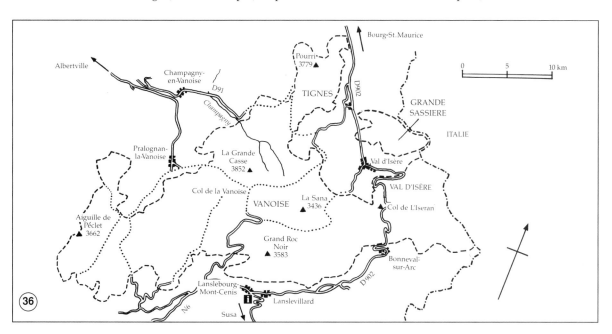

northern species in a marvellous mixture. The birds are similar to those of the Maritime Alps (see site 56), though with fewer large raptors. Among the mammals are Mountain Hare, Marmot and Chamois. This is fine, largely unspoilt walking country.

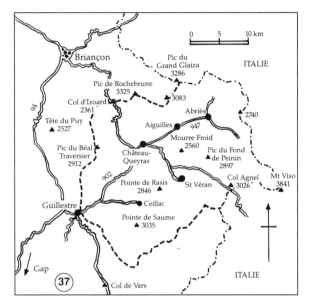

38. L'Étang Noir

Location: About 25km north of Bayonne, just inland near Seignosse.
Access: Via the N10 and D122; by footpaths and raised walkways from the reserve centre.
Timing: April–September.

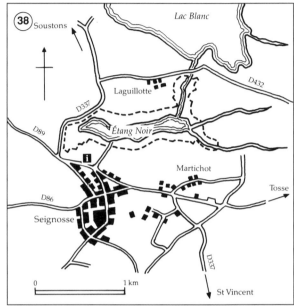

Combe du Queyras, a glorious area of the French Alps.

Fen carr in L'Étang Noir nature reserve.

A shallow lake surrounded by carr, reedbeds and heathland; the reserve centre has helpful displays and information. The reserve's main importance is botanical; among its 430 recorded species are Water Chestnut (with numerous spiny floating fruits), Hampshire Purslane, Lax-flowered Orchid and many aquatics. Great-crested Grebe, Water Rail, Teal and Shoveler breed, Edible Frogs abound, and dragonflies are reasonable. You will not doubt the abundance of mosquitoes.

39. Parc National des Pyrénées Occidentales

Location: The central high mountains of the Pyrenees.
Access: Good roads into the area; thereafter open access on foot.
Timing: Interesting all year; best May–September/ October.

Covering 457 sq km in total, the park encompasses most of the highest and best scenery of the central Pyrenees on the French side. The scenery is wonderfully diverse: peaks soar above huge cirques with waterfalls, snowfields, pastures, meadows and extensive beech, oak and conifer woods. The lavish flora has many specialities – often with the specific name *pyrenaica* – including Pyrenean Columbine, Pyrenean Lily, Pyrenean Gentian and Pyrenean Ramonda, not to mention saxifrages, germanders and representatives of many other groups. The floral displays at middle altitude can be quite spectacular.

The range of birds is equally good, with many uncommon species: Griffon Vulture is now widespread and doing well, Lammergeier is scarcer but established, Wall Creeper is quite frequent, Golden and Short-toed Eagles are widespread, and both kites are regularly seen. The mammals include substantial populations of Chamois (Isard), some Marmot (although less common than in the Alps), Wild Boar, Wildcat, Genet and the curious little Pyrenean Desman, a mole-relative dwelling in mid-altitude streams. Among the

many butterflies are Gavarnie Blue, Clouded Apollo, Mountain Clouded Yellow and Gavarnie and Lefèbre's Ringlets; there are numerous other insects.

Outside the park, most of the range is of interest. To the west, the **Vallée d'Ossau** is a superb place for raptors, especially Griffon Vulture. Further west, the vast beechwoods of the **Forêt d'Irati** are probably the last refuge of the Brown Bear in France, though you would be lucky to catch a glimpse of one.

Magnificent peaks soar above the Cirque du Gavarnie in the Pyrenees.

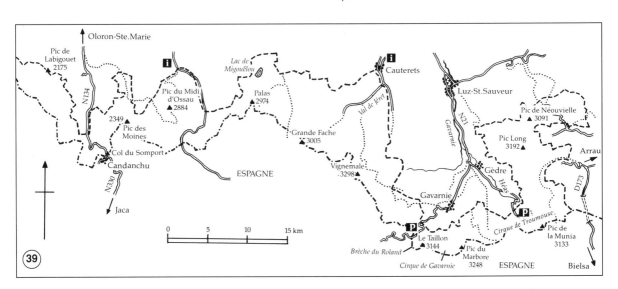

40. Forest of Grésigne

Location: About 30km east of Montauban.
Access: The D115, then the D87 to the forest; access on foot is open.
Timing: May–September.

The gentle slopes of this beautiful managed oak and beech woodland provide great places to see breeding raptors and other woodland birds – e.g., Goshawk, Booted and Short-toed Eagles, Honey Buzzard, Middle Spotted Woodpecker and Hawfinch. The flowers are good, too, with Violet Limodore, Red Helleborine, Military Orchid, Bath Asparagus and Large Self-heal among a rich mixture of woodland species. Butterflies abound in the sunny rides and clearings.

41. Aveyron Gorges

Location: Along the Aveyron, south of Villefranche de Rouergue and north of Albi.
Access: Via numerous minor roads; access on foot is generally open.
Timing: Generally best May–July; some birds good in winter.

An impressive limestone gorge with cliffs, riverside woodlands and surrounding areas of limestone plateau. Crag Martin, Alpine Swift, Peregrine, Eagle Owl, Hobby, Golden Oriole and many others breed. Wall Creepers overwinter around the cliffs and on the castles at Penne and Bruniquel. The plant life is rich and varied, with numerous orchids and other lime-stone plants. Butterflies like Adonis Blue and large Fritillaries abound.

42. Millau Causses

Location: Just east of Millau, on the N9/E11.
Access: Mainly open grazing land.
Timing: Late April to October.

Between Millau and the Cévennes proper lie three major *causse* (limestone-plateau) areas – the Causses Méjean, Noir and Larzac. This wild, scarcely populated area, grazed seasonally by sheep, is very hot in summer and very cold in winter. Among the abundant lime-loving flowers are over 40 orchid species, including rarities like Lady's Slipper and some intriguing Bee Orchid relatives endemic to this area (e.g., Aveyron Bee Orchid); other frequent flowers are Alpine Aster, wintergreens and Dutchman's Pipes in the pine woods. The rich bird-life includes several shrikes, Orphean Warbler, Blue Rock Thrush, Hoopoe, Stone Curlew, Ortolan Bunting and a good range of raptors, large and small. There are plentiful insects – superb butterflies, numerous grasshoppers and crickets, Praying Mantis, Glow-worm and many moths. Among the reptiles are Wall and Common Lizards and several snakes.

43. Gorges du Tarn

Location: Stretching 15–45km northeast of Millau, towards Florac.
Access: Easy road access via the D907; many paths.
Timing: All year; best April–September.

A major feature of the *causses* region, with spectacular cliffs and villages. Peregrine, Short-toed Eagle, Eagle Owl, Alpine Swift, Blue Rock Thrush, Chough and many other birds breed, with Griffon Vulture around Le Rozier. The rich and varied flora has a good assortment of orchids, splashes of pink Rock Soapwort, and many Mediterranean species including Pink and Yellow Flaxes. The numerous butterflies include Scarce and Common Swallowtails and Cleopatra.

The **Jonte Gorges**, joining the Tarn at Le Rozier, are well worth visiting for similar flowers and birds, plus a sizeable colony of Griffon Vulture.

44. Col de Montmirat Area

Location: Between Mende and Florac on the N106.
Access: Open.
Timing: April–September.

At 1046m, the col gives access to some fine mountain country just outside the Cévennes National Park (site 45). Two soil-types meet here, giving a wide range of flowers: Yellow Gentian, several pasque-flowers, Elder-flowered Orchid, Arnica, several narcissi and many others abound in the meadows and pastures. Buzzard and Long-eared Owl breed, and Golden Eagle visit regularly. Butterflies include Clouded Yellow, Apollo, Swallowtail and several Fritillaries.

45. Cévennes National Park

Location: Between Mende and Alès.
Access: Open from numerous roads.
Timing: May–September.

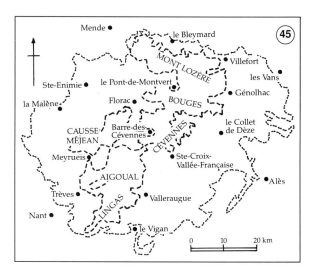

This is a superbly varied mountainous and wooded area, culminating in Mont Aiguoal (1567m) and Mont Lozère (1699m). The soils vary greatly from acidic to limestone, and the consequently wide range of habitats includes coniferous and deciduous (oak and beech) woodland, montane grassland, bogs and cliffs. The overall flora is extremely rich – over 40 orchids, for example – and the birds include Booted, Short-toed and Golden Eagles, visiting Egyptian and Griffon Vultures, harriers, Rock Sparrow, Rock Bunting and many more; this is an excellent place to see raptors. The mammals include Red and Roe Deer, Wild Boar, Red Squirrel and Beech Marten.

46. Olette Reserves

Location: Massifs to the north and south of Olette, on the N116 in the eastern Pyrenees.
Access: Open on foot from minor roads leading to Mantet (south of Olette) or Nohèdes (north of Olette).
Timing: Best late May to late August.

These two extensive reserves encompass all that is best in the Pyrenees except very high peaks. Habitats include beech, oak and spruce woodland and open mountain pastures. The varied geology, from limestone to acidic rocks, gives rise to a correspondingly diverse flora. Among the many breeding birds are Capercaillie, Golden Eagle, Eagle Owl and Dipper. Pyrenean Desman is widespread in suitable habitats here, and the secretive Genet occurs locally.
    Nearby, to the east, the fine, isolated **Mont Canigou** (2784m) towers above the surrounding countryside. You can explore it on foot or by jeep. The whole area makes magnificent walking country.

47. Fanges Forest

Location: 50km west of Perpignan, just north of the D117 near Quillan.
Access: The D117 and D109 encircle the forest; access on foot is open.
Timing: April–September.

In the beautiful, remote Fanges Forest.

A beautiful, remote region of mixed fir, beech and spruce woodland – partly on limestone but with some more acid areas – and occasional cliffs and crags. The generous flora has a good range of orchids and a number of Pyrenean specialities, like Pyrenean Fritillary and Pyrenean Honeysuckle. Birds breeding here include Honey Buzzard, Goshawk and Red Kite. Some of the rides are excellent for butterflies.

48. La Massane Forest

Location: About 10km southwest of Argelès-sur-Mer.
Access: Restricted to paths.
Timing: April–September.

These extensive managed deciduous woodlands on the lower slopes of the easternmost outpost of the Pyrenees are particularly noted for their insects; about 1250 beetle species have been recorded, and the other insects are equally good. Among the butterflies are sizeable populations of several larger Fritillaries and Great Banded Grayling. There are reasonable birds and flowers.

49. Ardèche Gorges

Location: Stretching 25–45km northwest of Orange.
Access: Minor roads run close by; access is open from there.
Timing: All year for birds; best late April–August.

Superb gorges cut mainly into limestone, with vegetation varying greatly according to aspect and slope; parts have been declared a nature reserve. The very rich bird life includes Bonelli's and Short-toed Eagles, Goshawk, Hobby, Honey Buzzard, Scops and Eagle Owls, Alpine Swift and Bee-eater. The plants are an interesting mixture of Mediterranean, mountain and northern species, from *Cistus* species to Dwarf Iris and Peony. The butterflies include the magnificent Two-tailed Pasha, which feeds on Strawberry Tree; among the other insects are Praying Mantis, ascalaphids (large dragonfly-like antlion relatives), numerous grasshoppers and cicadas. Genet has been recorded, but you would be lucky to see one.

50. Camargue

Location: South of Arles, at the mouth of the Rhône.
Access: Numerous roads, notably the D36 and D570, pass through; access from them is variable, and prohibited in the main central reserve.
Timing: Good all year; best April–July.

This is probably France's most famous wildlife site, and its reputation is well deserved. An extensive low-lying area comprising lagoons, marshes, saltmarshes, reedbeds, woodland, dunes and other habitats built up on the Rhône delta, it is best known for its many breeding birds, like the spectacular Greater Flamingo,

Greater Flamingo silhouetted in a Camargue sunset.

Little and Cattle Egrets, Purple, Squacco and Night Herons, Red-crested Pochard, Gull-billed, Little and Whiskered Terns, Bee-eater and Golden Oriole – and the numbers are as impressive as the variety. This is also a good winter site for wildfowl and waders.

There are other features of interest. The reptiles include Stripeless Tree-frog, Viperine and Montpellier Snakes, Pond Terrapin and several lizards; among the amphibians are numerous frogs and toads. The plants are best on the extensive dunes in the south, with Sea Daffodil, Cottonweed, Broomrape, Sand Crocus and many others. Invertebrates include plentiful dragon-flies and impressive numbers of aestivating Mediterranean Snail (*Theba pisana*). The information centres are recommended; they are marked on most maps and signed from the roads.

51. Crau Plain

Location: About 25km southeast of Arles, either side of the N568.
Access: Mainly open.
Timing: April–August.

This strange place, unique in France, is much more like southern Spain. An extensive stony plain, hard to cultivate and grazed by huge wandering flocks of sheep, it is best known for its birds – less for their abundance than for their rarity. They include Pin-tailed Sand Grouse (the only breeding site in France), Little Bustard, Stone Curlew, Calandra Lark, Lesser Grey Shrike and Roller. The flora includes various specialized plants.

52. Les Alpilles

Location: To the northeast of Arles.
Access: Via the D5 and D24; generally open on foot.
Timing: March–July.

An impressive though not especially high range of bare limestone hills rising steeply from the Provence plain. This is a good place to see a mixture of Provence birds, especially those favouring scrub or cliffs, like Egyptian Vulture (now rare), Bonelli's and Short-toed Eagles, Alpine Swift and occasional Eagle Owl; smaller birds include Dartford and Subalpine Warblers, Blue Rock Thrush and Wall Creeper. It is also good for flowers, especially in spring, when numerous orchids appear – e.g., Early Spider, Late Spider, Brown Bee and Giant Orchids and Violet Limodore, with the rarer *Orchis provincialis* here and there. The insects include a good range of Provence species, notably grasshoppers, crickets, Praying Mantis, cicada and butterflies. The citadel village of Les Baux is a good centre and merits a visit in its own right.

53. Luberon Natural Regional Park

Location: North of Aix-en-Provence, between Cavaillon and Manosque.
Access: The D943 and other roads pass through; from them access on foot is open.
Timing: April–August.

A superb area of limestone hills and gorges, notably the impressive Combe de Loumarin. Over 1000 flowers have been recorded, orchids being particularly frequent. A substantial forest of planted cedar is now maturing. There are over 130 species of breeding birds, including many raptors.

54. Port-Cros National Park

Location: An island south of Le Lavandou, near Toulon.
Access: By boat, mainly from Le Lavandou, then on foot.
Timing: Spring–summer.

France's smallest National Park, more like a reserve than a park, was established to prevent further exploitation of the extensive semi-natural Mediterranean forest; it includes also a substantial area of sea around the island. There is a small village at the island's northwest corner, but the rest is largely undisturbed.

The woodlands are mainly Holm and Cork Oaks, Aleppo Pine, Strawberry Tree, Phoenician Juniper and Myrtle – quite different from the mainland's scrubby hillsides. Wildlife has to be sought out: Eleanora's Falcon, Cory's Shearwater and Peregrine breed; Tyrrhenian Painted Frog is found; the reptiles include two gecko species and Ladder and Montpellier Snakes; and Two-tailed Pasha Butterfly and Oleander Hawk-moth are among the insects. The unpolluted sea around the island is excellent for marine life, including extensive beds of Sea-ball (*Posidonia oceanica*). You can take a boat with a clear bottom from the island harbour for good views; diving and snorkelling are

Port-Cros, France's smallest National Park.

allowed. This is a very attractive place for a relaxing visit combining natural history with seashore pursuits.

55. Massif des Maures

Location: Between Toulon and Cannes.
Access: Via the D558 or D14; generally open on foot.
Timing: Spring–summer.

A superb area of wooded rolling hills; unlike most of Provence, the rocks are acid. There are extensive areas of garrigue, maquis and heathland as well as pine and chestnut woods. Here you find several species of Sun-rose *Cistus*, with both species of the curious little parasite *Cytinus* flowering profusely at their bases. Other maquis flowers – Lavender, Large Mediterranean Spurge, *Anemone hortensis*, Thyme, etc. – are common, and there are abundant Violet Limodore under the pines. A feature is a substantial population of Hermann's Tortoise (its only French site); there is an exhibition and rehabilitation centre at nearby Gonfaron. Other reptiles of interest are Ocellated Lizard, Terrapin and Ladder Snake. Over 60 butterfly species have been recorded, and the birds include attractive species like Roller, Bee-eater, Woodchat Shrike, Golden Oriole and Hoopoe.

Garrigue alive with flowers in the Massif des Maures.

56. Mercantour National Park

Location: To the north of Nice, along the main ridge of the Maritime Alps.
Access: Several roads cross the area (the Col de Bonette, at 2802m, is normally closed until June); open access on foot.
Timing: Of interest all year; April–September generally best.

The whole of the Maritime Alps is of tremendous interest to the naturalist – as well as being extremely attractive, and superb for walking. The National Park includes most of the best areas, such as that above Le Boréon, the Col de La Cayolle, La Madonne de la Fenestre Valley, the Gordolasque Valley and the Cime de Bonette area. The flowers are spectacular, with fine displays of many widespread Alpine species as well as some Maritime Alps specialities, like *Crocus versicolor*, *Primula marginata*, *Viola valderia* and an extraordinary saxifrage, Ancient King (though it rarely flowers). Of the well over 2000 species found here, 40 are endemic to the area. The many birds include Nutcracker, both choughs, Golden and Short-toed Eagles, Lammergeier (beginning to re-establish) and Snow Finch. The list of mammals is impressive, and they are often easy to see, especially Marmot, Chamois and Ibex; Mouflon, Red and Roe Deer, Wild Boar and Mountain Hare are also found. The insect fauna is lavish, with a marvellous range of butterflies and about 100 endemics.

It is well worth taking the long walk to the **Vallée des Merveilles** to see the 100,000 or so Bronze Age carvings scattered through the valley.

CORSICA (CORSE)

57. Désert des Agriates

Location: On the north coast between L'Île Rousse and St Florent.

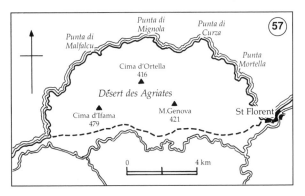

Access: No roads; open to walkers or four-wheel-drive vehicles.
Timing: April–August.

The virtually uninhabited 'desert', a large roadless area jutting into the sea north of the D81, has extensive areas of maquis and bare rock. Sardinian and Subalpine Warblers and other birds abound. On the coast around Loto and Punta Mortella a lovely mosaic of virtually undisturbed coastal habitats is protected as a reserve. Although not as species-rich as some parts of Corsica, this is a fascinating area to visit, if only for its wildness.

58. Lake Biguglia

Location: On the northeast coast, just south of Bastia.
Access: Easy access from the minor road running around the lake.
Timing: All year.

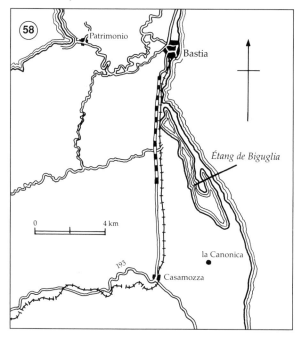

L'Étang de Biguglia, easily Corsica's largest lake, represents about half the island's open water. It is influenced by both the sea, at the north end, and freshwater sources, and there are variable amounts of reedbeds and saltmarsh vegetation. Best known as a bird site, it has breeding populations of Marsh Harrier, Bee-eater, Kingfisher, Cetti's, Fan-tailed, Great Reed and other warblers, Red-crested Pochard and Purple Heron. Passage times are excellent, with a wide variety of species stopping over, and a reasonable number of waterfowl and Coot winter here. The area is good for dragonflies and amphibians.

59. Asco Valley

Location: Between Corte and Calvi.

Access: Open access on foot from the D47/D147.
Timing: Best April–July.

A superb valley with stony plains, high mountains and a wide range of habitats including maquis, Corsican Pine forest and high-altitude grassland. Golden Eagle, Bearded Vulture, Corsican Nuthatch, Crossbill, Alpine Chough, Alpine Accentor and Citril Finch are among the birds, and this is a good place to see Corsican botanical specialities like *Crocus corsicus* and *C. minima*, Corsican Hellebore, the Snowflake *Leucojum longiflorum* and *Cyclamen repandum*. The reptiles include Bedriaga's and Tyrrhenian Rock Lizards.

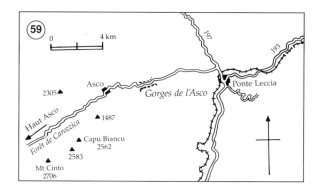

Haut Asco, at the head of the valley, is worth visiting, and the island's highest peak, **Monte Cinto** (2706m), is close by. The GR20 long-distance footpath passes through this excellent high-altitude walking country.

60. Spelunca Gorge and Forest of Aitone

Location: Either side of the D84 from Porto east to the Col de Vergio.
Access: Open access with many paths.
Timing: Best April–July.

The wild and rocky Spelunca Gorge.

A wild and little known area, worthy of extensive exploration. Breeding birds in this mountainous wooded gorge and the area above it include Goshawk, Red Kite, Corsican Nuthatch, an endemic Treecreeper subspecies, Citril Finch and Raven, while Golden Eagle pass through and may breed. The rich flora includes many Corsican specialities.

61. Scandola Nature Reserve

Location: On the coast about 16km northwest of Porto.
Access: By boat from Calvi or Porto (landing restricted) or by very long walk.
Timing: Best March–July.

An isolated coastal site protected as a strictly enforced reserve. Osprey (its only French site), Rock Dove, Blue Rock Thrush, Pallid and Alpine Swifts and Peregrine Falcon breed, while among the flowers are Corsican Storksbill (endemic), the Thrift *Armeria soleirolii* and a rich mixture of coastal and maquis plants. The reptiles and amphibians are exceptional – three gecko species plus Tyrrhenian Wall Lizard, Tyrrhenian Painted Frog and Corsican Brook Salamander – and the offshore marine life is likewise rich.

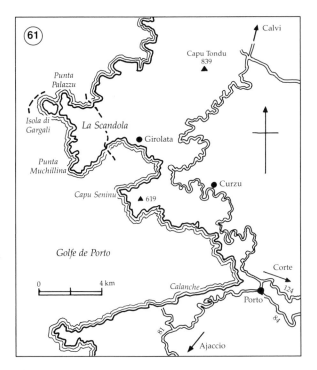

62. Vizzavona Forest and Monte d'Oro

Location: Beside the N193 midway between Corte and Ajaccio.
Access: Open on foot at all times.
Timing: Best March–August.

A beautiful area of managed forest reaching up to Monte d'Oro (2389m). Much of the forest is natural

beech, with Corsican Pine higher up, and the woodland flora includes many more northerly species plus Corsican specialities like *Crocus corsicus*. Among the birds are Corsican Nuthatch, Dipper, Common Redstart, Citril Finch, Goshawk and Red Kite, with Golden Eagle on the higher slopes.

63. Bonifacio Area

Location: Corsica's southernmost tip.
Access: Generally open.
Timing: Best March–July.

Separated from the rest of the island by the Trinity Mountains, this is one of the mildest parts of Corsica. Unlike most of the island, which has granite or other acid rocks, here there is an extensive area of limestone with a quite different flora and fauna. The flowers are especially rich. The numerous orchids include Bee Orchid relatives and masses of Pink Butterfly and Long-spurred Orchids. Among the many other interesting flowers are Corsican Storksbill, a dwarf yellow Crucifer (*Morisia monanthos*), several Sand Crocus species and the endemic little Composite *Evax rotundata*. The birds include breeding Cory's Shearwater, Spanish Sparrow, Rock Sparrow, Spotless Starling and other southern species. The intertidal and marine life on the limestone rocks is also very rich.

The **Îles Lavezzi**, accessible by boat from Bonifacio, are a nature reserve with breeding seabirds and interesting flowers and reptiles. The **Golfe de Rondinara**, an attractive bay midway between Bonifacio and Porto-Vecchio, has low dunes, sheets of Sand Crocus, pools with amphibia and, offshore, extensive beds of Sea-ball.

Sand Crocus on the dunes at Bonifacio.

SWITZERLAND

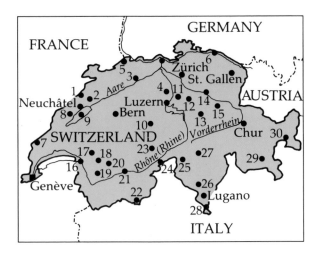

Switzerland, with an area of only 41,293 sq km, is about ⅓th the size of France. It is generally considered the most mountainous country in Europe, and its name is synonymous in the popular imagination with the Alps, clean air, pure water and nature. In fact, its mountainous terrain and relatively high population have put great pressure on any lower-lying and flatter areas, almost all of which are either intensively farmed or heavily built-up.

The country divides roughly into: the Jura Mountains, mainly limestone, which run across the northwest; the central plains, which occupy almost a third of the area; and the Alps, which dominate much of the south and east. In lowlands and mountains alike there are numerous lakes, some of which, such as Neuchâtel, are of great importance for birds. There are also scattered peatland areas, remnants of lakes that have filled in since the last ice age (many of the lowland ones have been drained). In the Alps, and to a large extent in the Jura, almost everywhere is of interest. The sites described here have been selected either as the very best or because they are protected areas, relatively free from developments and agriculture; omission does not imply that an area lacks interest.

Nature conservation is generally well organized, though complicated by the independence of the 26 cantons. There is only one National Park, but many areas are protected by the state in other ways – as nature reserves, landscape-protection areas or national monuments. The voluntary sector is strong, particularly the Swiss League for the Protection of Nature (LSPN), which now manages over 500 reserves.

1. Doubs Valley

Location: Between Morteau and St Ursanne, northwest of Bern, roughly along the French border.
Access: Minor roads cross the valley, and one road follows it west of St Ursanne; unrestricted on foot.
Timing: Best April–July.

A 60 km+ stretch of the beautiful, deeply incised wooded Doubs Valley, with steep deciduous woodland, lakes, gorges and waterfalls. The limestone sustains a rich flora in both open grassland and rocky areas and in the woods. The Snake's Head Fritillary, flowering at the end of April, still occurs in a few alluvial meadows. Honey Buzzard, Red Kite and various smaller woodland birds are found. The river itself is reasonably clean, and has stoneflies, caddis-flies and dragonflies – e.g., Banded Agrion and Club-tailed – and good fish populations.

2. Chasseral

Location: Northeast of Neuchâtel (Neuenburg), between St Imier and La Neuveville.
Access: Minor road over Col des Pontins and Col de Chasseral; access on foot largely unrestricted.
Timing: April–October; busy at weekends and in holiday periods.

This is excellent walking country, with superb views. At 1607m, Chasseral is the highest peak of the Swiss Jura. There are large areas of spruce, fir, beech and mixed woodland plus limestone grassland and rock outcrops. The flora is good, with many orchids – e.g., Lady, Military, Red Helleborine and Late Spider – plus Monkshood, Mountain Kidney Vetch and Martagon Lily. The butterflies include Adonis Blue, High Brown Fritillary and Scarce Swallowtail; Hazel Grouse, Capercaillie, Red and Dark Kites, Buzzard and other birds breed. The mammals include Marmot and Chamois, both reintroduced and now thriving and reasonably tame. There is an LSPN reserve just northwest of Le Chasseral.

The **Weissenstein**, further east, is rather similar, with limestone hills (to nearly 1450m) covered in mixed

Peaks or lowlands, almost everywhere in Switzerland is of interest to the naturalist.

woods and areas of grassland and scrub.

3. Belchen-Passwang Region

Location: About 15km southeast of Basle (Basel), around Waldenberg on road 12.
Access: Road 12 and minor roads over Passwang give good access; largely unrestricted on foot.
Timing: Best April–October.

An area of fine Jura limestone scenery, considered the type area for many geological formations. The unspoilt hills rise to over 1200m, with beech, yew and spruce forests and open grasslands and cliffs. The rich flora includes glacial-relict species like Mountain Avens and Yellow Whitlow Grass. Honey Buzzard, Red Kite, Woodlark, Capercaillie, Serin and many other woodland birds breed. This is beautiful walking country, with some skiing in winter.

Just north, between Arlesheim and Liestal, the **Plateau of Gempen** is another interesting area.

4. Reuss Valley and Lake Baldegg

Location: Respectively 15km and 30km southwest of Zürich.
Access: Road 1 crosses the valley and minor roads enter it. Road 26 passes by Lake Baldegg; access is limited to the shore.
Timing: Some interest all year; best April–July.

Two wetland areas of considerable interest. Along the course of the Reuss are various marshes and lakes, with a good breeding-bird list – Great-crested Grebe, various wetland warblers, Marsh Harriers and many others – plus Beaver, Otter, Lynx and abundant Marsh Frog. The wetland flora includes uncommon species like Siberian Iris.

Lake Baldegg, a reserve some 15km southwest of the valley, is good for breeding and wintering wetland birds.

5. Lake Klingnau

Location: On the River Aare, about 30km northwest of Zürich, close to the German border.
Access: Road 5 passes close by; tracks and paths lead into the reserve.
Timing: All year for birds.

An artificial lake, about 4km long, constructed to supply water for a power station. The silted areas at the southern end have a mixture of wetland habitats. This is a good place for breeding birds – Marsh Harriers, Reed and Sedge Warblers, Red-crested Pochard, etc. – for migrant birds – over 250 species recorded – and for wintering wildfowl in high numbers.

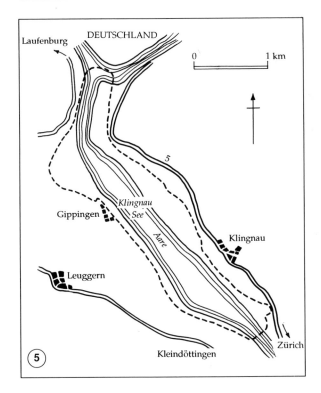

Lac de Joux, seen from Dent du Vaulion.

Yellow Gentian, Wolfsbane and Monkshood, lilies and a few Alpines. Butterflies abound, notably both Swallowtails. Red and Dark Kites, Honey Buzzard, Ring Ouzel, Citril Finch, Nutcracker, Woodlark and Ortolan Bunting breed.

8. Creux-du-Van and Areuse Gorges

Location: North of Lake Neuchâtel, just south of road 10 at Noiraigue.
Access: Unrestricted on foot from road 10.
Timing: Best April–October.

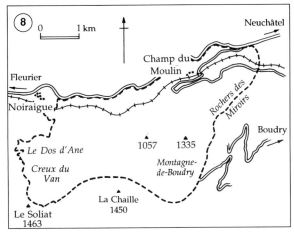

1100ha of impressive limestone scenery with a dramatic cirque at the Creux and fine gorges along the river, this is excellent walking country. The extensive woodland areas show strongly marked contrasts between north- and south-facing slopes: the northern slopes have mainly coniferous woodland, the southern slopes a mixture of broadleaves, grassland and scrub. The ample flora mixes lowland and upland species: crocuses, gentians, snowbells, Alpine Pasque-flower and the rare Woolly Hawkweed. The mammals are of special interest: Chamois, Ibex, Lynx (reintroduced), Marmot and at least 10 bats. Wall Creeper, Goshawk and several woodpecker species breed.

6. Untersee

Location: A subsidiary lake of Lake Constance (Bodensee), lying just west of Konstanz.
Access: Road 13 runs along the shore; access by minor roads and paths.
Timing: All year for birds.

The Swiss southern shore of this arm of Lake Constance has some small reserves and larger no-shooting zones; more is protected along the German north side (see page 104). There are reedbeds, mudflat areas, sandbars and other lake habitats associated with the route of the Rhine (Rhein), and this is a fine place for wetland birds at all stages, particularly wintering wildfowl like Pochard, Red-crested Pochard, Tufted Duck and Goldeneye. The amphibians and dragonflies are also of interest.

7. Joux Valley Area

Location: About 20km northwest of Lausanne, along the French border.
Access: Minor roads enter the area southwards from Vallorbe; access on foot is mainly open.
Timing: Some interest all year; best April–August.

A large region of limestone mountains and intervening valleys, together with Lac de Joux, partly protected as a nature reserve. There are extensive areas of beech, sycamore and mixed woods, with limestone grassland on higher areas, reaching 1483m (Dent de Vaulion), and some striking limestone cliffs. The good flora includes many orchids, Stemless Carline, Large

9. Lake Neuchâtel

Location: 40km west of Bern.
Access: Main roads run along the north side; the more important south side has minor roads and tracks. Mostly open on foot.
Timing: Interesting all year; best April–July.

Most of the southern and eastern sides, known locally as the Swiss Camargue, are of great interest. An interrupted protected area covers a 40km stretch of marshland, reedbeds and waterfront, with breeding birds including Goosander, Purple and Grey Herons, Water Rail, Little Bittern, several marshland warblers, Black-headed Gull and various ducks. In winter the lake becomes very important for wintering wildfowl. The flora is good, especially in Fanel Bay at the eastern end, where there are hay meadows and further wetlands; Marsh Helleborine, Marsh Gentian, various sedges and Marsh Orchids occur here. Over 30 dragonflies and damselflies and over 400 butterflies and moths have been recorded.

The LSPN runs an information centre and laboratory at its **Champ-Pittet Reserve** at Cheseaux Noréaz, just east of Yverdon – open daily April–October (not Mondays) – from where you can arrange a guided walk.

10. Hagleren-Glaubenberg Area

Location: About 25km southwest of Lucerne (Luzern).
Access: A minor road west from Sarnen crosses the Glaubenberg Pass, and minor roads east from Flühli enter the area; unrestricted on foot.
Timing: Best May–September.

This area of bog, moorland and mountain-pine forest, rising to about 2000m, is more reminiscent of northern Scandinavia than of Switzerland. Some of the bogs (e.g., Hagleren) are protected as reserves. The scanty flora has species of interest like sundews, Bog Rosemary, Marsh Bilberry, Rannoch Rush, the rare rush *Juncus stygius* and numerous sedges, including *Carex vaginata*; this is also a good area for lichens and fungi. Due to its position, the site tends to have a high proportion of its rainfall in summer, with dry autumns.

11. Lake Zug (Zugersee)

Location: Just east of Lucerne (Luzern), southwest of Zug.
Access: Main roads encircle the lake; minor roads run to the shore.
Timing: Some interest all year; best April–July.

The most interesting areas for the naturalist of this sizeable (about 15km long) body of water are the northern and western sides, from near Cham to south of Küssnacht, including reedbeds, marshland, open water, woodland and some meadows. Yellow Rattle, Marsh Orchid, Purple Loosestrife, various sedges and Flag Iris flower, and the breeding birds include marshland warblers, Lapwing, Little Bittern and Nightingale; Curlew has recently become extinct here.

Nearby **Lake Lucerne** (Vierwaldstätter See) is worth a visit, especially at its southern end (Urner See). Just east of Lake Zug, between Vorder Geissboden and Walchwil, the **Zugerberg bog area** is an interesting reserve, with good plants and insects.

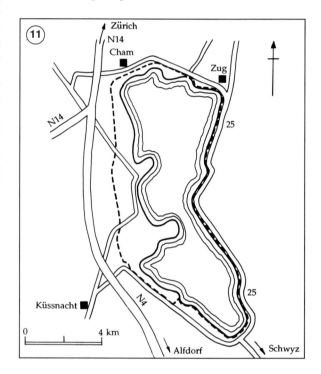

12. Rothenthurm Peatlands

Location: 15km east of Zug, just west of road 8 near Einsiedeln.
Access: From road 8 south of Biberbrugg; unrestricted on foot.
Timing: Best May–August.

An extensive bog and forest area in a relatively low-lying region (rising to about 900m); the bogs are among the most important in Switzerland. The flora includes most bog species – Bog Moss, Deer Grass, Marsh Bilberry, sundews, sedges, Cranberry, cotton-grasses and many others – together with species requiring slightly different conditions, like Bird's-eye Primrose; other acid-loving species like Arnica and May-lily occur in different habitats. The good dragonfly fauna includes White-faced Darter, Four-spotted Chaser and Common Hawker. Among the breeding birds are Tree Pipit, Woodlark, Quail, Whinchat and Nightingale.

13. Silberen and the Hölloch Cave

Location: About 40km southeast of Lucerne (Luzern), 18km southeast of Schwyz.
Access: Minor roads lead into the area from Schwyz and Glarus; unrestricted on foot. Hölloch Cave is open daily throughout the summer.
Timing: Best May–July.

The area around Silberen (2319m) is probably Switzerland's most impressive karst region (over 1000ha). The ample flora includes many specialized limestone-pavement species, like Rue-leaved Saxifrage and Mountain Avens, plus more widespread limestone flowers like orchids and the uncommon shrubby Yellow Coris (actually a St John's Wort). Capercaillie, Hazel Grouse, Ptarmigan, Sparrow-hawk, Crossbill and others breed.

Hölloch Cave is the second longest measured cave in the world (133km); a small part is open to the public. It has an interesting specialized cave fauna and flora and superb stalagmites and stalactites. There are many smaller caves in the area.

14. Kaltbrunner Riet Reserve

Location: At the eastern end of Lake Zürich, about 45km southeast of Zürich.
Access: From minor roads between Uznach and Benken; access on foot only.
Timing: Best April–September; visitor centre open daily end-March to June and at weekends.

This small area of wetland habitats surrounded by highly cultivated land on the plain at the eastern end of the lake is an oasis of interesting species. Over 400 flowers occur, including Siberian Iris, various Marsh Orchids and Slender Centaury. Among the butterflies are three Large Blues, including Alcon Blue and (reintroduced) Dusky Large Blue, and there are also numerous dragonflies. Black-necked Grebe, Water Rail and various ducks breed. There is an information hut and an observation tower.

15. Murg Valley (Murgtal)

Location: South of Lake Walen (Walensee), close to Liechtenstein.
Access: A minor road runs into the area south from Murg; access on foot is unrestricted.
Timing: May–October.

A beautiful stretch of northern Alpine scenery, protected as an area of great landscape value, with beautiful woods, lakes, waterfalls, moorland and pastures. The higher woods are mainly Arolla and Mountain Pines, but lower down is an interesting natural woodland of chestnuts, two lime species and Norway Maple, with interesting shrubs like Bladder-nut – a combination more generally characteristic of areas further south and east. The whole area is superb unspoilt walking country.

16. Rhône Delta, Lake Geneva (Lac Léman)

Location: At the eastern end of Lake Geneva, just west of Villeneuve.
Access: By minor roads off roads 9 and 21; footpaths through the delta.
Timing: Good for birds all year; otherwise best April–July.

The extensive and growing delta where the Rhône enters Lake Geneva has a mixture of freshwater habitats; a large part is managed as a nature reserve. The rich wetland flora has several orchids – e.g., Fen Orchid and Marsh Helleborine – and other uncommon species like Marsh Gentian. Among the 68 breeding birds are grebes, Kingfisher and Sedge, Reed and other wetland warblers, and this is also an important area for wintering wildfowl – tens of thousands at peak times – including Pochard, Tufted Duck and Goldeneye. Over 30 dragonfly and damselfly species have been recorded, and there are good butterflies, Hawkmoths and other moths. Beaver are seen occasionally, and Water Vole and other wetland species are frequent. Many of the area's 17 reptiles and amphibians – including Crested Newt, Pool Frog and Viperine and Smooth Snakes – are rare.

Pastures thick with narcissi above Lake Geneva.

17. Vanil-Noir

Location: About 20km northeast of Montreux, just northeast of Château d'Oex.

Access: Minor roads from Grandvillard or Flendruz; unrestricted on foot.
Timing: May–October.

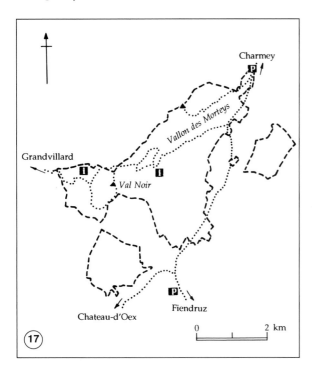

An extensive, beautiful area of calcareous pre-Alpine mountains, reaching 2389m at Vanil-Noir and 2236m at Dent de Ruth. Habitats include mixed coniferous and beech woods, Alpine pastures, limestone cliffs and marshes. The flora is extremely rich, especially around the Vallon des Morteys, northeast of Vanil-Noir peak; species include Variegated Monkshood, Monte Baldo Anemone, Alpine Poppy, Mount Cenis Pansy and other lime-lovers. Among the mammals are Marmot, Chamois, Ibex and Beech Marten, and the good range of mountain and forest birds includes Golden Eagle, Rock Partridge, Ptarmigan, Wall Creeper and Snow Finch. This is fine walking country – indeed, most parts can be reached only on foot.

18. La Pierreuse

Location: About 20km east of Montreux; southeast of Château d'Oex.
Access: By minor road from L'Etivaz (on road 11).
Timing: May–September.

A large area (over 3000ha) of superb mountain country, protected both to conserve wildlife and to maintain a traditional method of agriculture and cheese-making. The flora includes most of the species expected in the mid-range calcareous Alps. Chamois, Ibex, Marmot and wild goats are among the resident mammals, and Golden Eagle, Capercaillie, Red-backed Shrike, Pygmy Owl and Peregrine Falcon among the resident birds. Butterflies abound.

19. Derborence

Location: Northwest of Sion, in the upper Rhône Valley.
Access: A minor road leads into the area north from Conthey; access on foot is open.
Timing: April–October.

A large forest, one of probably only two remaining Swiss virgin forests (the other is at Chaltenbrunnen, east of Interlaken). Its history is interesting: after a major rockfall in the 18th century devastated an area of pasture and woodland and killed several people, the largely unexploited forest was completely abandoned. It consists mainly of Silver Fir and spruce, and there are some huge old trees – 71 of them have a diameter over 1m and a height over 35m. The flora includes many heath and woodland species, notably bilberries, Mountain Avens, wintergreens, saxifrages and Ghost Orchid. Breeding birds include Nutcracker, Black Grouse and Black Woodpecker, with Golden Eagle in the area. Among the mammals are Chamois, Ibex and Marmot.

20. Gelten-Iffigen

Location: In the Bernese Oberland, between Sierre and Zweisimmen.
Access: By minor roads south from Gstaad or Zweisimmen; pay-parking at the ends of the roads; access on foot unrestricted.
Timing: May–October.

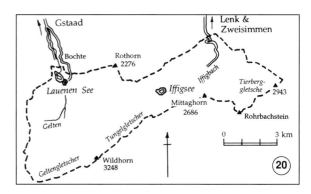

A marvellously unspoilt area (about 4000ha) of mountain country, reaching to over 3000m, with extensive woodlands, pastures, lakes, waterfalls and marshlands; the Geltenschuss Falls are exceptionally beautiful and dramatic. Unmarred by roads and cablecars, this is ideal walking country. Most of the area has calcareous rocks, and the lavish flora features a wide range of lime-loving Alpine species plus many woodland plants like Coral-root, Creeping Lady's Tresses, wintergreens and helleborines, together with fen species like Marsh Orchid, Marsh Felwort and Alpine Monkshood. Nutcracker, Water Rail and Marsh Warbler (at Lauenensee), Golden Eagle and both choughs breed.

Glassy, reed-fringed lake set in the unspoilt mountain country of Gelten-Iffigen.

The marshes around the lake are good for amphibians.

21. Pfynwald/Finges Forest

Location: On the south side of the Rhône Valley, immediately east of Sierre.
Access: Road 9 runs through the site; unrestricted on foot.
Timing: April–October.

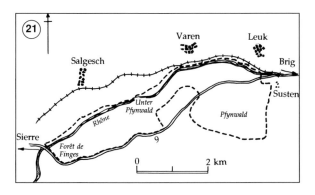

A large area of Scots Pine woodland with lakes, pastures and riverside gravel habitats. This part of Switzerland has a relatively low rainfall and hot sum-

mers, and the flora is a curious mixture of southern, eastern-steppe and northern species: Large Yellow Rest-Harrow, Dwarf Orchid, Red Helleborine, Bladder Senna, *Onosma vaudensis*, Goldilocks, etc. This is a good place for butterflies, dragonflies, grasshoppers and crickets. Scops Owl, Kingfisher, Rock Bunting and Bonelli's Warbler breed, and Beaver is resident.

22. Valais: Matterhorn (Cervin)/Monte Rosa Area

Location: Running south to the Italian border from Zermatt and Saas-Fee.
Access: Minor roads go close by the two towns; railways and cablecars go up beyond them.
Timing: May–September.

An exceptionally spectacular area of the Alps, culminating in the Matterhorn (4478m) and Monte Rosa (4634m). The whole area has a lavish flora – collectively, probably the richest in Switzerland – plus good birds, mammals and insects, and is marvellous for combining walking with natural history. Both calcareous and acid-rock types occur, and hence there is a wide range of flowers, among them Twinflower, Edelweiss, numerous primula species, Rock Jasmine, gentians, orchids – including Lady's Slipper, Red Helleborine and Military – Pasque-flower, anemones and others too numerous to detail. Birds include Ptarmigan, Golden Eagle, both choughs, Nutcracker, Citril Finch, Snow Finch and many more. Marmot are frequent and often tame – e.g., around Saas-Fee – while Chamois and Ibex can also be seen. Butterflies abound – Apollo, Clouded Apollo and many Blues and Browns – and the whole range of Alpine grasshoppers is present.

23. Grindelwald-Bernese Oberland Area

Location: The mountains south of Interlaken, as far as the Rhône Valley.
Access: Roads lead into the fringes of the area (e.g., to Lauterbrunnen and Kandersteg); cablecars, trains and paths thereafter. Higher areas include some difficult terrain.
Timing: May–October; some areas blocked by snow in early summer.

This vast area (about 1000 sq km) is much larger than most of our other sites, but it is impossible (and unnecessary) to subdivide it – the entirety is of supreme interest and of exceptional beauty, with high peaks – like the Jungfrau (4158m), Eiger (3970m) and Aletschhorn (4195m) – extensive forests, pastures and lakes, and superb glaciers. The Aletsch glacier is the longest (24km) and largest in the Alps. The remarkable flora, mainly on limestone, includes a marvellous range of Alpines, woodland species, meadow plants, orchids and wetland species. Breeding birds include Golden Eagle, Alpine and Common Chough, Wall Creeper, Grey-headed Woodpecker, Citril Finch,

The great ice wall of a glacier, Grindelwald.

butterflies, grasshoppers and other insects abound in the flowery meadows. This is a fine place for walking and for seeking semi-precious crystals.

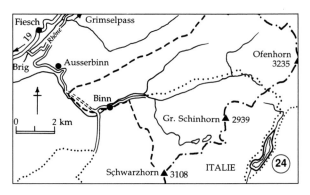

Nutcracker and many others. Alpine and meadow butterfly species abound, and among a reasonable range of dragonflies are Alpine species like *Somatochlora alpestris* and *Sympetrum pedemontanum*. And, of course, this is magnificent walking country: besides the mountain scenery there are some fine waterfalls, especially those in the Lauterbrunnen Valley and the extraordinary Trümmelbach Falls, where glacial meltwater comes down inside the mountain.

In the southeast of the area, not far from Brig, the LSPN has a nature reserve (at Aletschwald) and runs a centre in the impressive Villa Castel, offering regular courses as well as information. East of the area, on roads 6 and 19, **Grimselpass** gives access to some fine high-altitude country, much of it protected within a reserve; the Rhône glacier ends here. North of the area, just west of Interlaken, there is an interesting wetland reserve, the **Neuhaus-Weissenau**, on Thunersee.

24. Binntal, Haut-Valais

Location: 20km northeast of Brig, between road 19 and the Italian border.
Access: By minor road off the 19 to Binn; access unrestricted on foot.
Timing: May–September.

One of the most beautiful and remote Swiss valleys, this follows the course of the fast-flowing Binn up to a ring of mountains reaching over 3000m. There is a rich flora, with numerous Alpine species, and good breeding birds in the coniferous forests and high cliffs. The mammals include Red Deer and Ibex, and

25. Bavona Valley

Location: 35km northwest of Locarno, running up to the Italian border between Bignasco and San Carlo.
Access: By minor road through Bignasco from Locarno; unrestricted on foot.
Timing: May–September.

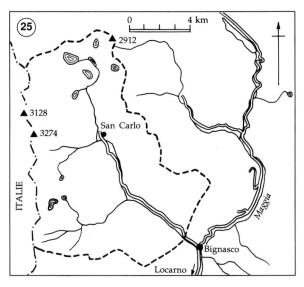

This remote, attractive mountain valley, with as many affinities to Italy as to Switzerland, has a rich flora and fauna. The reptiles are especially good: seven of Switzerland's eight snakes – Grass, Dice, Smooth, Aesculapian and Western Whip Snakes, Adder and Asp Viper – plus four of Switzerland's six lizards – Green, Wall, Sand and Common. Among the insects is Praying Mantis.

26. Tecino (Tessin) Delta, Lake Maggiore

Location: At the northern tip of Lake Maggiore, just east of Locarno.
Access: By footpath from Magadino or Tenero.

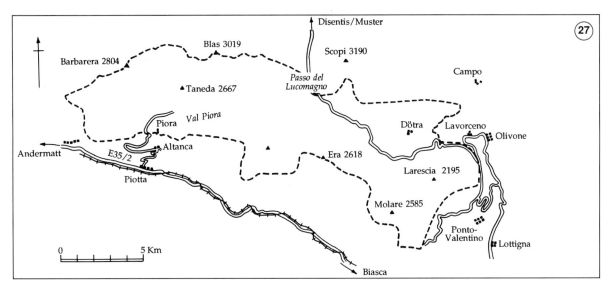

Timing: Good all year; best May–June.

Probably the only wholly intact Swiss delta, mostly protected as the Bolle di Magadino Reserve. Habitats include grassland, reedbed, open water and wet woodland. It is particularly important for birds, with over 240 species recorded and good numbers of breeding, passage and wintering birds. This is also a good place for reptiles, especially snakes – e.g., Dice, Aesculapian and Grass – and Green and Wall Lizards. The amphibians include Agile Frog, toads, Great-crested Newt and Fire Salamander.

27. Piora

Location: 15km southeast of Andermatt, north of road 2/E35.
Access: Minor roads north from the main road to Piora and other villages; access on foot unrestricted.
Timing: May–October.

An extensive area (3700ha) of mountains, including both acid and calcareous rocks with areas of coniferous forest, Alpine pastures, high moorland, cliffs and several lakes, notably Lake Ritom; the highest peaks reach over 2700m. The area's interesting flora includes two rarities: an Eyebright (*Euphrasia christii*) and a variety of Arctic Mugwort. Black Grouse and Nutcracker breed.

28. Monte San Giorgio

Location: Just south of Lugano, northwest of Mendrisío, enclosed by two arms of Lake Lugano on the Italian border.
Access: Various minor roads encircle and enter the site; access on foot is largely unrestricted.
Timing: Best April–July.

A varied low-mountain area (2500ha), rising to just under 1100m. Habitats include extensive broad-leaved woodlands – Sweet Chestnut, beech and oak – scrub, meadows and pasture land on a mixture of acid and calcareous soils. The rich flora includes European Michaelmas Daisy, Green Hellebore, Yellow Ox-eye and Hairy Fleabane. The southern influence is evident among the birds, which include Hoopoe and Orphean Warbler. Edible Dormouse, Polecat, Pine Marten, Fire Salamander and Common Tree-frog are all found.

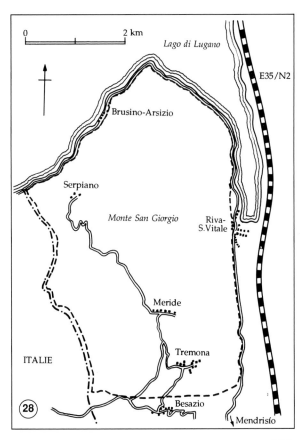

Across the arm of the lake, a few kilometres east on the Italian border, **Mount Generoso** is known for its exceptionally rich flora, including rarities.

29. Massif de la Bernina, Haute-Engadine

Location: The area enclosed by roads 27 and 29 south of St Moritz.
Access: Minor roads and cablecars lead in from the main roads.
Timing: May–October.

The Engadine Mountains occupy the southeast corner of Switzerland, next to Italy and near Austria. In the spectacular Haute-Engadine the peaks reach almost 4000m amid glaciers, lakes, Alpine pastures and forests. The splendid flora – enriched by the diversity of rock types, from calcareous to acid – combines widespread and central-Alpine species with some more eastern specialities. Among the many interesting species are King-of-the-Alps, several snowbells, numerous gentians, primulas, rock jasmines, pansies, saxifrages and the lovely *Clematis alpina*. Ibex are abundant, with particularly good numbers at Piz Albris, just north of road 29, and Marmot are widespread. Most Alpine bird specialities breed here, including Nutcracker, Alpine Chough, Snow Finch and Golden Eagle. The whole area is superb for walking, having ample facilities without being too busy.

Just west of St Moritz, **Les Tourbières de St Moritz et Celerina** is a peatland reserve with interesting features and a nature trail. North of St Moritz, between the Albula Pass and the Flüela Pass on road 28, lies another beautiful mountain area, culminating in **Piz Kesch** (3418m). Its rich flora begins with masses of crocuses in spring and continues right through the summer; most of the usual Alpine mammals and birds can be found here.

30. The Swiss National Park

Location: In the extreme southeast of Switzerland, southeast of Zernez to the Italian border.
Access: Road 28 runs through the park; otherwise access is on foot along marked trails.
Timing: May–October.

Switzerland's single National Park is something special. It is probably the most strictly controlled such park in Europe: there are no villages and minimal human interference. Although the area was exploited for timber and other resources until 1914, when it was declared a park, it has since then been allowed to develop naturally, thus providing an unrivalled opportunity to see communities and species unaffect-ed by mankind. It now covers about 17,000ha of mountainous country (to over 3150m) and includes extensive forests, pastures, lakes, cliffs and snowfields (but no significant permanent glaciers). The rocks are mainly calcareous, with some more acid outcrops.

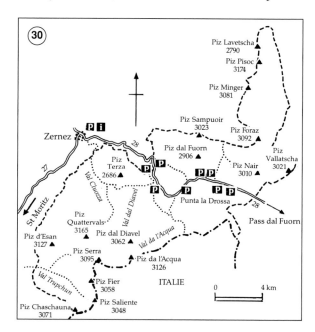

The flora is glorious. The forests are mainly of Mountain Pine, larch and Stone Pine, with a prolific ground flora of common species. The most impressive areas are the Alpine pastures, whose floral displays rival those anywhere else in the Alps. Over 650 species have been recorded; the list includes not just the widespread central-Alpine species but also plants that are otherwise mainly eastern or southern. Over 30 mammals are found: Ibex, Chamois, Marmot, Polecat, Red Deer, Snow Vole, Pine Marten and others, some being particularly tame and visible here. The birds are not exceptional, but most of the expected Alpine species occur in reasonable numbers and about 60 species breed, including Golden Eagle, Capercaillie, Ptarmigan, Tengmalm's, Eagle and Pygmy Owls, Ring Ouzel and Wall Creeper (there is usually a pair resident at the bottom of the Clemgia Gorge, at the park's extreme northeast). Reptiles and amphibians are limited by the altitude, though Alpine Newt is found. The most interesting insects are longhorn beetles, mainly in the woods, and butterflies, with Apollo and Small Apollo, Scarce and Common Swallowtails and numerous Blues, Hairstreaks, Fritillaries and Browns.

The information centre (with displays) at Zernez is excellent; it is open 1 June–24 October.

AUSTRIA

Austria, covering 84,000 sq km, has a population of about 8 million, most of whom live in towns or on the Danube-plain area; landlocked, it borders seven other countries. Along with Switzerland, it is the Alpine country *par excellence*, largely occupied by mountains and high hills that comprise a marvellous mixture of unspoilt habitats. It has other faces, though. The far east of the country is quite different: the extensive lowlands along the Danube have more in common with Hungary's steppe country than with

The Lienz Dolomites support a generous flora and are also a rewarding area for those in search of birds and insects.

western-European habitats, and the Neusiedler See (shared with Hungary) and adjacent Seewinkel area are internationally important wetlands.

Some 45 per cent of Austria's surface area is forested – a figure well in excess of the European average (exceeded only by Finland and Sweden) – and, although much of this is managed commercially, it represents a superb natural resource. The single National Park is at Hohe Tauern (site 6); its boundaries have not been fully ratified as the several states into which it spreads have different policies. Three other National Parks are under consideration. There are also hundreds of nature reserves (the larger ones are marked NSG on better maps) plus a number of landscape reserves (marked LSG), which are often of great interest. About 2800 species are recorded in the flora, and the fauna includes 83 mammals, 220 birds, 21 amphibians and 13 reptiles.

Austria is extremely rewarding to visit. In most of the mountainous regions, almost anywhere holds some interest; only in the far east and northeast are there significant areas without much semi-natural habitat.

1. Bangser Ried Nature Reserve

Location: On the Swiss border just northwest of Feldkirch.
Access: Unrestricted on foot from Bangs, just to the south.
Timing: April–September.

This area of wet meadows between the Ill and the Rhine (Rhein) has a rich flora including many widespread wetland species plus Marsh Gladiolus, Marsh Gentian, Siberian Iris and various orchids. The invertebrate fauna is likewise good, and includes the rare False Ringlet Butterfly.

2. Rhine (Rhein) Delta, Bodensee (Lake Constance)

Location: Just west of Bregenz, along the southern shore of the lake.
Access: Minor roads from Fussach; partly restricted to paths.
Timing: Some interest all year; best April–July.

A nature reserve protects about 1400ha of this area of marshland, reedbeds, open water and sand around the delta of the Rhine (Rhein) in the freshwater lake, the Bodensee. Among the birds breeding here are Little Bittern, Purple Heron, Red-crested Pochard, Black-tailed Godwit, Great-crested Grebe and several ducks, and passage and wintering wildfowl appear in reasonable numbers. This is also a good place for marshland plants like Siberian Iris and Marsh and Fen Orchids.

Reedbeds in Bodensee, in evening light.

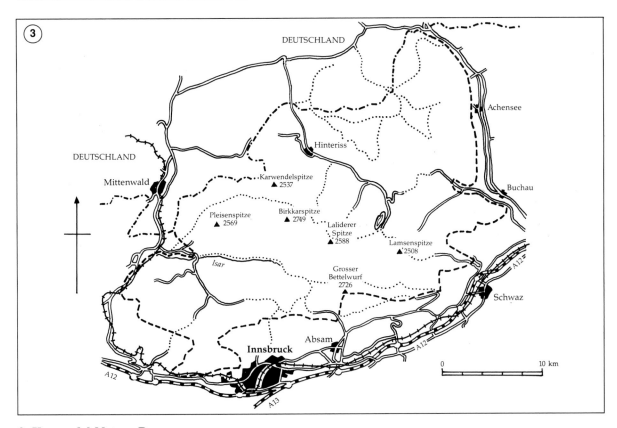

3. Karwendel Nature Reserve

Location: North of Innsbruck and the A12, up to the German border.
Access: By numerous minor roads (including several from Germany); access on foot is unrestricted.
Timing: Best April–October.

720 sq km of calcareous Alpine country, with peaks to 2700m (Birkkarspitze), deep valleys, extensive forests, pastures, meadows and small glacial lakes. The flora contains numerous Alpine species. Golden Eagle, Honey Buzzard, Capercaillie, Ptarmigan, Hazel Grouse, Black and Grey-headed Woodpeckers and many other birds breed, and there are good populations of Red Deer, Chamois, Wild Boar and Marmot.

The **Rissbach Valley**, running up to Ahornboden, has an interesting sycamore wood-pasture area above Hinteriss. It is believed to be very ancient in origin, though overgrazing had reduced the amount of natural regeneration to such an extent that a programme of replanting had to be undertaken recently.

4. Kaisergebirge (Emperor Mountains)

Location: Immediately east of Kufstein.
Access: Minor roads from Kufstein and Greisenau.
Timing: Best May–October.

A superb area of limestone mountains (to 2344m), with over 10,000ha protected as a nature reserve. The flora is extremely rich, especially in Alpines. Mammals of interest include Red Deer, Snow Vole and Mountain Hare, while the breeding birds include Golden Eagle, Capercaillie, several woodpeckers and Rock Partridge. Both Alpine and Fire Salamanders are found, and the ample insect fauna includes Apollo Butterfly.

5. Otztaler Alps

Location: A few tens of kilometres southeast of Landeck, along the Italian border.
Access: By minor roads up the Kaunertal or Pitztal Valleys, or up road 186 to the Timmelsjoch Pass; unrestricted on foot.
Timing: May–September for higher areas.

Many peaks in this beautiful area are over 3000m; it is unprotected and used for skiing, but many natural forest, pasture and high-Alpine habitats survive. A glorious flora thrives on the predominantly acid rock, including numerous gentians, primula species, Creeping Azalea, several snowbells, Alpine Clematis and various orchids; at lower levels the woods contain all the conifer-wood specialities like Twinflower, four wintergreens and May-lily in abundance. Birds of interest include Goshawk, Honey Buzzard, Citril Finch, Nutcracker, Snow Finch and many other Alpine and forest species. Butterflies are prolific.

Franz Josef's glacier in Hohe Tauern National Park.

Yellow Loosestrife fills a forest clearing in the Lienz Dolomites.

6. Hohe Tauern National Park

Location: In the high Alps between Lienz and Bruck.
Access: The Hochalpenstrasse and several other roads run through the park; unrestricted on foot.
Timing: May to late September for higher areas; very busy in July–August.

One of the finest high-altitude regions in Europe, with huge areas of Alpine habitats including impressive glaciers, the highest mountain in Austria – the Gross Glockner (3797m) – extensive Alpine pastures, screes, cliffs. moraines and lakes, and Austria's highest waterfall, the 400m Krimml Falls; lower down there are extensive forests. Although the rock is mainly acidic, the flora is rich and varied, with superb displays of Alpines, including numerous gentians, primulas (e.g., *P. minima*), saxifrages and rock jasmines, plus many further species at lower altitudes: Martagon Lily, Alpine Onion, orchids and others. Griffon Vulture (coming north from Yugoslavia), reintroduced

Bearded Vulture, Golden Eagle, Eagle Owl, various grouse relatives and Alpine Chough breed. Marmot are abundant and tame, and there are reintroduced Ibex. About 900 invertebrate species are recorded, including many butterflies and an Arctic Bumblebee. There are ample information centres and nature trails. Altogether, this is an exceptionally rewarding area.

7. Lienz Dolomites

Location: To the south of Lienz, along the Italian border.
Access: Minor roads off the 111, or from the Plockenpass; largely unrestricted on foot.
Timing: Best May–August for flowers, birds and insects.

A beautiful area of high calcareous peaks, similar to the Italian Dolomites (see pages 209–10) but slightly less dramatic and distinctly less busy. The generous flora includes many orchids – Lady's Slipper, Globe-flow-

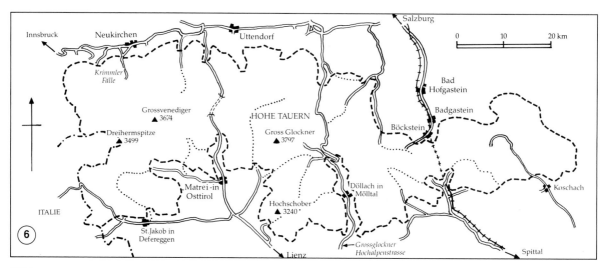

ered Orchid, Red Helleborine, etc. – Carnic and Martagon Lilies, Pasque-flower, Globeflower and many more, plus good conifer-wood flowers lower down. Golden Eagle, Eagle Owl and many woodland species breed, and butterflies abound. The nature reserve at **Mussen**, just northwest of Kotschach, is hard to locate and not especially better than the surroundings.

8. River Inn around Braunau

Location: 50km north of Salzburg, along the Inn where it forms the German border.
Access: Minor roads cross the valley; generally unrestricted access on foot.
Timing: All year.

Along the Inn to the east of Braunau, mainly the stretch as far as Obernberg (though the area of interest extends to Scharding), is a series of lakes produced by damming, with a mixture of associated wetland habitats, including carr, sandbars, reedbeds and grassland. These have developed a rich bird fauna: Night Heron, Little Bittern, Marsh Harrier, Black-tailed Godwit, Kingfisher and others breed, and numerous species, especially wildfowl and waders, occur on passage, often in abundance.

9. Purgschachen Moor

Location: Just east of Liezen, in the floodplain of the Enns.
Access: On foot from Selzthal; partly restricted.
Timing: April–September.

One of the best remaining peat bogs in Austria, now managed as a reserve. Its rich peat flora includes Bog Rosemary, Cranberry, Rannoch Rush and sundews;

Siberian Iris and Narrow-leaved Daffodil (*Narcissus stellaris*) occur in the surrounding grasslands. There is an interesting relict insect fauna, plus butterflies like Green Hairstreak.

10. Steinernes Meer Area

Location: South of Salzburg, enclosing the German Berchtesgaden National Park.
Access: The area itself is largely roadless, but minor roads run into it from east, south and west; unrestricted access on foot.
Timing: April–October.

A beautiful high-mountain area just south of the German border, reaching 2941m at Hochkonig. Habitats include lakes, highlands, coniferous woodlands and a few glacial features; the whole area is a nature reserve. The flora and fauna, broadly similar to those of Berchtesgaden (see page 105), include Honey Buzzard, Black Woodpecker, numerous Alpine flowers and much else.

Just west of Salzburg lies the **Untersberg**, an area of limestone mountains rising to almost 2000m with good flora and fauna; and about 7km southwest of Salzburg, towards Grossgmain, there is a Nature Park.

11. Niedere Tauern Mountains

Location: Between Tamsweg and Schladming.
Access: From the Tauern Pass or Solkpass, or by minor roads from Tamsweg or Schladming; unrestricted on foot.
Timing: April–October.

This high-mountain area has for many years been a proposed National Park. The rock is mainly acidic, and the

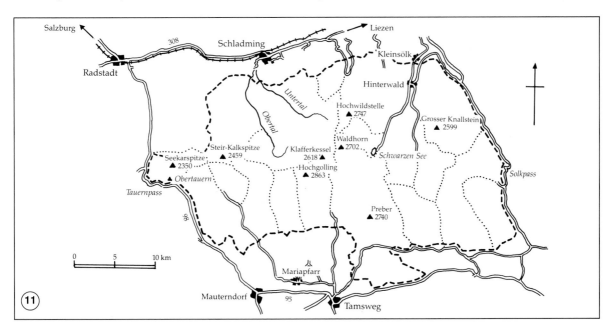

area has pastures, pine woodlands and high-altitude habitats (to 2863m), with a number of small glacial lakes and many waterfalls. Plants include Arnica, Bearded Bellflower, Small White Orchid, Hairy Alpenrose, Martagon Lily and various saxifrages and gentians, plus a good range of old-woodland species. Golden Eagle, Eagle Owl (very rare), Hazelhen, Capercaillie, Crag Martin, Rock Thrush and many other birds breed; Bluethroat breeds on one area of moorland.

Bearded Bellflower in the Niedere Tauern Mountains.

12. Nockberge National Park

Location: Just northeast of Seeboden and the Millstätter See.
Access: From road 99 or minor roads off it; unrestricted on foot.
Timing: April–October.

A fine forested mountain area, rising to 2400m; the parts of interest include land to the east and north of the park, like the Turracherhohe and Hagleiten areas. The rocks are mainly acidic, and there are bogs and moors as well as coniferous forests and pastures. Breeding birds include Tengmalm's Owl, Golden Eagle, Goshawk, various woodpeckers and an isolated outpost of Dotterel. The flora is dominated by acid-lovers – Trailing Azalea and Alpenrose, with several primulas, rock jasmines, Dwarf Soapwort, Alpine Clematis, gentians and others.

The Trogener Klamm, an impressive limestone gorge in the Karawanken Mountains.

13. Karawanken Mountains

Location: South of Klagenfurt, along the border with Slovenia.

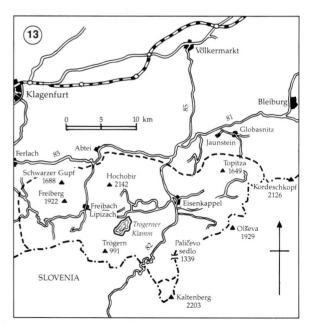

Access: From the 91/E61, 82 and various minor roads.
Timing: April–October.

The Karawankens are magnificent limestone peaks along the southern Austrian border, from south of Villach eastwards, with extensive mixed woodlands and high pastures surmounted by towering cliffs. The Trogener Klamm, southwest of Eisenkappel, is an impressive limestone gorge with a particularly rich and curiously mixed flora. Indeed, the area's flora is in general lavish, with many special plants like the striking *Lilium carniolicum*, Willow Gentian, Dwarf Alpenrose, bellflowers – e.g., *Campanula zoysii* and *C. thyrsoides* – Sowbread, several cinquefoils, Christmas Rose and numerous other attractive flowers. The range of breeding birds is also good, including many raptors and a broad spectrum of forest species.

14. Waldviertal Area

Location: North and east of Gmund, running up to the Czech border.
Access: Numerous roads through the area; ample access on foot.
Timing: All year; best April–July.

A diffuse region of interest with numerous scattered nature reserves and nature parks. The **Blockheide Eibenstein area** offers a curious landscape of granite rocks among a heathy and wooded landscape, with meadows and lakes; the **Thaya Valley** is of great interest, with good woods and cliffs; and the particularly rich **Geras area**, containing reserves and a Nature Park, is a good place to see mammals like Red Deer. The region as a whole is ornithologically important, with large numbers of Eagle Owl and a rich mixture of forest, wetland and cliff species. Butterflies of interest include Hungarian Glider and Scarce Copper.

15. Wildalpen-Rothwald Area

Location: In the mountains west of Mariazell, south of road 71.
Access: Road 24 passes through the area, and minor roads to Rothwald give good access; largely unrestricted on foot.
Timing: April–October.

This part of the east-central Austrian Alps lies within a series of large nature reserves; because it is hard to get to it is mostly unspoilt. The region is dominated by forest, partly managed but with an area of virgin forest, the **Urwald**, on the east side of the Durrenstein (1878m). Mixing beech, spruce, sycamore and fir on calcareous rock, the Urwald is believed never to have been managed, and features superb old trees and much fallen timber. The area is excellent for breeding forest birds – among them Capercaillie, Honey Buzzard, Hazel Grouse, Eagle and Tengmalm's Owls and Golden Eagle. Mammals include Red and Roe

Deer, Pine Marten and Badger. The invertebrate fauna has lots of deadwood species like longhorn beetle.

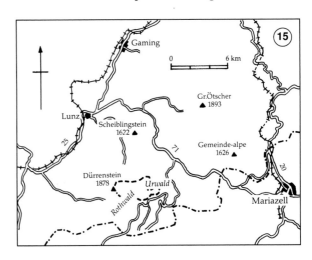

16. Hagensdorf Area

Location: About 15km southeast of Güssing, close to the Hungarian border.
Access: Minor roads through Hagensdorf and Luising.
Timing: Interesting all summer; best April–May.

A little-visited and relatively unspoilt corner of Austria, partly surrounded by Hungary. At the extreme eastern point of the 'finger' is the Schachblumen Reserve, declared for the superb displays of thousands of Snakeshead Fritillaries – *Schachblumen* is German for Fritillaries. Other flowers are Marsh Orchid, Water Dropwort and Yellow Star of Bethlehem. The surrounding woods are good for flowers and birds, including breeding Honey Buzzard, Grey-headed Woodpecker and Red-backed Shrike.

17. Lainzer Tiergarten and the Wienerwald

Location: Immediately west of Vienna (Wien)
Access: Numerous roads; the Tiergarten is open Easter–November, daily Wednesday–Sunday.
Timing: Best April–August.

An area of mixed forest. The various habitats of the Tiergarten, an old hunting forest protected from development, include woodland, pasture and water. Among the mammals, some fairly tame, are Wild Boar and Red, Roe and Fallow Deer. Black Stork, Honey Buzzard, Golden Oriole and a good selection of woodpeckers breed. The whole wooded area west of the Tiergarten – the Wienerwald – though more fragmented, is likewise of interest.

Further into the city, the **Schonebrune Palace Gardens** have some woodland and grassy areas with surprisingly good birds, notably Grey-headed Woodpecker. Southeast of Vienna, along the northern side of the Danube, is the **Lobau Reserve**, an interesting wetland area with good birds, flowers and amphibians; access is by minor roads and then marked tracks.

18. Marchauen Reserve

Location: 40km northeast of Vienna (Wien), north of Marchegg, along the Czech border.
Access: From Marchegg; limited to certain paths.
Timing: April–October.

An area of riverine marshland and woodland along the River March; the southern part of the protected area is a WWF reserve. This is an important place for breeding birds – Black and White Storks, Honey Buzzard, Saker Falcon, River Warbler, numerous owls and many others. Wild Boar and abundant Brown Hare are found. The splendid flora includes steppe species at the western end of their ranges; e.g., *Clematis integrifolia*, Moth Mullein, the Fleabane *Inula brittanica*, Summer Snowflake and the Maple *Acer tataricum*. Among the many invertebrates are Lesser Purple Emperor and Southern Festoon Butterflies.

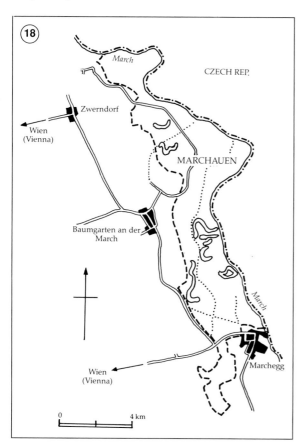

19. Neusiedler See

Location: About 50km southeast of Vienna (Wien), by the Hungarian border.
Access: Roads encircle the lake, and some reach the shore.

Timing: All year; best April–July.

Europe's fourth largest lake is some 30km long but shallow almost everywhere. The water, naturally moderately saline, is fringed by vast reedbeds, up to 6km wide in places – which can make viewing difficult but helps protect the lake from overuse. The whole area, together with Seewinkel (site 20), is essentially eastern-European steppe country, sharing more with Hungary than with the rest of Austria. It is especially important for breeding birds, like Bittern, Little Bittern, Great White Egret, Spoonbill, Purple Heron, numerous Marsh Harriers, vast numbers of Water Rail and many smaller species. White Stork still nest on nearby buildings. The surrounding area is likewise good, with Syrian Woodpecker (for example) being common, and the lake is notable for passage and wintering birds. The meadows by its north and west shores are attractive remnants of steppe grassland, with *Iris pumila*, the Pasque-flowers *Pulsatilla grandis* and *P. nigricans*, Feather-grass, Whorled Sage, Yellow Pheasant's Eye and many others. Among the reptiles is the rare Orsini's Viper; the butterflies include many Fritillaries.

Avocets on the Neusiedler See.

20. Seewinkel Area

Location: To the east of the Neusiedler See as far as the Hungarian border.
Access: By roads south from Neusiedl-am-See; some foot access.
Timing: Good for birds all year; best April–July.

This is contiguous with the Neusiedler See area (site 19) and similar to it in many ways, though also including open steppe country to the east. The western part is dominated by numerous and diverse soda lakes. It is extremely rich in birds, with most of the Neusiedler species plus, in the east, open-country birds like Stone Curlew, a few Great Bustard, Montagu's Harrier, Short-eared Owl and Bee-eater. There is a Bustard reserve east of Tadten. Other interesting species in this region include Steppe Polecat and Russian Tarantula, both at the far west of their range.

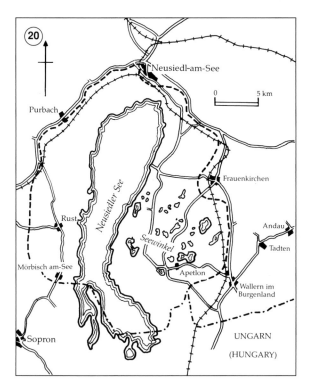

21. Hohe Wand

Location: About 15km west of Weiner Neustadt.
Access: A well signed minor toll road leads into the area.
Timing: Best April–September; exceptionally busy at peak periods.

An area of well forested (mainly pine) limestone hills with a dramatic cliff along the east. Wall Creeper, Capercaillie, Eagle Owl, Black Woodpecker, Nutcracker, Wryneck, Bonnelli's Warbler and many commoner species breed, and the mammals include Red Deer, Chamois and Red Squirrel. The flora is good, too, with numerous limestone species like pinks, flaxes and orchids. The small botanic garden at the top is as yet not very rewarding.

22. Hundsheimer Berg

Location: South and east of Hainburg and Bad Deutsch Altenberg.
Access: Roads encircle the site; open access on foot.
Timing: Best April-September.

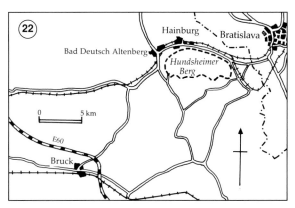

Almost on the Czech border, this area of low dry limestone hills (to 480m) has an extraordinarily rich flora, especially in the reserve area immediately north of Hundsheim. There are numerous *Allium* species, the attractive lupin-like *Cytisus austriacus*, Feather-grass, Fumana, Woolly Inula, the beautiful semi-parasite *Melampyrum nemorosum*, Globe Thistle, Cornelian Cherry, Jurinea and hundreds more calcicoles and steppe species. Birds of interest include Short-toed Eagle, Golden Oriole, Hoopoe, Serin, Barred Warbler, Woodlark and Red-backed Shrike. The invertebrate fauna, too, is extremely rich, including many representatives of the butterflies, moths, hoverflies and other groups.

HUNGARY

In marked contrast to Austria, its western neighbour, Hungary is a mainly lowland country, lacking major mountain ranges (the highest point is just over 1000m). Landlocked, it is highly cultivated and populous (almost 11 million people in an area of 93,000 sq km), yet it is surprisingly rewarding for the naturalist. The many wetland areas in the lowlands – including natural steppe lakes and marshes and artificial ponds and lakes – are ecologically very important, especially for birds. Extensive stretches of steppe grassland – a semi-natural habitat which has formed in the wake of forest clearance – support a good range of specialized birds and flowers. Such hills as do occur are often

Steppe grassland, rich with flowers, in Hortobágyi National Park.

wooded, sometimes with natural woodland. Many of these areas – e.g., the Aggtelek National Park (site 16) – are limestone, and provide a marvellous range of habitats, rich in flowers, insects, reptiles and birds.

Considerable areas of Hungary have some form of protection. The country's four National Parks (marked 'Nemzeti Park' on local maps) are treated separately below (sites 10, 15, 16 and 17). There are also numerous landscape-protection areas, nature-conservation areas and reserves (respectively 'TVK', 'TVT' and 'Reservatum' on maps); most are of interest, though often encroached upon by agricultural activities. One of the most attractive features outside the protected areas is the abundance of nesting White Stork, often on artificial platforms and frequently with several pairs in a single village. Indeed, bird numbers are generally high – Hungary is particularly rewarding for the birdwatcher.

1. Fertö tói (Neusiedler See)

Location: The southernmost part of the Neusiedler See, southeast of Sopron.
Access: By road 85 or, from Austria, by crossing southeast of Eisenstadt; minor roads enter the area.
Timing: All year.

The southernmost portion of this great lake, including some of its western shore, lies within Hungary, where it is protected within a landscape reserve; there are plans to link this with its Austrian counterpart (see page 160) to form a cross-border National Park. The habitats and species are essentially as for the Austrian site, with good breeding wetland birds and many passage migrants; extensive reedbeds make access to the lake difficult. Small numbers of Great Bustard are found in the more open parts of the surrounding plain.

2. Köszeg Hills

Location: On the Austrian border just northwest of Szombathely.
Access: Road 87 runs up to the area and minor roads enter it; access on foot is unrestricted.
Timing: Best April–October.

A wooded area (about 4000ha) of acidic hills, more Austrian than Hungarian in character. The forests are beech, spruce and Silver Fir, with some Horse Chestnut. This is botanically interesting terrain, with species like May-lily, Lily-of-the-Valley, Three-leaved Bitter-cress and a rare cress-relative, *Thlaspi goesingense*. The insects are particularly good, especially forest species like longhorn beetles, Stag Beetle, Praying Mantis and numerous butterflies. Red Deer and Chamois are among the mammals, while among the 100 or so breeding birds are Honey Buzzard and several woodpeckers. There are Fire Salamander in the woods, and crayfish are common in the clear streams.

Just north are the **Sopron Hills**, which have a similar character. About 50km to the south of Köszeg, in

the **Örség Hills Protected Area** (almost 40,000ha), the interest is more diffuse; despite much settlement and farming, the area has rich flora and fauna, fine forests and some historic villages.

3. Hanság

Location: South of Mosonmagyaróvár, west of Györ.
Access: By minor roads (one too new to appear on most maps) from Lébény and Jánossomorja; access on foot to some areas is restricted, with notices on the site.
Timing: Best April–September.

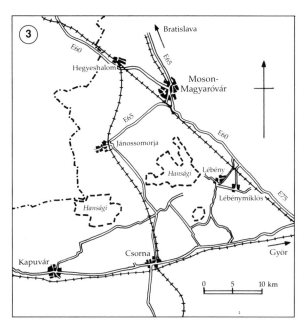

Although the local signs call this damp, low-lying peaty area (about 6000ha), with grazing meadows, ditches, canals and wet woodlands, a National Park, it is in fact a landscape-protection area. Among the numerous aquatic and wetland plants are all the duckweeds, many pondweeds, *Oenanthe aquatica*, Marsh Orchid, Meadow-rue and Yellow Iris, and this is also a good site for dragonflies, with Hairy Hawker and Norfolk Hawker among over 20 recorded species. The breeding birds are especially interesting: Purple Heron, Bittern, Black Stork, Montagu's and Marsh Harriers, Kingfisher, Whinchat and many more. Great Bustard are rare. The range of amphibians is good, though as yet incompletely recorded.

4. Gerecse Hills

Location: Immediately north of Tatabánya, running north to the Danube (Dunaj).
Access: By minor roads north from Tata and Tatabánya.
Timing: Gerecse best April–August; Tata Öreg-tóbest in winter.

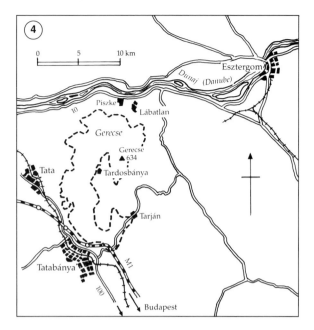

The 8600ha Gerecse Landscape-Protection Area comprises an attractive range of limestone hills with some steep cliffs, beech, lime, hornbeam and oak woods, and open grassy areas, plus considerable agriculture. The more natural areas enjoy an ample flora, with orchids, various garlic species, the Umbellifer *Smyrnium perfoliatum*, Field Eryngo, pinks, Mountain Germander and many others. Short-toed and Lesser Spotted Eagles, Honey Buzzard, Saker Falcon and Bee-eater breed, while butterflies like Marbled Whites are common in grassy areas.

The Old Lake in Tata (Tatai Öreg-tó), immediately south of the town, is important for wintering and migrating waterfowl, with huge numbers of Bean Goose in particular from about February onwards.

5. Vertes Hills

Location: About 40km west of Budapest, southwest of Tatabánya.
Access: Minor roads run through the site; access on foot is open except for two strict reserves.
Timing: Best April–October.

13,600ha of limestone hills, designated a landscape-protection area, with extensive beech and oak forests and some pine; the site is quiet and unspoilt, despite scattered villages. The breeding birds are extremely interesting; they include two or three pairs of Imperial Eagles, Honey Buzzard, Short-toed Eagle, seven woodpeckers, Woodlark, Collared and Red-breasted Flycatchers and Barred Warbler. Brown Hare are frequent and tame; Wild Boar and Fritillaries are common. The flora is rich, especially in open grassy or rocky clearings, with Black Broom, Tassel Hyacinth, Field Eryngo and several orchids.

6. Kis-Balaton Reserve

Location: At the extreme western end of Lake Balaton, immediately south of Keszthely.
Access: Road 76 passes through the site. Access is restricted, but you can see a great deal between the reserve and Lake Balaton. Permits can be acquired from Nyu-Kövizig, 9700 Szombathely, Vörösmarty U2.
Timing: All year.

A superb wetland area, several thousand hectares of open water, reedbeds, woodland and grassland on peat, once part of Lake Balaton (site 7). The breeding birds are especially important: there are good numbers of Black-necked Grebe, Squacco and Night Herons, Spoonbill, Little and Great White Egrets, Red-crested Pochard, three crakes, Whiskered and Black Terns and much else. Spring and autumn bring hosts of passage migrants, especially wildfowl; small numbers of White-tailed Eagle winter here. The far less significant flora includes the attractive local Purple Loosestrife *Lythrum virgatum*.

7. Tihanyi Peninsula and Lake Balaton

Location: The peninsula is on Lake Balaton's north side, southwest of Balatonfüred.
Access: Main roads (e.g., 7, 71) encircle the lake; tracks spread out from the minor road that runs out on to the peninsula.
Timing: Best April–September.

Lake Balaton is Hungary's premier resort area, and its shores are almost everywhere heavily developed and used. Though in summer the lake is almost devoid of birds because of the disturbance, in winter it is good for wildfowl. The Tihany Peninsula, a partly developed landscape-protection area, holds some attractive unspoilt habitats, especially in the centre and on the west. Birds breeding here include Golden Oriole, Scops Owl, Marsh Harrier, Purple Heron and Nightjar. The flowers match the area's Mediterranean appearance, with species like Pink Flax, the attractive pink everlasting plant *Xeranthemum annuum* and Globe Thistle. Butterflies, especially Marbled White, Hairstreak and Fritillary, abound on the peninsula, while among the dragonflies around the small lakes are abundant Emperor Dragonfly. This area is also noted for its reptiles and amphibians.

8. Lake Velence (Velencei-to)

Location: About 45km southwest of Budapest, 10km east of Székesfehérvár.
Access: Main roads (e.g., 70, M7) encircle the site, and minor ones go to the shore; access to the reserve areas is restricted.
Timing: Good all year; best April–July.

An exceptional wetland-bird site, its best part covering

about 1000ha. The lake itself is large and shallow, well used at the eastern end but very reedy and protected by a nature reserve at the west. There is always something to be seen. Highlights on the long list of breeding birds are Great White Egret, Spoonbill, Marsh Harrier, Savi's and Moustached Warblers, Bluethroat, Black Tern and Ruff. In winter good numbers of Bean Goose and other wildfowl use the lake. The flowers include abundant spikes of the purple *Lythrum virgatum*, and among the amphibians are Agile and Marsh Frogs.

Just to the southwest, the **Dinnyes Marshes Reserve** has good breeding waders and grebes and a feeding ground for storks and herons. Access is restricted, but you can see plenty from the roads and tracks.

9. Pilis and Visegrád Hills

Location: Within a bend of the Danube (Dunaj) about 20km north of Budapest.
Access: Minor roads lead off road 11, which runs along the site's northern side; vehicles are restricted on forest tracks, but access on foot is open.
Timing: April–October.

An attractive area of limestone (Pilis) and volcanic (Visegrád) hills; 23,000ha is protected. This is a very popular place for walking, and there are well marked trails. The hills are amply wooded with oak, ash and beech, and the rich flora – especially on the limestone

– includes Hungarian Thistle, the impressive Umbellifer *Ferula sadleriana* and Birds' Nest Orchid. Among the breeding birds are Saker, Lesser Spotted and Short-toed Eagles, Honey Buzzard, Collared Flycatcher and several woodpeckers. The reptiles are represented by Fire Salamander, Snake-eyed Skink and Smooth Snake. The plentiful insects include many grasshoppers, notably the rare *Stenobothrus curasius*. There are some interesting caves and, near Szentendre, an open-air museum (marked 'Skanzen' on maps).

A little further south, just west of Budapest, the **Buda Landscape-Protection Area** is another range of well wooded limestone hills with rich flora and fauna, including some endemic flowers and unusual spiders like *Eresus cannabarinus*.

10. Kiskunság National Park

Location: About 30km (northernmost point) south of Budapest.
Access: Numerous roads (e.g., 52, 54) pass through the park; access on foot is mainly unrestricted.
Timing: All year; best April–July.

Kiskunság National Park protects extensive areas of the Hungarian plain.

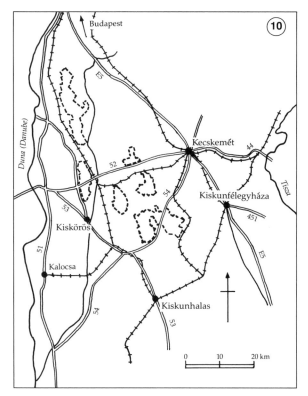

The park protects 30,628ha spread over a wide area of the Hungarian plain in six separate blocks – wherever, in fact, there was habitat left to protect. These cover a wide range of lowland habitats – salt lakes, steppe grassland, inland dunes, wetlands (including reedbeds) and woodlands. Visit the information centre at Liszt Ferenc in Kecskemét to get an overview of this complex area, and possibly to hire a guide. Among breeding birds here are Spoonbill, Great White Egret, Avocet, Black-tailed Godwit, various herons, Whiskered and Black Terns, Stone Curlew, Great Bustard and Roller. The flowers are impressive, especially on the steppe grassland, with masses of Spiny Rest-Harrow, the mallow-relative *Lavatera thuringiaca*, sages, the florists' *Gypsophila paniculata*, flaxes and many more, including rarities like the Globe-thistle *Echinops ruthenicus*. The reptiles are interesting – Sand Lizard and the rare Orsini's Viper, among others. There are colonies of the delightful little Souslik.

11. Ocsa Landscape-Protection Area

Location: About 25km southeast of Budapest, north of Dabas.
Access: Road E5 runs along the southwest of the site, and minor roads lead into it.
Timing: Best April–July.

A remnant of Danube Valley fen, this low-lying area (about 3500ha) is made up of alder woods, grazing marsh, reedbed, fen and open water. Marsh and Montagu's Harriers, Roller, Black and White Storks,

River and Moustached Warblers breed, and there are extensive beds of the sedge *Carex elata* and Cotton-grass, with a range of unusual wetland flowers like Swamp Nettle and Least Bur-reed, and the tall blue Bellflower *Adenophora liliifolia* in the damp grasslands. There is also a curious land crab, *Armadillidum zenckeri*. Tours and guides can be arranged at the visitor centre in Ocsa – don't forget the mosquito repellent!

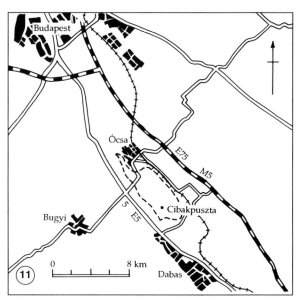

12. Gemenc Area

Location: Along the Danube floodplain, just west of Baja.
Access: Road 55 crosses the area (west of Baja) and minor roads enter it; access on foot is partly restricted.
Timing: Best April–July.

One of the wider areas – up to 10km across – of Danube floodplain, with extensive areas of willow/poplar forest and, on drier ground, oak, ash and elm. Breeding birds of interest include White-tailed Eagle (which also winters here), Black Stork, Night Heron, Black Kite and Kingfisher; mammals include Red Deer (notably large here), Otter and Beech Marten; flowers include Hungarian Narrow-leaved Ash, Hungarian Hawthorn and Marsh Gentian. The area is noted also for its fungi, and is a good place for river fish.

13. Tisza Valley North of Szeged

Location: North of Szeged, running north to Szentes.
Access: Roads 5/E75 and 45 pass either side of the area, and minor roads lead in; access on foot is largely unrestricted, though some areas are private or strict reserves.
Timing: All year.

The Péteri-tói Nature Reserve in the Tisza Valley, an excellent site for wetland birds.

An exceptional complex of wetland habitats protected within the Pusztaszer Landscape Reserve and several nature reserves. The whole area is of great importance for birds (it is a Ramsar site). Bittern, Little Bittern, Night Heron, Little and Great White Egrets, Avocet, Black-tailed Godwit, Moustached Warbler and many others breed, spring and autumn migration times bring new birds to the region, and large numbers of wildfowl and waders winter here.

Just to the northwest, alongside the main E75/5 road about 15km south of Kiskunfélegyháza, the **Péteri-tói Nature Reserve** comprises a lake with surrounding reedbeds and woodland. It has excellent breeding birds – e.g., Spoonbill and Great White Egret – good amphibians and dragonflies and an interesting flora, including abundant Cannabis.

14. Kardoskut Fehér-tó

Location: About 10km south of Orosháza, which is about 60km northeast of Szeged.
Access: By minor roads; access into the reserve is limited, but there is good viewing from the edge and the observation tower.
Timing: All year.

This shallow soda lake, partly fringed with reeds and varying seasonally in size and salinity, is very important for birds; about 500ha is protected as a strict reserve and Ramsar site. Bittern, Avocet, Black-tailed Godwit, Marsh Harrier and other birds breed, and hosts of wildfowl come here at migration times, including thousands of White-fronted Goose. Common Crane arrive in autumn, reaching peak numbers of about 10,000 at the end of October – a remarkable sight – with some staying on for the winter. A few Great Bustard and Stone Curlew are found on the surrounding plains.

15. Būkk National Park

Location: Immediately west of Miskolc.
Access: Minor roads from all directions; access on foot unrestricted.
Timing: Interesting all year; best April–July.

A quiet, attractive, unspoilt hilly forested region (just under 40,000ha), reaching almost 1000m with, as its core, a limestone plateau (about 800m) surrounded by mixed acid- and lime-rich rocks. There are also areas of grassland, cliffs, caves, a natural lake (at Hámor) and forests, mainly of beech but with Hungarian Oak, spruce, pine and sycamore. The rich flora has numerous orchids – e.g., Greater Butterfly and Lady's Slipper – together with Pasque-flower, Yellow Pheasant's Eye and a local subspecies of Dame's Violet. Butterflies abound, and the park is particularly good for longhorn beetles, notably the extraordinary *Cerambyx cerdo*, one of Europe's largest beetles, and the beautifully marked *Rosalia alpina*. Among the breeding birds are Imperial, Lesser Spotted and Booted Eagles, Red-breasted Flycatcher, Hazelhen and (reintroduced) Eagle Owl. Resident mammals include Wildcat, Beech and Pine Martens and (introduced) Mouflon. Snake-eyed Skink occurs along the woodland edges. A few of the hundreds of caves in the hills are open to the public. This is a marvellous area for walking.

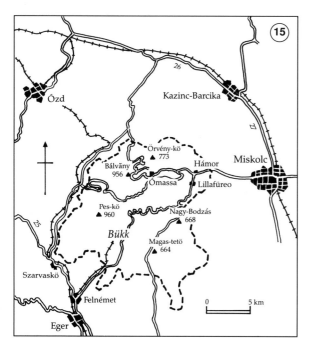

About 40km northeast of Bükk, just northwest of Sárospatak, lie the **Zemplén Hills**. Well wooded and unspoilt, rising to over 750m, this little-known site is of interest for its birds and mammals.

16. Aggtelek-Karst National Park

Location: On the Czech border, about 35km almost due north of Miskolc.
Access: Road 27 and many minor roads into the park; access on foot is unrestricted.
Timing: Best April–October.

About 20,000ha of limestone hills, considered one of the best examples of karst scenery in Europe. The hundreds of caves (many open to the public) have an interesting fauna. Over 400 species have been recorded in Aggtelek Cave, including a blind ground beetle (*Duvalius hungaricus*) and a white blind cave crab. The hills bear a rich flora, with many lime-loving species like orchids, Black Broom, Bladder-nut, the attractive perennial Cornflower *Centaurea triumfetti*, Yellow Pheasant's Eye and the endemic *Onosma tornense*, a

close relative of Borage. Birds breeding here include at least four eagle species, Honey Buzzard, Black Woodpecker and Rock Bunting. The butterflies are good, too, with abundances of species like Camberwell Beauty, various Fritillaries and Large Tortoiseshell.

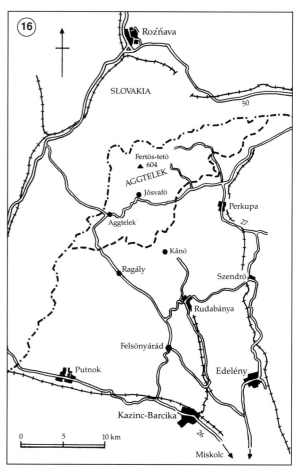

17. Hortobágyi National Park

Location: About 30km west of Debrecen.
Access: Road 33 runs through the centre of the park; minor roads enter it. Access on foot is unrestricted except to strict reserves, for which permits may be obtainable from the park's administrative offices (Debrecen, Böszörményi út 138; tel 52/19–206).
Timing: All year.

The 52,000ha park and the many adjacent sites of interest form one of the best areas anywhere in Europe for the naturalist, especially the birdwatcher; it really is exceptional for birds at all times. There is a marvellous mixture of steppe habitats, including salt lakes, steppe grassland, marshes, reedbeds, woodland and fresh water. In the wetland areas, the presence of large numbers of birds is something constantly felt, and virtually all Hungary's wetland species breed here, often in large numbers – Great White Egret, Spoonbill, Bittern, terns, grebes, herons, Pratincole, Aquatic Warbler, etc. – while Glossy Ibis, a regular visitor, sometimes nests. On the drier steppe areas, including the saline pusztas, are good numbers of Great Bustard plus many other open-country birds, like Red-footed Falcon, Short-toed Lark, Lesser Grey Shrike and Tawny Pipit. The area is of great interest also during migration times and through the winter, with hosts of wildfowl and waders at peak periods. White-tailed Eagle and a very few Slender-billed Curlew are rare visitors.

The flowers, though less spectacular, are likewise notable, especially the wetland, saltmarsh and steppe grassland species: Feather-grass, Spiny Rest-Harrow, flaxes, Lady's Bedstraw, Tuberous Bitter-vetch, Whorled Sage, the lovely pink *Lavatera thuringiaca*, the tall spikes of the Star-of-Bethlehem *Ornithogalum pyramidale* and many others. Resident mammals include the Marmot-like Suslik and herds of traditional Longhorn cattle.

The Marmot-like Suslik, a resident of Hortobágyi.

18. Dévaványa Bustard Reserve

Location: Between roads 4 and 47, about 25km south of Karcag, just north of Dévaványa.
Access: A minor road passes the entrance; access into the reserve is limited, but the centre and observation area are open on Tuesdays, Thursdays and Saturdays 9am–4pm.
Timing: April–November.

A 3000ha area of steppe set aside specifically for the protection of Great Bustard, with agriculture being strictly controlled in terms of both crops and their harvest times. The research and rescue station reintroduces Bustard to the wild, and has an exhibition explaining the research, with videos (various languages) about the area's wildlife. This region has Hungary's highest concentration of Great Bustard, so you certainly have a good chance of seeing one. Treesparrow nest in the observation hide and Roller, Red-footed Falcon and Shrike are common nearby, with Crane visiting on passage.

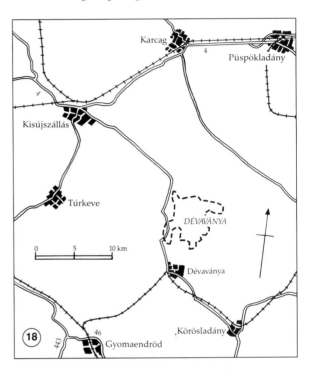

19. Szatmár-Bereg Plain

Location: About 80km northeast of Debrecen, on the Romanian and CIS borders.
Access: Roads 41, 491 and many minor roads pass through the site; unrestricted access on foot.
Timing: Best April–September.

A remote, little-visited area of plain and low volcanic hills, including woodlands and patches of peat bog, all protected within a 22,000ha landscape reserve. The extensive Hornbeam/Hungarian Oak woodlands have a rich flora, notably Carpathian Crocus (*C. heuffelianus*), Snake's Head Fritillary and Cranberry. Among the mammals are Wildcat and Pine and Beech Martens; birds breeding here include Hazelhen and Honey Buzzard. The Aesculapian Snake is frequent, butterflies are abundant and varied, and Carpathian Blue Slug has been reported.

ROMANIA

White-winged Black Tern in the Satchinez Reserve.

Romania is probably the least known and least visited of all European countries. It covers 237,500 sq km in the extreme east of Europe, bordering Bulgaria, the former Yugoslavia, Hungary, Ukraine and Moldova, with about 200km of Black Sea coast. Extensive mountain regions, notably the Carpathians, cover about one-third of the country; large areas of these are wooded and very unspoilt. But the most important feature of the country for the naturalist is the Danube and its delta, one of the major wetland sites of Europe.

Conservation and recording are not well advanced, though the present government is developing a conservation scheme and some of the damaging policies of the previous regime are being reversed. Despite difficulties of travel and language, Romania is very rewarding to visit.

1. Satchinez Reserve

Location: Far midwestern Romania, close to the borders with Hungary and the former Yugoslavia, about 25km northwest of Timişoara.
Access: Via minor road northwest from the E671 to Sachinez; the good area, including the reserve, lies south of the village.
Timing: April–August.

A marshy area around the headwaters of the River Stan Begej, partly protected as a reserve (marked 'NSG' on some maps), with areas of open water, reedbed and marsh. Breeding birds include Bittern, Little Bittern,

Purple, Night and Squacco Herons, Little Egret, Marsh Harrier, Black and White-winged Black Terns, Penduline Tit and various warblers. The clear water of the ponds supports a good aquatic flora, including White and Yellow Water-lilies and numerous sedges.

2. Retezat National Park

Location: About 100km east of Timişoara, or due south of Hunedoara, in the Carpathians.
Access: From Hunedoara through Haţeg and into the park; access on foot unrestricted. There is a skilift west of Vulcan.
Timing: May–September.

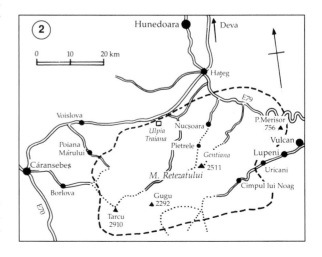

20,000ha of fine mountain country, rising to 2511m at Peleaga, with more than 20 peaks over 2300m. There are extensive areas of coniferous – spruce, Mountain Pine and Arolla Pine – and beech forest, plus high pastures, cliffs and lakes. Chamois, Lynx, Brown Bear (in good numbers) and Wild Boar all occur. Lesser Spotted and Golden Eagles, Capercaillie, Pygmy, Ural and Eagle Owls, numerous woodpeckers, Wryneck and Red-breasted Flycatchers and commoner species breed. The reptiles include Common Adder and Sand Viper. The flora is very rich in endemics and commoner plants – while this area is noted for its many hawkweed species, of more interest to the average visitor are the fine displays of mountain flowers and the rarities like the Knapweed *Centaurea retezatensis*, *Rubus retezaticus*, the Crucifer *Draba dorneri* and Edelweiss. The whole area is superb walking country, with a number of huts for long-distance walkers.

The **Little Retezat**, just south of the park, are limestone mountains with a rich flora.

3. Eastern Carpathians

Location: In the northeast, roughly between Baia Mare and Bacau.
Access: Via numerous roads (e.g., E576, E85, 15); generally open on foot.
Timing: May–September.

This vast and varied area of mountains holds a huge variety of interest; good centres from which to explore it include Viseu de Sus, Vatra Dornei, Bicaz, Ditrau and the spa of Tusnad, towards Brasov. This is a substantial area of serious mountain country, with many peaks over 2000m. There are acid and limestone areas, bogs, coniferous and deciduous forests, cirques, cliffs, gorges and small lakes. Birds breeding in the area include Golden Eagle, Honey Buzzard, Capercaillie, Black Grouse, Eagle Owl, Nutcracker, Sombre Tit and Chough. Chamois, probably reintroduced, are found, and the very rich flora – perhaps 1000 species in all – includes many interesting plants like *Rhododendron kotschyi*, *Iris hungarica*, a Speedwell *Veronica incana*, *Scorzonera purpurea* and *Echium rubrum*. There are numerous sphagnum species and many other bog plants in, for example, the large area of upland bog southwest of Vatra Dornei, and there are also good lichens, uncommon spiders like *Xysticus pini* and *Theridium undatum*, and lots of butterflies and dragonflies.

4. Danube Delta

Location: On the Russian border, where the Danube (Dunarea) meets the Black Sea.

Access: Minor roads lead to good centres (e.g., Tulcea, Sulina, Murighiol, Maliuc); access is on foot or by boat from these.
Timing: Good all year; best April–July.

The delta of the Danube, which has flowed through Europe for 2800km, is one of the largest and finest wetlands in Europe. It is vast, some 440,000ha in all, with about 56,000ha protected in reserves. The last communist government's plans to reclaim the delta in a series of polders have luckily been largely dropped, and it is now intended that the area be managed as the exceptional wildlife sanctuary it is. The breeding birds are too numerous even to highlight: the 160+ species include just about all the wetland and associated birds you could expect. Special features include large colonies of Dalmatian Pelican, Pygmy Cormorant, White Pelican, Great White Egret, Glossy Ibis, White-winged Black Tern, etc. In winter hosts of geese and ducks come, and at passage periods there are good waders, wildfowl, birds of prey and others. Also of interest are the rare reptiles: Aesculapian Snake, Orsini's Viper and Eremias Lizard (*Eremias arguta*), at its only European site. The delta habitats are good for amphibians and dragonflies. Over 60 species of fish have been recorded, and the mammals include Racoon-dog, Water Vole, Wild Boar and Wildcat. The rich aquatic flora encompasses species at the north of their ranges plus plants like Water Soldier, in great abundance.

In short, this offers an exceptional wildlife experience. The nearby Black Sea coast has holiday resorts, so there is no problem in getting to the area. Boat trips can be arranged at most of the waterside villages, and are essential for a full appreciation of the delta. Not a place to be rushed.

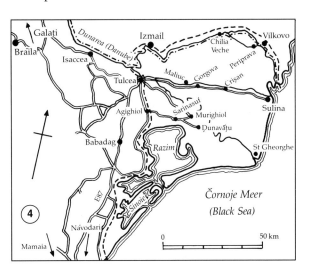

PORTUGAL

The northern half is very mountainous, with predominantly acid rock; the southern half is lower-lying, with limestone outcrops. Rainfall varies widely between the northern mountains – with, for example, the Serra de Estrela receiving 2825mm per year, the highest in the Iberian peninsula – and the Algarve, which is reliably warm in spring and hot in summer. Portugal has a solitary National Park and seven Natural Parks, plus a number of significant natural reserves.

The range of flora and fauna is broad for so small a country. About 3000 flowering species are native, and some 65 endemic. The birds are impressive, too, with good populations of raptors, seabird-breeding colonies, surviving populations of Great Bustard, White Stork and Black Stork, and some excellent coastal and wetland areas for wintering and passage birds. All in all, there is much to interest the naturalist.

Madeira, a self-governing province, is a group of small islands in the eastern Atlantic, some 900km to Portugal's southwest; the largest in the group is also called Madeira. The mild climate makes the island a popular winter resort, but the tourist trade has not adversely affected it as a place of wild and natural beauty. Large parts are legally protected to one degree or another, the biologically richest areas being designated natural reserves.

Of volcanic origin, Madeira itself rises steeply out of the ocean to a height of 1861m. The rugged terrain, cut by many and often very deep ravines, offers sweeping landscapes and coastlines with spectacular cliffs, including Cabo Girao, the world's second highest seacliff. All the high peaks and the large plateau of Paul da Serra are in the centre of the island.

A drive along the encircling coast road or across the island's centre via the high Encumeada Pass gives you a flavour of the place, but the best way to view the rich flora is to walk along the many levadas – artificial courses that transport water to all parts of the island. These follow the contours, often taking seemingly impossible routes; the walks range from easy to difficult, and you should go prepared. The higher parts of the island in particular are often shrouded in dense, disorienting fogs, which can descend quickly; on some walks there are steep drops.

The lowlands are for the most part affected by agriculture and development, but even here the unique native flora, a large Mediterranean element and exotic species introduced from many other countries combine to offer a wide range of plants not normally seen growing side by side.

Portugal, on the western seaboard of Europe, has a wholly Atlantic coastline, though the southeastern part of the country is similar in character to the Mediterranean countries. The population is roughly 10 million, largely rural in character and spread throughout the country's 92,082 sq km; Portugal has a much more lived-in feeling than neighbouring Spain (see page 183), and lacks the wilderness areas of that country.

OPPOSITE PAGE: *The Serra de Monchique in the western Algarve.*

The principal vegetation is laurissilva, an evergreen forest unique to the Azores, the Canaries and Madeira, where it is at its most extensive and best preserved, confined mainly to the central and northern parts of the island, like the Ribeiro Frio Valley. Although at its finest in September–October, when the endemic Lily-of-the-Valley Trees are in flower, it is always interesting for its abundant ferns and climbers. Many species are shrubs from groups more familiar for their herbaceous members, like shrubby sow-thistles, germanders and members of the cabbage family. The moss and lichen growth is very lush in this damp habitat.

The higher reaches are clothed in Tree Heather and the endemic Madeiran Heather and Madeiran Bilberry. Among the highest peaks, like Pico Ruivo (1861m) and Pico d'Arriero various rare endemics can be found.

Many specialized native plants are found on the cliffs, both inland and coastal. Among the best are those along the north coast between São Vicente and Porto Moniz; they support plate-like Aeonium and many endemic Compositae, like *Helichrysum* species.

There are few mammals and reptiles on Madeira, and all are small. The birds initially seem very familiar to northern-European eyes, but most differ sufficiently from their continental relatives to merit recognition as unique Madeiran subspecies. Look out, too, for flocks of wild canaries and in the laurissilva for the endemic Laurel Pigeon. The various seabirds are mostly confined to the smaller islands of the group.

The Azores (Açores) The nine islands and associated islets of the Azores (see page 181) lie about 1500km west of southern Portugal; of volcanic origin, they have a total area of 2344 sq km and a population of about 250,000. Much cultivated, they lack real wildernesses, except in some of the highest parts. Most of the native vegetation has gone; only about half the recorded plants are native.

Most interesting to the naturalist are the colonies of breeding seabirds. There are no endemic birds left (there was once a Laurel Pigeon subspecies), but the islands support most of the world's population of Cory's Shearwater and important populations of Bulwer's and Madeiran Petrels. The best time to visit the islands is March–July.

1. Peneda-Gerês National Park

Location: About 40km northeast of Braga.
Access: Minor roads run into the park; generally open access on foot.
Timing: Best April–October.

Portugal's sole National Park, 72,000ha of mountainous land along the Spanish border rising to 1545m at Mt Nerosa, is an excellent and scenic area for walking. Large areas of beech/Common Oak and pine forest deck predominantly granite slopes, and there are some fine granite cliffs and rock formations. 18 species in the reasonably rich flora are not found else-

Beechwoods in Peneda-Gerês National Park.

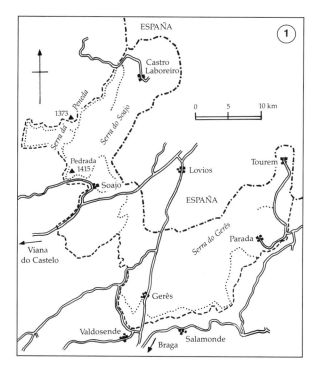

where. Plants of interest include the blue Borage-like *Omphalodes nitida*, the spring-flowering *Crocus carpetanus*, a few Alpines – e.g., Dogtooth Violet – and the endemic blue *Iris boissieri*. Among the mammals are Roe Deer, Wolf, Genet, Otter, Wild Boar and Beech Marten, plus a herd of small wild ponies. Golden Eagle, Booted Eagle, Scops and Eagle Owls, Red Kite and many smaller woodland birds breed. The reptiles, too, are interesting, with Lataste's Viper, Viperine Snake and the rare Schreiber's Green Lizard; among the amphibians are Marbled Newt and Midwife Toad.

2. Montesinho Natural Park

Location: North of Braganca, roughly between the N218 and the Spanish border.
Access: By minor roads from Braganca; unrestricted on foot.
Timing: April–October.

Wolf and Wild Boar may be seen in the huge mountainous area of Montesinho Natural Park.

This huge mountainous area (75,000ha), reaching over 1450m, has extensive forests of Common and Pyrenean Oaks and pines, plantations of Sweet Chestnut, and some heathy moorland on predominantly acid soil. The flora is interesting, with a number of *Cistus*, *Halimium* and *Erica* species, several daffodils (e.g., *Narcissus triandrus*) and French Lavender. Raptors breed in fair numbers – Golden Eagle, Short-toed Eagle, Montagu's Harrier, Peregrine Falcon and others – while Tawny Pipit and Ortolan Bunting are also found. There is still Wolf around, and Roe Deer and Wild Boar are reasonably common.

3. Alvao Natural Park

Location: Just northwest of Vila Real.
Access: Via minor roads N304 and N313 from Vila Real.
Timing: May–July for almost everything.

This small, mountainous park (7365ha) is a well-used area, with considerable amounts of cultivated land and plantations in among the matrix of woodland and moorland, on acid soil. The modest flora has a good range of leguminous shrubs, heathers and the rock-rose-like *Halimium* species. The birds include breeding Golden Eagle and Montagu's Harrier, and this may be one of Portugal's most important areas for breeding Tawny Pipit and Ortolan Bunting.

4. Upper Rio Douro

Location: Along the Douro (Duero in Spain) Valley, on the Spanish border south of Miranda do Douro.
Access: Minor roads lead into the area; unrestricted on foot.
Timing: April–September.

This site is of similar ornithological importance to Spain's Arribes del Duero (see page 191), on the other

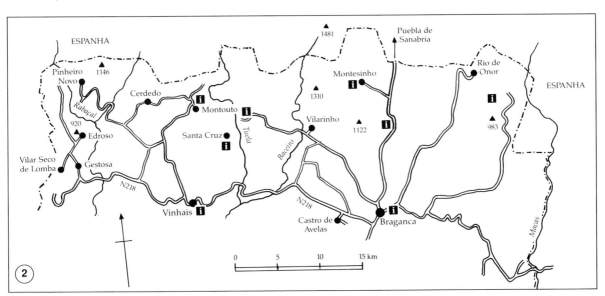

side of the valley. The most interesting part lies at the southern end of the border area, where the Douro turns westwards to the sea. Among the many interesting birds that breed here are important numbers of Black Stork, Egyptian and Griffon Vultures, Golden, Booted and Bonelli's Eagles, Lesser Kestrel, Peregrine, Red-necked Nightjar and Thekla Lark.

5. Berlenga Islands

Location: Off Peniche, 70km northwest of Lisbon (Lisboa).
Access: By boat from Peniche during the tourist season.
Timing: April–July.

A cluster of islands just off the coast; Berlenga itself is a nature reserve. This is an important area for feeding seabirds and as a breeding place for colonies of Cory's Shearwater, Guillemot, Shag and gulls. Blue Rock Thrush and Rock Sparrow are both widespread. This is also a good place to look at seashore life.

To the northwest are the more remote **Farilhoes**; to reach them you must make local arrangements. The only 'mainland' European population of Madeiran Storm Petrel breeds here.

6. Paúl de Arzila

Location: Just west of Coimbra, in the Rio Mondego Valley.
Access: Minor roads run through the reserve; access on foot is limited.
Timing: All year.

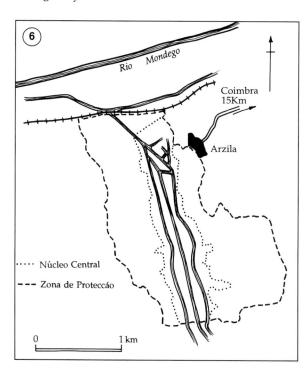

····· Núcleo Central

– – – Zona de Protecção

0   1 km

This small wetland reserve – 165ha of strict reserve plus 370ha of peripheral protected area – is a good site for wetland birds like Marsh Harrier, Little Bittern, Kingfisher, Purple and Grey Herons, Egret, Kite, White Stork and various warblers. Otter, Water Vole and seven other mammals are present, together with 10 reptiles and four amphibians.

7. The Upper Rio Tejo

Location: About 20km southeast of Castelo Branco, along the Spanish border.
Access: Limited, by very minor roads from Castelo Branco.
Timing: March–July.

A relatively remote area along one side of the steep-sided Tejo Valley, with the southern side in Spain (where the river is called the Tajo). The cliffs around here are a noted breeding area for Egyptian and Griffon Vultures, Black Stork, Short-toed, Booted and Bonelli's Eagles, Lesser Kestrel, Thekla Lark, Eagle Owl, Black Wheatear and others. There are also woodland and scrub areas, though increasing Eucalyptus cultivation is reducing the available habitat.

8. The Serras de Aire and Candeeiros Natural Park

Location: Between Leiria and Santarem.
Access: Numerous minor roads enter the site; the N1 skirts its western side.
Timing: April–August.

An attractive area of limestone hills – good walking country – with extensive mixed woodland (Cork, Lusitanian and Round-leaved Oaks) and areas of grassland and garrigue. The 500 or so species in the flora include many orchids and plants like the Clary *Salvia sclareoides* and the attractive yellow Fleabane *Inula montana*. Among the birds are an isolated population of Common Chough – breeding, unusually, in caves – plus Lesser Kestrel and Tawny Pipit. Bats are common, notably Greater and Lesser Horseshoe Bats.

9. Aveiro Estuary

Location: On the coast west of Aveiro.
Access: Various roads (e.g., N109, N327) encircle the site; some access on foot.
Timing: All year.

An extensive estuarine system where the Vouga and Agueda arrive at the coast but are prevented from reaching the sea by a long sandbar; among the habitats are sand, mudflats, saltmarshes, lagoons and saltpans. Marsh Harriers, Purple Heron, Egrets, Little Bittern, Black-winged Stilt, Little Tern and numerous warblers and other marshland birds breed, and this is also a good place for wintering and passage birds, with Osprey, Merlin and especially wildfowl and waders. At present only the San Jacinto dunes (good dune flora), at the tip of the spit coming down from the north, are protected as a reserve, so the remainder is disturbed and shot over at times. This is a complex area that takes time to appreciate.

10. Serra da Estrela Natural Park

Location: To the southwest of Guarda and the east of Coimbra.
Access: Numerous minor roads, including one up Torre; unrestricted on foot.
Timing: April–September.

100,000ha of this area of wooded granite mountains lies in the Natural Park, including Portugal's highest point, Torre (1993m). The mountains are rounded rather than craggy; the area's habitats include cliffs, lakes, heaths and extensive Pyrenean Oak woodland.

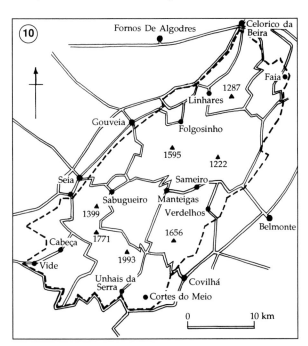

Heathers are well suited to the acidic rock of Serra da Estrela. This is Erica umbellatum.

The rainfall is very high, and the flora, though limited by the acid rock, is rich, with good heathers, shrubby legumes like *Cytisus purgans* and *Chamaespartium tridentatum*, daffodils like *Narcissus asturiensis*, *N. bulbocodium nivalis* and *N. rupicola*, and crocuses and other Alpines; there are several endemics. Short-toed Eagle, Hen and Montagu's Harriers, Chough, Ortolan Bunting and others breed. Some Wolf linger, but their numbers are declining. This is excellent walking country, with few difficult places.

11. Paúl do Boquilobo

Location: About 20km northeast of Santarem, just west of the Tejo Valley.
Access: From Golega, just to the north; access on foot unrestricted but difficult.
Timing: Best April–June; some birds in winter.

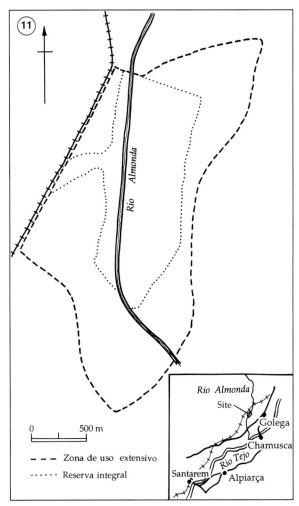

The reserve area comprises 529ha of marshland along the Rio Almonda, just above where it joins the Tejo (Tajo in Spain), with a lake surrounded by sedge-beds and pastures, and willow and alder carr. Little and

177

Cattle Egrets, Night and Purple Herons, Little Bittern and occasionally Spoonbill breed in Portugal's largest and most diversely mixed heronry. In winter there are Osprey and good numbers of ducks. Good displays of White Water-lilies can be seen.

12. Tejo Estuary

Location: Just east of Lisbon (Lisboa).
Access: Major roads encircle the site; minor roads and tracks lead into it.
Timing: Good all year for birds.

With its complex of habitats, this whole estuary is important for birds, though much has been reclaimed or affected by development; a substantial nature reserve (14,500ha) in its upper part contains a selection of the best habitats. Despite deterioration in recent decades, this is still one of the best wetlands in Europe. Purple Heron, Bittern, Little Bittern, Cattle and Little Egrets, Marsh and Montagu's Harriers, Black-winged Stilt, Avocet, Collared Pratincole, Roller and many others breed, and the wintering birds come in abundance, including important numbers of Avocet, Black and Bar-tailed Godwits, Grey Plover and many more.

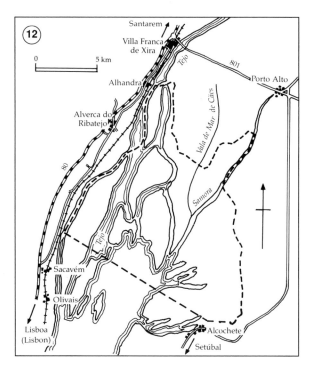

13. Serra de Arrábida Natural Park

Location: To the west–southwest of Setúbal.
Access: Numerous roads lead through the park, including the coast road (N379) from Setúbal. Largely unrestricted on foot.
Timing: Best March–July.

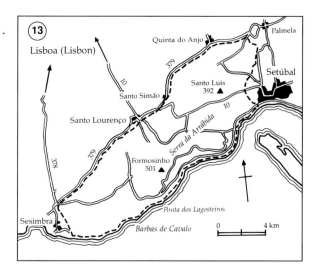

Almost 11,000ha of the best parts of a range of low limestone mountains, rising to just over 500m and retaining a reasonable forest and scrub cover, plus more open areas. Over 1000 plant species are recorded, including numerous orchids, *Fritillaria lusitanica*, the Peony *Paeonia broteroi*, Wild Tulip, other bulbs (e.g., daffodils, Star-of-Bethlehem) and many scrub or coastal species. Sardinian and Orphean Warblers, Black-eared Wheatear, Blue Rock Thrush and a few Eagle Owl breed, and there are some small colonies of breeding seabirds on the rocks offshore. Genet are relatively abundant.

14. Alentejo Plains

Location: Between Évora, Elvas and Monforte, running east to the Spanish border.

The Alentejo Plains, home of the Great Bustard.

Access: Numerous roads cross the area; generally open access on foot.
Timing: April–July.

This diffuse region of rolling plains, partly under cultivation, adjoining similar habitat in Spain, is Portugal's finest area for steppe birds like Great and Little Bustards, Black-bellied and Pin-tailed Sand Grouse, Thekla Lark, Great Grey and Woodchat Shrikes and Stone Curlew. The part around Elvas is currently the best but, as none of the area is protected, this may change.

15. Sado Estuary

Location: Directly southeast of Setúbal.
Access: Various roads (e.g., E90/E01, N253–1) encircle the site, and minor tracks go closer to the estuary. Access on foot is unrestricted.
Timing: All year.

An important wetland and estuary area, partly protected by a 23,000ha reserve; the north shore is industrialized and there are tourist developments on the ocean shore. Birds breeding here include Purple Heron, Little Bittern, Egret, Black-winged Stilt, Avocet, Pratincole and Marsh Harrier, and among the passage and wintering birds are Shearwater and hosts of waders. There are Otter in the area and Bottle-nosed Dolphin close offshore. On the east side, around Pinheiro, a broad tract of species-rich open Cork Oak forest has an understorey of *Cistus crispus* and *Genista scorpius*; here Golden Oriole and other open-woodland species breed.

16. Santo André Lagoon

Location: On the coast about 20km north of the Cabo de Sines.
Access: Easy from minor roads just inland.
Timing: All year.

The Lagoa de Santo André and the Lagoa de Melides, just to its north, are both good bird sites, being open brackish-water lagoons with extensive surrounding reedbeds and dunes and pine woodland nearby; parts are protected. Among the breeding birds are Purple Heron, Little Bittern, Baillon's Crake, Marsh Harrier, Red-necked Nightjar, Savi's, Great Reed and Fan-tailed Warblers and Great Spotted Cuckoo. This is also a good place for migrating birds, especially in autumn when all sorts of species turn up. The dunes are too forested for their flora to be of much interest.

17. Serra de Monchique

Location: About 25km north of Portimão, in the western Algarve.
Access: Easy from minor roads through the hills; the N265 goes through the centre.
Timing: Interesting all year; best April–June.

A range of partly wooded acidic mountains (to over 900m), a little inland from the Algarve and notably cooler and wetter than the coast. The hillsides were once well wooded with oak, but now there are extensive areas of Cork Oak and Eucalyptus, some still being planted. The interesting flora contains many widespread maquis-garrigue species, like Gum Cistus, French Lavender and *Daphne gnidium*; the pink *Rhododendron ponticum* is said to be native here, and another rare plant is the inconspicuous orchid *Gennaria diphylla*. Bonelli's Eagle, Short-toed Treecreeper and Golden Oriole breed. Fire Salamander can be found in damp shady areas, and lizards are abundant.

18. Cabo de San Vicente and Ponta de Sagres

Location: At the extreme southwest tip of Portugal.
Access: Good roads, notably the N268; unrestricted on foot.
Timing: February–June.

Nowhere else in Europe is quite like this area of hard dolomitic limestone, exposed to the full force of Atlantic gales. The flora is rich, interesting but not always easy to find. The local speciality *Cistus palhinhae* (a Portuguese endemic) is abundant, along with four other *Cistus* species; also of interest are the curious shrubby *Viola arborescens*, the Thrift *Armeria pungens* and monocotyledons like *Narcissus obesus*, *Bellevalia hackelii* and the distinctive Squill *Scilla vincentina*. Breeding birds include Chough, Peregrine, Stone Curlew, Little Bustard and Thekla Lark (comparatively easy to identify here, as Crested Lark is rare if not absent). This is a good place from which to observe sea migration.

Interesting and unusual species are worth searching for among the flora of Cabo de San Vincente.

19. Ria Formosa Natural Park

Location: The Algarve coast from west of Faro to east of Tavira.
Access: From minor roads to Ludo and Praia de Faro, or from Tavira at the eastern end; difficult in places.
Timing: All year.

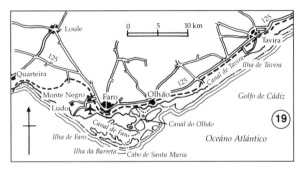

16,000ha of an enormous area of saltmarshes, mudflats and lagoons contained within a series of outer sandbars. The abundant birds include breeding Cattle and Little Egrets, a few Purple Gallinule, Night and Purple Herons, Little Bittern, Red-crested Pochard, White Stork, Collared Pratincole and Kentish Plover, with Azure-winged Magpie and Hoopoe in the nearby woods. The area is very important for wintering waders, wildfowl and raptors, and there is usually a good variety of passage migrants. The plants are more limited, but there are spectacular displays of the tall yellow parasite *Cistanche phelypaea* as well as good dune plants.

20. Burgau-Lagos Area

Location: On the western Algarve coast from Lagos westwards.
Access: Minor roads lead to the coast; largely unrestricted on foot.
Timing: February–June.

A diffuse site, consisting of separate parts of this limestone coast. **Ponta de Piedade** has breeding seabirds and Egret, with a reasonable clifftop flora. Around **Luz** the clifftop flora is good, and very attractive in April–May. West of **Burgau** all the undeveloped parts of the coast are rich in coastal, limestone or Mediterranean flowers, with many orchids, especially *Ophrys* species (Bee Orchid relatives), the impressive spires of *Nepeta tuberosa* and many bulbous species. Lesser Kestrel are found. The marshy area at **Vale de Barão** has abundant Marsh Frog and Terrapin, occasional Viperine Snake and an interesting flora, including naturalized Buttonweed.

To the east of Lagos, between the mouths of the Alvor and Odiáxere and just west of Portimão, the **Quinta da Rocha area**, although well cultivated, has a relatively unspoilt if unspectacular mix of Algarve habitats with an excellent range of birds and insects and, at the coastal end, marshes and mudflats.

The stark cliffs of Ponta de Piedade in the Burgau-Lagos area.

21. Castro Marim Reserve

Location: On the west side of the Rio Guadiana, just north of Vila Real de St António.
Access: Road 122 passes through the site; limited access by footpath and track from it.
Timing: All year.

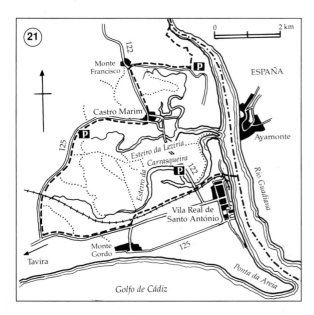

Greater Flamingo in the Castro Marim Reserve.

Marshes, lagoons, saltpans and other estuarine habitats with a rich bird fauna. Large numbers of Black-winged Stilt breed, as do White Stork, Little Bittern, Avocet, Collared Pratincole, Kentish Plover, Little Tern, Rufous Bush-Robin and possibly Lesser Short-toed Lark. Non-breeding birds typical of the nearby Spanish sites – e.g.,

Greater Flamingo and Spoonbill – are common, and this is a good passage and wintering area. Among the reptiles are Chameleon and Western Spadefoot Toad.

THE AZORES (AÇORES)

22. Pico da Vara (São Miguel)

At the eastern end of São Miguel, this site consists of Pico de Vara (1110m) and Pico Verde (931m), both partly covered by native Laurel forests. This is a good place for endemic Azores plants. The breeding birds include various endemic subspecies or races of more widespread birds, like Azores Bullfinch (its only known site), Azores Buzzard, Woodpigeon and Blackbird.

23. Coast of Flores

This rocky coast supports huge numbers of seabirds – Roseate Tern, Cory's and Little Shearwaters, Bulwar's Petrel and others. The whole island is very flowery (hence its name).

24. Monte Brasil (Terceira)

On the sides of this mountain is a rich flora of mainly endemic species.

25. Montanha da Ilha do Pico

This mountain, the highest point (2351m), on Pico, is protected as a reserve. It has a good flora and interesting volcanic geology.

26. Ilhéu do Topo

An island off São Jorge, with a rich flora, breeding seabirds and good seashore and marine life.

SPAIN

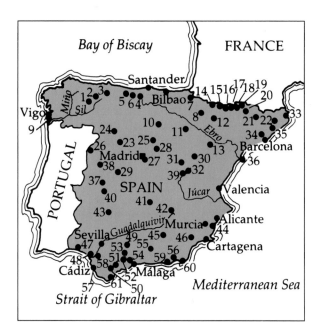

Spain, Europe's second largest country (504,782 sq km), has a relatively low population density, and is judged Europe's second most mountainous country (after Switzerland). The result is a land with a vast range of habitats and many unspoilt and genuinely wild areas. It is very varied, with everything from lowland salt lakes to very high mountains, from the driest point in Europe (Cabo de Gata) to the extremely wet mountains of northwest Spain.

The last decade or so has seen tremendous changes in Spain, as agriculture has intensified and expanded, tourism has developed dramatically and Spain's industries have blossomed. The countryside has changed for the worse, and many richly varied areas whose future had seemed assured have come under threat. In particular, water is at a premium everywhere in Spain, and the abstraction of groundwater for agriculture can deleteriously affect water-levels elsewhere.

Many plant and animal species can be seen only in Spain, or in Spain and Portugal; for many further species Spain is a last major refuge. Birds of prey, for instance – especially vultures and eagles – do much better in Spain (and are much more readily seen) than in most other countries.

OPPOSITE PAGE: *Floral display beside a footpath in the deep Ronda Gorge.*

Spain's special wildlife is probably more under threat than any other in Europe, yet conservation is in some ways well advanced. Nine National Parks together cover 1226 sq km, and there are also many Natural Parks and natural reserves, together covering a considerable area, although these are very variable in the degree of protection they provide. A further category of some relevance is the national hunting reserve; these are extensive and give some protection to habitat and certain species, but obviously do not constitute an ideal way of conserving wildlife.

The Balearic Islands Off Spain's eastern coast, the islands of this group (see page 202) are in many respects fragments of the Spanish mainland, but offshore – as if they were sierras poking above the surface, with the lower-lying land between them being submerged. With the exception of Menorca, which is made up of more acid rocks, most are essentially of limestone. Climatically, they are typically maritime, with a slightly milder and damper climate than on the adjacent mainland; spring starts early and winters in the sheltered lowland parts are mild.

Their flora and fauna differ in some ways from those of the mainland. Although some widespread Mediterranean species are absent, this is more than made up for by the addition of Balearic specialities, especially on Mallorca, and there are various endemic species, like *Paeonia cambessedessii* and the Mallorcan Midwife Toad (not identified until 1980). The northern mountains of Mallorca are as wild an area as anywhere, and consequently have populations of birds rare elsewhere, like Black Vulture.

The Canary Islands The National Parks of the Canaries, off the coasts of Morocco and Western Sahara, are part of the Spanish conservation system, but the islands have few ecological links with Europe, and are accordingly treated only cursorily here (see page 204).

1. Los Ancares Leoneses National Reserve

Location: In the Cantabrian Mountains north of Ponferrada, about 90km west of León.
Access: Small roads run through the site; open access on foot.
Timing: April–October.

A huge reserve on the southern slopes of the Sierra de Ancares, with woodland and scrub on the rounded mountainsides. This is a fine area for mammals, including Roe Deer, Wild Boar, Genet, Beech Marten, Wildcat and Red Squirrel; Wolf still occurs in the general area, and Bear used to. There are good populations of Capercaillie, Short-toed and Bonelli's Eagles, Goshawk and many woodland birds. Plants include several local daffodils (*Narcissus* species) – a feature of this area – as well as the taxonomically confusing Tongue Orchids characteristic of northwestern Spain.

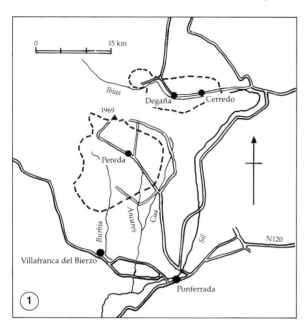

2. Degaña and Muniellos Reserves

Location: On the north slopes of the Ancares, south of Cangas de Narcea, about 100km northwest of León.
Access: Via minor roads, then generally open on foot.
Timing: Spring–autumn.

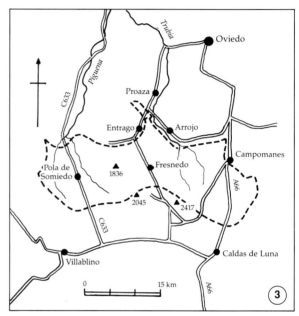

These two reserves cover a sizeable area on the flanks of the Cordillera Cantabrica. El Bosque de Muniellos is a mixed-oak wood of some 3000ha – one of the largest such stands in Europe – while Degaña is mixed, with more beech. The whole area has a very high rainfall. Thanks to the extensive forests, this is one of the best places in Spain for mammals, including Wild Boar, Chamois, Wildcat, Roe Deer and many

smaller mammals, plus Brown Bear and Wolf in small numbers. Among the breeding birds are Capercaillie, Black and Middle-spotted Woodpeckers and Golden, Bonelli's and Short-toed Eagles. This is an excellent site for *Narcissus*, with *N. triandrus*, *N. asturiensis*, *N. nobilis* and several others. Altogether, a superbly unspoilt area, if not as spectacular as the Picos de Europa (site 6).

3. National Reserve of Somiedo

Location: About 25km southwest of Oviedo.
Access: By small roads, then open on foot.
Timing: Spring–autumn.

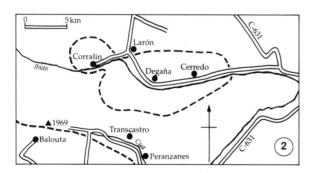

An extensive area of rounded ancient mountains, clothed with woodland and seamed with gorges and deep valleys. The 87,900ha reserve is one of the largest in Spain. The highest point is Peña Ubiña (2417m), and there are glacial lakes at Lagos de Saliencia. Brown Bear have their main Spanish stronghold here, though numbers have dwindled dramatically, and Wolf is found. The birds, much like those of Muniellos (site 2), include good Capercaillie populations. Among the plants are several daffodils and a range of mountain-pasture plants – e.g., Dogtooth Violet, gentians, fritillaries, Mountain Buttercup and, in wetter areas, Large-flowered Butterwort. The endemic Crucifer *Teesdaliopsis conferta* occurs in bare acid sites.

4. National Reserve of Saja

Location: About 25km south of San Vicente de la Barquera.
Access: Minor roads traverse the site; unrestricted access on foot.
Timing: April–October.

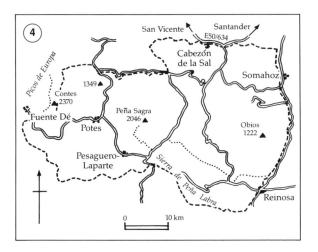

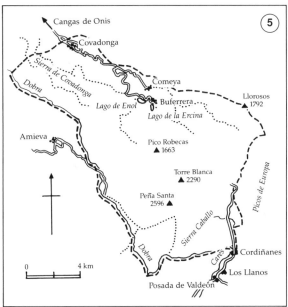

Spain's largest reserve area (180,000ha) lies on the northern slopes of the Cantabrian Mountains, reaching 2536m at Pico de Peña Prieta. It lies to the east of the Picos de Europa (site 6) and covers similar country, with superb limestone mountains, flower-filled meadows and extensive beech and oak woods on the lower slopes. It is botanically rich, even on the high peaks; the hay meadows have Tongue Orchid, Rampion and hundreds of other species, with *Crocus nudiflorus* and Meadow Saffron in autumn. Mammals include Red and Roe Deer, Wildcat, Chamois and a few Wolf; the area's Brown Bear have now disappeared. The bird life is prolific, with good numbers of large raptors, Griffon Vulture and many others.

To the south and southwest of Saja are two other important sites: the **Fuentes Carrionas Reserve** and the **Picos de Tres Mares area**, including the valley of Campóo; there are both calcareous and acid rocks here. This is the only Spanish site for Almond-eyed Ringlet Butterfly, a separate race from other European populations. The three areas together form one of the finest protected areas in Spain.

5. Covadonga National Park

Location: Southeast of Cangas de Onis.
Access: By minor road from Cangas through Covadonga; unrestricted foot access.
Timing: Best May–October.

A beautiful mountain area (17,000ha) adjacent to the Picos de Europa (site 6), this was Spain's first National Park (1916) and is an EEC Special Protection Area. The natural history is generally like that of the Picos, but with fewer hay meadows and móre woodland. Habitats include high-level beech and mixed-oak woodlands, extensive areas of pasture, often overgrazed, and several glacial lakes. Raptors are common. There is a feeding area for vultures – and smaller scavengers also feed there. Pyrenean Desman and Fire Salamander are found, and there is a small population of 'wild' Asturcón Horse near the lakes. Chamois are common.

6. Picos de Europa

Location: Inland from Llanes, on the north coast.
Access: The N621 and other roads run into the area; unrestricted access on foot.
Timing: Interesting all year; best April–October for flowers, birds and butterflies.

One of the finest ranges in Europe. The superb high limestone pinnacles of the Picos, with dramatic deep gorges between massifs, reach 2648m at Torre Cerredo. The climate is wet and misty, and the vegetation verdant: some 600 plants, including over 40 orchids, have been recorded in the hay meadows alone, and the higher peaks have numerous Alpine, Pyrenean and endemic species. Daffodils are a speciality. Among the birds, the raptors are noteworthy, with Griffon and Egyptian Vultures, Golden, Short-toed and Booted

Pastures full of daffodils, Picos de Europa.

185

Eagles and many smaller species; Wall Creepers dwell in some of the gorges; and there are six owl species. Among the mammals are good numbers of Chamois and an important though declining population of the rare Pyrenean Desman. Reptiles include Fire Salamander, quite common though rarely seen. Butterflies abound, especially in the higher pastures, to the extent that one-third of all Europe's butterfly species can be found here; of special note are Spanish Argus, Gavarnie Blue (as an endemic race) and Chapman's Ringlet.

Good starting points include Fuente Dé, the Mirador de Llesba and the Puerto de Pandetrave. This is superb walking country, with marvellous views and wildlife everywhere.

7. Monte Goramakil

Location: About 45km north of Pamplona, near the French border.
Access: Minor road to the summit; unrestricted access on foot.
Timing: May–October.

This modest peak (1090m) forms the northernmost outpost of the Pyrenees. There are some fine gorges with cliffs, on which nests a large colony of Griffon Vulture, along with Peregrine Falcon, Buzzard and other more widespread raptors. The floral and insect populations are moderate.

8. Sierra de Leyre

Location: 40km southeast of Pamplona, just north of the N240.
Access: Via the NA211; unrestricted access on foot.
Timing: Best April–October.

An attractive and little known range, reaching over 1350m, with several gorges. Griffon Vulture breed, and Lammergeier are often in the area. The flora includes an interesting mixture of Pyrenean and arid Spanish species, e.g., Pyrenean Saxifrage and the attractive blue *Catananche caerulea*. Pyrenean Desman and Pyrenean Brook Salamander are found.

9. Islas Cíes Natural Park

Location: Off the west coast, by Vigo.
Access: By boat from Vigo; some limitations on landing.
Timing: Best April–August.

This group of small (430ha in total) and virtually unin-habited islands is most important as a colony for seabirds, some of which – e.g., shags, guillemots and gulls – are rare in Spain; most noteworthy is Iberian Guillemot, of which all 150 or so surviving individuals breed here. There are also good numbers of wintering ducks and waders. The flora (about 260 species) includes the curious shrubby Crowberry relative, *Corema album*,

and the lovely Sea Daffodil. Among the reptiles are Bocage's and Iberian Wall Lizards and Fire Salamander.

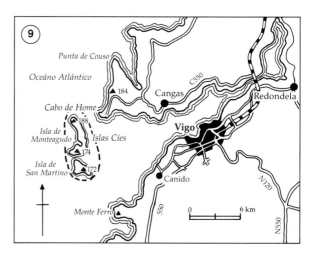

10. Sierras de La Demanda and de Urbion

Location: Between Burgos and Soria.
Access: Numerous minor roads; then unrestricted on foot.
Timing: April–October.

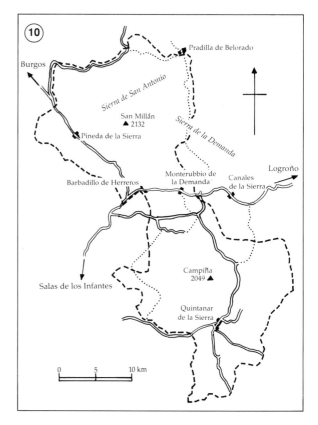

Within this rarely visited area are several contiguous reserves and hunting reserves, together covering a vast

The Rio Revinuesa on its way through the Urbion nature reserve.

stretch of mountainous country, reaching over 2250m and with many parts over 2000m. The plentiful bird-life has Booted Eagle, Honey Buzzard and Hen Harrier; the ranges of Treecreeper and Short-toed Treecreeper overlap here. The rich and varied flora includes a wealth of orchids and lowland species in the foothills and, higher up in the pastures, montane species like *Narcissus*, Tulip and Dogtooth Violet. Among the but-terflies are Long-tailed Blue, Cleopatra and Marbled Fritillary.

11. Dehesa del Moncayo Natural Park

Location: About 80km northwest of Zaragoza and 12km southwest of Tarazona.
Access: Via minor roads from Tarazona; unrestricted on foot.
Timing: April–October.

This 1388ha park consists mainly of the isolated Moncayo (2315m), with a minor road going up to the Sanctuario del Moncayo. The mountain is protected primarily as a botanical site, with a rich variety of plants in the woods and on the barer high slopes. Endemic or rare species include *Saxifraga moncayensis*, *Viola montcaunica*, *Ranunculus gregarius* and the attrac-tive rusty coloured Foxglove, *Digitalis parviflora*; among the orchids are Red Helleborine and Lady's Slipper Orchid. This is a good place for large raptors like Golden Eagle and Goshawk, and there is a big colony of Griffon Vulture nearby. Of note among the butterflies is the Iberian form of Blue-spot Hairstreak.

12. Sierra de La Peña

Location: About 100km southeast of Pamplona and 15km southwest of Jaca.
Access: Minor road to the monasteries; unrestricted access on foot.
Timing: April–October.

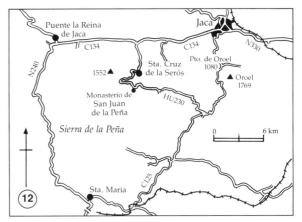

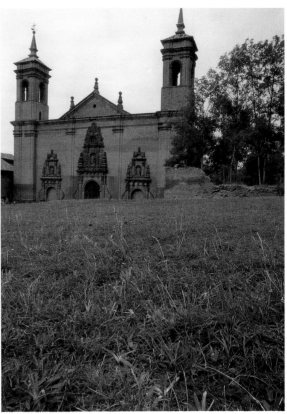

The monastery of San Juan de La Peña, surrounded by drifts of Merendera montana.

An attractive low-mountain area, with pine and oak forests giving way to scrub and pastures. The two monasteries, old and newer, are well worth seeing (and you can stay in the newer one). The rich flora has drifts of *Narcissus* species, Spanish Iris, orchids and others in spring, and incredible displays of the crocus-like *Merendera montana* in autumn. Griffon and Egyptian Vultures, Lesser Kestrel, Red Kite, Woodchat, Red-backed Shrike and many other birds breed. The butterflies, grasshoppers and crickets are particularly rich from late spring onwards.

13. Mediana-Belchite Steppe Country

Location: About 40km southeast of Zaragoza.
Access: The C222 runs through the area; unrestricted on foot.
Timing: Best April–July.

Extremely hot in summer and very cold in winter, this is – though partly threatened by irrigation schemes – one of the best preserved steppe areas in the arid Zaragoza region. It is most important for breeding steppe birds, among them good numbers of Black-bellied Sandgrouse, Stone Curlew and Dupont's and Lesser Short-toed Larks; a very few Great Bustard may be present. The flowers, though secondary, include typical dryland species like the shrubby blue Borage-relative *Lithodora fruticosa*.

The International Council for Bird Preservation is campaigning to purchase and manage a large reserve around here to demonstrate what can be done to protect steppe birds and habitat.

14. Puerto (Col) de Somport

Location: On the French border 25km north of Jaca.
Access: The N330 passes over the col; unrestricted access on foot.
Timing: April–October.

A 1632m pass through the Pyrenees, giving good access to high country on both sides of the border (the north side is in the French Pyrenees National Park – see page 135). The flowers can be spectacular; among them are specialities like Pyrenean Saxifrage on the cliffs as well as all the gentians, primula species, Lousewort, montane buttercups, *Corydalis* species, etc. The birds include Ptarmigan, Snow Finch, both Choughs and occasional Golden Eagle.

15. Viñamala National Reserve

Location: Northeast of Biescas and northwest of Torla.
Access: By minor roads to Balneario de Panticosa; then unrestricted on foot. Snow makes this site difficult to get to outside summer.
Timing: May–October; best June–July.

This superb high-Pyrenean site – with Ordesa (site 16) to the east and the Vignemale part of France's Pyrenees National Park (see page 135) to the north –

has fine peaks, glacial lakes and Alpine pastures; it is excellent for high-altitude walking. The lavish flora includes many Pyrenean specialities in addition to widespread species – gentians, daffodils, pasque-flowers, Dogtooth Violet, Edelweiss, several *Dianthus* species and many more, notably the gorge-side flowers in the Garganta del Escalar. Among the birds are Lammergeier, Golden Eagle, Chough and Ptarmigan, and there are abundant Chamois.

16. Ordesa National Park

Location: In the high Pyrenees just northeast of Torla.
Access: Minor road (HU360) to edge of park; unrestricted access on foot.
Timing: April–October; best May–July; busy at weekends and holiday times.

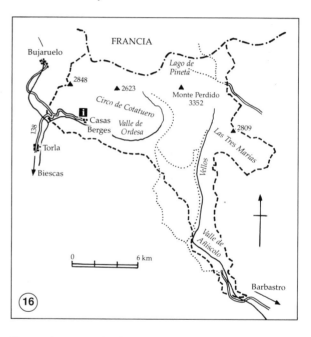

Not to be missed. This is one of Spain's most attractive and exciting places for the naturalist: both the 15,608ha park and the region around it are exceptionally interesting, with superb mountain and gorge scenery and a rich flora and fauna. Lower down are beech, pine and fir woodland, wintergreens, Dutchman's Pipes and masses of the lovely *Ramonda myconi*; higher up the woods give way to Alpine pastures, grazed mainly by cattle, with abundant montane and Alpine flowers – Edelweiss, Pyrenean Saxifrage, Ashy Cranesbill, Globeflower, Leafy Lousewort and many more. Among the breeding birds are Lammergeier, Golden Eagle, Wall Creeper, Chough, Citril Finch and numerous pinewood species. Chamois abound, and there are signs of Wild Boar everywhere, plus Otter in the river and Red Squirrel in the woods; a population of the rare Spanish Ibex is concentrated along the Faja de Pelayo, a rocky ledge in the Ordesa Valley. There are prolific

Common Rock-roses in the high Pyrenees, Ordesa.

butterflies, grasshoppers and crickets, including rarities like Spanish Argus. A refuge high on the slopes of Monte Perdido (3355m) gives access to the spectacular high country.

17. Los Circos National Reserve

Location: In the Pyrenees, straddling the HU640 from north of Bielsa to the French border.
Access: From the HU640 and minor roads; unrestricted on foot.
Timing: May–September.

This extensive hunting reserve adjoins Ordesa (site 16) to the west and the Benasque National Reserve (site 18) to the east. The superb Valle de Pineta runs into the west side of the reserve, with a road, a Parador (government-run high-quality hotel) and, at its head, a wonderful cirque. Habitats include coniferous and deciduous woodland, high pastures, cliffs, scree and lakes. The very rich flora has Pyrenean specialities like *Ramonda myconi*, English Iris, Martagon and Pyrenean Lilies, orchids and good high Alpines. Among the birds are Lammergeier, Golden Eagle, Chough, Wall Creeper and Ptarmigan. Butterflies abound – numerous Fritillaries, Skippers, Blues, Apollos, Mountain Clouded Yellows, migrating Long-tailed Blues and many others. This is great walking country, and there are some well marked trails.

18. Benasque National Reserve

Location: In the central Pyrenees northeast of Benasque.
Access: Via the C139 from Benasque; unrestricted on foot.
Timing: May–October.

This splendid high-mountain area, running up to the French border and encircling the highest Pyrenean peak, Pico de Aneto (3408m), has coniferous and beech forest, high Alpine pastures, screes, cliffs and glacial lakes. Here you can find spectacular and wild walking country, and solitude. The flora and fauna are much like those of the adjoining areas of Circos (site 17) and parts of Val de Aran (site 19) – in other words, this site is good for almost everything!

19. Val de Aran

Location: In the central Pyrenees around Viella.
Access: Numerous roads; access on foot largely unrestricted.
Timing: Best April–October.

This was once a curiously isolated high valley, part of Spain yet cut off from it by the Pyrenees. Now a major road tunnel gives all-weather access, and the valley is developing apace. It is still marvellous, but there is no doubt that many flowery meadows and pastures have disappeared as a consequence of agricultural improvements and tourist (skiing) exploitation. Good meadows can still be full of Horned Pansy, several daffodil species, Oxlip and Early Purple Orchid in spring, followed by masses of different flowers; the high pastures have gentians, fritillaries, primula species and many other Alpines. Raptors are slightly less abundant here than further west or south, but this is not to say that the birds – including Lammergeier – are uninteresting. Side-valleys are home to Pyrenean Brook and Fire Salamanders, Wild Boar are common in the woods, and Chamois and Marmot occur higher up. The valley is noted also for its butterflies, with common and rare species like Clouded Apollo, Silvery Argus and Alpine Grizzled and Chequered Skippers.

Flowery meadows in Riu d'Aguamaix, Val de Aran.

To the east, the huge **National Reserve of Alto Pallars-Aran** stretches as far as Andorra. Minor roads reach into the area from the C147; Puerto de la Bonaigua (2072m) gives easy access to high land at one edge of the reserve. This fine high-altitude area, rich in flowers, mammals, birds and invertebrates, is wonderful for walking.

20. Aigües-Tortes y Estany de Sant Maurici

Location: In the Pyrenees to the southeast of Viella.
Access: Minor roads from Espot (off the C142); open access on foot.
Timing: May–October.

Previously known as Aigües Tortes y Lago de San Mauricio National Park, this is another superb high-Pyrenean area (just under 10,000ha); after various difficulties, it is now well protected. There are extensive coniferous forests, large lakes and high peaks, reaching nearly 3000m. Most of the rock is more acid than in Ordesa (site 16), and as a result the flora is rather different, though still very rich. Species of interest include Water Saxifrage, Vitellina, several gentians, Martagon Lily, Snowbell and several rock jasmines (*Androsace* species). Lammergeier, Golden Eagle, Griffon Vulture, Capercaillie, Ptarmigan and many other high-mountain and forest birds are found. Chamois are frequent, and Otter and Pyrenean Desman occur in and around the rivers. The butterflies include Apollo, Large Blue, Mountain Clouded Yellow and dozens of others. This is magnificent walking country, with high-altitude refuges.

21. Cadí-Moixeroi Natural Park

Location: South of La Seu d'Urgell and Puigcerdá.
Access: The C1411, C1313 and numerous minor roads; unrestricted on foot.
Timing: May–September.

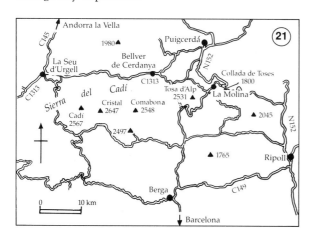

One of the many ranges in this part of Spain that are virtually indistinguishable from the main Pyrenean chain. The Natural Park (including the Sierra del Cadí

hunting reserve) covers over 41,000ha of this varied and wild area, with pine, beech and other forests on the lower parts giving way to flowery Alpine meadows. The rock is mostly limestone and the flora generally lavish: the pass at Collada de Toses (1800m) on the N152 is said to have the richest Alpine flora in the eastern Pyrenees. The birds include Golden and Short-toed Eagles, Capercaillie, Tengmalm's Owl and Black Woodpecker. Chamois are reasonably common and Red and Roe Deer, Wild Boar and others are found. Butterflies abound.

North of the C1313, reaching up to the Andorran border, the **National Reserve of Cerdanya** has similarly rich flora and fauna amid extensive Alpine pastures and woodlands.

22. Volcanic Zone of Garrotxa Natural Park

Location: About 40km northwest of Gerona, just east of Olot.
Access: Numerous minor roads; mostly unrestricted on foot (except farmland).
Timing: Interesting all year; best April–July.

This fascinatingly different area centres on numerous low cones left by volcanism. The area is farmed but well wooded, mainly on the hills, with beech, Pyrenean Oak and other species. Egyptian Vulture and a range of more widespread farmland and woodland birds are found. The reptiles and amphibians are of interest, with Marbled Newt, Fire Salamander, Three-toed Skink and Painted Frog. Among the mammals are Beech Marten and Wild Boar.

23. Embalse de San Jose

Location: On the Rio Duero, about 50km southwest of Valladolid.
Access: The C112 passes by the site.
Timing: All year; best April–July.

The damming of the Duero (Douro in Portugal) by the village of Castronuño has produced a large shallow lake along with extensive alluvial woodland and wetland vegetation, and this has become an important heronry, particularly for Grey and Night Herons, plus a few Little Egret. The marshland warblers – Cetti's, Great Reed, Fan-tailed, Savi's, etc. – are good, as are other characteristic wetland birds like Kingfisher and Great-crested Grebe.

To the east and north are some fine areas for steppe birds including Great and Little Bustards, Black-bellied Sand Grouse, Hobby and Dark Kite.

24. Villafáfila Area

Location: 40km north of Zamora.
Access: Minor roads to Villafáfila; easy access on foot.
Timing: April–July for breeding birds; winter for other birds.

Extensive semi-arid Meseta plains with some seasonal and saline lagoons and associated marshlands, though these latter are gradually disappearing. This is one of the best areas for steppe birds, with good numbers of breeding Great Bustard (an estimated 1000 birds) and somewhat fewer Little Bustard and Black-bellied Sand Grouse. The marshy areas and open water have kites, herons, storks, Kingfisher and other water birds; Spoonbill and waterfowl winter here.

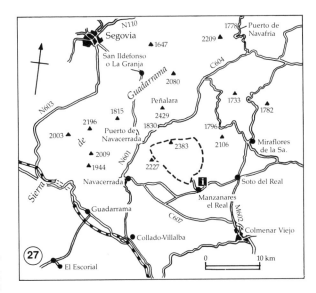

25. Montejo de la Vega

Location: About 15km south of Aranda de Duero, on the Rio Riaza just east of the N1.
Access: Minor roads from the N1, unrestricted on foot.
Timing: Best April–September, interesting all year.

A game refuge and nature reserve, partly managed by the WWF, with a limestone gorge and surrounding unspoilt scrub and grassland, plus poplar plantations on the valley floor. The scrub areas have a Mediterranean-like garrigue vegetation dominated by aromatic herbs with scattered irises and other bulbs. The site is particularly important for cliff-nesting birds like Egyptian Vulture, Griffon Vulture (a substantial population), several pairs of Peregrine Falcon and a colony of Common Chough, with surprising numbers of Dupont's Lark about. Golden Oriole, Hoopoe, Woodchat Shrike and other widespread birds occur in the woods and scrub.

26. Arribes del Duero

Location: On the Portuguese border, where the Huebra meets the Duero (Douro in Portugal), about 55km north–northwest of Ciudad Rodrigo.
Access: Good minor roads (e.g., the SA330 from Lumbrales), run into the area; unrestricted on foot.
Timing: Best April–October.

A sizeable area of fascinating and remote country stretching many kilometres northwards from the confluence of the Agueda and the Duero. Gorges and cliffs carved in the granite by the rivers make ideal nesting sites, and the area is excellent for breeding birds: Egyptian and Griffon Vultures, Golden, Short-toed and Bonelli's Eagles, Peregrine Falcon, Chough, Eagle Owl, Black Stork and many smaller or commoner species. Wild Boar are frequent in wooded areas, and there may still be a few Wolf. The area of interest runs over into adjacent Portugal (see page 175).

27. Sierra de Guadarrama

Location: Between Madrid and Segovia, closer to the latter.
Access: Via the N601 and many minor roads; largely unrestricted on foot.
Timing: Accessible all year; best April–July.

An attractive range of mountains, rising to 2429m at Peñalara though generally lacking substantial peaks, and including the fascinating 5000ha regional park just north of Manzanares el Real (where there is an information centre). Overall the flora and fauna are rich, though because of the proximity of Madrid parts of the area become very busy. Among the many birds are Black, Griffon and Egyptian Vultures, Spanish Imperial and Golden Eagles, several woodpeckers and owls, Alpine Accentor and Bee-eater. Ibex has been reintroduced, and Wild Boar, Fox and Red Squirrel are widespread. The flora includes interesting bulbs like *Crocus asturicus* and *C. carpetanus*, *Merendera montana*, pretty little daffodils (e.g., *Narcissus rupicola*) and many others.

The nearby **Embalse de Santillana reservoir**, just east of Manzanares el Real, is an important migration stopover and wintering area, and also features some breeding wetland birds.

Bee-eaters in the Sierra de Guadarrama.

191

28. Sonsaz National Reserve

Location: About 80km northeast of Madrid.
Access: Minor roads run eastward from the N1; unrestricted on foot.
Timing: April–September.

This huge reserve of mountainous wooded country, an eastward extension of the Sierra de Guadarrama (site 27), rising to 2273m at Pico del Lobo, includes an impressive beechwood area – the Hayedo de Tajera Negra Natural Park – and there are also woods of Pyrenean Oak, Scots Pine and other trees. Goshawk, several eagles, Red Kite, Honey Buzzard, Eagle Owl and many other woodland and scrub birds breed. The mammals, rather thin on the ground, include Roe Deer and Wild Boar. The woods are good for fungi.

29. Sierra de Gredos

Location: About 120km west of Madrid.
Access: Via the C502 and many other minor roads; unrestricted on foot.
Timing: Best April–October.

One of Spain's finest ranges, this rich, varied and extensive area rises to 2592m at Pico Almanzor. Particularly good parts are the high mountains north of Arenas San Pedro, the Puerto del Pico, on the C502, and the Cerro de Guisando, towards the eastern end. The rocks are predominantly acid, and the habitats include extensive mixed woodlands, scrub, high pastures, lakes and cliffs (e.g., the spectacular Circo de Gredos). A nature reserve surrounds the highest peaks; unfortunately, this is also the busiest area, especially since the road into the high parts was completed. The mountains are particularly good for Spanish Ibex, which are both common and reasonably tame. Among the abundant birds are many raptors (not least

the Spanish Imperial Eagle), Black-eared Wheatear, Pied Flycatcher and Bluethroat. White Stork breed in the nearby villages, with a few Black Stork nearby. The flowers include *Narcissus*, various heathers, *Cistus* species, shrubby legumes (e.g., Spanish Broom), Peony and many others. Among the butterflies are Spanish Chalkhill Blue, Long-tailed Blue, Spanish Argus, Great Banded Grayling, Scarce Swallowtail and numerous Fritillaries and Skippers.

30. Laguna de Gallocanta

Location: About 30km northwest of Monreal del Campo.
Access: By minor roads (e.g., TE400); unrestricted on foot.
Timing: Best in winter and at passage periods.

Spain's largest natural lake, at an altitude of about 1000m, is almost totally dry in summer but covers a huge area (about 1500ha) in winter. It is best known as a wintering site for hosts of waterfowl and especially of Common Crane, which gather here by the thousand and feed on the surrounding farmland: up to 22,000 may be present in March, just before they set off north. Other birds of note are Red-crested Pochard, Marsh Harrier and modest populations of steppe birds like Pin-tailed Sand Grouse, Stone Curlew and both bustards. The late-spring flowers are worth attention; they include such gems of the cornfields as the little Violet Horned Poppy and Pheasant's Eye.

31. Natural Park of Alto Tajo

Location: About 25km southwest of Molina de Aragón.
Access: By the GU914 from Molina, then minor roads; unrestricted on foot.
Timing: April–October.

Terraced slopes, Sierra de Gredos.

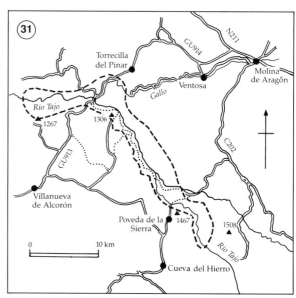

Near the headwaters of the Rio Tajo, with its impressive gorge, is this quiet, unspoilt area of limestone hills, rising to over 1300m. Habitats include pine woods, scrub and maquis, and large limestone cliffs. This is a good place for breeding Griffon and Egyptian Vultures, with Eagle Owl in the woods. The open hillsides have fine orchids, especially *Ophrys* species and Bug Orchids, and butterflies abound.

32. National Reserve of Los Montes Universales

Location: About 65km northeast of Cuenca, just west of Albarracín.
Access: By the TE903 and minor roads; unrestricted on foot.
Timing: May–September.

This huge national reserve (60,000ha) straddles the Universales and adjacent Albarracín ranges. Habitats include pine woodlands (partly planted), bare hillsides, scrub and cliffs. Among the birds are many large raptors – e.g., four eagle species – plus two vultures, Raven, Chough, Thekla and Dupont's Larks and many others. Brown Hare, Wild Boar, Roe Deer and Red Squirrel are found, and the numerous butterflies include Large Blue, Zephyr Blue, Damon Blue and Iolas Blue.

The **Sierra de Albarracín**, to the north, has equally rich flora and fauna, the flowers including a good selection of orchids, *Colchicum triphyllum*, the rock-dwelling Fumitory relative *Sarcocapnos enneaphylla* and the red Pasque-flower *Pulsatilla rubra*.

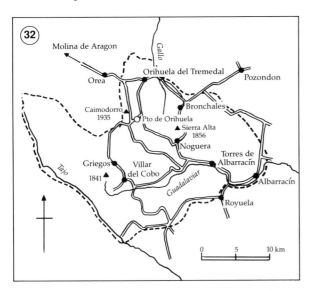

33. Aiguamolls de l'Emporda Natural Park

Location: On the Mediterranean coast east of Figueres.
Access: Minor roads to Castelló d'Empuries; access on foot is partly restricted to trails.
Timing: Some interest all year; best March–November.

One of Spain's best coastal wetlands. The park area divides roughly into two parts, both of very great interest: a northern freshwater-marsh part and a southern saltmarsh/lagoon area. Here 90 species of birds breed, including good numbers of Bittern, Black-winged Stilt, Marsh Harrier, Purple Heron, Garganey (its only Spanish site) and numerous warblers, plus a few Montagu's Harrier and Lesser Grey Shrike. All told, about 300 bird species have been recorded here, with a great variety coming through on passage or wintering here.

There is also a good range of amphibians, including Marsh and Painted Frogs, Marbled Newt, Natterjack and Western Spadefoot Toads and Stripe-necked Terrapins; among the reptiles are Three-toed Skink, Montpellier Snake and Spiny-footed Lizard, superbly colourful in its immature stages. The flora is of interest, too – good orchids and other flowers on the limestone hills and a whole range of marsh and saltmarsh plants. There is an information centre at El Cortalet, plus a number of marked trails.

Nearby sites include the cliffs and maquis just east of **Roses (Rosas)**, and the offshore **Islas Medes**, south of L'Escala, where there are some good seabird colonies and other breeding birds.

34. Sierra de Montserrat

Location: About 45km northwest of Barcelona.
Access: Via the NII and then a minor road; unrestricted on foot.
Timing: April–October.

This extraordinary range, nowhere reaching over 1250m but seeming higher owing to the dramatically eroded pinnacles and conglomerate buttresses, is a popular with tourists, especially because of the monastery with the Black Madonna and the nearness of Barcelona. The flora has many orchids plus Hepatica, Martagon Lily, the local *Globularia valentina*, the essentially Pyrenean speciality *Ramonda myconi* and, higher up, a rare saxifrage, *Saxifraga callosa cata-launica*. The birds include Peregrine Falcon, buzzards, Chough and Raven.

Nearby, west of the C1411, the **Sant Llorenc del Munt Natural Park** is worth a visit.

35. Montseny Natural Park

Location: 45km northeast of Barcelona.
Access: A good minor road through the park's centre; open access on foot.
Timing: Best April–September.

An attractive area (13,255ha) of granite mountains, reaching 1709m at Turo de l'Home. The woods include superb areas of beech forest along with Holm Oak, deciduous oaks and pine. The acid rock gives rise to a scanty but interesting flora, with abundant *Potentilla* and *Arenaria* species higher up plus an endemic saxifrage (*Saxifraga vayredana*), French Lavender, a local subspecies of Mountain Pansy and the saprophytic orchid, Violet Limodore. The butterflies are good, if hardly prolific; among them are an endemic race of Spring Ringlet, Two-tailed Pasha, Clouded Yellow and several Fritillaries. The good representative selection of woodland birds includes Short-toed Treecreeper and Goshawk.

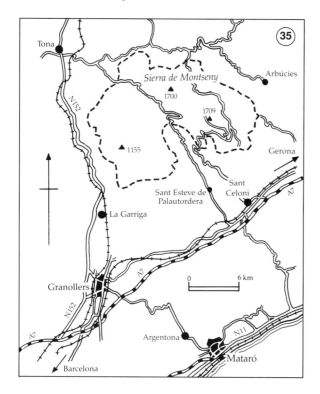

Paddy fields of the Ebro Delta, one of several important bird habitats.

Western Spadefoot and Stripeless Tree-frog (rare), with Spiny-footed Lizard and Large Psammodromus in the dunes. The modest flora includes good saltmarsh and freshwater plants, plus some interesting dune species like Sea Daffodil, Sea Medick, Large Rest-Harrow and *Limoniastrum monopetalum*.

A little inland, the **National Reserve of Puertos de Beseit** has impressive mountain scenery, good raptors and an interesting flora.

37. Monfragüe Natural Park

Location: About 25km south of Plasencia.
Access: Via the C524; unrestricted on foot outside the strict reserve area.
Timing: Interesting all year; best April–July.

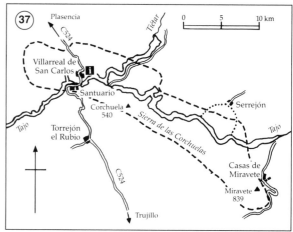

This area of exceptional ornithological importance and general interest, with about 18,000ha protected, combines cliffs and crags, dehesa vegetation, scrub and wetlands. The many breeding birds include Black Vulture (possibly its best area in the world), Griffon and Egyptian Vultures, Black Stork (good numbers),

36. Ebro Delta

Location: On the Mediterranean coast just east of Tortosa.
Access: Good minor roads into area; permits required for some areas.
Timing: All year for birds.

The Ebro Delta is a wetland site of international importance, somewhat similar to the Camargue (see page 137); you really need several days to appreciate it. There is a good information centre at Deltebre. Its primary importance is for birds: over 300 species have been recorded, their main habitats being the lagoons, reedbeds, dykes and paddy fields. Black-winged Stilt, Avocet, Collared Pratincole, Red-crested Pochard, Purple Heron and seven other herons, Little and Sandwich Terns, Slender-billed Gull, Marsh Harrier and many others breed. Vast numbers – up to 100,000 – use the site on passage or during the winter, especially ducks, waders and Greater Flamingo.

This is also a good place to see reptiles and amphibians – e.g., both Terrapins (now rare), Viperine, Montpellier and Horseshoe Whip Snakes, Painted Frog,

The Tagus Reservoir, Monfragüe Natural Park.

Spanish Imperial, Booted and Short-toed Eagles, Black-winged Kite, abundant Azure-winged Magpie, Golden Oriole, Hoopoe and Bee-eater. Most of the birds are present in force. Among the mammals are Pardel Lynx, Egyptian Mongoose and Wild Boar; the reptiles and amphibians are good, too, with Midwife Toad, Painted Frog, Marbled Newt, Bedriaga's Skink and others. The modest flora includes Tongue Orchid, Yellow Bartsia, Brown Bluebell (*Dipcadi serotina*) and masses of French Lavender and Gum Cistus. The river and associated wet areas have fine dragonflies, with *Onychogomphus* species and the striking red *Trithemis annulata*. This superb area is good for walking and general exploring; there is a very small information centre at Villareal de San Carlos.

38. Sierra de La Peña de Francia

Location: About 50km southwest of Salamanca.
Access: Many minor roads from Béjar; largely unrestricted on foot.
Timing: April–October.

This remote area of wooded acidic mountains, reaching 1732m at Peña de Francia, includes the **National Reserve of Las Batecuas**. The woods are of Pyrenean and other oaks, Sweet Chestnut and pine, with a heathy understorey often grazed by stock. The flora has various daffodils – e.g., *Narcissus bulbocodium*, *N. rupicola* and *N. triandrus* – various rock-rose relatives like *Halimium umbellatum* and the yellow *H. alyssoides*, and several heathers, including *Erica australis*. Among the birds are breeding Black and Griffon Vultures, Dark Kite, Hoopoe, Golden Oriole and particularly abundant Nightingale. As for the mammals, there are Roe Deer, Wild Boar and a few surviving Pardel Lynx.

A few kilometres southwest is the equally remote, wooded **Sierra de Gata**, with similar flora and fauna, including birds like the lovely Black-winged Kite and occasional Spanish Imperial Eagle.

39. Serranía de Cuenca

Location: To the northeast of Cuenca.
Access: Numerous minor roads enter the area; unrestricted access on foot.
Timing: Best April–July.

A superb range of mainly limestone mountains with a rich flora and some fascinating geological features. Several reserves lie within the range, notably the 26,000ha **Serranía de Cuenca Reserve** and the 60,000ha **Montes Universales Reserve** (site 32); the main concentration of places of interest lies along and in the environs of the Jucar Valley near Villalba de la Sierra. There are extensive forests of Scots Pine, mixed oaks and juniper, and the extremely rich flora includes numerous orchids, endemics and rock-dwellers like *Sarcocapnos enneaphylla* and *Antirrhinum pulverulentum*. Among the birds are Griffon and Egyptian Vultures, three eagle species, Chough and many woodland and scrub birds. Butterflies abound, notably Iolas Blue, Spring Ringlet and Spanish Gatekeeper. The whole area is good walking country.

40. Trujillo Area

Location: Between Trujillo and Torrecillas de la Tiesa, about 50km east of Cáceres.
Access: From the NV/E4 and minor roads; unrestricted on foot.
Timing: Best April–July.

An extensive tract of unprotected undulating countryside with granite outcrops, typical of the better parts of the Extremadura region. Large parts are covered by open dehesa woods. The breeding birds are very important, with a number of steppe species like Great and Little Bustards, Pin-tailed and Black-bellied Sand Grouse and Stone Curlew. In more wooded areas are found Azure-winged Magpie, Great Spotted Cuckoo and occasionally Black Stork. White Stork abound in the area, Montagu's Harrier is frequent, Lesser Kestrel

Crown Daisies and Bugloss mingle in a Cork Oak grove, Trujillo area.

breed in Trujillo, and Common Crane winter in the area.

41. Tablas de Daimiel National Park

Location: About 25km northeast of Ciudad Real.
Access: By well signed minor roads; restricted access on foot on trails with hides.
Timing: All year; best April–July.

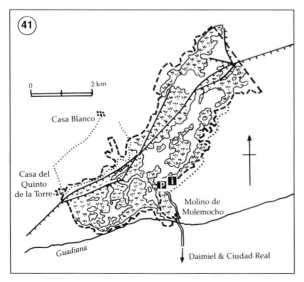

A small but important wetland area (just under 2000ha), with a good information centre and well organized walks and hides. The main habitats are seasonal open water and associated marshland; much of the habitat has been lost in recent years, though remedial measures currently under way may restore it to its former importance – at present it is well short of this, though still worth a visit. Breeding wetland birds include – or have included – Red-crested Pochard, Gadwall, Shoveler, Black-necked Grebe, several herons, Bearded Tit and Savi's Warbler, and numerous waterfowl and waders feed here on passage or in winter. Other features of interest include Marsh Frog, Tree-frog and Stripe-necked Terrapin.

About 40km northwest, the **Coto Nacional de Los Quintos de Mora** covers hilly wooded country, good for raptors and with a few Lynx.

42. Natural Park of Las Lagunas de Ruidera

Location: Straddling the N430 between Albacete and Manzanares.
Access: By minor roads from the N430; unrestricted access on foot.
Timing: All year for birds.

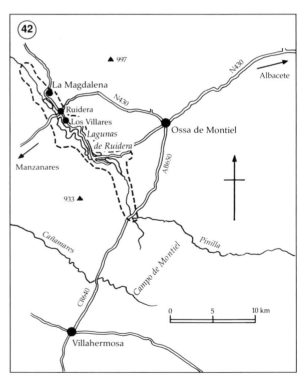

A beautiful chain of mainly natural lakes in otherwise dry rocky countryside, this limestone area has caves and subterranean water channels. The lakes – all different in size and depth, and invaded by vegetation to varying degrees – are good for breeding wetland birds and for wintering waterfowl, though not in spectacular numbers; species include Great-crested Grebe,

Shoveler and Red-crested Pochard. The information centre is near Laguna Santos Morcillo.

43. La Serena

Location: About 130km northwest of Córdoba, around Castuera.
Access: Minor roads (e.g., C413, C420) run through the site; easy access on foot.
Timing: Interesting all year; best April–June.

This remote and unpopulated piece of rolling steppe country – huge areas of dry grassland scattered with trees and shrubs and large cornfields – is very important for breeding steppe birds, including large populations of both bustards, Black-bellied and Pin-tailed Sand Grouse, Montagu's Harrier and Stone Curlew. Birds of prey are common. The flowers include cornfield weeds in fine displays and occasional masses of the pretty iris-like Barbary Nut.

44. Salinas de Santa Pola

Location: On the coast about 20km south of Alicante.
Access: Good views from roads, especially the N332; limited access into site.
Timing: All year.

This stretch of saline and freshwater lagoons on both sides of the main coast road south of St Pola is excellent for breeding wetland birds – Black-winged Stilt, Avocet, Red-crested Pochard, Kentish Plover, the rare Marbled Teal, etc. At other times there are Greater Flamingo and many waders, waterfowl and gulls.

45. Sierra de Cazorla y Segura

Location: About 100km northeast of Granada; about 30km southeast of Úbeda.
Access: Numerous minor roads; access on foot generally unrestricted.
Timing: Best April–October.

A superb limestone-mountain area largely covered by an enormous national reserve (about 750 sq km). The scenery is impressive – with peaks, gorges and woods – and the exceptionally rich flora includes not only widespread lime-loving plants, like orchids and rock-roses, but also many specialities: the superb pink-purple shrubby *Viola cazorlensis*, the Butterwort *Pinguicula vallisneriana*, the large pink Milkwort *Polygala boisseri*, various *Narcissus* species, *Trachelium caeruleum*, etc. Among the birds are Griffon Vulture, Chough, Golden Oriole and Azure-winged Magpie. Mammals of interest include Red Squirrel, Pine Marten, Red Deer, Genet and Wildcat. There are also many and varied butterflies and other insects. The information centre at Torre del Vinagre has a botanic garden, plus a nearby zoological

The Rio Guadalquivir in Sierra de Cazorla.

garden. The whole area is excellent for walking and touring.

46. National Reserve of Sierra Espuña

Location: About 40km southwest of Murcia, just north of Totana.
Access: Via minor roads north from the N340; unrestricted access on foot.
Timing: All year; best April–June.

An attractive wooded mountainous area (about 10,000ha), rising to over 1580m, with forests of Maritime Pine and spectacular cliffs. Mouflon, introduced in 1970, have done well – there are an estimated 700 in the higher parts of the park. Among the birds are Griffon Vulture, Golden Eagle and a small colony of Black Vulture. The prolific butterflies include the local Nevada Grayling.

47. Las Marismas del Odiel

Location: Just southwest of Huelva.
Access: A minor road runs through the reserve; reasonable access on foot.
Timing: All year.

A moderate-sized Natural Park (about 400ha) holding beach, mudflats, saltpans, saltmarshes and associated habitats, with two integral reserve areas. Little Egret (large numbers), Purple and Grey Herons, Spoonbill and Little Tern breed, and can be readily seen away from their nests on the Isla de Enmedio. Among the plentiful birds feeding here on passage or during the winter are Greater Flamingo, Black and Whiskered Terns and many waders. This is a good area for saltmarsh and coastal scrub flowers, including numerous *Cistus* species. There are also Chameleon and other reptiles.

48. Coto Doñana National Park

Location: About 50km southwest of Seville (Sevilla), west of the Rio Guadalquivir.
Access: Good roads; access into the park is controlled.
Timing: All year; best February–June. High summer should be avoided.

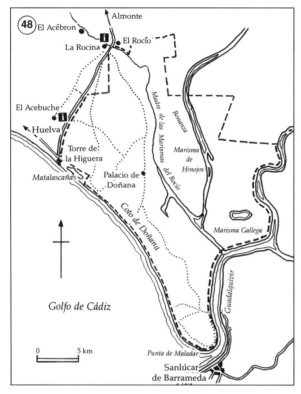

Spoonbills in flight at El Rocío in the Coto Doñana National Park.

- Take the official tour (by four-wheel-drive) from the El Acebuche centre over an 80km loop of the southern part of the park. You should book in advance, but don't be put off trying on the spur of the moment.
- Use the hides and walks at El Acebuche and Acébron Palace for good views of many wetland species.
- Visit the bridge and area south of El Rocío for fine birdwatching.
- Walk eastwards from El Rocío along the northern edge of the park for some fine woodlands, scrub and wetland areas.
- Explore the dunes in both directions from Matalascañas.

Not far away, on the east side of the Guadalquivir Estuary, the saltpans at **Bonanza** have many of the same wetland birds as Doñana, with a good area of coniferous forest nearby.

Almost certainly Spain's most famous and important wildlife site, and among the most important in Europe, this is a huge area (165,000ha) of the habitats around the Guadalquivir Delta: dunes and beach, extensive marshlands, lagoons, woodlands and heathy scrub. Its overall value is enormous, with vast quantities of breeding birds, including many rarities like Spanish Imperial Eagle, Purple Gallinule (the park's emblem), Marbled Teal and Red-crested Pochard. There are great abundances of Spoonbill, Black-winged Stilt, Flamingo, egrets, terns, gulls, kites and Azure-winged Magpie. The mammals and reptiles are likewise of note: Pardel Lynx, Wild Boar, Red and Fallow Deer, Spur-thighed Tortoise, Lataste's Viper, Spiny-footed Lizard, Ocellated Lizard and many more. Dragonflies and damselflies abound in the wetter areas, while dry-area insects like Antlion, Dung Beetle and butterflies do well. Even the flowers are of interest, especially on the dunes and heathy areas, where there are many different *Cistus* species, the pretty little snowflake *Leucojum trichophyllum* and rare thrifts like the impressive *Armeria gaditana*. Many of the finest areas, especially the extensive breeding colonies, are closed to the public. The best ways to see the park are:

49. Córdoba Lagunas

Location: About 45km south of Córdoba.
Access: Via the C329; access on foot is partly restricted.
Timing: All year; best April–June.

A series of natural and artificial freshwater and saline lakes, some designated as reserves, with an information centre at Laguna de Zónar and a good hide at Laguna del Rincon. Birds breeding in the area include the rare White-headed Duck, Purple Gallinule, Marsh Harrier, Purple Heron and other wetland species. Wintering birds include Greater Flamingo and good numbers of duck and waders.

50. Sierra de Grazalema Natural Park

Location: About 15km west of Ronda, north of Ubrique.
Access: Minor roads encircle the area; access on foot is generally open, but a few areas need permits.
Timing: All year; best March–July.

A superb area for flowers, fine scenery and much else. The key area is roughly bounded by Ubrique, El Bosque and Grazalema, though the area towards Cueva de la Pileta is also good. Besides many wide-spread limestone and mountain plants there are numerous endemics and rarities, like the beautiful white-spiked *Ornithogalum reverchonii*, the huge grey-leaved, yellow-flowered *Centaurea clementei*, *Biscutella frutescens* in yellow showers, the endemic rock-dwelling Poppy *Papaver rupifragum*, several local saxifrages, *Putoria calabrica* in pink cushions, and the pretty Toadflax *Linaria platycalyx*. There are fields of blue lupins, masses of orchids, good cornfield weeds and stands of the very rare Spanish Fir *Abies pinsapo*.

Numerous Griffon and Egyptian Vultures, Chough, Bonelli's Eagle, Black and Black-eared Wheatears, Eagle Owl and many other birds breed. Among the numerous butterflies are Moroccan Orange-tip and Cleopatra. The whole area, excellent for walking, deserves at least a few days of your time.

The edge of a cornfield ends in a riot of colour, Sierra de Grazalema.

51. Ronda Gorge

Location: In Ronda, 35km northwest of Marbella.
Access: Paths lead into the gorge, and a road-bridge crosses it.
Timing: Best February–July.

This dramatic deep gorge, crossed by several bridges and running through the lovely little town of Ronda, is a breeding site for Chough, Alpine Swift, Blue Rock Thrush, Rock Dove, Black Redstart and a colony of Lesser Kestrel. Excellent views can be had from the main bridge, and paths down into the gorge give access to different areas. The interesting flora includes local specialities – e.g., the branched white *Crambe filifolia* – plus various orchids. Moorish Gecko occurs in the gorge.

The surrounding area is generally extremely rich in flowers: at the start of the season displays of the Juno Iris, *Iris planifolia*, herald the arrival of a great variety of species.

52. Teba Gorge

Location: About 30km west of Antequera on the C341.
Access: The C341 crosses the gorge, and a small path enters it.
Timing: Best March–June.

The gorge is that of the Rio de la Venta near where it enters the Embalse del Guadalteba-Guadalhorce, a few kilometres east of Teba. You can get good views of breeding Egyptian Vulture, Bonelli's Eagle, Black Kite, Chough, Black-eared Wheatear and Blue Rock Thrush. There is also a broad if unspectacular range of limestone flowers and butterflies.

53. Lago de la Fuente de Piedra

Location: About 20km northwest of Antequera (northwest of Málaga).
Access: By minor road from Fuente de Piedra; access is limited to periphery and tracks.
Timing: All year; best March–June.

The largest saline lake in Andalucía (about 2400ha), now managed as a key nature reserve; there is an information centre near Fuente de Piedra. The site's particular importance is as Europe's largest Greater Flamingo breeding colony; in 1990, 14,000 pairs reared 10,400 young! Other birds breeding here include Black-winged Stilt, Avocet, Kentish Plover,

Lago de la Fuente de Piedra, the largest saline lake in Andalucía.

Gull-billed Tern, Slender-billed Gull, Marsh Harrier and, in recent years, a few White-headed Duck. In winter the lake becomes much larger and supports great numbers of duck and others. The flora is limited, but there are fine displays of the little pink Sea-heath. Local amphibians include Parsley Frog and Western Spadefoot Toad.

A few kilometres southwest, alongside the N342, is the **Laguna Dulce**, a small lake reserve with a good range of breeding birds and attractive displays of flowers.

54. Torcal de Antequera

Location: About 12km south of Antequera.
Access: The C3310 from Antequera leads into the site; paths from there.
Timing: Best April–October.

This marvellous karst area (1170ha), with fantastically shaped pinnacles, has a very rich flora, including 30 orchids – e.g., Yellow Bee Orchid and Pink Butterfly Orchid – the dwarf blue *Iris subbiflora*, common around the pinnacles, and *I. xiphium*, frequent on the south sides of the hills. Other interesting species are *Ranunculus rupestris*, the Bugloss *Echium boisseri*, with its tall spikes, the tiny purple *Arabis verna*, yellow *Viola demetria* and a local Saxifrage, *Saxifraga biternata*. The birds include Griffon and Egyptian Vultures, Chough and Black Wheatear; butterflies abound. This is good walking country, with well marked paths.

Fantastic karst formations, Torcal de Antequera.

55. Sierra Nevada

Location: To the southeast of Granada.
Access: The GR420 leads from Granada into the highest part; unrestricted access on foot.
Timing: Access to the higher parts is restricted to April–October.

Though it lacks the peaks and grandeur of the Pyrenees, this is a major range, including Mulhacén (3478m), Spain's highest peak. This fascinating and extensive area, good for walking, merits at least sev-

The 'Hedgehog Zone' of the Sierra Nevada.

eral days of your time. Because they are southern and isolated, the mountains have developed a remarkable endemic flora and some endemic insects. Plants of the higher zones include the bluish *Crocus nevadensis*, the yellow *Narcissus nevadensis* and the tiny purple Crucifer *Ptilotrichum purpureum*. Slightly lower down – in the 'Hedgehog Zone' – are hundreds of species, including the superb blue hummocks of the legume *Erinacea anthyllis* and the unusual spiny cushions of a yellow Crucifer, *Vella spinosa*. There are good butterflies, from widespread species like Painted Lady to rarer ones like Nevada Blue, Glandon Blue in a local form and Spanish Fritillary. The birds include Golden Eagle, Chough, Black Wheatear and Alpine Accentor.

56. Tabernas Badlands

Location: 25km due north of Almería.

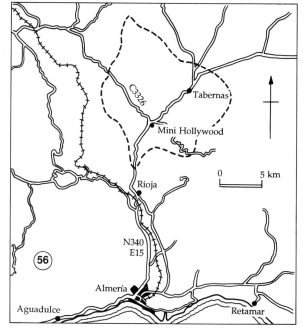

Access: The N340 and C3326 pass through the site; unrestricted access on foot.
Timing: Accessible all year; best February–June.

A number of Westerns have been filmed in this semi-desert area – typical badland country, with bare hill-sides falling into canyons that carry mere trickles of water. It becomes extremely hot by early June. Though sparse, the plants are interesting, mixing desert and saline steppe species – False Esparto Grass, *Fagonia cretica*, the beautiful pinkish-red Sea Lavender *Limonium insigne*, etc. At the bottoms of the canyons grow many members of the Goosefoot family, parasitized by the broomrape-like *Cistanche phelypaea* in its white form, plus the curious fungus-like spikes of *Cynomorium coccineum*. Among the birds are Black-bellied Sand-Grouse, Black Wheatear, Bee-eater and Trumpeter Finch. The insects are rather meagre, though the impressive *Empusa pennata* is quite common.

57. Cádiz Bay

Location: Beside Cádiz.
Access: By road, especially the NIV.
Timing: All year.

The site comprises not only the bay but also the used and neglected saltpans just to its south and east. Although disturbed and threatened, the site is still excellent for birds, easily seen from the roads and banks. Little Tern (probably the largest population in Spain), Avocet, Black-winged Stilt, Oystercatcher and Kentish Plover are among the breeding birds, and visitors include White Stork, Greater Flamingo (which gather in good numbers before breeding), Little Egret and numerous wildfowl and waders. On the saltmarshes you can see the impressive yellow spikes of the parasitic *Cistanche phelypaea*.

58. Laguna de Medina

Location: About 12km southeast of Jerez de la Frontera.
Access: Via the C440, then marked paths.
Timing: Good all year except middle to late summer.

This medium-sized lake, with associated wetlands, lies in an important strategic position for migrating birds. It varies greatly in size, often drying out in summer. Birds breeding here include the rare Crested Coot, the beautiful Purple Gallinule, Sardinian and Great Reed Warblers and grebes; at other times there are Greater Flamingo, huge numbers of coots, White-headed Duck, Marbled Teal and Red-crested Pochard. In autumn, hosts of Hirundine gather here to roost before leaving Europe. There are Ocellated Lizard around the lake and Viperine Snake and Stripeless Tree-frog in the wetter areas.

59. Punta Entinas-Sabinar and Roquetas de Mar

Location: On the coast about 20km southwest of Almería.
Access: Minor roads lead to the site; easy access on foot.
Timing: All year; best January–June.

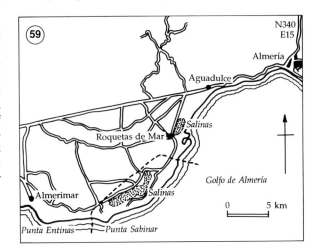

The western part of this site is a Natural Park, with saltmarshes and dunes; the part further east, towards Roquetas, is unprotected. The whole area is hemmed in with glasshouses and messy with rubbish. Numerous saltmarsh plants like Sea-blite, Glasswort and Tamarisk are found. The rich bird-life includes Little Egret, Greater Flamingo, Avocet, Black-winged Stilt and numerous waders and waterfowl on the wetter areas, while the scrub on the dunes sustains Crested Lark, Great Grey Shrike and Dartford Warblers. Lastase's Viper is occasionally seen.

60. Cabo de Gata

Location: On the Mediterranean coast 25km southeast of Almería.

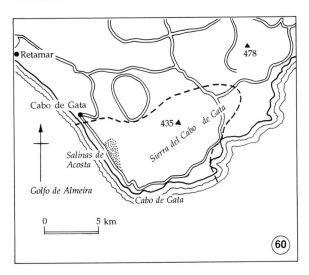

Access: Minor roads from Almería; unrestricted on foot.
Timing: All year; best February–June (very hot in summer).

This is usually adjudged Europe's driest place, with an annual rainfall under 10cm. From here, the arid Sierra del Cabo runs inland to the northeast. The interesting flora has local and endemic species like the Toadflax *Antirrhinum charidemi*, the pale-blue Sea Lavender *Limonium thouinii* and the curious shrubby *Periploca laevigata*, with its great twin-horned fruits. Many commoner species thrive on the low dunes, among them Sea Daffodil and the Sea Lavender *Limonium sinuatum*. The birds include Bonelli's Eagle and Black Wheatear; among the reptiles an isolated outpost of Italian Wall Lizard is of interest.

The nearby saltpans of **Salinas de Acosta** are superb for wetland birds, with numerous gulls, waders and waterfowl and many Greater Flamingo.

61. Gibraltar

Location: On the south coast, just east of Algeciras.
Access: By road from mainland Spain; good foot access to parts.
Timing: Best spring and autumn.

Although developed and overused, Gibraltar still has features of interest. The rock is limestone, so the flora is reasonably rich, with Gibraltar Candytuft a speciality. The mammals include the famous Barbary Ape, a Macaque whose origins are still uncertain. This is the only place in Iberia where Barbary Partridge breed, though they were originally introduced. Especially when a westerly wind is blowing, Gibraltar is excellent for watching spring and autumn migrations, with multitudes of Honey Buzzard and Dark Kite and smaller numbers of eagles, ospreys, harriers and vultures passing through on their way to or from Africa.

62. Northwest Mountains (Mallorca)

Location: Between Andratx and Pollença.
Access: The C710 runs along much of the chain and the C711 crosses it; minor roads and tracks lead off these.
Timing: Interesting all year; best March–August.

The northern mountains of Mallorca and their associated coastline comprise a superb wilderness area, worthy of National Park status but protected only by scattered reserves. Many peaks exceed 1000m; the highest is Puig Major (1436m). The lavish flora combines widespread Mediterranean species and Mallorcan specialities, particularly in the higher areas. Plants of interest include *Cyclamen balearicum*, *Crocus cambessedessii* (autumn-flowering), a robust parsnip (*Pastinaca lucida*), the Balearic form of primrose and a buttercup (*Ranunculus weyleri*). Puig Major's northern slopes (Puig Tomir) offer good opportunities to see the flora, while the C110 south of Puig Major enters reasonably high country.

The birds include breeding Black Vulture, Peregrine and Eleonora's Falcon, and the reptiles False Smooth Snake and Gecko. Butterflies abound, among them Two-tailed Pasha (on the Strawberry Trees) and the Balearic form of Common Blue. It is worth spending several days exploring this superb wild walking country.

63. Puerto de Pollença Area (Mallorca)

Location: The northern tip of Mallorca.
Access: The PM221 runs right to the tip of the peninsula; unrestricted, if often difficult, access on foot.
Timing: All year, especially March–May and September–October.

This spectacular rocky limestone peninsula, ending at Cabo Formentor, juts out into the Mediterranean. The flora is especially rich, with several endemics and rarities. Red Peony (*Paeonia cambessedesi*) flowers in April,

THE BALEARIC ISLANDS

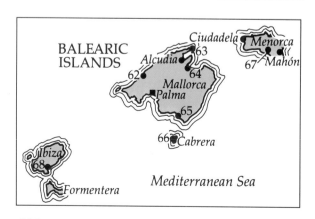

Spring flowers near Puerto de Pollença.

and the St John's Wort *Hypericum balearicum*, *Senecio rodriguezii*, *Erodium reichardii* and the Foxglove *Digitalis dubia* thrive. Dwarf Fan Palm is common, as are many other Mediterranean coastal or scrub species. Among the birds breeding here are the lovely Eleonora's Falcon, Marmora's, Subalpine, Melodious and Dartford Warblers and Blue Rock Thrush. The headland is a good place to watch passing seabirds, occasional raptors and Dolphin.

The beautiful and unspoilt **Boquer Valley**, cutting across the base of the peninsula from Puerto de Pollença to the north coast, has fine flowers, birds and reptiles. The beach is great for swimming or looking at seashore life.

64. Albufera Marsh Nature Reserve (Mallorca)

Location: Near the coast south of Puerto de Alcudia.
Access: Signed from the C712, with access on foot-trails. Permits must be obtained from the Reception Centre (open 9am–7pm in summer and 9am–5pm October–March).
Timing: All year; April–June probably best.

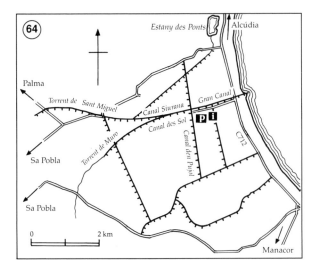

An important 800ha marshland nature reserve known also as S'Albufera. Trails radiate from the reception centre and car park at Sa Roca, and there are good hides. Hundreds of pairs of marshland warblers – e.g., Great Reed and Moustached – breed, as do Marsh Harrier, Purple Heron, Little Bittern and many other species. Osprey, Black Tern, Spoonbill and Red-footed Falcons are among the scores of regular visitors. The flowers are quite good, especially if the adjacent sandy and wooded areas are included: there are good orchids, many dune plants and, by the car park, plenty of Squirting Cucumber.

65. Salinas de Levante Area (Mallorca)

Location: Just west of the southernmost point of the island.

Access: The PM604 and other good minor roads into the area; access to private areas permitted only on working days.
Timing: All year.

An area of saltpans, lagoons and coastal marshes, known also as Lagunas de Salobrar de Campos. The area is important for passage and wintering birds, especially waders. Numerous Black-winged Stilt, Avocet, Kentish Plover, Little Egret and Night Heron breed, and raptors like Osprey and Marsh Harrier appear regularly. The surrounding drier agricultural land has good breeding populations of birds like Hoopoe, Bee-eater, Stone Curlew and Great Grey and Woodchat Shrikes.

To the southeast, at **Cabo Salinas**, the island's southernmost point, looking across the straits to Isla de Cabrera (site 66), there are high limestone cliffs with good flowers and views of seabirds.

66. Isla de Cabrera

Location: Just south of the southern tip of Mallorca.
Access: By boat from Colonia Santa Jordi (Mallorca); exploration permits from the Tourist Office in Palma (Mallorca).
Timing: Spring to late summer.

This small island, used for military training, is under consideration as a reserve or National Park. It is important for breeding seabirds, especially Cory's and Manx Shearwaters, Storm Petrel, Shag, Eleonora's Falcon, Audouin's Gull and a pair of Osprey. The boat trip to the island offers the chance of good views of some of these, and you may well also see Dolphins and Whales. On the island itself, a Cabrera subspecies of Lilford's Wall Lizard is abundant and tame. There is good snorkelling to be had in the clear coastal waters near the landing area.

67. Menorca

Location: About 30km east of Mallorca.
Access: By air, or by ferry from Mallorca or the mainland.
Timing: All year; best March–June.

Although much smaller and less diverse than Mallorca, with poorer flora and fauna, Menorca holds much of interest. Good habitats include coastal limestone and acid cliffs, coastal marshlands, rocky beaches and maquis scrub. There are Balearic and specifically Menorcan flowers, including *Paeonia cambessedessii* (as on Mallorca), Menorcan Loosestrife, the shrubby *Daphne rodriguezii* and *Hypericum balearicum*. On the east side, at the reserve near El Grao, there are good bird areas and a marsh called Albufera; there are further good sites for birds near Son Bou on the south coast. The reptiles are especially interesting – Lilford's Wall Lizard, Moroccan Rock Lizard (originally introduced) and Italian Wall Lizard.

68. Ibiza

Location: About 85km southwest of Mallorca.
Access: By air, or by ferry from Mallorca.
Timing: All year; best spring.

This small island, composed mainly of limestones and well wooded, has a rich flora containing attractive species like the orchid *Ophrys bertolonii*, Chaste Tree and Barbary Nut. Its birds include Audouin's Gull and many migrants. The Ibiza Wall Lizard dwells here (and on Formentera, the island just south). Good areas include the cove and headland at Aubarca, on the north coast, and the saltpans at the southern tip.

   Formentera, much smaller, has some good limestone cliffs, dunes near La Mola and saltpans at the northern point.

THE CANARY ISLANDS

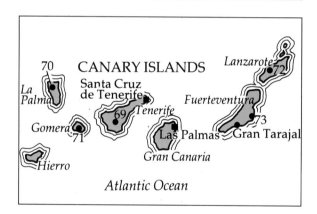

The extraordinary peak of El Teide dominates the island of Tenerife.

Tenerife (site 69) and is more forested (with Canary Laurel and pine). Flowers of interest in the park include the Bugloss *Echium gentianoides*, *Viola palmensis* and *Pterocephalus porphyranthus*.

71. Garajonay National Park (Gomera)

This covers about 10 per cent of Gomera, a small and relatively undeveloped island west of Tenerife. The area is heavily wooded with laurel, and the forests have the characteristic species associated with that tree: Laurel and Long-toed Pigeons, numerous ferns and a good insect fauna.

72. Lanzarote

The island that is closest of the group to the African coast, this has the most desert-like character. The **Timanfaya National Park** protects a substantial area of lava flows on the west side. Large areas of the interior remain unspoilt; the best area for flowers is on the **Famara Ridge** (to 700m) at the island's northern end. The animal life is very limited, though there is an interesting large lizard, *Lacerta atlantica*, on the lava flows and elsewhere. Immediately north of the Famara Cliffs, the Graciosa group of islets forms the **Graciosa Natural Park**. Like Fuerteventura (site 73), Lanzarote is excellent for diving and snorkelling.

73. Fuerteventura

The most interesting areas on this island are the dunes and hills of the **Jandía Peninsula**, at the southwestern end, and the **Corralejo dune complex** in the far north, where there is a rich flora with many endemics. Like Lanzarote, Fuerteventura is excellent for diving and snorkelling.

69. Tenerife

The major island of the group, this is volcanic in origin and dominated by the extraordinary El Teide (3710m), the highest peak in the islands and, indeed, higher than anything on mainland Spain. The **Cañadas del Teide National Park** encompasses the huge caldera, a wholly volcanic landscape that is home to many endemic plants, including the Bugloss *Echium wildpretii*, with impressive spikes that can reach 2m, *Cistus osbeckifolius* and *Centaurea arguta*; the highest part of the cone has the endemic Pansy *Viola cheiranthifolia*. The mammals and birds are rather sparse, although Blue Chaffinch, Canary Pipit and Barbary Partridge are found in the park or in the lower woods.

70. National Park of the Caldera de Taburiente (La Palma)

This is at the centre of the island of La Palma. Of volcanic origin, the island has a higher rainfall than

ANDORRA

Andorra, with an area of only 468 sq km and a government that is effectively a coalition of Spanish and French interests, has recently developed as a low-duty area and ski-resort, and its roads and mountains are increasingly busy. It has no National Parks or major nature reserves, and its wilder mountains are being

Andorra has no major nature reserves but there are some fine areas for walkers and botanists. LEFT: Spring Crocus splashed across a mountain pasture above Soldeau. RIGHT: Alpenroses in high altitude Black Pine forest.

spoilt by ski-related developments, but the flora and fauna – fairly typical of the central-eastern Pyrenees, with more affinities to Spanish species than to French – as yet remain good. Virtually all the mountain country along the French border and around the Pic de Casamanya is superb for serious walking, while further south there is some fine country towards Pics del Pessons and the border with Spain.

The road over the Pas de la Casa (an unattractive ski resort) and the Port d'Envalira (2407m) offers direct access to superb mountain pastures, with good flowers and insects. North of Soldeu, a track runs into the mountains up an attractive and flowery valley which is well worth a visit. Further west, the roads from Andorra La Vella up to Arinsal, or to El Serrat and beyond, pass through a fine variety of mountainous country, eventually reaching high altitudes. If you can get away from the worst development areas you can see a fine range of Pyrenean birds, mammals, flowers and insects, and everywhere large raptors like Golden and Short-toed Eagles and Peregrine Falcon.

ITALY

Italy has an area of 322,460 sq km and a population of over 57 million. Although generally thought of as a peninsular country, it has a substantial area of land north of the peninsula, reaching up to Austria and almost to Germany. Overall, it has a wonderful variety of habitats – the high Alps and the Dolomites, the Apennines further south, extensive areas of limestone, marshes along the coast, many woodlands and some 5000km of varied coastline – and there are its two major Mediterranean islands, Sicily and Sardinia.

Despite popular belief to the contrary, Italy is ornithologically significant, and there is much to interest the visiting birdwatcher: important populations of many coastal birds – e.g., Cory's Shearwater and Slender-billed Gull – as well as substantial numbers of wetland and mountain birds and raptors. The plant life is rich and varied, and includes many endemics. Reptiles and amphibians are especially important, with 62 recorded species, many of them rare and endangered, like Italian Agile Frog, Loggerhead Turtle and Horvath's Rock Lizard.

OPPOSITE PAGE: *The Natural Park of Monte di Portofino covers a delightful stretch of undeveloped coastline.*

It can be difficult to find Italy's nature. Away from the higher mountains the country is much farmed and has many industries, notably tourism. It also has the highest per capita number of hunters of any European country. The five National Parks offer a reasonable degree of protection to habitats, and there are many regional natural parks – of greatly varying quality – and nature reserves, both private and state-owned, which are likewise very variable in their size, importance and degree of accessibility.

Sardinia A large (24,000 sq km) and important island, Sardinia (see page 217) is in most respects quite different from mainland Italy. Predominantly granite, though with outcrops of limestone, it has some moderately high mountain areas and some very wild country, and remains much less developed than most of the mainland. It is a wonderful place to visit, with its many unspoilt habitats and its vast range of characteristic Mediterranean flowering species, alongside some endemics and rarities. Birds of interest include Marmora's Warbler and Eleonora's Falcon, many of the reptiles are either endemic or shared only with Corsica (see page 139), and there is a substantial population of Mouflon in the central mountains. The only drawback is that widespread hunting decimates many birds and mammals outside the protected areas – and can make matters very unpleasant for the visitor.

Sicily The largest Mediterranean island (25,708 sq km), Sicily (see page 219) has a typical Mediterranean climate, although slightly cooler than on some of the Greek islands. Along its north coast is a pronounced spine of limestone mountains – the Madonie and Nebrodi ranges – with the active volcano Etna (3323m) in the east; all three areas are nature reserves, but hunting takes a sad toll of the birds, especially the raptors. In spite of extensive grazing, the island has a rich flora – especially at the roadsides, off which the shepherds wisely keep their flocks.

1. Gran Paradiso National Park

Location: About 15km south of Aosta, near the French border.
Access: By minor roads from Aosta; unrestricted on foot.
Timing: April–October.

Italy's oldest and most famous National Park, covering 730 sq km of superb Alpine country and rising to 4061m at Gran Paradiso. Geologically very diverse, the park has a wide range of habitats, including spruce, pine and larch woodlands, lakes, Alpine pastures, cliffs and snowfields. Among the flowers are gentians, bellflowers, various primula species, Martagon Lily, Black Vanilla Orchid and the whole range of Alpine and coniferous-wood species. The birds include all you might expect, notably Golden Eagle (6–8 pairs), Rock Partridge, Eagle Owl (4–6 pairs), Alpine Chough and Black Woodpecker. The most famous mammal is Ibex, now abundant – the park is credited with having ensured Ibex's survival throughout the Alps. Chamois, Marmot and Mountain Hare are among the other mammals, while the prolific butterflies include Apollo, Peak White and Southern White Admiral.

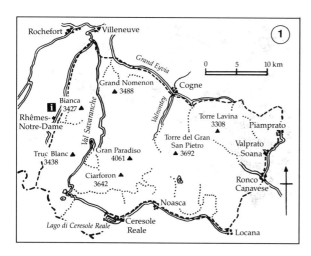

Gran Paradiso National Park protects some superb Alpine country.

The park is adjacent to France's Vanoise National Park (see page 133). The whole area holds considerable interest, although, on the Italian side outside the protected areas, hunting pressure is severe.

2. Alpe Veglia

Location: About 15km southeast of Brig (Switzerland) and east of the Simplon Pass.
Access: Minor road from Bertonia; unrestricted on foot.
Timing: May–October.

A small protected area high in the Alps. The valley has larch forests and extensive Alpine pastures. The mammals include Chamois, Beech Marten and Mountain Hare, and among the birds are Golden Eagle (occasional), Alpine Chough, Ptarmigan and Alpine Accentor. Flowers abound: gentians, primulas, Cowslip and Oxlip, saxifrages, Spring Crocus, etc. The whole region is fine walking country and of great interest, although unprotected areas tend to be heavily shot over.

3. Stelvio National Park

Location: Just northeast of Tirano, on the Swiss border.
Access: The SS38 and minor roads run through the park; unrestricted access on foot.
Timing: April–October.

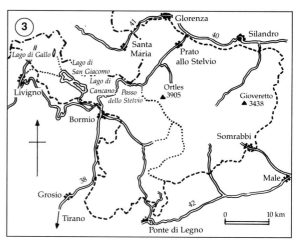

This superb Alpine area (over 1370 sq km), reaching 3905m at Ortles and lying partly alongside the Swiss National Park (see page 152), contains extensive stretches of coniferous woodland, Alpine pasture, cliffs and lakes, plus Italy's largest glacier. The mixture of rock types and an altitude range of 350m–3905m make for an ample flora, including high Alpines like the Dwarf Rampion *Phyteuma humile*, several gentians, Sticky Primrose and endemics like *Saxifraga vandellii* and *Primula daonensis*; lower down are pasque-flowers, orchids, Martagon Lily and many others. The butterflies include Apollo and Dark Green Fritillary, and among the mammals of interest are Ibex (introduced), Roe and Red Deer and Marmot. Over 130 species of birds have been recorded, including Golden Eagle, Eagle Owl, Hazel Grouse, Rock Partridge, Black Woodpecker and Alpine Chough, many in abundance.

4. Adamello-Brenta Natural Park

Location: Straddling the SS239 about 25km northwest of Trento.
Access: Minor roads from the SS239; unrestricted on foot.
Timing: May–October.

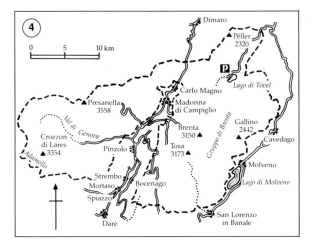

A beautiful mountain area, relatively undisturbed, with peaks reaching over 3000m and large areas of native coniferous woodland, Alpine pastures, cliffs and some lakes. The birds are of great interest: Golden Eagle, Honey Buzzard, Hazel Grouse, Ptarmigan, Capercaillie, Tengmalm's and Eagle Owls and many forest species. The flora is varied, with high-Alpine species plus many old-coniferous woodland flowers like One-flowered Wintergreen and Dutchman's Pipes.

5. Natural Park of Panaveggio-Pale di San Martino

Location: About 40km southeast of Bolzano-Bozen, around the Rolle Pass.
Access: From the SS50 and minor roads; unrestricted on foot.
Timing: April–October.

A beautiful area of the Dolomites, largely on calcareous rock but with some acid; the two rock types meet at the Rolle Pass to give an interesting mixture of flowers. The park's habitats include extensive coniferous forest, lakes, Alpine pasture, cliffs and high mountains (to over 3000m). The flora is rich and often spectacular, including Dolomite specialities like Dolomite Bellflower, the yellow Poppy *Papaver rhaeticum* and *Primula tyrolensis*. The more acid rock supports fine

displays of Arnica, plus Small White Orchid, rampions, Bearberry and heathers. Golden Eagle, Eagle Owl, Capercaillie, Black and Hazel Grouse, several woodpeckers and many other birds breed, and Chamois, Marmot and Red Deer are found.

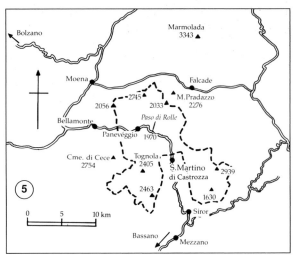

Alpine meadow with Arnica, on the Rolle Pass, Panaveggio-Pale di San Martino.

6. Cortina Dolomites

Location: To the north of Cortina d'Ampezzo.
Access: The SS51, SS49/E68 and numerous others traverse the area; access on foot generally unrestricted. A toll road leads to the Tre Cime de Laváredo.
Timing: April–October.

This arc of mountains includes some of the finest of the Dolomites; there is a series of protected areas, from **Puex Odle Park** in the west to **Dolomiti di Sesto (Sextener-Dolomiten)** in the east. The area around the **Tre Cime de Laváredo (Drei Zinnen)** is particularly spectacular and rich in wildlife. The flora is magnificent, in terms of both abundance of flowers and range of species, with plants

A beautiful pink Cinquefoil clings to a rocky slope high in the Cortina Dolomites.

like the beautiful pink Cinquefoil *Potentilla nitida* and the yellow Poppy *Papaver rhaeticum*, plus gentians, saxifrages and louseworts. Among the birds are Alpine Chough, Golden Eagle, Crossbill, Capercaillie, Eagle Owl and many other forest and Alpine species. Red and Roe Deer, Marmot, Wild Boar, Red Squirrel and Chamois are found in the area, and the lakes – e.g., the small Lago di Antorno – have interesting dragonflies.

Northwest of Merano, running up to the Austrian border, the **Texel-Gruppe Natural Park** is another good Dolomite area.

7. Fusine Natural Park

Location: In the Julian Alps about 20km southwest of Villach (Austria), close to the Slovenian border.
Access: A minor road leads into the park; unrestricted on foot.
Timing: April–October.

This small (450ha) but beautiful Natural Park is almost contiguous with Slovenia's Triglav National Park (see page 222). The centrepoint is the glacial lake of Fusini, with some superb Dolomite peaks immediately to its south (out of the park area). The area has a fine cross-section of Dolomites wildlife, with a rich flora, good butterflies, Golden Eagle, Capercaillie, Chamois, Beech Marten and much else of interest.

The adjacent **Tarvisio Forest** – protected to varying extents – has a rich natural history. Bear are believed to be still in the area.

8. Mouth of the River Isonzo/Foci dell'Isonzo

Location: Just southwest of Monfalcone.
Access: Minor roads traverse the area; open access on foot to some parts.
Timing: All year.

These estuarine and marine habitats around the mouth of the River Isonzo, with mudflats, sandflats and lagoons, are partly protected as reserves. Marsh Harrier, Grey and Purple Herons, various marshland warblers

and other birds breed. The area is particularly good in winter, when there are large numbers of wildfowl and waders, like Curlew and Velvet and Common Scoters. Unusually for southern Europe, Eider are found.

Just to the west lies the **Laguna di Grado**, a large tidal lagoon.

9. Argentera Natural Park

Location: In the Maritime Alps, on the French border some 30km southwest of Cúneo.
Access: By minor roads from Cúneo; unrestricted on foot.
Timing: April–October.

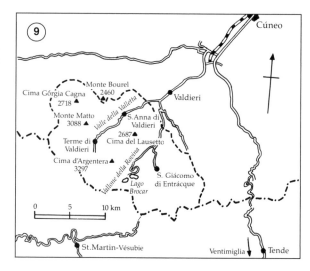

Large Pinks, one of many species among the Argentera's splendid flora.

A beautiful high mountain area running up to the border, where it adjoins part of France's Mercantour National Park (see page 139). The Argentera's splendid flora includes many Maritime Alps specialities like those on the French side. Golden Eagle, Lammergeier (recently reintroduced on both sides of the border), Alpine Chough and many other birds dwell here, and Ibex and Chamois are common. The whole region is superb walking country.

10. Mezzola Lake

Location: The northern tip of Lake Como.
Access: The SS36 runs along the lake's east shore.
Timing: All year.

This lake and its associated marshy areas, where the River Mera and a minor stream flow into it, offer good territory for marshland and wetland birds, with breeding Purple Heron, Marsh Harrier and Water Rail; Honey Buzzard and Golden Eagle are found nearby. This is also a good place for waterfowl on migration or in winter, including up to 50 Ferruginous Duck on passage.

11. Monte di Portofino Natural Park

Location: On the coast about 30km east of Genoa (Génova), just south of Santa Margherita Lígure.
Access: Minor roads to San Rocco or Portofino; unrestricted on foot.
Timing: All year; best March–June.

One of the few pieces of undeveloped land along this stretch of coast. The hilly peninsula has areas of beech, Sweet Chestnut and Strawberry Tree forest, plus Hop Hornbeam and other trees. Among the many flowers are *Orchis patens* (rare elsewhere in the region), Short-spurred Orchid, Hepatica, Scorpion Vetch, Maidenhair Fern and *Anemone trifolia*, with an attractive mixture of Mediterranean, northern and Atlantic species. There are also interesting lichens on the bare limestone or conglomerate – e.g., *Toninia*

The hilly Portofino peninsula supports an attractive mixture of Mediterranean, northern and Atlantic plant species.

caeruleonigricans. The birds include Hobby and Sparrow-hawk, the reptiles Ocellated Lizard (at the eastern end of its range), Italian Wall Lizard (at the western end of its range) and geckoes. Wild Boar, Red Squirrel and Beech Marten represent the mammals.

12. Lake Superiore di Mantova

Location: Immediately west of Mantova.
Access: The SS10 runs past the site's south; access on foot is variable, but easy in places from minor roads.
Timing: All year.

An important wetland complex, including the lake and associated habitats up the Mincio Valley, partly protected as a nature reserve and Ramsar site. Among the habitats are marshes, canals, open water, reedbeds and woodland; Purple Heron, Little Bittern, Marsh Harrier, Little Crake, Kingfisher, Garganey and various wetland warblers breed. In winter various ducks, Bittern and Cormorant spend time here.

13. Gulf of Venice (Laguna di Venezia)

Location: All around Venice.
Access: By minor roads and by boat.
Timing: All year.

A great stretch of coastal lagoon with associated mudflats, saltmarshes and open waters of variable salinity; most is unprotected and suffers pollution and disturbance, but it still retains a rich bird fauna, with Little Egret, Black-winged Stilt, Avocet, Purple and Night Herons, Marsh Harrier, Kingfisher and many others breeding and large numbers of waterfowl, grebes, coots and gulls to be seen in winter.

East of Venice, the **Valle Zignano** lagoon near Caorle is likewise of interest, as is the **Marano Lagoon**, further east, which is a Regional Park.

14. Po Delta

Location: About 80km northeast of Bologna.
Access: Numerous minor roads thread the area, and the SS309 passes by the site's west side; in some parts access is limited.
Timing: All year.

The Po Delta is bounded by Ravenna in the south, Ferrara in the west and Venice in the north. Much has been reclaimed for agricultural use, but large tracts of wetland habitat remain. At the south end, on either side of the River Lamone, 13km north of Ravenna, the **Punte Alberete Reserve** (run by the WWF) is the breeding place for a great many birds including Little Egret, Purple, Common and Night Herons and occasional Glossy Ibis. The flowers include Water-lily, Lax-flowered Orchid and Greater Water Parsnip, and among the butterflies are Large Copper.

Further north, there are areas of interest on the salt-pans and lagoons south of Comácchio, with the **Valle**

Little Egret displaying breeding plumage, Po Delta.

Bertuzzi (another lake) and the nature-reserve area of the **Forest of Mesola**. North and east of this, the newest part of the delta is contained within the **Natural Park of Delta Padano**, which includes many habitats of interest.

15. Lake Massaciuccoli and Surrounds

Location: About 20km north of Pisa, within a triangle of motorways.

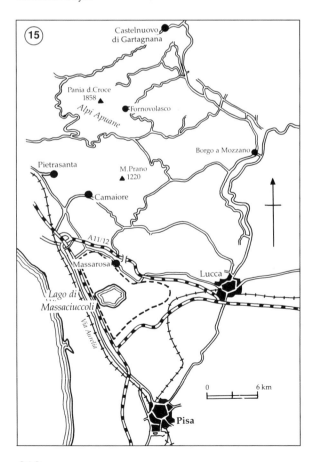

Access: By minor roads from the east; within the reserve, walkways give access to hides.
Timing: All year

This large shallow lake and its extensive associated reedbeds and marshes are part of the much larger Natural Park of Migliarino-San Rossore, and form a very important area for birds (partly managed as a reserve by the Italian bird-protection organization LIPU, which has built good hides): about 250 bird species have been recorded, of which about 50 breed – e.g., Bittern, Little Bittern, Purple Heron, Black-winged Stilt, Moustached and Cetti's Warblers and Marsh Harrier. In winter there are good numbers of ducks, plus terns, gulls and other waterfowl on passage. The aquatic flora is rich, and the surrounding marsh has Common Sundew (rare in Italy). The area is also good for amphibians and dragonflies.

About 20km northeast lies the start of a superb area of the Apennines, the **Natural Park of Alpi Apuane**, running northwards as far as Monte Pisanino (1945m), with some parts protected as strict nature reserves. The park has good breeding birds of prey – Eagle Owl and others. Just north again, around the village of **Corfino** (15km north of Castelnuovo di Garfagnana), is a superb protected mountain area with laid-out walks and a rich flora.

16. Bolgheri Wildlife Refuge

Location: South of Cécina, close to the coast.
Access: By minor road from Cécina; walkway to site.
Timing: All year.

An area of coastal habitats – dunes, marshes, reedbeds, open water, etc. – partly managed by the WWF as a reserve with access and hides. Purple and Night Herons, Black-winged Stilt and other birds breed, numerous birds visit on passage, and many ducks winter here. This is also a good place to see mammals, some quite tame – Crested Porcupine, Wild Boar, Roe Deer, Pine Marten and Otter. Reptiles of interest include Hermann's Tortoise and Pond Terrapin.

17. Valle del Farma

Location: About 35km south of Siena, close to Lamalesa.
Access: By the SS223 to Lamalesa, and then by tracks; unrestricted access on foot.
Timing: Best March–August.

An extensive hilly wooded area around the valley of the River Farma. The woods are very mixed, with different trees according to aspect and soil. This is a good area for birds of prey, including Honey Buzzard, Black and Red Kites, Short-toed Eagle, Montagu's Harrier, Lanner Falcon and Eagle Owl. Alpine Newt is found here, unusually far south.

18. Maremma Natural Park

Location: On the coast about 15km south of Grosseto; just north of site 19.
Access: A minor road from Spergoláia reaches the coast at Marina di Alberese; buses from Alberese go right into the park (Wednesdays and weekends only); unrestricted access on foot.
Timing: All year; best March–July.

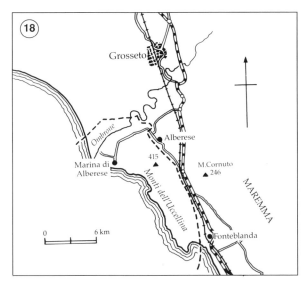

An attractive protected area (7000ha), largely unspoilt, combining low limestone hills (to 415m) with coastal marshland and dunes. Short-toed Eagle, Peregrine, Wryneck, Hoopoe, Woodchat, Lesser Grey and Red-backed Shrikes, Roller and many other birds breed, and the reptiles include Hermann's Tortoise and good snakes and lizards. Crested Porcupine (probably a Roman introduction), Wild Boar, Pine Marten and a fine local breed of Long-horned Cattle are among the mammals. There is a good range of dune flowers like Sea Daffodil, Sea Bindweed, numerous asphodels and a few orchids, and the scrub on the hills is home to various other flowers.

Marshland in Maremma Natural Park.

19. Orbetello and Monte Argentario

Location: On the coast about 100km northwest of Rome (Roma); just south of site 18.
Access: Minor roads run through area; Argentario is generally open, but the WWF reserve at Orbetello is open only on Thursdays and Sundays.
Timing: All year; best March–June.

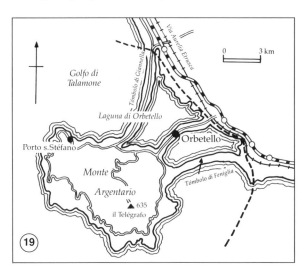

The rocky promontory of Argentario and the lagoons around Orbetello make an attractive combination. Part of the northern lagoon is a WWF reserve, and the protection has dramatically increased the numbers of resident birds. Little Egret, Black-winged Stilt, Montagu's and Marsh Harriers, Stone Curlew, Bee-eater and numerous warblers breed, and another range of birds – e.g., Hoopoe and Sardinian Warbler – populates the sandbar south of the lagoons and the scrub on Argentario, while there are abundant and varied migrant and wintering birds on the lagoons. The flora is less spectacular, but has a good range of coastal and Mediterranean species like Grape Hyacinth, Star of Bethlehem and Sand Crocus. Argentario is a good area for orchids, notably Provence Orchid and a local variant of Late Spider Orchid (*Ophrys holoserica exaltata*).

A few kilometres southeast, close to the shore, the freshwater **Lago di Burano** is another important site for breeding and visiting birds.

20. Vico Lake Nature Reserve

Location: About 60km northwest of Rome (Roma), a few kilometres east of Vetralla.
Access: Minor roads encircle the lake; there is ample parking and unrestricted access on foot.
Timing: All year.

A nature reserve comprising a volcanic lake with marshes plus the wooded slopes of the crater to the north and east. The lake is an important bird site, with breeding Little Bittern, Kite, Great Crested Grebe,

Kingfisher and Marsh Harrier. In winter there are good numbers of waterfowl, including a few Red-crested Pochard. Among mammals of interest are Fat Dormouse, Wild Boar, Wildcat and Crested Porcupine, and there is a good selection of marshland and old-woodland plants like the pretty blue *Anemone apennina*, Bird's Nest Orchid and Alpine Squill.

The larger **Lago di Bracciano**, about 15km south, is of some interest, though much more disturbed and with a less good marginal habitat.

21. Abruzzo National Park

Location: About 110km due east of Rome (Roma), in the high Apennines.

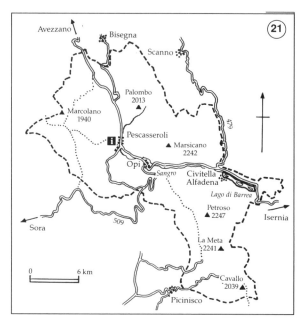

Abruzzo National Park, one of the best areas in Europe for naturalists.

Access: The SS83 and several other roads run through the park; access is generally unrestricted.
Timing: Fascinating all year; difficult November–March.

It is impossible to do justice to this superb wooded mountainous region, one of the finest areas for the naturalist in Europe yet little known outside Italy. There are over 1200 flowers, 300 birds, 40 mammals and 30 reptiles and amphibians – and all amid exceptional scenery! The mammals include small populations of Brown Bear and Wolf (which can be seen in an enclosure near Civitella Alfadena or in the Pescasseroli zoo). Golden Eagle, Peregrine, Eagle Owl and many other birds breed. The flowers are too varied to summarize, but there are good high Alpines, the endemic Iris *Iris marsica* and fine orchids – e.g., Lady Orchid, Early Spider Orchid, a species of Lizard Orchid (*Himantoglossum adriaticum*) and Green-winged Orchid.

22. Lake Varano and Lake Lésina

Location: The northwestern Gargano Peninsula.
Access: Roads (including the SS89) and tracks around the sites; partly open on foot.
Timing: All year.

A pair of large lakes, close to the shore and separated from each other by a rocky headland. Lésina, the more interesting and accessible of the two, has a sizeable nature reserve at its eastern end where Bittern, Kingfisher, Marsh Harrier and Great Reed Warbler breed. The lakes are important in winter – with large numbers of ducks, Cormorant and coots – and at passage periods. Though largely afforested, the dunes support quite a good flora, including *Cistus clusii* in one place.

The **Trémiti Islands (Isole Trémiti)**, about 25km offshore and accessible by boat from Térmoli or Rodi Garganico, support some good seabird colonies (with a few Peregrine), but are too disturbed to be outstanding.

23. Gargano Peninsula and Forest of Umbra

Location: On the Adriatic coast to the north of Manfredónia.
Access: Ringed by major roads (A14/E55 and especially SS89), with numerous minor roads; generally unrestricted access on foot.
Timing: Best March–July.

This exceptional place is botanically extremely important, and has good birds and interesting reptiles, too. About 2000 flowers have been recorded on the peninsula, including an extraordinary 61 orchids as well as many rarities and specialities; there are wonderful displays of coastal flowers in the undeveloped sections. Away from the resort areas, everywhere offers something of interest. In the centre, the Foresta d'Umbra has further interesting plants and a selection of breeding birds – e.g., White-backed and Black Woodpeckers,

North coast of the Gargano Peninsula, with Rosemary growing in the foreground.

Short-toed Eagle, Honey Buzzard and Eagle Owl, and possibly Egyptian Vulture nearby – plus mammals including Roe and Fallow Deer and Wild Boar.

24. Salina di Margherita di Savoia

Location: On the Adriatic coast between Manfredónia and Barletta.
Access: Good views from the SS159; access into the reserve is limited.
Timing: All year.

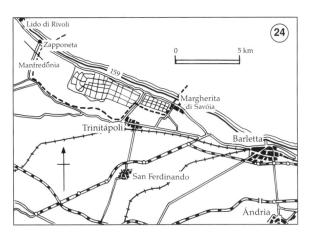

Important for birds at all seasons, this site includes extensive government-owned saltpans (partly a reserve) of varying salinities, plus saltmarshes and grazing land. Black-winged Stilt, Avocet, Little Tern, Kentish Plover, Calandra Lark and others breed, and this is also an important area for passage and winter birds, with large numbers of waders and wildfowl and small groups of Common Crane and Spoonbill.

At **Frattarolo**, 9km south of Manfredónia beside the main SS159, there is a good WWF wetland reserve.

25. Circeo National Park

Location: On the coast about 90km south of Rome (Roma), around Sabaudia.
Access: The SS148 leads to the park, and many roads traverse it; access is unrestricted except in the forest area to the east.
Timing: Interesting all year; best March–June.

Italy's smallest (7450ha) and possibly busiest National Park, straddling an area of desirable beach within striking distance of Rome, protects some of the last remaining Pontine marsh habitat, including lakes, marshes, forest and a rocky limestone promontory culminating in Monte Circeo (541m), as well as Isola Zannone (reached by ferry from Terracina to Ponza, and thence to Zannone), which supports some good seabird-breeding colonies. On the mainland, the marshes and lagoons are good for birds all year; over 230 species have been recorded. The dunes bear a good range of flowers, including Sea Medick, Sea Holly, broomrapes and storksbills, plus an assortment of lizards. Monte Circeo has a rich flora of woodland and scrub species like *Cyclamen repandum*, *Prasium majus*, Strawberry Tree and various orchids. An attractive variety of Italian Wall Lizard is abundant, and the superb Two-tailed Pasha is among the butterflies.

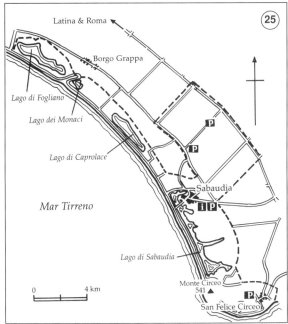

26. Vesuvius

Location: Just southeast of Naples (Napoli).
Access: Minor roads climb towards the top, and there is a cablelift.
Timing: Best April–July.

The great volcanic cone of Vesuvius rises to 1281m. It

has been long enough since the last eruption for good flora and fauna to develop, including the impressive shrubby Mount Etna Broom and the endemic ash-grey lichen *Stereocaulon vesuvianum*, found in abundance. The birds include Rock Thrush, Sardinian and Subalpine Warblers and occasional raptors.

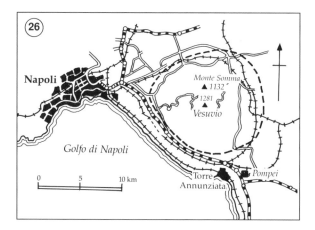

27. Capri

Location: At the southern point of the Bay of Naples.
Access: By ferry from Naples (Napoli) or Sorrento; unrestricted on foot.
Timing: March–September.

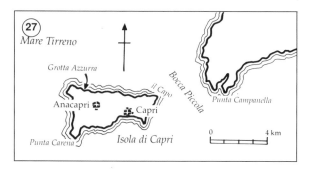

A small limestone island, popular for holidays but retaining much of interest. Peregrine and Manx and Cory's Shearwaters breed around it, and Alpine Swift are found locally; this is also an excellent place to watch passage migrants. Flowers abound, especially in early spring; the extensive list includes orchids – e.g., Early Spider Orchid varieties, Pink Butterfly Orchid and *Orchis italica* – and Sand Crocus. Among the butterflies is the Cleopatra.

28. Lattari Peninsula

Location: The southern arm of the Bay of Naples.
Access: Many minor roads across the hills; access on foot is generally open.
Timing: Best March–May.

A range of limestone hills forms the peninsula.

Despite much tourism and a good deal of agriculture in the interior, the flora is still very rich, especially among the orchids – aside from many widespread species there are local specialities like the *oxyrrhynchos* and *exaltata* variants of Late Spider Orchid and the Early Spider Orchid subspecies *sicula*. Among many other garrigue/scrub plants are *Arisarum proboscideum* and the very rare fern *Woodwardia radicans*. The reserve of **Vallone del Ferriere**, above Amalfi, is especially recommended. The scrub birds include Sardinian Warbler.

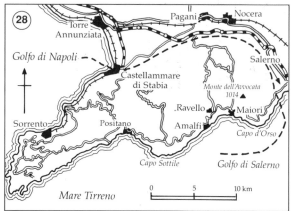

Italian Wall Lizard seen in the Lattari Peninsula.

29. Le Cesine

Location: On the coast near Lecce, in Italy's 'heel'.
Access: By the SS611 and track.
Timing: All year.

A large coastal lagoon and associated habitats, managed as a reserve by the WWF. Black-winged Stilt, Gull-billed Tern and others breed here, but the area's particular importance is as a staging post for a huge

216

variety of migrants. The flora, too, is rich, with 320 species recorded.

30. Monte Pollino Regional Park

Location: To the north of Castrovíllari, Calabria.
Access: By minor roads from Mormanno and from the north; largely unrestricted on foot.
Timing: April–October.

This beautiful, forested, deep-gorged mountain area, a proposed National Park since 1971 and partly protected by nature reserves, includes the highest bits of the southern Apennines. Birds breeding here include Golden and Short-toed Eagles, Black and Red Kites, Honey Buzzard, Lanner and Peregrine Falcons, Eagle Owl and many more; the gorge of Raganello is particularly good for raptors. There is a small area of Bosnian Pine, and the generally rich flora includes Alpine species. Among the mammals are Wild Boar, Otter, Crested Porcupine and Wildcat.

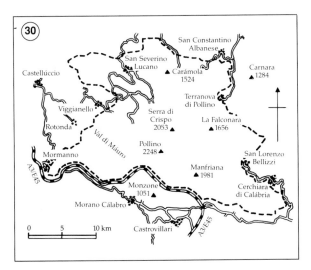

31. Calabria National Park

Location: In the 'toe' of Italy between Rossano and Catanzaro.
Access: Major and minor roads traverse the area; unrestricted on foot.
Timing: All year; best April–July.

Declared a National Park in 1968, with boundaries drawn in 1978 to cover 13,452ha, this is still not properly protected. Nevertheless, a large area of high-quality and very varied wooded mountainous habitat remains, in three separate blocks. Predominantly granite and mica-schist rocks sustain fine forests of larch, beech, Silver Fir and a mixture of other trees. The flowers in the acid areas are moderately good. Asp Viper and the local Spectacled Salamander are among the reptiles. Birds breeding here include Honey

Buzzard, Kites, Short-toed Eagle, Lanner Falcon and Black Woodpecker, while the mammals include a few Wolf, Wildcat, Beech Marten, Forest Dormouse and various deer.

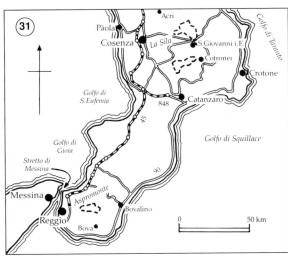

SARDINIA

32. Maddalena Archipelago

Location: Just off Palau, near Sardinia's northern tip.
Access: By ferry from Palau.
Timing: April–August.

These partly inhabited islands, as yet unprotected, have important seabird colonies and good scrubland birds. Here you can find Cory's and Manx Shearwaters, Audouin's Gull, Shag, Peregrine Falcon, Common Tern, Marmora's Warbler and others. There is also good seashore life, and you can get fine views of birds at sea from the boat and from the islands themselves.

Capo Testa, just west of Santa Teresa Gallura, has some impressive rock formations and a superb flora (including rarities). **Isola Asinara**, at Sardinia's north-western tip, has some good seabird colonies.

33. Monte Albo Region

Location: South of Siniscóla, just west of the SS131.
Access: A minor road runs along the ridge; unrestricted access on foot.
Timing: April–July.

A fine limestone area, with peaks to 1127m (Monte Albo) and superb gorges and cliffs. Among the birds breeding here are Golden and Bonelli's Eagles, Peregrine Falcon, Griffon Vulture, Raven and Common Chough, plus a few Marmora's Warbler. There are also some Mouflon, but not protected as in Gennargentu (site 34). The rich though well grazed flora includes many orchids, peonies and the local version of Sea Daffodil, *Pancratium illyricum*, which flowers in spring.

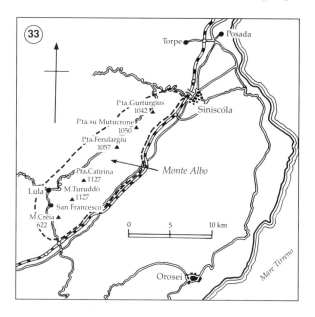

34. Gennargentu

Location: In the central mountains, within the trapezium formed by Nuoro, Dorgali, Lanusei and Láconi.
Access: Many roads (e.g., SS295, SS198) cross the area; largely unrestricted on foot.
Timing: April–October.

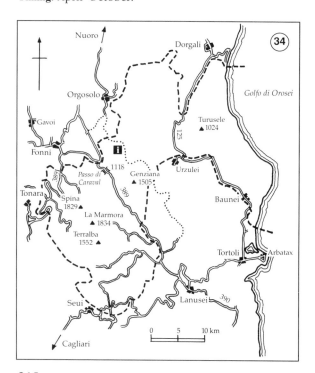

An impressive, wild, partly wooded mountain area – perhaps the finest wilderness in Italy. The park – still not formally declared or protected – also includes some rugged coastland. The extensive woodlands are of Holm Oak and pine, and the moorland, scrub and mountain habitats reach almost 2000m. A large herd of Mouflon thrives within an area officially protected from grazing by domestic animals. Golden and Bonelli's Eagles, Goshawk, Griffon and Egyptian Vultures and good numbers of Eleonora's Falcon breed, and along the coast are some sizeable colonies of Manx and Cory's Shearwaters and Audoin's Gull. The Tyrrhenian Swallowtail Butterfly occurs. The flora contains many acid woodland and scrub species, but some of the limestone areas are also of special botanical interest, especially at Monte Novo San Giovanni (1316m). There is an information centre and animal enclosure at Funtana Bona.

The area around the Bay of Orosei is exceptionally good for reptiles and amphibians, and has been proposed as a special reserve for their conservation. Among the 18 species recorded here (out of a total of 25 known in Sardinia) are European Leaf-toed Gecko, Sardinian Cave Salamander, Tyrrhenian Painted Frog and, offshore, Loggerhead Turtle.

35. Sinis Peninsula and Gulf of Oristano

Location: To the south and west of Oristano, on the west coast.

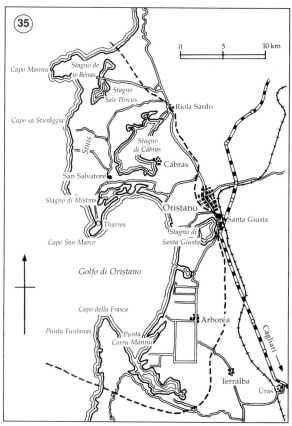

Access: Many minor roads; ample access on foot.
Timing: All year.

Of international importance, this superb complex of wetlands covers a large area. Aside from the saltpans scattered throughout the area, key sites are: the large lagoons of **Cabras** and **Mistras**, west of Oristano; the LIPU (Italy's bird society) reserve at **Sale Porcus Lake**, by the coast northwest of Oristano; and the lakes of **San Giusta**, **S'Ena Arrúbia** and others to the south. Birds breeding here include Bittern, Little Bittern, Purple Heron, Red-crested Pochard, Marsh Harrier, Purple Gallinule, Avocet, Black-winged Stilt and many others. A good range of birds, especially wildfowl, winter here, and there are often thousands of Flamingo. The flowers and reptiles on the dunes and on the peninsula's scrub areas are also interesting. The southern tip of the peninsula, around Tharros, is worth visiting for views of the marine wildlife in its clear warm waters.

36. Giara de Gésturi

Location: About 30km southeast of Oristano, on the SS197 just north of Barúmini.
Access: Unrestricted but roadless; best from Gésturi or Tuili.
Timing: Best April–July.

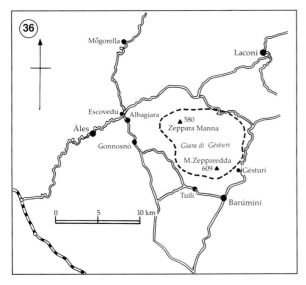

A strange plateau area, reminiscent of parts of western Spain, with Cork Oak among boulder-strewn grassland and some lakes. Little Bustard, Buzzard, Dark Kite, Goshawk, shrikes, Bee-eater, Hoopoe and Golden Oriole breed, and there is a herd of about 200 small 'wild' horses. The rich flora includes 16 orchid species, *Narcissus tazetta* and many other grassland flowers.

The **Altopiano della Campeda**, about 60km north (just south of Bonorva), has similar habitats and breeding birds, including Stone Curlew.

37. San Pietro Island

Location: Off the southwest coast.
Access: By boat from the island of San Antíoco or from Portoscuso; unrestricted on foot.
Timing: March–October.

This small island is inhabited – Carloforte is the main town – and has some tourism, but is still relatively unspoilt. Large areas of Mediterranean scrub sustain a good range of scrub birds – e.g., Marmora's Warbler and Blue Rock Thrush – and reptiles like Western Whip Snake, Tyrrhenian Wall Lizard and Ocellated Skink. The island's highlight, recently acquired by LIPU (the Italian bird-protection organization) as a nature reserve, is the large colony of Eleonora's Falcons around Capo Sandalo and Cala Fico.

38. Cagliari Wetlands

Location: East and west of Cagliari.
Access: Various roads traverse the area; some access on foot.
Timing: Good all year for birds.

Despite the proximity of Sardinia's capital, there are superb wetlands here, especially the lake at Molentargius and the saltpans to Cagliari's west; a large part is classified as a Ramsar wetland. Avocet, Black-winged Stilt, Slender-billed Gull, Little Tern, Gull-billed Tern, Marsh Harrier, Purple Gallinule, Cattle Egret, Little Bittern and many others breed, and the passage and wintering birds are important, with many waders and wildfowl and variable numbers of Flamingo.

A little to the west, the southern region of the **Iglesiente Massif**, especially around Monte Arcosu and Monte Carávius, is protected forest and mountain country, partly a WWF reserve, with good flowers and excellent breeding raptors and vultures.

SICILY

39. Stagnonie di Marsala

Location: On the west coast immediately south of Trápani.
Access: Off the coast road running south from Trápani.
Timing: October–June.

Drainage has destroyed most of Sicily's coastal wetlands, but the Stagnonie di Marsala covers a 10km by 3km area, of which 3700ha is a regional nature reserve with a shallow (about 1m on average) lagoon, saltpans

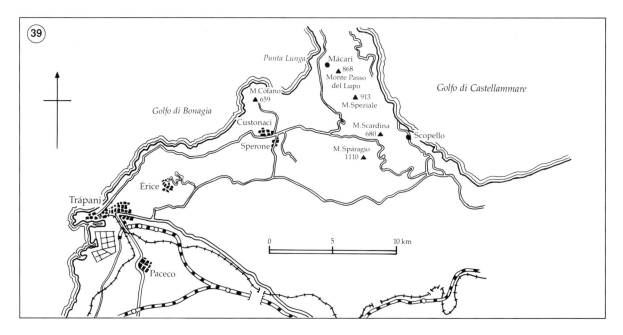

and several islands. The northern part is sheltered from the open sea by Isola Grande. The surroundings are saltmarsh backed by agricultural land. As well as an estimated 21,000 waders there are migrating Spoonbill and large numbers of Garganey. Nesting birds of note are Kentish Plover, Black-winged Stilt and Little Tern.

40. Zingaro

Location: About 8km west of Castellammare del Golfo, near the village of Scopello.
Access: From Scopello (visitor centre).
Timing: April–June.

Part of this unspoilt stretch of coastline was made a reserve in 1980. The area offers diverse habitats – sea-cliffs, stony beaches, sandy beaches and dunelands. Paths lead from the reserve towards Monte Speziale (913m), where numerous orchids grow under the bushes of the garrigue, including the endemic *Ophrys. lunulata*. Dwarf Fan Palm and the intensely blue-flowered *Lithodora rosmariniflora* are spectacular. Fan-tailed Warbler and Cirl Bunting are common, and on the peninsula there are Peregrine Falcon, Golden and Bonelli's Eagles and Rock Partridge.

41. Madonie

Location: South of the coast between Palermo and Cefalù.
Access: South from Cefalù on various roads, or from Palermo on the SS188 via Piana di Albanesi.
Timing: April–October.

Rising to 1979m at Carbonara, south of Cefalù, the Madonie are Sicily's highest mountains after Etna. Ski-resorts are the most recent threat to the area; over-grazing and extensive forest clearance started earlier. High stone-strewn plateaux provide suitable terrain for a wide range of orchids, including the endemic *Ophrys lunulata*, *O. pallida* and *Orchis brancifortii*. Extensive forests remain, but the proximity of Palermo means that hunting has eradicated all but the smallest mammals. The Lago di Piana di Albanesi is one of several large, open-water areas important as resting places for migrants. Breeding raptors in the region include some 4–6 pairs of Red Kite and three pairs of Egyptian Vulture, plus Golden and Bonelli's Eagles and Lanner and Peregrine Falcons.

Flowery slopes in the Madonie, highest mountains in Sicily after Etna.

42. Nebrodi Mountains

Location: Along the north coast west of Messina.
Access: From Cefalù to the north side of the range or, to its south side, from the SS120.
Timing: Spring-autumn for flowers.

A wild limestone region of high, rounded slopes, imposing cliffs and dense, ancient forests of oak and beech, with about 140,000ha designated a Natural Park. Mammals found in the forest include Fox, Marten and Wildcat; large raptors like Red Kite, Golden Eagle and Peregrine breed in the area. In May the open woodlands have a colourful spring flora with Cyclamen, Paeony and a selection of bulbs – *Romulea bulbocodium*, *Crocus vernus*, Grape Hyacinth and *Narcissus tazetta* – plus numerous orchids, including both pink and yellow Roman Orchid (*Dactylorhiza romana*), *Orchis tridentata*, *O. provincialis*, *O. italica* and *O. morio*. Bee Orchids, including the endemic *Ophrys lunulata* and the rare *O. lacaitae*, can be found in open rocky areas that have not been overgrazed.

43. Etna

Location: 30km north of Catánia.
Access: Jeeps and minibuses run to the main crater during April–October.
Timing: Spring for the flowers.

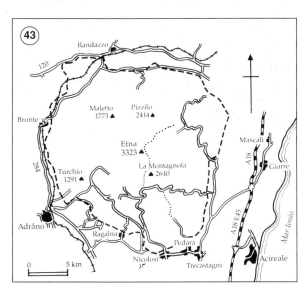

Rising from just above sea-level to 3323m and snow-capped much of the year, Etna is an imposing sight and an obvious tourist attraction. As a giant, isolated lava cone it has numerous endemic plant species: extensive areas are covered in yellow Broom or pink *Astragalus siculus*. The climb to the summit is arduous but botanically fascinating, going from an extensively cultivated lower zone (olives, carobs, vines, figs, oranges) to chestnut and hazel and then to Black Pine, which thins out into beech and Etna Birch; the highest zones harbour little flora other than assorted mosses and lichens. Hunting has severely reduced the numbers of Marten and Porcupine. The birds include Rock Thrush, Rock Partridge and several woodpecker species.

44. Straits of Messina, Monte Peloritani

Location: Between Messina and Réggio di Calábria.
Access: From Messina, via the 114 coast road north and south of the town.
Timing: Mid-April to mid-May.

The straits form a bottleneck through which huge numbers of migrant birds make their way, including Black Stork, Honey Buzzard, Black Kite, Egyptian Vulture, Marsh Harrier, Golden Eagle, Booted Eagle, Red-footed Falcon and Hobby. Depressingly, hunting turns spectacle into tragedy, with raptors faring badly—especially Honey Buzzard (early May): folklore has it that a Calabrian male must shoot one or be cuckolded. Monte Ciccia and the part of Monte Peloritani near Messina form good vantage-points, with a varied terrain of farmland, garrigue, maquis and broad-leaved woodland; several pairs of Red Kite breed.

45. Isole Eólie o Lipari

Location: Off Sicily's northeast coast.
Access: By boat from Milazzo (two hours to Vulcano, the nearest) or, to Stromboli, from Messina.
Timing: All year; best April–October.

The Eólie Isles and rock-stacks – the main islands are Vulcano, Lipari, Salina, Panarea, Stromboli, Filicudi and Alicudi – are essentially scrub-covered volcano tops; Stromboli is still active. They are partly farmed, and there is some tourism. The garrigue and maquis are botanically interesting, but the main attraction is the bird-life. Breeding birds include Dartford Warbler, some 300 Cory's Shearwater, some 8–10 pairs of Peregrine Falcon and, breeding in late summer and feeding on autumn migrants, several colonies of Eleonora's Falcon (20–30 pairs all told).

46. Pantani di Capo Passero

Location: On the southwest coast, 25km south of Noto.
Access: The road from Noto to Pachino leads to the site.
Timing: October–June for resident and migrant birds.

This complex of shallow saltpans, with a surrounding vegetation of Salicornia and reeds, is part of a local and regional nature reserve; it almost dries out in July–September. One major threat – a proposed marina – has been removed, but hunting is a perennial problem. Its status as an EEC Special Protection Area acknowledges its importance for passage waterfowl: Squacco Heron, Little Egret, Glossy Ibis (in spring), Spoonbill, Greater Flamingo, Garganey, Slender-billed and Audouin's Gulls and Gull-billed, Caspian and Black Terns.

YUGOSLAVIA

At the time of writing, the former Yugoslavia is riven by civil war. For the purposes of this book the region is treated largely as if it were still a single nation, although it is unlikely that the territory will ever enjoy that status again. We cannot predict which parts will be protected in the future, or know what damage has already been done to previously protected areas. The information given in this section should therefore be regarded charitably: it is only as accurate, up-to-date and complete as is practical. The term 'Yugoslavia' is sometimes used as a regional description in the text, for convenience.

The area is one of Europe's most exciting for the naturalist – a substantial region of mountainous and varied land almost twice as large as Greece. Its position is strategic, not just culturally but also ecologically: it straddles the distribution areas of Mediterranean, Balkan/Asian and central-European species. Both flora and fauna are rich in species from different distributions and in endemics.

The northern part is mainly low-lying, with extensive plains in the Danube (Dunav) Valley; there is relatively intensive agriculture and the character is akin to Hungary and parts of western Romania. In the far northwest an area of high mountains, rising to 2864m and generally considered part of the Alps, lies adjacent to similar areas in Austria and Italy. The remainder is almost entirely mountainous, or at least hilly, with huge areas of sparsely populated, often forested land on a variety of rock types. The predominant rock is limestone: Yugoslavia is the type area for karst scenery, with extensive limestone pavements, cliffs, gorges and caves.

Although the coast is long and convoluted, with many offshore islands, the width of actual coastal habitat – e.g., grazing marshes or saltmarsh – is generally small. Until recently tourism, concentrated along the Adriatic coast, caused the loss of many remaining coastal habitats, and some of these cannot readily re-form. Inland, especially along the Greek and Albanian borders, there are some important large lakes, several of which are major ornithological sites.

1. Triglav National Park (Slovenia)

West of Bled, on the Austrian and Italian borders, 84,000ha of superb limestone mountain scenery in the Julian Alps, rising to Yugoslavia's highest point at Triglav (2864m). Lower down are extensive beech

Cliffs and forest in stark contrast, Triglav National Park

forests; above them are coniferous forests, Alpine pasture, cliffs, screes, glacial lakes and karst scenery. The lavish flora mixes general Alpine and localized species. The butterflies are notably varied and abundant. Mammals of interest include Ibex, Chamois, Mouflon, Alpine Marmot and Wildcat. Among the breeding birds are Golden Eagle, Ptarmigan and Rock Partridge.

2. Postojna Caves (Slovenia)

Part of a complex cave system under karst landscape. The main cave, about 16.5km long, sustains a specialized cave fauna, most famously the Olm, a virtually blind amphibian, confined to Yugoslavia and one Italian site, which lives and breeds neotenously (in a permanently immature state, retaining external gills).

There are also specialized Crustacea, harvestmen, spiders and moths. The nearby **Pivka and Planina Caves** are also of interest. The whole area has a rich limestone flora.

3. Risnjak National Park (Croatia)

About 40km east-northeast of Rijeka, the park covers 3000ha of fine limestone mountains – rising to 1528m at Risnjak itself – forested with mixed beech and fir, grading into Oriental Hornbeam and Hop Hornbeam and then into Dwarf Pine at the highest levels. The rich flora has many orchids. The mammals include Brown Bear and Wildcat, and the breeding birds Ural Owl (at the edge of its range), Honey Buzzard and Red-breasted Flycatcher.

4. Plitvice National Park (Croatia)

About 100km south of Zagreb, northwest of Bihác, this was Yugoslavia's most famous National Park, 19,000ha of excellent walking country, and formerly visited by vast numbers of people from abroad. The central feature is a string of lakes linked by a series of beautiful waterfalls built up from tufa deposits. The surrounding forests and grasslands are full of interest, with a rich flora. Mammals include Brown Bear, Wild Boar, Otter and many smaller species. Numerous woodpeckers and other forest species breed here.

5. Fruška Gora National Park (Serbia)

Near Novi Sad, about 70km northwest of Belgrade (Beograd), a wooded hilly area along the Danube (Dunav), with an extensive area of natural limewood. There is an ample flora; breeding birds of interest include Black and White Storks, Eagle Owl and Imperial Eagle. To the northwest, just east of Osijek, the extensive marshland area around the confluence of the Danube and Drava is of great ornithological interest.

6. Djerdap National Park (Serbia)

Situated in the Danube (Dunav) Valley from Golubac to Tekija and stretching 100–170km east of Belgrade on the Romanian border, the park protects 64,000ha of the impressive gorge carved here by the Danube; damming for hydroelectricity has produced a long, thin lake, and this is an important area for wetland birds. The rich flora has a distinctly Asian flavour and includes a number of endemics.

7. Paklenica National Park (Croatia)

Just inland from the west coast between Karlobag and Zadar, a 3600ha area of impressive limestone peaks, two gorges and some fine beech, Downy Oak and mixed forests. The woodland flowers are mainly of widespread species, but higher on the rocks are a number of specialists. The breeding birds include Egyptian and Griffon Vultures, various raptors, Blue Rock Thrush and Wall Creeper. A very few Brown Bear (probably), Wild Boar, Red Squirrel and other mammals are found. Immediately north of the park lie the **Velebit Mountains**, a large area of unspoilt, partially wooded limestone mountains, with rich flora and fauna.

8. Kornati National Park (Croatia)

Off the coast south of Zadar, northwest of Split, these limestone islands, 109 of which are significant, scattered over an area of 32,000ha, have marvellous unspoilt karst scenery. Their vegetation is open garrigue with small patches of denser scrub and Holm Oak and olive forest; there is a good bulb flora. Shag, Common Tern, Eleonora's and Peregrine Falcons, Ortolan Bunting and several shrikes breed.

9. Krka National Park (Croatia)

In the valley of the River Krka, running inland for 75km from Sibenik, northwest of Split, this unusually shaped 14,000ha park follows virtually the whole of the river's course. There are superb series of waterfalls over limestone dams, several lakes, deep gorges and extensive woods of Downy and Holm Oak, Hornbeam and Hop Hornbeam. The flora is rich. Golden Eagle and several other raptors breed. A little further north along the coast is the 3000ha **Lake Vrana (Vransko Jezero)**, with a small bird reserve.

10. Mljet National Park (Bosnia)

The western part of Mljet, offshore northwest of Dubrovnik; a wonderfully unspoilt part of the Adriatic. The 3100ha park occupies the whole of Mjlet's hilly western end, which has escaped the deforestation of most of the rest of the Mediterranean coast, and is still almost wholly covered in evergreen forest. The herbaceous flora is quite rich, though characteristically less varied than in cleared areas of garrigue. Introduced Mongoose have seriously depleted the numbers of reptiles though a few remaining species are of interest.

11. Sutjeska National Park (Bosnia)

Between Dubrovnik and Sarajevo, this attractive mountainous wooded park (17,250ha), reaching 2386m at Maglic, contains extensive woodlands, mountain pastures, lakes and waterfalls. The most important part is the strict reserve of Perucica, comprising 1434ha of virgin forest. The flora of the Alpine grasslands is rich and varied. The mammals include Brown Bear, Wolf, Chamois, Roe Deer and Wild Boar. To the northeast, about 50km west of Titovo Užice, the 22,000ha **National Park of Tara** has a good mixture of upland habitats broken by much agricultural land.

Karst region, Sutjeska National Park.

12. Durmitor National Park (Montenegro)

About 85km north of Titograd, along the River Tara near Žabljak, a magnificent 33,000ha tract of country-side comprising a western mountain area, rising to 2522m (Bobotov Kuk), and an eastern 'tail' which follows the spectacular Tara Gorge (over 1000m deep in places). Habitats include glacial lakes, cliffs, extensive forests of oak and conifers, plus a range of karst features. The lavish flora includes some specialities, together with attractive bulbous species and many rock Alpines. Brown Bear live in the area, and the rich breeding-bird community includes Golden Eagle, Capercaillie and Rock Partridge.

13. Biogradska Gora National Park (Montenegro)

The park, about 65km north of Titograd, covers 3400ha of superb mountain country, rising to over 2100m, with stretches of high grasslands and five major natural lakes. The area is largely wooded, including some fine virgin forest of sycamore, beech and ash with a rich beetle and fly fauna and numerous forest birds. The mammals include Wolf, Brown Bear, Red and Roe Deer, Wildcat, Badger and Wild Boar.

14. Lovćen National Park (Montenegro)

To the west of Cetinje, this 2000ha park is generally considered one of the most attractive places in Yugoslavia, with wooded limestone mountains up to 1749m (Štirovnik) and beautiful views of the coast.

The forests have a rich mixture of trees and shrubs. Over 1200 flowering species have been recorded; there are numerous orchids in open areas. Imperial and Golden Eagles, Honey Buzzard, Rock Partridge and Alpine Swift breed. Among the mammals, Beech Marten and Red Squirrel are common.

15. Skadarsko Jezero National Park (Montenegro)

The large, freshwater Lake Skadar (Scutari) is shared with Albania; the Yugoslavian side has about 20,000ha of open water and wetlands, with marshy deltas where rivers enter the lake. It is very important for birds; among the many breeding here are Dalmatian Pelican, Pygmy Cormorant, Whiskered Tern and various herons and wetland warblers; the lake is also good for wintering wildfowl. Bonelli's Eagle and other raptors are found at Morača Gorge, to the north. Amphibians of interest include Common Tree-frog, Agile Frog and the beautiful Green Toad; the water-based Dice Snake is common.

16. Mavrovo National Park (Macedonia)

About 65km southwest of Skopje, close to the Albanian border, Yugoslavia's largest National Park covers just over 73,000ha of beautiful, partly wooded mountainous country, with more than 50 peaks over 2000m and rich flora and fauna throughout. The mammals are particularly good, with Bear together with Wolf, Lynx, Chamois and Roe and Red Deer. Golden, Imperial, Lesser Spotted and Booted Eagles, Egyptian, Griffon and Bearded Vultures and many other birds breed.

17. Galicica National Park (Macedonia)

Between Lakes Ohrid and Prespa, in the extreme south of the country, this is a little-known 23,000ha area of mainly mountainous country at the southern end of the Dinaric Mountains. The forests, largely natural, have an extremely high concentration of different species of woody plants. Birds breeding in the mountain area include many raptors and forest species, and among the resident mammals are a few Bear and Wolf. The two lakes are of great importance for birds, especially in winter. Lake Prespa is shared with Albania and Greece, and is dealt with in more detail on page 230.

18. Pelister National Park (Macedonia)

Northeast of Lake Prespa and west of Bitola. A wooded mountainous area (10,400ha), reaching 2601m at Pelister, with an extensive forest of Macedonian Pine and, above the tree-line, Alpine pastures and glacial lakes. Bear, Wolf and Lynx are present in small numbers. The flora is rich, especially in higher rocky pastures. Breeding birds include raptors and several woodpeckers.

BULGARIA

Bulgaria covers 110,912 sq km in the far southeast of Europe, bounded by Romania, Turkey, Greece and the former Yugoslavia. It is one of the least accessible and least known countries of Europe, and our coverage here can be no more than a sketch.

It is a varied country, with extensive mountainous regions, especially in the south and west, large areas of river-valley plains, and a long coastline on the Black Sea. Thanks to this diversity, and its position in the Balkans, it has a very rich flora and fauna, including a number of endemics. Larger mammals like Wolf and Brown Bear still occur in the wilder areas.

Nature conservation is not well advanced, though some initiatives have been brought forward in the past three years. Sreburna (site 2) and Pirin (site 5) have been declared World Heritage Sites, and a number of biosphere reserves have been established. Visitors are welcome at any of the country's nature reserves; ideally they should obtain advance permits from the Ministry of Environment, 67, William Gladstone Str., BG-1000, Sofia. The south and west are especially rewarding but travel is difficult without your own transport.

Diverse habitats in the Rila Mountains support an exceptionally varied flora and an abundance of interesting bird species.

1. Rusenski Lom National Park

Location: About 20km southeast of Ruse.
Access: Via the E70 and minor roads; access open on foot.
Timing: May–October.

2230ha of valley deciduous forest, with fine Sessile and Turkey Oaks, Silver Lime, hornbeam, beech and others. Eagles, Goshawk, Eagle Owl, Hoopoe and many other birds breed. Wildcat and Roe Deer are resident, and there is a rich flora.

2. Sreburna Reserve

Location: On the Romanian border in the northeast, 18km west of Silistra.
Access: On foot from Sreburna village. Guided tours are available from the visitor centre.
Timing: Good all year; best April–July.

A superb 750ha wetland site, recognized as of international importance. The lake and surrounding wetlands support about 100 breeding bird species, including a good population of Dalmatian Pelican plus Pygmy Cormorant, eight herons, Spoonbill and Glossy Ibis. The area has a rich aquatic and marshland flora, 21 species of reptiles and amphibians and 39 recorded mammals. The site is now being carefully managed in a way befitting its importance.

3. Vitosa National Park

Location: Just south of Sofia.
Access: By minor roads south from the city.
Timing: May–October; busy at weekends and during holiday periods.

A beautiful mountain area (26,500ha), rising to 2290m at Cherni Vrûh, with a marvellous variety of habitats: coniferous and deciduous woodlands, cliffs, screes, glacial lakes, Alpine pastures, bogs and marshes. Easily accessible from Sofia, this is a superb walking area. The rich and varied flora includes specialities like Frivald's Frog Orchid *Pseudorchis frivaldii*, the beautiful Janka Lily *Lilium carniolicum jankae*, the yellow-flowered Columbine *Aquilegia aurea*, and numerous gentians, bellflowers, saxifrages and crocuses. Altogether, over 2600 plants have been recorded and over 120 bird species, including many mountain specialities. Red and Roe Deer and Wild Boar are among the mammals.

4. Rila Mountains

Location: About 70km south of Sofia.
Access: Via route 2 south from Sofia, then east on the 164 to Kocerinovo; Rila Monastery is signed.
Timing: Best May–October.

This huge, marvellous mountain area, not protected by a National Park, has some fine areas of coniferous woodland, deciduous woodland, pastures, upper mountain slopes, lakes, bogs and other montane habitats, notably Bulgaria's highest mountain, Mount Moussala (2925m). The flora is of phenomenal interest, with too many species, both endemic and widespread, to mention individually: there are gentians (e.g., *Gentiana frigida*), orchids (e.g., *Nigritella nigra*), primulas (e.g., *Primula deorum*), saxifrages, pinks, snowbells and many more, often in great abundance. This area is also very fine for birds, with mountain species like Golden and Booted Eagles, Alpine Accentor, Alpine Chough, Rock Nuthatch, Wall Creeper, Shore Lark and many more. Chamois, Red Deer and Brown Bear are resident.

Rila Monastery is a good centre and fascinating in itself. There are scattered ski-resorts (with lifts) and good trails. This area needs time to explore and appreciate.

5. Pirin (Vikhren) National Park

Location: Roughly between Sandanski and Bansko, close to both Greece and Macedonia.
Access: Minor roads off route 279; open on foot.
Timing: April–October.

A superb region of high mountains, rising to 2914m (Vikhren), the park covers 29,500ha, and there are many areas of interest outside this. Extensive woodlands, high pastures, lakes, screes, bogs and other habitats, partly on limestone, contribute to an exceptional flora, rivalling that of the Rila area (site 4). Specialities include *Crocus veluchensis*, *Haberlea rhodopensis*, *Potentilla apenia* – the list includes over 50 endemic to the Balkan region and 20 endemic to Bulgaria, with many in superb displays. The bird list is like that of Rila, though there is more chance of seeing vultures. This is also a good area for butterflies.

Eastwards from here, the mountains along the Greek border, partly known as the **Rhodope Mountains**, are superb.

ALBANIA

Albania, with an area of just under 29,000 sq km, is Europe's least accessible nation; very little is known about its current natural history and the detailed organization of its conservation strategy. Recent events in Eastern Europe and the former Yugoslavia seem only to have enhanced Albania's isolation, and there is little likelihood of its becoming fully opened to visitors in the near future.

For the naturalist, it is – or would be – a very rewarding country to visit. There are extensive forests, several ranges of mountains reaching to over 2000m, a convoluted coastline, and four large natural lakes shared with Greece and/or Macedonia/Montenegro. The flora is rich and varied, though there are probably few species that do not occur in its neighbour countries. Albania's birds and mammals are not well recorded, but there are believed to be significant populations of some of the species that occur in Macedonia and/or northwestern Greece; e.g., Lammergeier, Griffon Vulture, Lesser Kestrel, White-backed Woodpecker, Bear and Wolf.

As far as is known, these are the best sites for seeing wildlife.

1. Lake Shkodra (Skadarsko Jezero)

In the north of the country (by Shkodër), with about 15,000ha in Albania and the rest in Montenegro (see page 224), this lake is important for breeding and visiting birds.

2. Lake Ohrid (Ohridsko Jezero)

About 85km southeast of Tiranë (Tirana), the Albanian part of this lake used to be of as much ornithological interest as the part in Macedonia (see page 224), but agricultural developments are believed to have taken their toll.

3. Lake Prespa (Prespansko Jezero)

Just southeast of site 2, and shared with Greece and Macedonia. Although it is of ornithological importance in the latter two countries – especially Greece (see page 230) – its value in Albania is currently uncertain.

4. Thethi National Park

This 4500ha area of mountains in the north of the country, due south of Ivangrad, has forests of beech and fir and good populations of Bear, Lynx, Chamois and various large raptors.

5. Lura National Park

About 50km northeast of Tiranë (Tirana), this covers 3000ha of mountainous forested area, reaching 2246m at Mal i Dejës. There are good populations of Bear, Lynx and large raptors, including Golden Eagle.

6. Dajtit National Park

3000ha of hilly forested country just north of Tiranë (Tirana), reaching 1612m at Mal i Dajtit.

7. Divjaka National Park

On the coast about 30km southwest of Tiranë (Tirana), this 1000ha park has dunes and coastal woodland. It is closed in winter.

8. Tomorri National Park

About 90km southeast of Tiranë (Tirana) and covering 3000ha of mountainous country, reaching over 2400m. There are extensive forests and high pastures.

9. Llogara National Park

Close to the coast southeast of the Karaburuni Peninsula, 120km south of Tiranë (Tirana), this covers 3500ha and rises to over 1650m. Habitats include pine woodland and pastures on limestone. There is a rich flora; Golden Eagle and other raptors breed.

GREECE

Although it covers only about 132,000 sq km, little over half the area of the United Kingdom, Greece is, to the naturalist, one of the most important and attractive – and most complex – countries in Europe. Apart from the many hundreds of islands (see page 240) – stretching across the Aegean to the Turkish coast, along the Adriatic coast to beyond the borders of Albania, and out as far as Crete in the Mediterranean – the mainland itself is endlessly convoluted and indented, with a coastline over 15,000km long. Greece has very few lowlands but some substantial mountain areas, especially in the southern Peloponnese (Pelopónnisos), through the centre of the mainland, along the northern borders, and around the great bulk of Olympus (Olimbos; 2917m). One's overall impression is of bare hills, especially in the south, where most visitors go. In fact, forest covers about 19 per cent of the land, though most of this is concentrated in the mountains and the north.

A great feature of the Greek countryside is the number of archaeological sites, ranging from prehistoric to medieval Byzantine and often in attractive and unspoilt areas. In a sense, one could find thousands of similar unspoilt areas elsewhere in Greece, but a few archaeological sites are picked out below as worth a visit – aside from offering you the chance to combine two interests they have the added bonus of being goat-free and hence flower-filled; often, too, there are tame lizards and birds. Out-of-season or early-morning visits are recommended for all such tourist sites.

The flora of Greece is outstandingly rich (at least 6000 species, with additional species being discovered or named all the time), combining Asian, African and European elements with over a thousand endemics and frost-intolerant species that survived the last ice age here. The country is rich also in other forms of wildlife. The birds include eastern species like Cretzschmar's Bunting, Sombre Tit and Long-legged Buzzard, while among the mammals are Jackal and Souslik. There are 68 reptile and amphibian species, and Greece is the only country which has areas where all three European tortoises occur, as well as breeding Loggerhead Turtles.

Conservation and landscape protection are by European standards not well organized or funded. Although there are 10 National Parks, these are generally unstaffed and have none of the infrastructure associated with others in Europe. There are also Aesthetic Forests and Natural Monuments, the last of which may correspond roughly with nature-reserve areas.

Greek names are transliterated for use outside Greece, and thus often exist in several different versions. Usually the differences are minor and present no problem. Here we give variants when it seems sensible to do so.

Crete The large island of Crete (see page 241) is, in effect, a long, narrow range of limestone mountains, in three main blocks, with narrow coastal strips on the north. Despite tourism, many of its mountain areas are wilderness, with a fascinating flora and numerous birds and insects. Like much of the Mediterranean area, it was once heavily forested; little true forest now survives, the land being largely covered instead by maquis and phrygana (garrigue). There has been no land connection to the island for 10 million years, and this isolation has led to 10 per cent of the island's 2000 flowering species being endemic, as is one mammal, the Cretan Spiny Mouse.

March–April is the best time to visit for the spring flowers at low level; the weather is then usually pleasantly warm. By the end of April rainfall has virtually

OPPOSITE PAGE: *Ancient monasteries surmount the cliffs of Meteóra.*

petered out, and the lowlands are dry, even though the White Mountains are still under snow. The mountain flowers are at their best from May onwards.

1. Préspa National Park

Location: Where Albania, Greece and Macedonia meet, about 160km northwest of Thessaloniki.
Access: By minor roads north from Kastoría or west from Flóriná. A sensitive border area at present. The causeway between the two lakes provides the best views.
Timing: Some interest all year; best April–July.

The park covers 25,800ha, including virtually all of Mikrí (small) Préspa (about 5000ha) and the small Grecian part of Megalí (big) Préspa. At an altitude of about 800m, Mikrí Préspa is a large shallow lake with extensive reed- and sedge-beds, except on the western side. It is very important for breeding wetland birds, especially both European Pelican species – Dalmatian and White – with about 500 individuals altogether; others are Spoonbill, Pygmy Cormorant, Little and Great White Egrets and Purple Heron, with birds like Golden Eagle breeding in the surrounding hills. There are Jackal and Wolf in the area around the lakes, and possibly Bear. Over 1000 species of flowering plants have been recorded in the park, and there is an endemic fish, *Barbus prespensis*, in the lake.

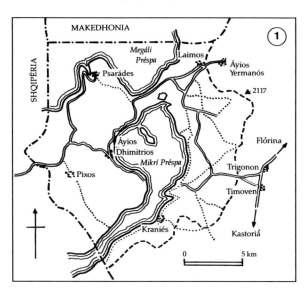

2. Kastoría Lake and Adjacent Lakes

Location: In a line running from Kastoría northeast towards Édhessa, close to the Yugoslavian frontier.
Access: The E65, road 2, the new road from Neápolis to Kastoría and many minor roads run into or through the site.
Timing: Some interest all year; best March–July.

A string of substantial freshwater lakes with associated wetland habitats. Collectively they form an important site for birds, though these are underrecorded and largely unprotected, except in some no-shooting areas. Good numbers of wetland birds breed here, including Purple, Grey and Night Herons, Ferruginous Duck, Marsh Harrier and Kingfisher (quite tame on the edge of the town), while Glossy Ibis, both pelicans, Roller, terns and many others visit. A large population of continental-race Cormorant winters near Kastoría. Among the amphibians are Agile Frog and Tree-frog.

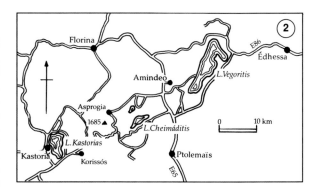

Cormorants roosting in poplars beside Kastoría Lake.

3. Aliákmon Delta

Location: About 30km southwest of Thessaloníki, just east of road 1.
Access: Via road 1, then the old main road into Néa Agathoúpolis, then northwards on tracks.
Timing: Best March–July.

The formerly rich Axios Delta to the north of here is now mainly agricultural, and the southern area is losing its value due to alteration of the river flow and agricultural encroachment. However, there is still a large area of good, flat coastal habitats – saline and brackish lagoons, grazing marshes, saltmarshes and mudflats – sustaining many breeding birds like Purple Heron, Little Egret, Little Bittern, Black-winged Stilt, Stone Curlew and Collared Pratincole. Numerous birds pass through, notably gulls, terns, Glossy Ibis and lots of waders, and the numbers of birds wintering here can also be good, depending on water-levels. The flora has salt-tolerant species like Glasswort, Tamarisk and several sea lavenders in abundance.

About 20km south, at **Alyki**, just south of Piona, reached via the old main road towards Kateríni, an area with saltpans and a lagoon supports a very large gull colony, including Mediterranean and Slender-billed Gulls and much else. The heathland around the lagoon and saltpans was identified in the 1980s as a key site for reptiles, including tortoises and large lizards, but was burnt and partly ploughed before conservation proposals could be implemented.

4. Lake Kerkini

Location: About 65km north of Thessaloníki, and about 30km northwest of Serres (Sérrai), in the Strymon (Strimón) Valley.
Access: Via road 63 and minor roads to Virónia, then tracks around the lake.
Timing: Good all year; best March–July.

A large reservoir, created about 40 years ago, then raised by a further 4–8m in 1982. Although the rise in water-level flooded many good areas, the important wetland-bird colonies are re-establishing themselves – just about all of Greece's wetland birds (except the two pelicans) nest here, some in large numbers. Also, many birds use the area at migration times, and winter numbers of wildfowl, pelicans, Great White Egret and Common and Pygmy Cormorants are high. In sum, the lake has large numbers of birds at all seasons, though at the time of writing these were being adversely affected by the low water-levels from which Greece as a whole was suffering.

The wild and well wooded **Beles Mountains**, northwest of here on the Bulgarian-Macedonian border, are home to many raptors.

5. Cholomon Mountains and Chalcidice (Khalkidhikí)

Location: The peninsula to the southeast of Thessaloníki.
Access: Via road 16 and minor roads; largely unrestricted on foot (for Mount Athos see below).
Timing: March–June and September–October.

The Chalcidice Peninsula is made up of a broad 'base' at the north, with three 'fingers' pointing southwards – from west to east these are Kassándra, Sithonía and Athos (Ayion Óros). The Cholomon Mountains run roughly east–west across the peninsula, reaching over 1150m, and are surprisingly well wooded, with oak, chestnut and hornbeam, plus Strawberry Tree and Kermes Oak below. The rich flora includes orchids like Violet Limodore and Red Helleborine. Booted and Short-toed Eagles, Eagle Owl, Long-legged Buzzard, four woodpeckers and Ortolan and Cretzschmar's Buntings breed, and the butterflies include Cardinal and Two-tailed Pasha. The three 'fingers' have, away from the resorts, a good range of unspoilt habitats including woodland, garrigue and dunes, and rich flora and fauna to match.

Athos is an extraordinary place. Virtually all a self-governing area, run by a council of monasteries, it remains largely unspoilt and well wooded, with interesting wildlife. Access is restricted to males, who must apply through the Greek Tourist Office with a recommendation from their embassy.

Sithonía is one of the few areas set aside for underwater activities by the National Tourist Organization.

6. Lake Kóronia and Lake Vólvi

Location: Directly east of Thessaloníki, north of road E90/2.
Access: Minor roads encircle the lakes; unrestricted access on foot.
Timing: March–July.

These two freshwater lakes and their connecting marshy land cover about 2400ha; Kóronia is generally the more interesting, but the eastern end of Vólvi is a reserve. Many wetland species – e.g., Marsh Harrier, White Stork, Little Bittern, Squacco, Night and Purple

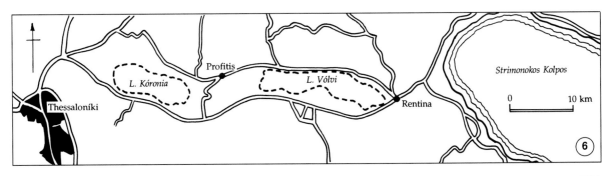

Herons and Penduline Tit – breed here, and the wintering birds, though often disturbed by shooting and fishing, can attain large numbers, mainly of grebes and ducks. In the marshes between the lakes are Dice Snake, several frogs and Pond Terrapin. Chaste Tree and Christ's Thorn are abundant around the lakes, and this is also a good place for dragonflies, including Norfolk Hawker and *Lindenia tetraphylla*.

Just east of Lake Vólvi the main road passes through the wooded **Rentina Gorge**, with limestone cliffs above and good raptors and flowers.

7. Lake Vistónis and Pórto Lágo

Location: On the coast southwest of Komotoní.
Access: Direct from the E90, which bisects the area; unrestricted access on foot.
Timing: Interesting all year; best April–June.

About 10,000ha of mixed coastal and wetland habitats, relatively unspoilt by agriculture or development. Vistónis is a very large lagoon, connected directly to the sea at Pórto Lágo and fringed with reedbeds and scrub; the area also supports dunes, scrub, open patches, saltmarshes and saltpans. The whole site is very important for breeding and passage birds: Squacco, Night and Purple Herons, Little and Great White Egrets, Pygmy Cormorant, Avocet, Black-winged Stilt, Spur-winged Plover, Roller and many others breed, and the range of migrant and non-breeding species is huge – especially in the saltpans.

Along the coast to the east are several other interesting lagoons and associated habitats, **Lake Mitrikou** being the largest.

8. Évros Delta

Location: About 25km east of Alexandroúpolis, on the Turkish border.
Access: Road 2 runs just north of the main site, and tracks lead into it; the southern and eastern parts are a restricted border zone, requiring permits from police or military in Alexandroúpolis.
Timing: All year; best April–June and September–October.

Once one of the finest wetlands in Europe, this is still, despite steady deterioration, an excellent site for birds, with a good range of the usual wetland species breeding as well as eastern specialities like Spur-winged Plover, Isabelline Wheatear and Masked Shrike; wildfowl and waders winter here, although their numbers are much lower than they used to be. The habitats include freshwater and brackish lagoons, dunes, offshore islands, saltmarshes and estuarine woodlands. The site has good saltmarsh plants, but otherwise an undistinguished flora. The amphibians and reptiles include Tree-frog, Pond and Stripe-necked Terrapins and Dice Snake.

About 10km north of Alexandroúpolis, the **Ávas**

Gorge has good flowers and is excellent for vultures, eagles, Eagle Owl and three buzzards, as well as many other rock-loving and scrub-dwelling birds. **Dadia** forest, nearby, is superb for raptors.

9. Pindos (Píndhos) Mountains 1: Grammos-Smólikas Area

Location: About 50km north of Ioánnina.
Access: Road 20 crosses the area and minor roads enter it; unrestricted access on foot, except towards the Albanian border.
Timing: April–October.

The Pindos Mountains dominate the northwestern corner of Greece, with Smólikas (2637m) the highest peak. The rocks of this northernmost Greek section, more varied than the usual limestone, include schists and serpentine, often highly eroded. Still wild and unspoilt, the region has extensive forests of beech and pine and a lavish flora, with unusual violets like *Viola magellensis* and *V. orphanidis*, the purple-flowered Butterwort *Pinguicula hirtiflora*, bellflowers like *Campanula hawkinsiana*, anemones, fritillaries, gentians and many others. Egyptian and Griffon Vultures, occasional Lammergeier, several eagles, Honey Buzzard, Chough, Rock Partridge and many other birds breed. The mammals include Wildcat, Wild Boar and probably Wolf and Brown Bear. Butterflies abound, among them Southern White Admiral, Silver-washed Fritillary, Swallowtail and Cleopatra. This is good walking country – but for experienced walkers only: trails and villages are few and far between.

Bare but dramatic hills in the Grammos area of the Pindos range.

10. Pindos (Píndhos) Mountains 2: Vikos-Aóos National Park

Location: About 35km north of Ioánnina, near Monodéndri.

Access: Road 20 north from Ioánnina, then minor roads to Monodéndri and other villages; the Vikos Gorge is signed from the main road. Access on foot is unrestricted.

Timing: April–November; best May–June. Snow may limit access to higher areas in spring.

The park covers 12,600ha of superb mountainous country, with the extraordinary Vikos Gorge, running north from Monodéndri, as its centre-point; the Aóos Gorge, ending at Kónitsa, is almost equally spectacular. There are extensive forests of beech, pine, lime, sycamore and Greek Fir, plus Montpellier Maple scrub and many patches of open limestone grassland and rock. The lavish flora includes specialities like *Ramonda serbica*, a Knapweed (*Centaurea pawlovskii*), a Valerian (*Valeriana epirota*), various saxifrages (including *Saxifraga marginata*), the attractive purple *Aubretia deltoidea*, a Soapwort (*Saponaria calabrica*), pinks, hellebores and orchids; the exceptionally good lichens have yet to be properly recorded. Egyptian and Griffon Vultures breed, as do occasional Lammergeier, Short-toed, Booted and Golden Eagles, Shore Lark, Wall Creeper, Cretzschmar's Bunting and many others. Wolf, Bear, Chamois, Otter and Wild Boar are among the resident mammals. The prolific butterflies include Southern White Admiral, Alcon Blue, Ilex Hairstreak, Fritillary and Swallowtail. This is excellent walking country, with some marked trails, but is not for the inexperienced.

Ayía Paraskevi monastery perched high in the Vikos Gorge.

11. Pindos (Píndhos) Mountains 3: Pindos National Park and Katáras Pass Area

Location: The pass is on the E92 about 40km east of Ioánnina; the park lies north of the pass.

Access: The E92 gives access to high areas; minor roads lead north into the park and south into other good areas.

Timing: Best May–October; snow may lie into early summer.

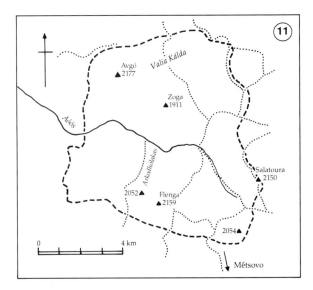

This large area of wild country – the park itself covers 10,000ha to the north of the road, and the area around the pass and the mountains to its south offer further good terrain – reaches 2295m at Peristéri, and 2177m within the park at Avgó; the 1690m pass is a good starting point for high-altitude exploration. There are extensive forests of beech, Black and Bosnian Pines, fir, oak and hornbeam, and the area's flora is lavish: numerous orchids, irises, lilies, fritillaries, crocuses, *Colchicum* species, tulips, saxifrages, etc., with a good mixture of widespread species and local specialities. Vultures, eagles, Honey Buzzard, Lanner Falcon, shrikes and eight woodpeckers (including Three-toed, at the southern edge of its range) breed; the mammals include Bear, Wolf, Jackal and Wild Boar. The butterflies, abundant in the open areas, are much as for the other Pindos sites.

Métsovo, just on the west edge of the area, is surrounded by excellent beechwoods and mountain meadows, and makes a good base. The whole area is grand for walking, though with few facilities.

12. Lake Pamvótis (Lake Ioánnina)

Location: Immediately east of Ioánnina.

Access: Major and minor roads encircle the lake, and tracks and causeways lead closer; ferries run to an island.

Timing: Best March–July.

A medium-sized freshwater lake, about 8km long, largely surrounded by a reed fringe; although somewhat polluted from the development around the west side, it is still a rich wetland habitat. The breeding birds include Little Bittern, Purple and Squacco Herons, Moustached and Great Reed Warblers and Kingfisher, and migrants can include Glossy Ibis, several terns, harriers and gulls. Among the amphibians are Marsh Frog and Tree-frog; Terrapin and Grass and Dice Snakes represent the reptiles; the flora contains Great and Common Reeds, Arrowhead, Flowering Rush and Water-lily; and Darter and Emperor Dragonfly are among the dragonflies.

About 20km southwest of Ioánnina is the historic amphitheatre at **Dhodhóni**; much quieter than most Classical Greek sites, it has good flowers and reptiles. The mountain of **Astaka** (1596m), about 25km north of the town, has good flowers and birds. The marshes on the coast just north of **Igoumenítsa**, about 50km west of Ioánnina, are of interest for breeding wetland birds like egrets and Black-winged Stilt.

Though heavily developed on its west side, the lake at Ioánnina is still a rich wetland habitat.

13. Metéora

Location: About 70km west of Larissa, by the main E92/6 road from Larissa to Ioánnina, near Kalabáka.
Access: A clearly signed minor road leads from Kalabáka around the site; access unrestricted except by the topography.
Timing: Best March–October; oppressively busy in high summer.

An extraordinary place: dramatic conglomerate and limestone pinnacles and cliffs are made even more interesting by the series of ancient monasteries on their tops. Metéora is an excellent place to watch cliff-dwelling birds like Egyptian Vulture, Short-toed and Bonelli's Eagles, Chough, Raven, Alpine Swift and Crag Martin; both White and Black Storks occur in the area. Among the plants are various orchids, pinks, sun-roses, Dragon Arums and Sand Crocuses – a typical mixture of Greek limestone flowers.

14. Mount Olympus (Olimbos) National Park

Location: About 50km north of Larissa, just west of the main E75/1 motorway.
Access: Minor roads encircle the mountain; the easiest route to high levels is via Litókhoron, on the east side, and on to Prionia at 1100m.
Timing: April–October; higher areas snow-covered well into early summer.

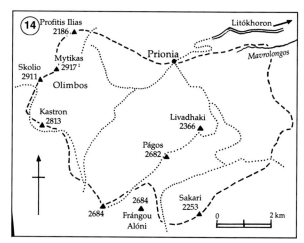

Greece's highest mountain (2917m) is the focus of this 4000ha park, which lies mainly on the mountain's east; the area of interest extends well beyond the park. The lowest slopes have open maquis, like so many Greek hills; then come fine forests of beech, Black and Balkan Pines and Greek Fir; and above about 2000m these give way to high pastures and cliffs. Olympus is one of the finest botanical sites in Europe, its flora including over 1700 species (23 endemics) and with more still being discovered or named; probably the best known is the attractive pur-

The mist-shrouded Enipevs Valley, Mount Olympus National Park.

ple-flowered *Jankaea heldreichii*, a relict species from before the last ice age. Not surprisingly, in view of its rich plant life, Olympus is also good for almost all other groups, including reptiles, butterflies, moths, beetles and lichens, though there is much still to be recorded; the mammals include Wolf, Jackal, Chamois, Red Deer and Wildcat. The breeding birds are important, covering the whole range from lowland-scrub through forest to high-altitude species: Griffon, Black and Egyptian Vultures, several eagles, Tengmalm's and Eagle Owls, Rock Partridge and many others. This is a fine place for mountain walking: there are signed footpaths (including part of a Europath) and several refuges. Note, though, that the ascent should not be undertaken lightly.

The area of interest extends southwards into the lower **Káto Olympus**, while on the mountain's north side there are good gorges near **Vróndou**.

15. Gulf of Árta (Amvrakikós Kólpos)

Location: On the west coast of mainland Greece, south of Árta.
Access: Main roads encircle the site and minor roads lead into it; access on foot is mostly unrestricted.
Timing: All year.

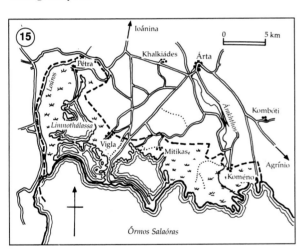

Though the whole gulf is of some interest, the main attraction is the enormous area (about 25,000ha) of coastal wetland habitats on its northern side – lagoons, saltmarsh, reedbeds, mudflats and sandy areas. Collectively these form an excellent area for birds, though one gradually declining in value because of inadequate protection. A small colony of Dalmatian Pelican plus good numbers of more widespread species like Little Bittern, Purple, Squacco and Night Herons, White Stork, Ferruginous Duck, Spoonbill and many warblers breed; away from the wetlands there are breeding Stone Curlew, Collared Pratincole, Roller, Bee-eater, Penduline Tit and Short-toed Lark. Many birds stop over on migration, and late-winter numbers of wildfowl can be high.

16. Missolonghi (Mesolóngion) Marshes

Location: On the southwest point of mainland Greece.
Access: Road 48 runs just north of the site, and minor roads enter it.
Timing: All year.

Rather like site 15 but slightly smaller, this wetland complex, with lagoons, saltmarsh and grazing marshes, is important for breeding birds, especially for many wetland species – e.g., Little Bittern, Purple Heron, White Stork, Water Rail, Marsh Harrier and Little Tern. The numbers of birds on passage are high, and this is a good place to see wintering wildfowl and raptors.

Just to the north, the **Arákinthos Mountains** have good flowers and impressive cliffs with breeding vultures, eagles and others.

17. Mount Oeti National Park (Iti Óros)

Location: About 20km southwest of Lamía, off the E75/1.
Access: Difficult; via minor roads to Ipáti, then on foot.
Timing: May–October.

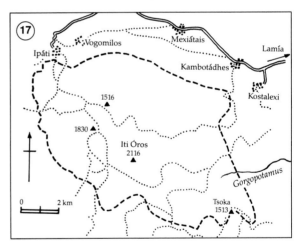

A remote and little visited mountain area (7210ha), rising to 2150m at Oeti, with extensive Greek Fir forests. The rich flora includes many orchids, the beautiful Lily *Lilium chalcedonicum*, *Viola graeca* and *Asperula oetaea*, while the list of mammals features Wolf, Chamois, Stone Marten, Roe Deer, Wild Boar and a naturalized form of Wild Goat. Peregrine Falcon, several eagles, Honey Buzzard, Eagle Owl, Rock Partridge and numerous woodpeckers breed. Alpine Newts occur in the lake. There are few facilities within the park.

The marshes just southwest of Lamia on the **Sperchios (Spérkhíos) Delta** are of some interest for wetland and coastal birds despite agricultural and other depredations.

18. Mount Parnassus (Parnassós) National Park

Location: About 120km northwest of Athens (Athínai), just north of site 19.
Access: Road 48 runs south of the main mountain, and minor roads (including one to a high-altitude ski-centre) climb towards the top; access on foot is unrestricted.
Timing: Best April–November; higher parts may be inaccessible until early summer.

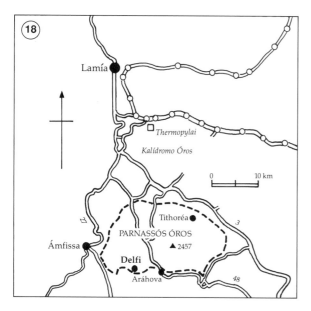

Despite ski-related developments, a large area of genuine wilderness survives on and around the mountain, which reaches 2457m; the park itself covers 3600ha, though the demarcation seems of little relevance on the ground. There are wide spreads of pine and Greek Fir woods, cliffs, limestone pavements and extensive pastures. The flora includes over 1000 recorded species: in spring there are drifts of crocuses – e.g., *Crocus pallasii* and *C. veluchensis* – and *Colchicum catacuzenium*, and there are crocuses again in autumn, alongside plants like the pretty

Mount Parnassus National Park in winter.

pale-yellow *Sternbergia colchiflora*. Golden, Booted and Short-toed Eagles, Shore Lark, Rock Thrush, Alpine Accentor and occasionally vultures breed here, and Fox, Jackal, Badger and Wild Boar are among the resident mammals.

19. Delphi

Location: On road 48 just southwest of Mount Parnassus (Parnassós).
Access: Well signposted via the 48; you need to pay at the site itself, but access is open to the surrounding area.
Timing: All year; best for flowers March–April. Go early in the morning or out of season.

Although very close to Parnassus (site 18), Delphi is very different. The archaeological site is very flowery away from the few herbicided areas: on the walls, species like the Golden Drop *Onosma frutescens*, the yellow-flowered *Alkanna graeca* and the Bellflower *Campanula rupestris* are common; Giant, Sawfly and other orchids and bulbs like *Bellevalia dubia* (in spring), *Colchicum boisseri*, *Crocus cancellatus* and two

Limestone cliffs tower above the ancient historical site at Delphi.

Sternbergia species (in autumn) are also found. Green Lizard are common and tame; the birds include the lovely Rock Nuthatch, Serin and Black Redstart.

Nearby, the limestone maquis and cliffs sustain an ample flora plus Sombre Tit, Rüppell's Warbler, Cretzschmar's and Ortolan Buntings and other birds, with vultures, eagles, Crag Martin and Alpine Swift overhead. Butterflies abound – e.g., Clouded Yellow and Painted Lady all year.

20. Párnitha National Park

Location: Immediately north of Athens (Athínai).
Access: Roads and lifts climb the south face; access on foot is unrestricted.
Timing: Best April–July; very busy in summer and at weekends.

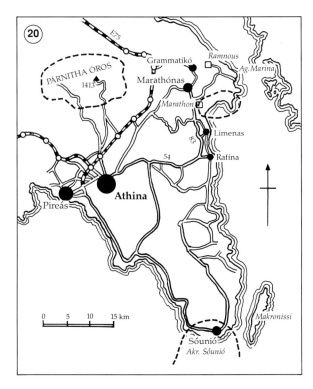

The park covers 3840ha within a much wider area of interest. It is of limestone, with characteristic maquis scrub, bare rock and, higher up, pine and Greek Fir forests. There are over 1000 recorded flowers, among them good orchids (e.g., Horseshoe, Mirror, Woodcock and Four-spotted Orchids) and, at greater altitudes, many bulbs like crocuses and squills, with near-Alpine plants towards the peak (1413m). The range of breeding birds is quite good – Short-toed Eagle, Peregrine Falcon, Rüppell's and Sardinian Warblers, etc. – though the populations of the larger species suffer from human interference. Tortoises, Green Lizard and Whip Snake are among the reptiles, and butterflies abound in May–June. The park is good for walking, with well marked trails and a refuge at the top.

Just to the east of Athens, the 1019m limestone mountain **Hymettus (Imitós)** has similar flora and fauna, with particularly good orchids.

21. Marathón Marshes

Location: On the coast about 30km northeast of Athens (Athínai) and just southeast of Marathón.
Access: Via roads 54 and 83 from Athens, then by minor roads and tracks; access to some areas restricted by military and airport use.
Timing: Some interest all year, depending on water-levels; best March–June.

This 1000ha area of coastal marshes, lagoons and dunes, while very patchy in quality – and losing interest by the year – is currently good for breeding wetland birds like Little and Baillon's Crakes, Purple, Grey and Night Herons, Marsh Harrier and several warblers, plus drier-ground species like Tawny Pipit, Short-toed Lark and Roller. It generally has fine migrants, especially in spring, but much depends on the prevailing water-levels. The amphibians and dragonflies are notable.

The nearby **Marathón Lake** (well signed locally) is a reservoir of relatively little interest except as a gull roost and for some good limestone hills round about.

Inky storm clouds brooding over the Marathón marshes.

22. Soúnion National Park

Location: About 60km southeast of Athens (Athínai), at the tip of the peninsula.
Access: Well signed via roads 91 and 89; access on foot is unrestricted, except for the area around the temple of Poseidon, where you must pay.
Timing: All year; best March–May.

The park nominally covers 4250ha. Unlike National Parks elsewhere, it is not composed of wild, unspoilt scenery – indeed, in terms of natural history it is just a typical piece of Greek coast. Spring flowers include excellent orchids—e.g., Horseshoe, Yellow Bee (subspecies *murbeckii* and var *melena*), Mount Carmel, Sawfly, Four-spotted and Pink Butterfly – plus the attractive dwarf Iris *Iris pumila* and Crown Anemone. In autumn there are masses of the pretty little Daffodil *Narcissus serotinus*, yellow *Sternbergia lutea* and the beautiful Greek Saffron Crocus. Rock Nuthatch, Sardinian Warbler and Blue Rock Thrush breed, and this is a good place to see migrant birds, whether on land or passing by at sea. Green and Common Wall Lizards are the main reptiles.

The headland, with its imposing 5th-century temple ruins, covers only a small area. To the north are several fine stretches of limestone hills with open maquis, rich in flowers and accessible directly from the road. The coast nearby is good for rock-pool life and snorkelling.

23. Kalogria Area

Location: On the west coast about 30km southwest of Patra (Pátrai).
Access: Minor roads off the E55/9; mainly unrestricted on foot.
Timing: All year; busy at weekends and during holiday periods.

A remarkably unspoilt – even though unprotected – collection of maritime habitats, including dunes, coastal pine woodland, brackish pools, large lagoons and a small range of limestone hills. There are good flowers on the hills, and the largest lagoon (just southeast of Kalogria) has breeding Water Rail, Little Bittern, Black-winged Stilt, Kingfisher, Marsh Harrier and others, plus reasonable numbers of wintering ducks, occasional Dark Kite and harriers, abundant dragonflies and amphibians and frequent Dice Snake. The dune flowers include Sea Daffodil, Cottonweed, Sea Spurge, Sea Holly and the spiny *Echinophora spinosa*.

Some distance south, the lagoons and marshes by **Pírgos** are still of some interest, though they have been partly reclaimed. The historic site of **Olympia**, to Pírgos's east, has good flowers.

24. Mount Helmos and Panahaiko Mountains

Location: About 50km southeast of Patra (Pátrai), in the northern Peloponnese (Pelóponnisos).
Access: By minor roads climbing steeply southwards from the main E65/8A coast road; access on foot is unrestricted.
Timing: April–October.

A magnificent wild area of mainly limestone mountains, reaching 2341m at Mount Helmos, with extensive forests of pine and Greek Fir and, higher up, wide areas of rocky pasture. There are some dramatic gorges and cliffs, especially where the valleys of the Selinous and Vouraïkós cut through. This is a good site for birds of prey, including Griffon Vulture and Golden and Short-toed Eagles. The flora is generally lavish,

and the higher peaks bear many specialities – e.g., Greek Fritillary, several bellflowers (and close relatives), saxifrages, a Columbine (*Aquilegia ottonis*) and a Germander (*Teucrium aroanium*); the Marsh Orchid *Dactylorhiza cordigera* is also found. You need time to explore this extensive area fully; the high parts may not be accessible until June.

About 25km southeast of Mount Helmos, the medium-sized freshwater **Lake Stimfalías** has reedbeds that can be good for breeding birds and migrants, though often conditions are too dry.

25. Epidaurus (Epídhavros)

Location: About 40km southeast of Kórinthos (Corinth), in the Peloponnese (Pelóponnisos).
Access: By road 70 from Kórinthos.
Timing: All year; best March–May.

A major archaeological site with a rich natural history. The whole area is good for flowers, especially in early spring and in autumn, when they form lovely displays. They include many orchids of interest – e.g., Yellow Bee and Eyed Bee Orchids and Horseshoe and Tongue Orchids – plus Crown Anemone, Tassel Hyacinth, irises, broomrapes, crocuses and *Colchicum* species. Among the birds are Rock Nuthatch, Black Redstart and Sardinian Warbler, and the reptiles include Hermann's Tortoise. Butterflies abound.

Mycenae (Mikinai), 30km southwest of Kórinthos, is another good classical site with fine flowers, and the whole peninsula south from Epidaurus is also of interest, especially in February–April.

26. Mystra and the Taígetos (Taíyetos) Mountains

Location: Immediately south of Spárti (Sparta), in the southern Peloponnese (Pelóponnisos).
Access: Roads 82 and 39 pass through; open access except at Mystra, where a fee is charged.
Timing: Interesting all year; best February–May, with high areas best May–July.

The Taígetos are superb limestone mountains, reaching 2407m at Mt Taígetos itself. The whole region is extremely good for flowers, most notably at Mystra, a Byzantine city on the eastern slopes close to Spárti, where grazing is excluded from the city area. Here and elsewhere there are many orchids, especially the Bee Orchid group, together with Greek Snowdrop, cyclamens, *Anemone fulgens*, several tulips, crocuses and Autumn Crocus. Away from the site, the gorges of Parori (just above Mystra) and Langádha have very rich floras, though how much you see depends on how recently the goats have been through! The butterflies include Scarce Swallowtail and the fabulous Cleopatra. Breeding birds include Golden and Short-toed Eagles in the hills and many widespread scrub and woodland species.

The forested mountain areas are largely roadless, but can be approached on foot from higher villages like Ayios Ioánnis. The E4 footpath passes through the area, but no long walks here should be undertaken without adequate preparation.

27. Máni Peninsula

Location: The central of the three westerly 'fingers' of the Peloponnese (Pelóponnisos), several tens of kilometres due south of Spárti (Sparta).
Access: Road 39 and minor roads into the area; access on foot largely open.
Timing: All year; best February to early May.

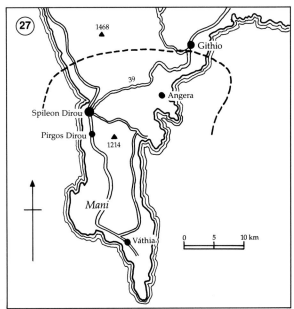

Site of the Byzantine city of Mystra, near Spárti.

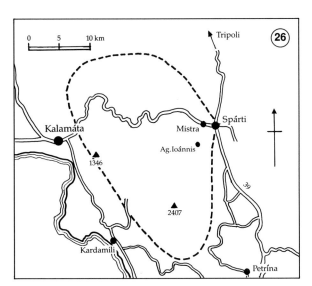

Bright floral carpet in olive groves on the Máni Peninsula.

This remarkable peninsula, bare and rocky, with limestone mountains rising to over 1200m along the centre, is very unspoilt, having settlements (with some interesting old churches) only on its fringes. The flora is especially rich, including various endemics and a wide range of orchids like *Ophrys reinholdii*, Mirror Orchid, a variety of Bug Orchid, Horseshoe Orchid and more widespread species; *Lilium chalcedonicum* occurs locally. In late autumn at least three crocuses appear in abundance – *Crocus goulimyii*, *C. niveus* and *C. boryi* – together with profuse Cyclamen. The birds are somewhat sparse, but include Peregrine, Short-toed Eagle and, very locally, Eagle Owl; and the extreme south is good for migrants. There are good butterflies, with a few species in evidence virtually all year. There are fine caves at Pírgos Dhiroú, and it is well worth browsing in the rock-pools around the coast.

THE ISLANDS

28. Corfu (Kérkira)

Location: In the Ionian Islands, west of the mainland.
Access: By ferry from Igoumenítsa or direct by air; generally open access on foot.
Timing: March–June.

A large island with a well developed tourist industry, and notably greener than the average piece of Greece thanks to an annual rainfall of about 115cm. Despite recent developments, it is a superb place for natural history – especially in the north, where there are mountains, lagoons and woods. The marvellous flora includes at least 44 orchids – with a peak of flowering

in late March through April – plus fritillaries, crocuses, anemones and many others. The birds are good, too: Cretzschmar's Bunting (at the west of its range) and many more widespread species breed, and numerous birds of many species arrive during passage periods, especially spring. The rich insect fauna has many butterflies, fireflies, crickets and Praying Mantis, and there are also geckoes, Nose-horned Viper and various lizards and frogs, plus Hermann's Tortoise.

29. Cephalonia (Kefallinía; Aenos) National Park

Location: Off the west coast, due west of Patra (Pátrai).
Access: By boat from Patra.
Timing: March–July.

The park covers 2800ha on the east side of Cephalonia, protecting the area around Mount Aenos. Of particular importance is the surviving relict of Greek Fir (*Abies cephalonica*) forest, for which this is the original type locality. The underlying rock is limestone, and the whole area has a very rich flora. Other features include Jackal and a good range of reptiles. Griffon Vulture breed on the island.

30. Zákinthos

Location: West of the Peloponnese (Pelóponnisos), southwest of Patra (Pátrai).

Saltpans near Alikes, on the southern tip of Corfu, an important site for migratory birds.

Dafori Bay on the beautiful island of Zákinthos.

240

Access: By regular ferries from Killíni and Katákolon, or by air.
Timing: March–August.

This lovely island offers a wide spectrum of natural-history interest – hills (in the interior), woods, dunes, marshland and open water. Cretzschmar's Bunting and other birds breed, and spring sees many migrant birds as well as superb wild flowers, including numerous orchids. The island's main claim to fame is as one of the few – and probably the best – remaining sites where Loggerhead Turtle breed. Sadly, tourism is putting paid to this: the turtles have abandoned one of their erstwhile main breeding beaches. The principal remaining area is on the south coast, east of Laganás, where a Turtle Information Centre is open during the summer. Other parts of interest are the dune areas – with flowers and lizards – and the marshlands along the south coast, where there are Tree-frog and Stripe-necked Terrapin.

31. Lésvos (Lesbos; Mylíni)

Location: Just off the Turkish coast.
Access: By air, or by ferry from Thessaloníki or Kaválla; transport is needed on the island.
Timing: March–June and September–October.

Lesbos, the third largest Greek island, holds much of interest: allow at least several days. The spring flora is very rich, with a wealth of orchids including some rarities like *Comperia comperiana*, *Ophrys rheinholdii* and *Orchis anatolica*; other flowers include fritillaries, tulips, *Iris spuria* and, in the western hills, Yellow Azalea, a predominantly Turkish species here in its only European site. Birds breeding on Lesbos include eastern species like Krüper's Nuthatch and Cinereous Bunting, plus storks, Levant Sparrow-hawk and Lanner and Eleonora's Falcons. Especially recommended are the western hills and the marshes and saltpans at the head of the Gulf of Kalloní.

32. Rhodes (Ródhos)

Location: Just off southwest Turkey.
Access: By air or by ferry.
Timing: Early March to August.

Although a popular and well developed holiday resort, Rhodes – a large and mountainous island, at the far southeast of Greece's territory – has many wild areas. The ample flora includes specialities like Rhodes Peony plus a wealth of orchids – including many *Ophrys* species (e.g., Horseshoe Orchid) and *Orchis sancta* – the distinctive Dragon Arum and a scarlet form of Turban Buttercup, both common. Among the reptiles and amphibians are 'Rhodes Dragon' (Agama Lizard) and Tree-frog. There are good butterflies, including Southern Festoon; but 'Butterfly Valley' (near Petaloúdhes), the island's prime feature, actually

gets its name from the Jersey Tiger Moth, millions of which gather in a shady spring-fed valley to aestivate. It is a wonderful sight; the peak time is July–August.

CRETE (KRITÍ)

33. Omalós and Lévka Óri

Location: Western Crete, south of Khánia.
Access: By good road from Khánia to the Omalós plateau.
Timing: April–July; flowers best in May–June; snow-covered in winter.

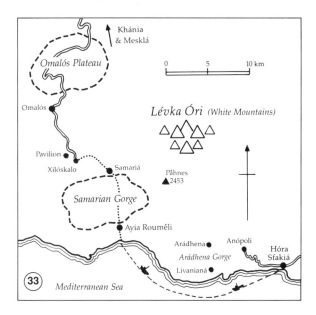

The Ammoutsera Valley, Lévka Óri (White Mountains).

The Omalós plateau, at about 1000m, is a fertile well cultivated area. In May *Tulipa bakeri* flowers in rocky places between the fields, and on the limestone at the edges of the plateau grow *Daphne sericea*, Dittany, *Cyclamen creticum* and yellow *Orchis pauciflora*. From the tourist pavilion at the southern end of the plain a path leads west into an outlying block of the Lévka Óri (White Mountains), where, in May, there are colourful Crocus, Chionodoxas and low, blue-flowered bushes of *Anchusa caespitosa*. Lammergeier are seldom out of the skies and Bonelli's Eagle and Peregrine Falcon are not infrequent.

34. Samaria Gorge

Location: Western Crete, between the Lévka Óri and the sea.
Access: From Omalós; in season, boats leave from the harbour near Ayía Roumeli at the foot of the gorge.
Timing: Spring–autumn; in winter torrents make the gorge impassable.

Once a wilderness, this is now a much publicized tourist attraction, tramped annually by thousands. The 16km walk starts with the descent of the Xyloskalon (literally 'wooden stairs'), where there are rock plants, Crossbill and Citril Finch, and often raptors overhead. In the gorge are found several orchids plus endemics like Cretan Ebony, *Petromarula pinnata* and White Peony (near Samaria); also in the gorge are Blue Rock Thrush and Crag Martin. In early summer butterflies abound in the flowery meadows. There is a (slim) chance you might see the native Cretan Goat (Kri Kri).

From Chora Sfakíon you can reach two far less frequented gorges: from Komithades, 5km to the east, runs the **Imbros Gorge**; near Anopoli, 12km northwest, is the **Aradhena Gorge**, reached by a steep mule-track down the rockface. Both have flora and fauna similar to those of the Samaria Gorge.

35. Phaestos (Phaistos)

Location: Midway along the southern coast.
Access: From road 97 and minor roads.
Timing: March–April.

The site of the Minoan palace of Phaestos commands a view northwards over the snow-capped peaks beyond the central plain. Wild flowers abound: Gladiolus, anemones, Turban Buttercup and orchids – *Orchis italica*, Monkey Orchid and the endemic *Ophrys cretica* are on the surrounding hillsides and bordering the walk to the summer palace at Ayía Triadha. Close to this palace, near the River Geros, there are marshes sustaining Pond Terrapin, Tree-frog, feeding herons, numerous warblers (including Sardinian and Rüppell's) and Penduline Tit. To the west of Ayía Galíni are scrub-covered hills rich in orchids; most impressive is the large form of the Late Spider Orchid (in late April). To the east, Lesser Kestrel and Alpine Swift breed on the cliff-faces, and Hoopoe and Nightingale are common.

Wild tulips on the Gious Kambos plain, near Phaestos.

36. Mount Jouktas

Location: Near Knossos, 5km southeast of Iráklion (Heraklion; Candia).
Access: From Arkanes, south of Knossos, a narrow road leads up to a radio mast.
Timing: Spring/autumn for flowers.

Mount Jouktas (811m) offers a good introduction to Cretan flora. The slopes are covered with scented Thyme, Origanum, Sage and *Cistus* shrubs, making up the phrygana. Bushes shelter numerous bulbs like Gladiolus, Grape Hyacinth and Iris, plus orchids – Pink Butterfly Orchid, Giant Orchid and the endemic *Ophrys cretica*. Two endemics grow in the rock crevices: *Cyclamen creticum* and *Alyssoides cretica*. Around Arkanes the weeds include Crown Daisy (in its bicoloured form) and Mandrake. In autumn the flora is less diverse but has – as well as the Mandrake flowers – the curious Lily *Biarum davisii* and an Autumn Crocus, *Colchicum cupanii*. Butterflies appear in early spring; they include Scarce Swallowtail and Eastern Festoon.

37. Lato and Sitía

Location: Respectively about 50km and 70km east of Iráklion (Heraklion; Candia) on the main coast road, road 90.
Access: From road 90.
Timing: March–June for flowers; October for flowers and Eleonora's Falcon.

High in the hills to the west of Ayios Nikólaos is the ancient city of Lato, in spring a flower-filled ruin offering displays of plants like yellow Turban Buttercup, Dragon Arum and, on walls, *Petromarula pennata*. From here the road leads up to the highly cultivated Lasithi Plain, where at roadsides and field-edges there are orchids – various Bee Orchids plus *Orchis prisca*, *O. anatolica* and *O. pauciflora*. The path to the Dhiktean Cave is edged with flowers; birds around here include Corn Bunting, Hoopoe and Woodchat Shrike. The mountains are of a good height for Alpine flowers and vultures.

Some 25 per cent of the world population of Eleonora's Falcon breeds on islands off Crete's northeast coast, and Sitía is an excellent place to see them, often hunting in the evenings in flocks around the coast.

TURKEY

Turkey is a vast country (780,000 sq km) with a terrain largely comprising high mountains and plateaux. Here Europe meets Asia. The climate is determined both by the sea and by the proximity of the Asian landmass – so that, for example, Istanbul swelters in summer but endures bitterly cold winters. Towards the southwest and south the winters are milder, but the Toros Mountains behind the coastal strip remain snow-capped even through the broiling summers.

The sites discussed here are all in the coastal regions of western Turkey, which, because they have been inhabited and cultivated for millennia, are much like the landscapes of the rest of the Mediterranean. Although there are ancient forests elsewhere in Turkey, little extensive woodland remains here in the west. However, the spring flowers, the butterflies and the birds will gladden the heart of any naturalist. The presence of high mountains away from the coast and

Belgrade Forest, within easy reach of Istanbul, is an excellent area for birdwatchers and botanists.

high plateaux beyond, reminiscent of central Asia, brings many eastern birds to the coast, and Turkey is unrivalled in Europe for migrating birds. Of the 9000 or so flowering species listed in the flora, roughly one in three is unique to Turkey – and almost every range offers a new crocus species. The bulb flora is truly remarkable, with many of the forerunners of familiar garden plants – Iris and Tulip, for example – originating here. Sadly, collecting for sale to the ready overseas market has done great damage, and some species are on the verge of extinction in the wild. The WWF and the Fauna and Flora Preservation Society (FFPS) have joined forces with Turkey's Society for the Protection of Nature (DHKD) to develop a programme to replace wild collecting with cultivation – thereby protecting both the plants and the villagers' livelihood.

1. Samsun Daği (Dilek Yarimadasi)

Location: On the west coast opposite Sámos.
Access: Open from the north side via Güzelçamli, from the south via Karine. For Ephesus (entrance fee), approach from Selçuki.
Timing: All year; perhaps best in spring (April onwards). Go early in the day to beat the crowds.

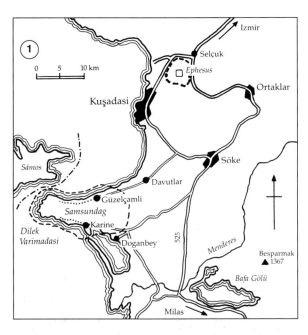

The 11,000ha National Park, an east-west range reaching nearly 1240m, offers a wide range of habitats with steep slopes, canyons and peaks in the interior grading to rocky bays and sandy and gravel beaches at the coast. Maquis forms about two-thirds of the vegetation, protecting many orchids (e.g., Monkey and Woodcock); the rest is pine woodland. Anatolian Leopard has disappeared, but there are several pairs of Peregrine Falcon, Eleonora's Falcon (outside the breeding season), Krüper's Nuthatch and Spectacled Warbler.

Ephesus, to the north, is worth a visit, not only for the ruins but also, away from them, for the wildlife. The flowers include Woodcock, Mirror and Early Spider Orchids, Scarlet Anemone, Golden Henbane and Giant Fennel. Between the site and the sea there are often Nightingale, Woodchat Shrike and feeding White Stork, which perch on roofs in nearby Selçuk.

2. Manyas-Kuş Cenneti National Park

Location: West of Apolyant, about 15km south of Bandirma.
Access: Controlled within the reserve: nesting birds may be viewed closely only from the observation tower. Elsewhere access is unrestricted where approach permits; a track runs from Kuş Cenneti Golyaka on the western side.
Timing: All year; spectacular during the breeding season and spring and autumn passage times.

64ha of the 16,800ha lake comprises Turkey's only ornithological and smallest National Park. The lake is surrounded by fields; hunting is prohibited over the whole of it. The park is reached through a small poplar wood where there are butterflies in spring: Camberwell Beauty, Large Tortoiseshell, Scarce Swallowtail and Eastern Festoon. An enclosed viewing tower (you need binoculars or a telescope) provides a view over a flooded wood where trees almost creak under the weight of nesting birds. Cormorant and Pygmy Cormorant dominate the upper layers, Little Egret and Glossy Ibis nest in the reeds, and Grey Heron and Spoonbill occupy the mid-zone. Some 30 pairs of Dalmatian Pelican nest on platforms built for them near the water, and in September over 3000 White Pelican pause on migration.

Away from the reserve, many of the birds can be watched from the village of **Eskisigirci**, where White Stork nest on the roofs and the fishermen seem oblivious to the pelicans floating optimistically around their boats.

3. Istanbul and Surrounds

Location: At the southwestern tip of European Turkey.
Access: Open. The Çamlica Hills are reached from the suburb of Usküdur, on the Asian side of the Bosporus. Belgrade Forest is north of Istanbul, between Bentler and the Black Sea; it is open during daylight hours (protected by the DHKD), and there is a small entrance fee.
Timing: All year; May–July for flowers.

Good sites lie within easy reach of the overcrowded and traffic-polluted city of Istanbul. Within the city itself are Common and Alpine Swifts, a heronry in Gülhane Park, Europe's only population of Palm Dove in the streets, and Shearwater on the Bosporus.
The **Çamlica Hills** are a Mecca for birdwatchers dur-

ing the spring and especially autumn, when the migrant numbers are swelled by young birds. Passage times see vast numbers of White and Black Storks, Honey Buzzard, Black Kite, Levant Sparrow-hawk, Egyptian Vulture and Short-toed, Lesser-spotted and Booted Eagles, often flying so high you need a telescope to watch them. In spring the hills have displays of Wild Iris, Grape Hyacinth and others.

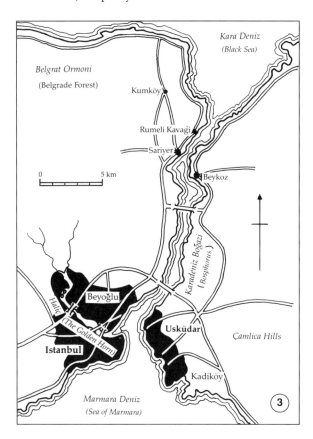

Belgrade Forest has attractive wildflowers – e.g., Cyclamen, *Iris sintenisii* and Water-lilies – and birds including numerous warblers, Kingfisher and Greater, Middle and Lesser-spotted Woodpeckers. Armies of Edible Frog make spring noisy, and there is the occasional herd of Water Buffalo. At weekends the forest is popular with walkers and joggers.

4. Apolyant

Location: About 35km west of Bursa.
Access: Open. From a narrow road to Gölyazi (Apolyant); a track runs to Mustafa Kemalpaşa. There are good views to the north from the main road and to the west from the track between Uluabat and Kumkadi.
Timing: All year.

Known also as Uluabat Gölü and as Apolyont Gölü, this large lake (13,400ha) has extensive wet meadows,

reedbeds and water-lilies on its southwestern side and Tamarisk along the Mustafa Kemalpaşa River, which feeds it. There are several islands; on one, connected to the shore by a causeway, is the village of Apolyant, the erstwhile centre of a crayfishing industry that was wiped out by pollution. Caspian Pond Tortoise and Tree-frog thrive in the reeds, but the great feature of the lake is the range of birds breeding there: Great Crested Grebe, Little Bittern, Little Egret, Spoonbill, Montagu's and Marsh Harriers, Night, Purple and Squacco Herons and colonies of Pygmy Cormorant.

5. Uludağ

Location: About 15km south of Bursa.
Access: Open, although the heights are snow-covered until late May. You can take a cablecar to Sanalan (1635m) or go by minor road from Bursa to the ski-resort.
Timing: April–August.

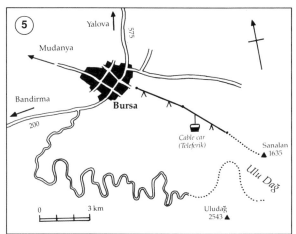

Crocuses seen in May at the edge of the melting snows in the Uludağ Massif.

The great whale-back of the Uludağ Massif, the highest in Western Anatolia (2500m), dominates the Ottoman city of Bursa; some 11,388ha of the massif is a National Park. In recent years deforestation and grazing have been deployed to create ski slopes. Near the summit sheets of crocuses – *C. biflorus* (blue) and *C. gargaricus* (yellow) – appear in May at the edge of the melting snow; they flower earlier lower down, followed by Alpine Squill, fritillaries and a pink form of Common Primrose.

The winding road to the resort moves through beech forest to pine and low juniper in the heights. Forest birds include Crossbill, Krüper's Nuthatch, Black Woodpecker, Tengmalm's Owl, Goldcrest and Firecrest. Near the screes are found Raven, both Choughs, Shore Lark and Red-fronted Serin, while among the large raptors breeding in the area are Golden Eagle and Lammergeier, plus Egyptian and Black Vultures. There is also a relict population of a race of Apollo Butterfly (*Parnassius apollo graslini*).

6. Dalyan

Location: On the south coast about 50km west of Fethiye.
Access: Open access to the lake and wet meadows, approached on paths north of Dalyan. Access to Istuzu beach is barred at night June–September, when turtles are laying and hatching.
Timing: All year; best late March onwards.

The large lake, Koycegiz Golü, surrounded by stands of *Liquidambar orientalis*, can be explored in a boat hired from Dalyan. This is an important site for wintering waterfowl as well as, in spring, Pygmy Cormorant and large numbers of nesting Little Egret, Glossy Ibis and Purple and Night Herons. The river connecting the lake to the sea is reached by cutting across fields of cotton whose irrigation ditches are alive with Marsh Frog, Caspian Pond Tortoise and Dice Snake; White Stork feed in the fields, and Corn Bunting and Wagtail are common. Several breeding pairs of Lesser Pied and Smyrna Kingfishers have been recorded.

Dalyan Estuary, where Loggerhead Turtles make their nesting grounds throughout the summer.

Between Dalyan and the sea lies ancient **Kaunos**. Rock Nuthatch breed in the ruins, and spring flowers and butterflies are prolific. The dune-backed Istuzu beach is a protected nesting-ground for Nile Soft-shelled, Loggerhead and Green Turtles, although Jackal and Wild Boar dig up the nests and there is some disturbance from tourists.

MALTA

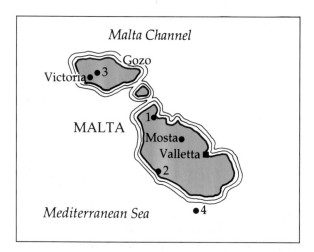

The Maltese Archipelago – Malta, Gozo and some small outlying islands, with a total area of about 320 sq km – lies well south of parts of the African coast. It is consequently very hot in summer and generally mild or even warm in winter, and its flora and fauna reflect this. Moreover, since Malta is composed almost entirely of limestone, its flora is rich.

Such factors favour a fine natural history – but sev-

Sand dunes with Sea Daffodils at Ir-ramla, Gozo.

eral things militate against them. First, Malta's high population density affects all but the most remote habitats. Second, in the absence of much planning or other control, there is extensive development, rubbish-dumping, bulldozing and general destruction almost everywhere. Third, the unpleasant hunting pressure – indeed, levels of shooting and trapping make it almost impossible for any bird or mammal to live for long – even machine-guns are used for the slaughter. Visiting Malta can be a depressing experience for the naturalist.

1. Ghadira Nature Reserve

Location: In Mellieha Bay, in the island's northwest, by the main road.
Access: On foot; at weekends and holidays only, unless by arrangement with the warden (on site).
Timing: All year.

A small area of brackish water, of varying salinity, with surrounding scrub and marshland and a wider no-shooting area around that. The birds include herons, egrets, grebes, Water Rail, Kingfisher and wildfowl, and this is a good place for passage and wintering waders, including up to 100 Ruff. The reptiles include a small Chameleon population and a Western Whip Snake variant. The flowers are mainly saltmarsh species: Golden Samphire abounds, and the very rare

Broomrape *Orobanche densiflora f. melitensis* occurs on nearby dunes; the rare Tasselweed *Ruppia drapensis* grows in the pools. There are hides, walkways and an information centre.

The Maltese Ornithological Society hopes to open a reserve in nearby **St Paul's Bay** in 1994.

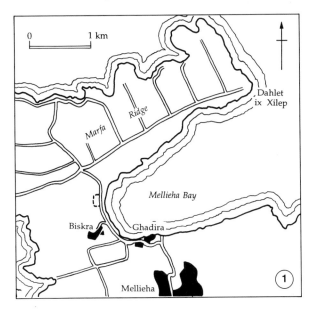

2. Dingli Cliffs

Location: On the coast south of Rabat and Dingli.
Access: Minor roads along the clifftop; access partly open on foot.
Timing: February–November.

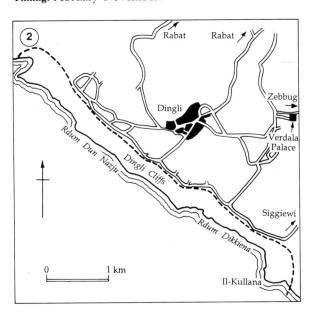

Although messy in places and regularly shot over, these limestone cliffs have a rich flora, including

many orchids, two daffodils – *Narcissus serotinus* and *N. tazetta* – the curious milkweed-relative *Periploca laevigata* and Sea Squill.

3. Gozo

Location: About 6km northwest of Malta.
Access: By ferry from Marfa Point.
Timing: Some interest all year; best February–June and autumn.

Despite having quite a dense population, Gozo is much less spoilt than Malta. Areas of interest include:

- the cliffs at Ta'Cenc, midway along the south coast, where there are breeding colonies of Storm Petrel, Manx Shearwater and Blue Rock Thrush
- the dunes at Ir-ramla, northeast of Xaghra, where there are abundant Sea Daffodil, the spiny Umbellifer *Echinophora spinosa*, Sea Holly, Yellow Horned Poppy and various bulbs
- the well visited but generally unspoilt rocky slopes around Dwejra Point and Fungus Rock, at the island's far west, which have a good flora.

Near where the ferry from Malta leaves for Gozo, the **Marfa Ridge** is another good botanical locality, especially at its southwest end; among others, *Erica multiflora* abounds.

4. Filfla Islet

Location: About 8km off the south coast of Malta, near Blue Grotto.
Access: By permit from the Environment Ministry in Valletta.
Timing: April–September.

This impressive 6ha rocky islet has some fine seabird-breeding colonies; it is particularly important for Storm Petrel, Cory's Shearwater and a local variant of Herring Gull. There are also an endemic lizard, *Podarcis filfolensis filfolensis*, and two endemic species of terrestrial snail.

The tiny islet of Filfla is important for its seabird colonies.

CYPRUS

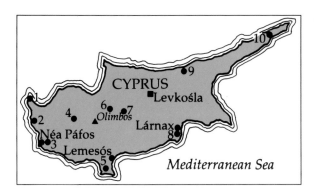

With an area of 9251 sq km, Cyprus is the third largest Mediterranean island. It escaped the ravages of the last ice age, and has a staggering diversity of rock types and natural habitats. Thus, even though about 46 per cent of the land is under cultivation, the island supports some 1800 flowering species. Its strategic location has made it virtually a 'collecting basket' for wildlife, with contributions from Asia Minor, Africa and the Mediterranean countries. It thus offers us the opportunity to see plants and animals which we could otherwise find only by making separate journeys further afield.

Until about a million years ago the Troödos to the south and the Kyrenia Mountains to the north stood as the hearts of two separate islands. The channel between them then silted up to form the central plain (Mesaöria), today a heavily cultivated and grazed area which reveals its past in the form of fossil shells exposed after winter rains. The long-term isolation of the ranges from each other and from neighbouring landmasses aided the evolution of some 120 endemic flowers and several endemic animals – butterflies, birds and even races of shrews and mice.

Geologically the island can be split into three broad regions: the northern mountains, mainly limestone; the southern mountains, volcanic heights flanked with chalks and limestone; and the central plain, formed of comparatively recent deposits, with schists forming conical hills at its edges. This geological diversity creates added interest in the four main habitat types: coastal, cultivated land, low hillsides and mountains.

About 18 per cent of the island is covered by 'forest', although this is a much more open type of wood-

OPPOSITE PAGE: *View towards the Troödos Mountains, from Limassol.*

land than the word would suggest to northern Europeans. The bird life is varied, especially in the mountains, and the island straddles spring and autumn migration routes. There are comparatively few mammals – 16 species, including eight bats – but surprising ranges of reptiles and amphibians.

To sample the wildlife at its most diverse, avoid the hot summer months: although many endemic flowers persist in the mountains through June–July and plants at the coast go on flowering all year, in the lowlands the ground bakes. Bulbs start to flower with the first rains in October–November, anemones appear at Christmas, and orchids grow in abundance in the lowlands from February. Spring sees the real explosion of colour on the plains and lower hills. The weather is unpredictable and rapidly changeable until late March. Summer temperatures can exceed 40°C inland, with a slightly more tolerable 35°C or so on the coast.

Hunting is widespread; although the netting and liming of small birds is illegal it goes on unabated. Energetic campaigning by local groups has awakened environmental awareness, and the island has just gained its first National Park, the Akamas Peninsula (site 1). The political division since the 1974 Turkish invasion means that the north, recognized by Turkey alone as a republic, cannot easily be reached by visitors to the south.

1. Akamas Peninsula

Location: The extreme northwest tip, west of Polis.
Access: Open, but keep to the paths.

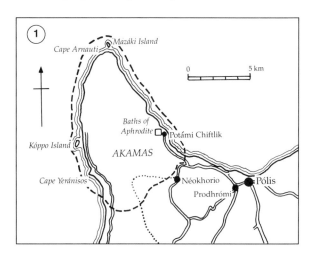

Cyclamen in spring on the Akamas Peninsula.

Timing: All year for scenery; spring and autumn for migrants; spring (from January) for flowers.

This peninsula is a National Park. The heights are covered by scrub and occasional pockets of coniferous woodland; near the shore are scrub and farmland. The geology is varied, with cliffs and deep gorges of limestone plus outcrops of serpentine and other igneous rocks. The flora is rich, especially in the gorges: there are hillsides of cascading Cyclamen in spring, various orchids, an endemic Alyssum (*A. akamassicum*) on the serpentine, and, more frequent in the north near Myrtou, local populations of *Tulipa cypria*.

Well hidden gorges provide nesting sites for Lammergeier and cave roosts for most of the island's Fruit Bat population. Increasing numbers of Black Francolin, a pair of Peregrine Falcon, Cyprus Wheatear and Cyprus Warbler breed. Autumn and spring passage migrants favour the north shore; they include Squacco and Night Herons, Little Egret, Common Crane, Garganey, Teal, Roller, Collared Flycatcher and Rüppell's Warbler.

2. Lara

Location: 25km north of Paphos, beyond Aghios Georghios.
Access: A track to the bay leads off an unsurfaced road north from Aghios Georghios. Open all year.
Timing: January–April for wildflowers; June–September for turtles.

Lara, a sweeping sandy beach, is the site of an ambitious turtle conservation project run by the Fisheries Department; both Green and Loggerhead Turtles nest here. Coast flowers include *Medicago maritima*, *Centaurea aegiophila*, *Ruta chalepensis* and, in high summer, Sea Daffodil. The *Cistus* scrub behind the beach is a riot of colour in March and April when *Gladiolus triphyllus* is in bloom.

Inland from Aghios Georghios, the **Peyia Forest** commands views over the coast and, although a comparatively recent plantation, has been colonized by numerous wild orchids and Bee Orchids.

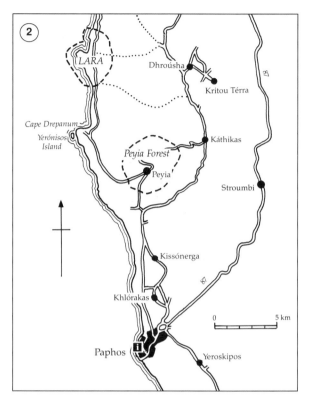

3. Paphos Area

Location: To the east and west of Paphos.
Access: Open from the B6, B7 and secondary coastal roads.
Timing: January–May for flowers; March–April for migrants; late summer–autumn for Eleonora's Falcon.

In the past decade or so coastal development near Paphos has proceeded at an alarming pace, but the town still serves as a useful centre. High cliffs to the east at Cape Aspro (near Pissouri) are home to colonies of Eleonora's Falcon (other sites are within the sovereign base, to which there is no open access) and several pairs of Peregrine Falcon. The narrow coastal strip from Aghios Georghios in the west to the Khapotami River is backed by agricultural land and much tourist development, including Paphos Airport. However, this is one of the main breeding areas for Black Francolin and a resting area for migrants – Night, Squacco and Purple Herons, Little Egret, various harriers, Lesser Kestrel, Collared Pratincole and Roller. Coastal flowers include several Stock species and bushes of *Fagonia cretica*.

4. Stavros Tis Psokhas

Location: Northwest of the Troödos Massif.
Access: All year round, either from Kykko or by going from Polis to Lyso and then east on forest roads.

Timing: All year for birds; early summer for flowers.

A forest station in the extensive Paphos Forest, which includes the Cedar Valley. The forest is the stronghold of the native Mouflon (*Ovis musimon*), shy and seldom seen wild – several are kept penned at the station. Numerous small roads lead to hidden valleys and peaks (Zakharou, Tripylos) where large raptors nest: one or two pairs of Imperial Eagle, several pairs of Lammergeier and three pairs of Bonelli's Eagle. Smaller birds include Hoopoe, Cyprus Scops Owl, Nightingale and Woodlark. The rich flora has the native Cedar *Cedrus libanii brevifolia*, several endemics (e.g., *Cyclamen cyprium*) and abundant orchids.

5. Akrotiri Salt Lake

Location: Just north of the RAF base.
Access: Take the road to the RAF base from Kolossi, west of Limassol. The shore is open, but do check with the officer at the camp gate.
Timing: Winter for wintering birds; spring and autumn for passage birds. The lake dries out in summer.

This site – a Permanent Game Reserve, with shooting permitted in the surrounding area – is of major importance for wintering and passage species. The lake is surrounded by reedbeds and marshes, with citrus

Striking mosaic left on the dried-out bed of the salt lagoon at Akrotiri.

groves and vineyards near Bishop's Pool (which takes treated effluent from the Akrotiri sewage plant); it is threatened by irrigation requirements and by the damming of source rivers. Anything up to 10,000 Flamingo, 3000 Pintail, 1000 Shelduck and a few Ruddy Shelduck winter on the lake, and in autumn thousands of Common Crane visit on passage. Spring migrants include Purple and Squacco Herons, with varying numbers of White Stork and Demoiselle Crane (up to 100 can 'stay overnight'). Marsh Harrier is the commonest spring raptor – with occasional Hen, Montagu's and Pallid Harriers – and Imperial Eagle has been seen over the Phasouri reedbeds. In spring the lakeside scrub has Green Toad, Tree-frog and Cyprus Bee Orchid, plus occasional Scorpion.

6. High Troödos

Location: A massif occupying much of the south of the island.
Access: Open from the B9 from Kakopetria or the B8 from Platres.
Timing: Birds all year; March (when the snow melts) onwards for flowers.

Snow can remain in pockets until April – the name of the peak Khionistra (1951m) means 'snow-pit'. Spring starts late but with numerous choice plants, including many endemics: *Crocus cyprius* and *C. hartmannianus*, *Corydalis rutaefolia*, *Ranunculus cyprius* var *cadmicus*, *Onosma troodii*, *Allium troodii* and *Epipactis troodii*; these do not form large-scale displays; the effect is more of a huge rock garden. Paths lead through the open mountain scenery and forests of Black Pine and Foetid Juniper, where endemic Coal Tit, Pied Wheatear, Jay, Crossbill and Short-toed Treecreeper live. One of the nature trails follows the Krios River down to Platres; posts indicate plants of interest en route. In early summer several orchids grow along the stream-bank. Around the Caledonia Falls the rare Cyprus Butterwort grows out of reach.

Extensive forests to the northwest, below Khionistra, offer Peony in May; near Prodhromos thrives a red parasite, *Orobanche cypria*; and near Kykko Monastery there is an endemic buttercup, *Ranunculus kykkoensis*.

7. Troödos Foothills

Location: Around the Troödos Massif.
Access: On well maintained dirt roads. Suitable 'access points' are, working clockwise around the massif, Kakopetria (to the north), Alona, Agros (for Pitsillia region), Makheras, Odhou and then Vavla, Omodhos and Mallia.
Timing: Spring for flowers; spring and autumn for walking.

The area is geologically very varied, underlying volcanic rocks having pushed up through chalks. Although it is much cultivated for vines and fruit, there are many 'pockets' of wild country and a rich flora, with numerous endemics. The road from Aghios Iraklidheos, near Pera (southeast of Nicosia), to Makheras Monastery epitomizes the changes, first following a dry chalk valley with orchids and Grape Hyacinth, and then coming to volcanic soils with *Cistus* and lavender bushes.

Around Makheras itself grow typical trees of the lower Troödos – *Arbutus andrachne* and *Quercus alniifolia*. Endemic flowers include *Crocus hartmannianus* and *Chionodoxia lochiae* in early spring and *Cyclamen cyprium* in autumn. The varied birds include Cyprus Scops Owl, Cyprus Warbler and Chukar. On the chalk hills you find various orchids as well as butterflies like Cleopatra, Southern White Admiral and Cyprus Festoon.

8. Larnaca Salt Lake

Location: Immediately southwest of Larnaca Airport.
Access: Open. From the B4 take the signposted road to Tekke Hala Sultana for the lake; the pine plantations are accessible from the next turning, the minor road to Dhromolaxia.
Timing: November–March for Flamingo; January–April for orchids and other flowers. The lake dries out in summer.

This system of four shallow salt lakes, three of which are interconnected, covers 658ha. An airport runway cuts through one of the lakes, and the area is threatened by pollution. About 2000 wintering Flamingo are visible from the tourist pavilion, and Black-winged Stilt, Calandra Lark, Cyprus Wheatear, Cyprus Warbler, Little Egret and others breed. Among the passage migrants in spring are Night, Squacco and Purple Herons, Glossy Ibis, Spoonbill, Avocet and Stone Curlew.

Agricultural land and scrub surround the lakes. To the west lies an area of open pine plantation with numerous orchids and Bee Orchids, including Giant Orchid and the endemic *Ophrys kotschyii*. Anemones, Turban Buttercup and Giant Fennel flower in grassland alongside the road to the Tekke.

9. Kyrenia Mountains (Pentadhaktylos)

Location: Northern Cyprus.
Access: Only from Turkey, normally by air.
Timing: All year for birds; spring for flowers.

The limestone pinnacles of the Pentadhaktylos have a 'Gothic' look. Their northerly and southerly aspects are quite different, the former being much lusher, with cyclamens, anemones and Turban Buttercup everywhere. Woods are of Aleppo Pine with Funeral Cypress and dense maquis. A mountain road runs from St Hilarion west along the range for 30km via the highest peak, Kyparrisovouno (1023m), offering stupendous views and abundances of birds, lizards and flowers – but do avoid detours in case you encounter the military.

Only the eastern approach to Buffavento is open to the public. Here Lammergeier wheel, and there are hosts of mountain birds: Blue Rock Thrush, Alpine Swift, Cretzschmar's Bunting and Raven. On the cliffs around St Hilarion and Buffavento grow endemic plants of the northern range: *Arabis cypria*, *Phlomis cypria* and *Brassica hilarionis*. Around Halevga there are large numbers of orchids including the endemic *Ophrys kotschyii*.

10. Karpas Peninsula

Location: The northeastern 'panhandle'.
Access: From the northern side of the Kyrenia Mountains go east along the coast road and then turn south via Kantara or via Komi Kebir; from south of the Kyrenia range go via the coast road from Famagusta (Gazimağusa).
Timing: All year for birds (especially spring and autumn); January to midsummer for flowers.

Long, sparsely populated, but here and there highly cultivated, with an 8000ha National Park, the peninsula is a continuation of the limestone ridge of the Pentadhaktylos, with a gently hilly spine rising to 364m at Pámboulos. There are lavish spring displays of anemones, Turban Buttercup, poppies and Gladiolus. Orchids and numerous other lime-loving plants grow in uncultivated pockets. The 'panhandle' provides a flight-path into the island for colourful migrants—Roller, Golden Oriole, Bee-eater, etc. – and a nesting area for Black Francolin. Turtle – mainly Loggerhead – come ashore to lay on the sandy beaches to the east of Cape Plakoti (Yassi Burnu), not far from the 16th-century monastery church.

The **Klidhes Islands** are Cyprus's last eastern outpost. They are home to Peregrine Falcon and are one of the few places in Cyprus where seabirds – Shag and Audouin's Gull – nest.

Spectacular bloom of the orchid Ophrys kotschyi, *found on the Karpas Peninsula and several other sites.*

SELECTIVE GLOSSARY

Aapa mire Large sloping mire (q.v.) with ridges and depressions.

Aestivation The opposite of hibernation – the stopping of all activity during the hot, dry summer.

Breckland An area of East Anglia, in England, whose special geology and climate favours a group of species that have more in common with eastern Europe; e.g., Stone Curlew and the Spring Speedwell *Veronica verna*.

Calcareous Rich in lime.

Carr Wet woodland.

Causse Dry limestone plateau area.

Dehesa A form of land use, with scattered Cork Oak in pasture.

Dolerite A base-rich volcanic rock.

Dune slacks Damp or flooded areas within a dune system.

Eutrophication The process whereby a body of water acquires unnaturally high levels of nutrients and pollutants, leading to a loss of flora and fauna.

Garrigue Low, open scrub, rich in flowers.

Karst Limestone scenery, with a collection of features such as swallowholes, caves and limestone pavement.

Kettle-hole Deep hollow, usually filled with water, caused by a block of ice melting after glaciation.

Laurrisilva Natural Laurel forest.

Lek A displaying ground for some species of birds – e.g., Black Grouse.

Lochan Small loch.

Machair Flowery pasture developed where calcareous sand has blown over soil, normally on the coast.

Maquis Tall, dense scrub.

Mire A wetland on peat.

Phrygana Scrub on dry hillsides.

Polder Low-lying area of land reclaimed from the sea.

Puszta Level, flowery grassland.

Ramsar site Wetland site considered of international importance, as defined under the Ramsar Convention (named after Ramsar, a place in Iran).

Saxicolous Habitually growing on rocks.

Schist A type of rock, often crumbly and rich in lime.

Serpentine A type of rock, rich in bases and minerals, that often supports a distinctive flora.

Tundra Land with a permanently frozen subsoil layer, thus supporting a reduced range of vegetation.

Turlough Lake fed largely by groundwater.

Whin Sill A volcanic intrusion running across the north of England; hence, rock similar to this.

RECOMMENDED READING

Arnold, E., and Burton, J.: *A Field Guide to Reptiles and Amphibians of Britain and Europe*, Collins, London, 1978

Askew, R.R.: *The Dragonflies of Europe*, Harley Books, Colchester, 1988

Bacon, L.: *Mountain Flower Holidays in Europe*, AGS, Surrey, 1979

Bibelriether, H., and Schreiber, R.L.: *Die NationalParke Europas*, Süddeutscher Verlag, München, 1990

Campbell, A.C.: *Hamlyn Guide to the Flora and Fauna of the Mediterranean*, Hamlyn, London, 1976

Campbell, A.C.: *Country Life Guide to the Seashore and Shallow Seas of Britain and Europe*, Hamlyn, London, 1984

Chinery, M.: *Collins Guide to the Insects of Britain and Europe*, Collins, London, 1986

Chinery, M.: *Butterflies and Day-Flying Moths of Britain and Europe*, Collins, London, 1989

Davies, P., Davies, J., and Huxley, A.: *Wild Orchids of Britain and Europe*, Chatto & Windus, London, 1986

Davies, P., and Gibbons, B.: *Photographic Guide to the Flowers of South Europe*, Crowood Press, Marlborough, 1993

Dickson, G.: *Green Guide: Mushrooms and Toadstools of Britain and Europe*, New Holland, London, 1992

Flegg, J.: *Photographic Field Guide to the Birds of Britain and Europe*, New Holland, London, 1993

Gibbons, B.: *Green Guide: Seashore Life of Britain and Europe*, New Holland, London, 1992

Gibbons, B., and Brough, P.: *Hamlyn Photographic Guide to the Flowers of Britain and Northern Europe*, Reed, London, 1992

Goodden, R., and Goodden, R.: *Green Guide: Butterflies of Britain and Europe*, New Holland, London, 1992

Gooders, J.: *Where to Watch Birds in Britain and Europe*, Christopher Helm, London, 1988

Gooders, J.: *Field Guide to the Birds of Britain and Europe*, Kingfisher Books, London, 1990

Grey-Wilson, C.: *The Alpine Flowers of Britain and Europe*, Collins, London, 1979

Grimmett, R., and Jones, T.: *Important Bird Areas in Europe*, ICBP and IWRB, Cambridge, 1989

Heinzel, H., Fitter, R., and Parslow, J.: *The Birds of Britain and Europe, with North Africa and the Middle East*, Collins, London, 1985

Jahns, H.M.: *Guide to the Ferns, Mosses and Lichens of Britain and Northern and Central Europe*, Collins, London, 1983

Macdonald, D., and Barrett, P.: *Collins Field Guide to the Mammals of Britain and Europe*, Collins, London, 1993

Press, Bob: *Photographic Field Guide to the Trees of Britain and Europe*, New Holland, London, 1993

Press, B., and Gibbons, B.: *Photographic Field Guide to the Wild Flowers of Britain and Europe*, New Holland, London, 1993

Raine, P.: *Mediterranean Wildlife: The Rough Guide*, Harrap-Columbus, London, 1990

The Foreign Birdwatching Reports and Information Service, run by Steve Whitehouse, offers reports by amateur birdwatchers of birding trips to all parts of Europe. These are useful for planning visits and knowing what to expect. Catalogue/information from: S. Whitehouse, 5 Stanway Close, Blackpole, Worcester WR4 9XL, UK; tel. 0905 54541.

Recommended maps

Good maps are essential for finding sites and making the most of unfamiliar territory. It is not practicable, in a book of this size, to recommend a whole range of maps for each country. For general use, I suggest one or more of those listed below. All are adequate for route-and site-finding, and often show National Parks and other protected areas.

- The **Michelin** maps and atlases, at the largest scale available – 1:200,000 for France, progressively smaller for countries away from France. The larger-scale maps mark many protected areas.
- The **RV Verlag** atlases, especially that for Central Europe, which covers 10 main countries at 1:300,000, with many National Parks and even some nature reserves marked (as 'NSG').
- The **Geocenter International Country Map** series, covering all Europe, usually at 1:800,000. These are excellent for route-planning; National Parks and other protected areas are often clearly marked. **Freytag & Berndt** issue a similar series.
- The **Mairs Geographischer Verlag General Karte** maps, at 1:200,000, cover Germany and a number of nearby countries, such as Austria and northern Italy, and mark protected sites very clearly. They are the ideal for use in the areas they cover.

Larger-scale maps are usually best obtained in the relevant country; often they are available from a site's information centre. Most good map suppliers operate a mail-order service.

INDEX OF PLACES

Page numbers in *italics* refer to photographs; *p = passim*
Placenames in **bold** refer to sites given individual entries
The symbol >> refers to another entry in the index

Aberlady Bay 40
Abernethy Reserve 38
Abisko National Park 10–12, *11, 12*
Abruzzo National Park 214, *214*
Açores >> Azores
Acosta, Salinas de 202
Adamello–Brenta Natural Park 209
Aenos, Mount 240
Affric, Glen 36
Aggtelek Cave 168
Aggtelek–Karst National Park 113, 163, 168
Agriates, Désert des 139–40
Agueda, River 176, 191
Aiguamolls de l'Emporda Natural Park 193
Aigües–Tortes y Estany de Sant Maurici 190
Aiguoal, Mont 137
Aillebrack 60
Ainsdale dunes 49
Aitone, Forest of 140–1
Akamas Peninsula 251–2, *252*
Akrotiri Salt Lake 253, *253*
Albania 227
Albarracín, Sierra de 193
Albo, Monte 217–18
Albufera (Menorca) 203
Albufera Marsh Nature Reserve (Mallorca) 203
Albula Pass 152
Alentejo Plains 178–9, *178*
Aletschhorn 149
Algarve 173, 179, 180
Aliákmon Delta 230–1
Alikes *240*
Alkmaardermeer 82
Allt nan Uamh Valley 35
Almanzor, Pico 192
Almindingen, Forest of 29
Almonda, Rio 177
Alpe Veglia 208
Alpi Apuane, Natural Park of 212
Alpilles 138
Alps 132, 133–4, *134*, 139, 143, 149, 152, 155, 207, 208, 222; *see also* Dauphine Alps; Julian Alps; Maritime Alps; **Otztaler Alps**
Altmühltal Naturpark 102
Alto Pallars–Aran, National Reserve of 190
Alto Tajo, Natural Park of 192–3
Alvao Natural Park 175
Alvor, River 180
Amsterdamse Waterleidingduinen 84

Amvrakikós Kólpos >> Árta, Gulf of
Anatolia 247
Anciennes Troufferies 76
Andalucía 199
Andelys, Les 123
Ånderdalen National Park 5
Andorra 190, 205, *205*
Andorra La Vella 205
An Eileann, Loch *37*
Anglesey 41
Ängsö National Park 14
Anlier, Forests of 76
Annacoona 60
Annecy Lake 132
Antrim Coast (North) 57–8, *58*
Antwerp 68
Aóos Gorge 233
Apennines 207
Apolyant 246
Apolyont Gölü >> Apolyant
Apremont, Gorge et Platières de 126
Aradhena Gorge 242
Arákinthos Mountains 235
Aran Isles 62–3
Aran, Val de 189–90, *189*
Arcachon Basin 129
Arcosu, Monte 219
Ardèche Gorges 137
Ardennes 77
Ards Country Park 56
Arenas San Pedro 192
Areuse Gorges 145
Argentario, Monte 213
Argentera Natural Park 210–11, *210*
Argonne Forest 123
Arnside Knott 48
Arribes del Duero 175–6, 191
Arriero, Pico d' 174
Árta, Gulf of 235
Asco Valley 140
Ashridge Estate 52
Asinara, Isola 217
Aspro, Cape 252
Astaka 234
Athos 231
Augustów Marshes 116
Austria 153–61
Auvergne 130
Ávas Gorge 232
Aveiro Estuary 176–7
Aveyron Gorges 136
Avgó 233
Aviemore 38
Axios Delta 230–1
Ayion Óros >> Athos
Azores 174, 181

Babia Góra 119

Babiogórski 119
Balaton, Lake 164
Baldegg, Lake 144
Balearic Islands 183, 202–4
Ballard Point 54
Ballater 38
Ballochbuie Forest *38*
Balranald Reserve 35
Banagher Forest 57
Banc d'Arguin 129, *129*
Bangser Ried Nature Reserve 154
Barão, Vale de 180
Barle, River 52
Barre des Écrins 132
Bass Rock 40
Bavona Valley 150
Bayerischer National Park 102, *102*
Bayerischer Spessart Naturpark 100–1
Bayerischer Wald Naturpark 102
Bedford Levels 51
Beinn Eighe >> Eighe, Beinn
Belchen–Passwang Region 144
Beles Mountains 231
Belgium 67–76
Belgrade Forest *244*, 246
Belorussia 117
Bempton Cliffs Reserve 49
Benasque National Reserve 189
Benbane Head 58
Benbecula 35
Berchtesgaden National Park 105, 157
Berlenga Islands 176
Bernese Oberland 149–50
Bernina, Massif de la 152
Bertuzzi, Valle 211–12
Beskid Mountains 118
Białowieza Forest 115, 117
Biebrza Marshes 115, 116
Biesboch 87, *87*
Bieszczadzki National Park 119
Biguglia, Lake 140
Binnensee 92
Binntal, Haut–Valais 150
Biogradska Gora National Park 224
Birkkarspitze 155
Bishop's Pool 253
Black Sea 170, 171, 225
Black Tor Copse 54
Blakeney Point 50
Blanc, Mont 120, 133
Blankaart Lake 68
Blankenberge 68
Blanket Nook 57
Blasket Islands 64
Blåvandshuk 26

Blockheide Eibenstein area 159
Bobotov Kuk 224
Bodensee 104, 145, 154
Bohan–Membre Natural Park 75
Bois du Parc 126–7
Bolgheri Wildlife Refuge 212
Bolle di Magadino Reserve 151
Bonaigua, Puerto de la 190
Bonanza 198
Bonifacio Area 141, *141*
Boquer Valley 203
Børgefjell National Park 7, *7*
Bornholm 28–9, *28*
Borrowdale 47
Boschplaat Reserve 80
Bosherston 44
Bosnia 223
Bosporus 245
Boswachterij Schoorl 82
Botranges 73
Boubínsky Prales 111
Bourgneuf Bay 125
Bouverans, Lac de 128
Bracciano, Lago di 214
Braemar 38
Brandon, Mount 64 ·
Brasil, Monte 181
Braunau 157
Breadalbane Range 39
Břeclav 113
Brecon Beacons National Park 45–6, *45*
Brecon Mountains 45, *45*
Breen Forest 58
Breidafjordur *xii*, 1
Brenne Area 125
Bridestones 49
Brière Regional Natural Park 124
Broadland Conservation Centre 50
Brocken 97
Brockhole 48
Brownsea Island 54
Buda Landscape–Protection Area 165
Bükk National Park 167–8
Bulbin, Ben 60
Bulgaria 225–6
Bullerö and Långskår Reserve 14
Burano, Lago di 213
Bure Marshes 50
Burgau–Lagos Area 180, *180*
Burren 62–3, *62*
Buttermere 48

Cabras Lagoon 219
Cabrera, Isla de 203
Cader Idris 41

Cadí–Moixeroi Natural Park 190
Cádiz Bay 201
Caenlochan 38, *38*
Caerlaverock 40
Cagliari Wetlands 219
Cairngorms 31, 36–8
Caithness 34
Calabria National Park 217
Caldera de Taburiente, National Park of the 204
Caledonia Falls 253
Camargue 137–8, *138*, 194; Swiss 146
Çamlica Hills 245–6
Campeda, Altopiano della 219
Campóo, River 185
Cañadas del Teide National Park 204
Canary Islands 174, 183, 204
Canigou, Mont 137
Cantabrica, Cordillera 184, 185
Cantal, Plomb du 130
Capri 216
Carávius, Monte 219
Carpathians 119, 170, 171
Carra, Lough 60
Casa, Pas de la 205
Casamanya, Pic de 205
Castle Gregory Peninsula 64
Castro Marim Reserve 181, *181*
Cazorla y Segura, Sierra de 197, *197*
Cephalonia National Park 240
Cerdanya, National Reserve of 190
Cerisy Forest 122–3
Cervin >> Matterhorn
Cévennes 136
Cévennes National Park 136–7
Chaine des Domes 130–1
Chambord Park 126
Champalle and Poilvache 72
Champ–Pittet Reserve 146
Chasseral 143–4, *144*
Chère, Roc de 132
Cherni Vrúh 225
Cheseaux Noréaz 146
Cheviot Hills 47
Chiemgauer Alpen Reserve *90*, 105
Chiemsee 105
Chiltern Hills 52
Chiny, Forest of 76
Cholomon Mountains 231
Ciccia, Monte 221
Cime de Bonette 139
Cinto, Monte 140
Circeo National Park 215
Clara Bog 63
Clare, County 55
Clare Island 59, *59*
Clemgia Gorge 152
Cley 50
Coire Fee 38, *38*
Col de Somport >> Puerto de Somport
Connemara National Park 59–60
Constance, Lake >> Bodensee
Copinsay 33
Córdoba Lagunas 198
Corfe Common 54
Corfino 212
Corfu 240, *240*
Corralejo dune complex 204

Cors Caron 44
Corse >> Corsica
Cors Fochno 43
Corsica 120, 139–41, 207
Cortina Dolomites 209–10, *210*
Coto Doñana National Park 198, *198*
Coto Nacional de Los Quintos de Mora 196
Covadonga National Park 185
Craig Cerrig Gleisiag 46
Craig–y–Cilau 46
Crau Plain 138
Creeslough Wood 56
Cressbrookdale 49
Crete 229–30, 241–3
Creux–du–Van 145
Croatia 222–3
Crom Castle estate 60, *61*
Cronkley Fell 48
Crotoy, Le 123
Cuenca, Serranía de 195
Cueva de la Pileta 199
Cyprus 251–4
Czech Republic 106–8, 111–12

Dafori Bay *240*
Dajtit National Park 227
Dale 44
Dale of Cottasgarth 33
Dalyan 247, *247*
Danube (Dunaj, Dunav) 102, 153, 170, 223; Delta 171; Marshes 113; Valley 107, 166, 222, 223
Dark Peak area 49
Dartmoor National Park 53–4, *53*
Dart, River 54
Dauphine Alps 132
Deelerwoud Reserve 85
Dee Valley 38, *38*
Degaña Reserve 184
Dehesa del Moncayo Natural Park 187
Delphi 236–7, *236*
Delta Padano, Natural Park of 212
Den Helder 80
Denmark 23–9
Dent de Ruth 148
Dent de Vaulion 145, *145*
De Putten Nature Reserve *82*
Derborence 148
Der–Chantecoq 127
Derrynane National Historic Park 64
Derwentwater *30*
Dévaványa Bustard Reserve 169
Dhiktean Cave 243
Dhodhóni 234
Diepholzer Moorniederung 96
Dilek Yarimadasi >> Samsun Daği
Dinant Area 71–2
Dinant Reserve 72
Dinaric Mountains 224
Dingle Peninsula 64
Dingli Cliffs 249
Dinnet 38
Dinnyes Marshes Reserve 165
Divjaka National Park 227
Djerdap National Park 223
Doll, Glen 38
Dollard 81, 92
Dollart Reserve 91–2

Dolomite Mountains *153*, *156–7*, *156*, 207, 209–10, *210*
Dolomiti di Sesto 209
Dombes Area 131
Dôme, Puy de 130
Donna Nook 50
Doubs Valley 143
Douro, Rio 175–6, 190, 191
Dove, River 49
Dovedale 49
Dovrefjell National Park 8
Dowrog Common 44
Drava, River 223
Draved Skov 28
Drei Zinnen 209
Drentsche A 81
Druidibeg, Loch 35
Drunense Duinen 88
Duero >> Douro
Dulce, Laguna 200
Dümmer Naturpark 95–6
Dunaj, Dunav >> Danube
Dundrum Bay 61
Dundrum Inner Bay 62
Dunfanaghy Area 56
Dunkery Beacon 52
Dunstable Down 52
Dunwich 51–2, *51*
Durlston Head 54
Durme Valley 68
Durmitor National Park 224
Durrenstein 159
Dwejra Point 249
Dwingelderveld National Park 84
Dyfi Estuary 42–3, *42*
Dyje, River 113

East Friesian islands 91
Ebeltoft Vig 25
Eben–Emael 71
Ebro Delta 194, *194*
Écrins National Park 132, *132*
Eiger 149
Eigg 35
Eighe, Beinn 36, *36*
Eire >> Ireland
Ejer Bavnehog 23
El Rocío 198
El Teide 204, *204*
Embalse del Guadalteba–Guadalhorce 199
Embalse de San Jose 190
Embalse de Santillana reservoir 191
Emperor Mountains >> Kaisergebirge
Ems Estuary 81, 92
Encumeada Pass 173
Engadine Mountains 152
England 46–54
Enipevs Valley *234*
Enmedio, Isla de 197
Entinas–Sabinar, Punta 201
Eólie o Lipari, Isole 221
Ephesus 245
Epidaurus (Epídhavros) 238
Eriskircher Ried 104
Er Lannic 124
Erne, Lough 60–1, *61*
Errisbeg/Roundstone bog complex 60
Escaut, River 68
Eskisigirci 245
Espie, Castle 61
Esrum Sø 27
Esthwaite Water 48
Estrela, Serra da 173, 177, *177*
Etna 207, *220*, 221

Europa, Picos de 184, 185–6, *185*
Évros Delta 232
Exmoor National Park 52, 54

Fair Head 58
Fair Isle 32
Faja de Pelayo 188
Falsterbo 16
Famara Ridge 204
Fanges Forest 137, *137*
Farilhoes 176
Farma, Valle del 212
Farndale 49
Farne Islands 46, *46*
Federsee 103
Fédrun, Île de 124
Ferrand, Puy 130
Ferriere, Vallone del 216
Fertö tói (Neusiedler See) 163
Fetlar 32
Fetzachmoos 104
Fico, Cala 219
Filfla Islet 249, *249*
Finges Forest >> Pfynwald/Finges Forest
Finland 17–21
Flagbakken Hill 24
Flevoland 83, 85
Flores, Coast of 181
Flüela Pass 152
Flumen, Gorge du 128
Foci dell'Isonzo >> Isonzo, River
Fontainebleau Forest 126, *126*
Fonteintjes, Les 68
Formentera 204
Formentor, Cabo 202
Fort–Mahon–Plage 123
Forvie, Sands of 38
Foula 32
Foyle, Lough 57
France 120–41
Franchard, Gorges de 126
Francia, Peña de 195
Fränkische Schweiz–Veldensteiner Naturpark 101
Franz Josef's Glacier *156*
Frasne Lake 128
Fréhel, Cap 122
Fruška Gora National Park 223
Fuente Dé 186
Fuente de Piedra, Lago de la 199–200, *199*
Fuentes Carrionas Reserve 185
Fuerteventura 204
Fungus Rock 249
Furfooz Natural Park 72
Fusine Natural Park 210
Fyns Hoved Reserve 27

Gabcikovo 113
Gairloch Conservation Unit 36
Gait Barrows 48
Galdhøppiggen 3, 8
Galibier, Col du 132
Galičica National Park 224
Gallocanta, Laguna de 192
Garajonay National Park 204
Gargano Peninsula 214–15, *215*
Garphyttan National Park 13–14
Garrotxa Natural Park 190
Gata, Cabo de 183, 201–2
Gata, Sierra de 195
Gelten–Iffigen 148–9, *149*

Geltenschuss Falls 148
Gemenc Area 166
Gempen, Plateau of 144
Generoso, Mount 152
Geneva, Lake 147, *147*
Gennargentu 217, 218
Geras area 159
Gerecse Hills 163–4
Gerlachovsky Stít 110
Germany 91–105
Geros, River 242
Ghadira Nature Reserve 248–9
Giant's Causeway 58, *58*
Giara de Gésturi 219
Gibraltar 202
Gibraltar Point 49–50
Gill, Lough 64
Gious Kambos *242*
Girao, Cabo 173
Glas Maol 38
Glaubenberg 146
Glenade Lough 60
Glenamoy Bog 59
Glendalough 63, *63*
Glendalough Valley 63
Glengarriff Wood 65
Glenveagh Castle *56*, 57
Glenveagh National Park 56–7
Glomdalen Valley 7
Goeree 86–7
Gomera 204
Goramakil, Monte 186
Gordolasque Valley 139
Gotland 16
Gouffre Natural Park >> Lesse and Lomme Nature Reserve
Gower Peninsula 44–5
Gozo 248, *248*, 249
Grabenstätt 105
Graciosa Natural Park 204
Grado, Laguna di 210
Gramat, Causse 129–30, *129*
Grammos–Smólikas Area 232
Grande, Isola 220
Grande Cassé, La 133
Grande Fagne 72
Grand–Lieu Lake 125
Grand Mont Point 124
Grand Veymont 132
Gran Paradiso National Park 207–8, *208*
Grassholm 43–4
Grazalema 199
Great Britain 31–54
Great Skellig 64
Gredos, Circo de 192
Gredos, Sierra de 192, *192*
Greece 229–43
Greek Islands 240–1
Grésigne, Forest of 136
Gressåmoen National Park 7
Grevelingen Lake 86
Gribskov 27
Grimselpass 150
Grindelwald–Bernese Oberland Area *142*, 149–50, *150*
Groote Peel *78*, 88
Grosser Beerberg 100
Gross Glockner 156
Gründlen Ried 104
Guadalquivir Delta 198
Guadarrama, Sierra de 191, *191*, 192
Gudená, River 27
Gudenåens og Skjern Åens Kilder Natural Park *22*, 27
Gugny 116
Guisando, Cerro de 192
Gülhane Park 245
Hadrian's Wall 47

Hagensdorf Area 159
Hageven 70
Hagleiten area 158
Hagleren–Glaubenberg Area 146
Halevga 254
Hamar, Keen of 32
Hamburgisches Wattenmeer National Park 92
Hámor 167
Hamra National Park 13
Handa Island 33, *33*
Hanság 163
Hantsholm Reserve 24, *24*
Harbottle Crags 47
Hardangervidda National Park 9, *9*
Harderbroek marsh area 83
Harderwijk Area 84–5
Harskampse Zand 85
Harthorpe Burn *46*
Harz Mountains 91, 97, *97*; *see also* Hoch Harz National Park
Haut Asco 140
Haute–Engadine 152
Haute–Savoie Mountains 133
Hautes Fagnes 73, *73*, 99
Havergate 52
Hayedo de Tajera Negra Natural Park 192
Hebrides 35
Heidenhäuschen Reserve 100
Hellevoetsluis 86
Helligdommen *28*
Helmos, Mount 238
Hermaness *32*
Hessischer Spessart Naturpark 100
Hickling Broad 50, *50*
Hierdense Beek 84
High Force 48
High Harz >> Hoch Harz
High Tatras >> Vysoké Tatry
Hindsholm Natural Park 27
Hjälstaviken Bird Reserve 14
Hoch Harz National Park 97
Hochkonig 157
Hoge Veluwe National Park 85, *85*
Hohe Tauern National Park 154, 156, *156*
Hohe Wand 161
Hölloch Cave 147
Holme Dunes 50
Holyhead Island 41
Holy Island (Lindisfarne) 46
Hornborgasjön 14, *14*
Horn Head 56
Hornstrandir Landscape Reserve 1
Hortobágyi National Park *162*, 168–9, *169*
Horusicky Rybník 112
Hüfingen Orchid Woods 102–3, *103*
Hulshorsterzand 84
Hundsheimer Berg 161
Hungary 162–9
Hymettus 237

Ibiza 204
Iceland 1–2
Idwal, Cwm and Llyn 41
Iglesiente Massif 219
Île de Noirmoutier Peninsula 125
Ilha do Pico, Montanha da 181
Imbros Gorge 242
Imitós >> Hymettus

Inch Lough 57
Inchnadamph 35
Inch Spit 64
Ingleton *48*
Ingolstadt 102
Inn, River 157
Invernaver 33
Inverpolly 34–5, *34*
Ioánnina 234, *234*
Ioánnina, Lake >> Pamvótis, Lake
Irati, Forêt d' 135
Ireland 55–65
Ir–ramla *248*, 249
Iser Mountains 107
Islas Cíes Natural Park 186
Ismaninger Teichgebiet 105
Isonzo, River 210
Istanbul Area *244*, 245–6
Italy 207–21
Iti Óros >> Mount Oeti National Park
Ivinghoe Beacon 52

Jandía Peninsula 204
Jasmund National Park 93
Jauberton, Vallée du 126
Jizerské Hory 107, *107*
Jokulsargljufur National Park 2
Jonte, Gorges de la *121*, 136
Jotunheimen National Park 8
Jouktas, Mount 243
Joux, Lac de 145, *145*
Joux Valley Area 145
Jucar Valley 195
Julian Alps 222
Jungfrau 149
Jura Mountains 101, 143
Jutland (Jylland) 23

Kaisergebirge 155
Kallesmaesks Hede 26
Kalloní, Gulf of 241
Kalmthoutse Heide 69, *69*
Kalogria Area 238
Kaltbrunner Riet Reserve 147
Kampinoski National Park 116–17
Karaburuni Peninsula 227
Karawanken Mountains 158–9, *158*
Kardoskut Fehér–tó 167
Karkonoski National Park 117
Karlsö Islands 16
Karpas Peninsula 254, *254*
Karwendel Gebirge, German 104–5
Karwendel Nature Reserve 104, 155
Kassándra 231
Kastoría Lake 230, *230*
Katáras Pass 233
Káto Olympus 235
Kävsjön, Lake 15
Kefallinía >> Cephalonia
Kennemerduinen 84
Kerkini, Lake 231
Kérkira >> Corfu
Khalkidhikí >> Chalcidice
Khapotami River 252
Kielder Forest 47
Kilfenora 62
Killard 62
Killarney National Park 65
Kis–Balaton Reserve 164
Kiskunság National Park 165–6, *165*
Klidhes Islands 254
Klingnau, Lake 144
Knockan 35
Kongens Mose 28

Kongsvoll 8
Königssee 105
Kónitsa 232
Kootwijker Zand 85, *85*
Kornati National Park 223
Kóronia, Lake 231–2
Kőszeg Hills 163
Koycegiz Gölü 247
Krimml Falls 156
Krios River 253
Krití >> Crete
Krka National Park 223
Krkonose National Park 108
Kvigtind 7
Kykko Monastery 253
Kynance Cove 54, *54*
Kyparrisovouno 254
Kyrenia Mountains 251, 254

La Cayolle, Col de 139
La Demanda, Sierra de 186–7
La Gabrière 125
Laganás 241
Lainzer Tiergarten 159–60
Lake District National Park *30*, 47–8, *47*
La Massane Forest 137
Lamb's Head 64
La Mola 204
Lamone, River 211
Langádha Gorge 238
Lanzarote 204
La Peña, Sierra de 187–8, *187*
La Peña de Francia, Sierra de 195
Lara 252
Larnaca Salt Lake 254
Larzac, Causse 136
Las Batecuas, National Reserve of 195
La Serena 197
Las Lagunas de Ruidera, Natural Park of 196–7
Las Marismas del Odiel 197
Lathkilldale 49
Lato 243
Lattari Peninsula 216, *216*
Lauterbrunnen Valley 150
Lauwersmeer 81
Lavezzi, Îles 141
Lawers, Ben 39, *39*
Laxa, River 2
Le Boréon 139
Łebsko 115
Le Cesine 216
Le Chasseral 143
Lednice Area 112–13
Leighton Moss 48
Léman, Lac >> Geneva, Lake
Lemmenjoki National Park 18–19
Le Rozier 136
Les Baux 138
Lesbos >> Lésvos
Lésina, Lake 214
Lesse and Lomme Nature Reserve 75
Lesse Valley 72
Lésvos 241
Leuvenumse Bos 84
Levante, Salinas de 203
Leven, Loch 39, *39*
Lévka Óri (White Mountains) 230, 241–2, *241*
Leyre, Sierra de 186
Liathach 36
Lienz Dolomites *153*, 156–7, *156*
Liereman Reserve 69–70
Liesjärvi National Park 21
Limassol *250*

Lindisfarne 46
Linnansaari National Park
19–20
Liszt Ferenc 166
Little Danube 113
Little Retezat 171
Little Skellig 64
Littondale 48
Lizard 54, *54*
Llogara National Park 227
Lobau Reserve 159–60
Lobo, Pico del 192
Loch Druidibeg Reserve 35
Loch Garten 38
Lochnagar, Mount 38, *38*
Loe Pool 54
Løgstør Bredning 24, *24*
Loonse en Drunense Duinen 88
**Los Ancares Leoneses National
Reserve** 183–4
Los Circos National Reserve
189
**Los Montes Universales,
National Reserve of** 193, 195
Lot Valley 130, *130*
Lough Navar Forest 60
Loumarin, Combe de 138
Lovćen National Park 224
Lozère, Mont 137
Luberon Natural Regional Park
138
Lucerne, Lake 146
Lui, Ben 39
Lüneburger Heide 69, 94, *95*
Lura National Park 227
Luxembourg 77, *77*
Luxembourg Natural Park
77, 99
Lydford Gorge *53*

Macdui, Ben 37
Macedonia 224, 227
MacGillycuddy's Reeks 65
Maddalena Archipelago 217
Madeira 173–4
Madonie 207, 220, *220*
Madonne de la Fenestre
Valley 139
Maggiore, Lake 150–1
Magharee islands 64
Magilligan Point 57
Maglic 223
Makheras 254
Malá Fatra 108–9, *109*
Malham Cove and Tarn 48
Mal i Dejës 227
Mallorca 183, 202–3
Malta 248–9
Maly Dunaj 113
Maly Tisy 112
Máni Peninsula 239–40, *239*
**Manyas–Kuş Cenneti National
Park** 245
**Marais Poitevin Regional
Natural Park** 128
Marano Lagoon 211
Marathón Lake 237
Marathón Marshes 237, *237*
March, River 160
Marchauen Reserve 160
Maree, Loch 36
Maremma Natural Park 213,
213
Marfa Ridge 249
Margherita di Savoia, Salina di
215
Mariapeel/Marienveen 89
Maritime Alps 134, 139
Märkische Schweiz Naturpark
96
Marsala, Stagnonie di 219–20

Martin Mere 49
Marwick Head 33
Marzelle, La 125
Massaciuccoli, Lake 212
Massacre Forest 128
Massif Central 130
Maten 71
Matterhorn 149
Maures, Massif des 139, *139*
Mavrovo National Park 224
Mechelse Heide 71
Medes, Islas 193
**Mediana–Belchite Steppe
Country** 188
Medina, Laguna de 201
Megalí Préspa 230
Meijendel Dunes 84
**Meissner–Kaufunger Wald
Naturpark** 97–8
Meissner Nature Reserve 98,
98
Méjean, Causse 136
Melides, Lagoa de 179
Menorca 183, 203
Mera, River 211
Mercantour National Park
139, 211
Merveilles, Vallée des 139
Mesaöria 251
Mesola, Forest of 212
Mesolóngion Marshes >>
Missolonghi Marshes
Messina, Straits of 221
Metéora *228*, 234
Mettnau Peninsula 104
Meuse, River 76
Mezzola Lake 211
Michalovce, Lake 111
Middelburg 87
Midi, Aiguille du 133
Miedriene, Mount *118*
Migliarino–San Rossore,
Natural Park of 212
Mikrí Préspa 230
Milicz Ponds 117
Millau Causses 136
Mincio Valley 211
Mindelsee 103, *103*
Minsmere 51–2
Mirador de Llesba 186
Missolonghi Marshes 235
Mistras Lagoon 219
Mitrikou, Lake 232
Mljet National Park 223
Moines, Île aux 122
Molentargius 219
Mols Bjerge Natural Park 25
Molsbroek 68
Monchique, Serra de *172*, 179
Monfragüe Natural Park
194–5, *195*
Mongan's Bog 63
Monk Dale *49*
Monsal Dale *49*
**Montagne St Pierre (De Sint
Pietersberg)** 71, 89
Montenegro 224, 227
Monte Pollino Regional Park
217
**Monte di Portofino Natural
Park** *206*, 211
Montejo de la Vega 191
Montmirat, Col de 136
Montesinho Natural Park 175
Montseny Natural Park 193–4
Montserrat, Sierra de 193
Moor House Reserve 48
Morava, River 107, 113
Morbihan, Gulf of *124*
Morecambe Bay 48
More Coigach, Ben 34–5
Morfa Harlech 41

Morgam–Viibus 18
Morrone Birkwood 38
Morteys, Vallon des 148
Mount Oeti National Park 235
Mount Olympus National Park
234–5, *234*
**Mount Parnassus National
Park** 236, *236*
Mourne Mountains 61, 62, *62*
Moussala, Mount 226
Muckross Peninsula 65
Muddus National Park 12
Muick, Coyles of 38
Muick, Glen 38
Muir of Dinnet Reserve 38
Mulhacén 200
Mullagh Mor 62
Mullet 59
Mullion 54
Mumbles 45
Muniellos Reserve 184
Murg Valley 147
Murgtal >> Murg Valley
Müritz National Park 93–4, *94*
Müritz See 93
Murlough Nature Reserve
61–2, *62*
Mustafa Kemalpaşa River
246
Mylíni >> Lésvos
Mystra 238, *239*
Myvatn, Lake 1, 2, *2*

Nacung, Lough 57
Nant Ffrancon *41*
Neagh, Lough 61
Nebrodi Mountains 207, 221
Nerosa, Mt 174
Ness Wood 57
Netherlands >> Holland
Neuchâtel, Lake 143, 146
Neuhaus–Weissenau 150
Neusiedler See 154, 160, *160*,
161; *see also* Fertő tói
Neuwerk 92
New Forest 52–3, *53*
Newborough Warren *41*
Niedere Tauern Mountains
157–8, *158*
**Niedersächsisches Wattenmeer
National Park** 91–2
Nissum Fjord 24–5
Nízke Tatry National Park 109
Nockberge National Park 158
Noir, L'étang de 134–5, *134*
Noordhollands
Duinreservaat 82
Nordeifel Naturpark 99
Norfolk Broads 50, *50*
Norfolk Coast (North) 50, *50*
North Bull Island 64
Northern Ireland >> Ireland
North Ronaldsay 33
Northumberland National Park
46–7, *46*
Northwest Mountains
(Mallorca) 202
Northwest Peninsula (Iceland) 1
**North York Moors National
Park** 49
Norway 3–9
Noss 32
Noup Head 33
Novo San Giovanni, Monte
218
Novozámecky Rybnik 107
Noyalo, Étang de 124
Nymindegab 26

**Ocsa Landscape–Protection
Area** 166

Odiáxere, River 180
Oeti, Mount 235
Ogof–ffynnon–ddu Reserve
46
Ohrid, Lake 224, 227
Ohridsko Jezero >> Ohrid,
Lake
Oisterwijkse Vennen 88
Ojcowski National Park 118
Öland 15–16
Olette Reserves 137
Olimbos >> Olympus
Olympia 238
Olympus 229, 234–5
Omalós 241–2
Oost–vaarders Plassen 83
Oostvoorne 86
Orbetello 213
Ordesa National Park 188–9,
189, 190
Orford Ness 52
**Orient Forest Regional Natural
Park** 127, *127*
Oristano, Gulf of 218–19
Orkney Isles 32–3
Oro, Monte d' 141
Orosei, Bay of 218
Őrség Hills Protected Area
163
Ossau, Vallée d' 135
Otztaler Alps 155
Oude Landen 68–9
Oulanka National Park *17*, 19
Ouse Washes 51
Øvre Anarjåkka National Park
6
Øvre Dividal National Park 6
Øvre Pasvik National Park 6,
6
Oxford Island 61
Oxwich Bay 45

Padjelanta National Park 12
Paklenica National Park 223
Pálava 112–13
Pálava Hills 112
**Pallas–Ounastunturi National
Park** 18, *18*
Pamvótis, Lake 233–4, *234*
Panahaiko Mountains 238
**Panaveggio–Pale di San
Martino, Natural Park of**
209, *209*
Pandetrave, Puerto de 186
Pantani di Capo Passero 221
Papa Westray 33
Paphos Area 252
Parikkala 21
Parnassós >> Mount
Parnassus National Park
Párnitha National Park 237
Parori Gorge 238
Paul da Serra 173
Paúl de Arzila 176
Paúl do Boquilobo 177–8
Pays de Monts Forest 125
Peak District National Park
49, *49*
Peatlands Country Park 61
Peitz 97
Pelister National Park 224
Peloponnese (Pelopónnisos)
229
Peloritani, Monte 221
**Pembrokeshire Coast National
Park** 43–4, *44*
Peñalara 191
Peneda–Gerês National Park
174–5, *174*
Pentadhaktylos >> Kyrenia
Mountains
Pen–y–Fan 45, 46

Pera 254
Perdido, Monte 189
Peristéri 233
Perucica 223
Pescasseroli Zoo 214
Petaloúdhes 241
Péteri–tói Nature Reserve 167
Petkeljärvi National Park 20–1
Peyia Forest 252
Pfynwald/Finges Forest 149
Phaestos 242, *242*
Phaistos >> Phaestos
Piana di Albanesi, Lago di 220
Pico, Puerto del 192
Picos de Tres Mares area 185
Piedade, Ponta de 180
Pieljekaise National Park 13
Pieninski National Park 110, 119
Pieniny National Park 110
Pierreuse 148
Pilat, Dune du 129
Pilat, Mont 131
Pilat Natural Regional Park 131
Pilis Hills 165
Píndhos Mountains >> Pindos Mountains
Pindos Mountains 232–3, *232*
Pindos National Park 233
Pineta, Valle de 189
Piora 151
Pírgos 238
Pírgos Dhiroú 240
Pirin National Park 225, 226
Pivka Cave 223
Piz Kesch 152
Plakoti, Cape 254
Planina Cave 223
Plitvice National Park 223
Plöckenstein 148
Po Delta 211–12, *212*
Poland 115–19
Pollença, Puerto de 202–3, *202*
Poole Harbour 54
Port–Cros National Park 138–9, *139*
Port d'Envalira 205
Pórto Lágo 232
Portugal 173–81
Postojna Caves 222–3
Predannack 54
Prespa, Lake 224, 227
Préspa National Park 230
Prespansko Jezero >> Prespa, Lake
Prieta, Pico de Peña 185
Puertos de Beseit, National Reserve of 194
Puex Odle Park 209
Puffin Island 64
Puig Major 202
Puig Tomir 202
Punta Mortella 140
Punte Alberete Reserve 211
Pupplinger Au Reserve 104
Purbeck, Isle of 54, *54*
Purgschachen Moor 157
Purl's Bridge 51
Pusztaszer Landscape Reserve 167
Puy de Sancy Area 130
Puy–Mary/Plomb du Cantal area 130
Pyhä–Häkki National Park 19
Pyhätunturi 19
Pyhätunturi National Park 19

Pyrenees 135, *135*, 186, 188–90, *189*, 205
Pyrénées Occidentales, Parc National des 135, 188

Queyras, Combe du *134*
Queyras Regional Natural Park 133–4
Quinta da Rocha area 180
Quoile Pondage 61

Råbjerg Mile dune *23*, 24
Radolfzell 104
Rahasane Turlough 63
Ramsey 43
Rathdrum woods 63
Rathlin Island 58
Rathlin O'Birne 58
Ravenglass 48
Raven Nature Reserve 65
Reisa National Park 5
Remoray Lake 127–8
Rentina Gorge 232
Retezat National Park 170–1
Reuss Valley 144
Reykjavik Area 2
Rhine (Rhein) Delta 86–7, 154
Rhodes 241
Rhodope Mountains 226
Rhône Delta 147
Rhône Valley 131
Rhum 35
Ria Formosa Natural Park 180
Ribble Estuary Area 49
Ribblesdale 48
Ribeiro Frio Valley 174
Riddagshausen–Weddeler Teichgebiet 96
Rila Mountains 225–6
Rincon, Laguna del 198
Ringkøbing Fjord 25–6, *26*
Risnjak National Park 223
Rissbach Valley 155
Ritom, Lake 151
Riu d'Aguamaix *189*
Robin Hood's Bay 49
Rocher Cuvier Chatillon 126
Roches d'Orival 123
Ródhos >> Rhodes
Roe Estuary 57
Rohrsee 104
Rolle Pass 209, *209*
Romania 170–1
Rømø 28
Ronda Gorge *182*, 199
Rondane National Park 8–9
Rondinara, Golfe de 141
Roquetas de Mar 201
Rosa, Monte 149
Roses (Rosas) 193
Roskilde Fjord 27
Ross Lough 60
Rothenthurm Peatlands 146
Roudsea Wood 47
Rouge, Aiguilles 133
Rouge Poncé Forest Reserve 75
Rouvroy 76
Ruivo, Pico 174
Runde Island 8
Rusenski Lom National Park 226

Saaristomeri >> Southwestern Archipelago National Park
Sächsische Schweiz National Park 98–9, *99*
Sado Estuary 179
Sagres, Ponta de 179
St Flour Area 131
Saint–Hubert Forest 75
St Moritz 152

St Paul's Bay 249
Saja, National Reserve of 184–5
S'Albufera 203
Sale Porcus Lake 219
Saliencia, Lagos de 184
Salinas, Cabo 203
Salobrar de Campos, Lagunas de 203
Saltfjellet–Svartisen National Park 6–7, *7*
Saltfleetby 50
Samaria Gorge 242
Samsø Island 27
Samsun Daği 245
Sancy, Puy de 130
Sandalo, Capo 219
Sandflot 9
San Giorgio, Monte 151–2
San Giusta Lake 219
San Jacinto dunes 177
San Juan de La Peña *187*
San Pietro Island 219
Santa Pola, Salinas de 197
Sant Llorenc del Munt Natural Park 193
Santo André Lagoon 179
Santos Morcillo, Laguna 197
San Vicente, Cabo de 179, *179*
São Miguel 181
Saone Valley 131
Sardinia 207, 217–19
Sarek–Padjelanta Complex of National Parks 12
Sárospatak 168
Sarzeau 124
Satchinez Reserve 170, *170*
Savelsbos 89, *89*
Scandola Nature Reserve 141
Scarrif Island 64
Schachblumen Reserve 159
Scharhörn 92
Schermützelsee Nature Reserve 96
Schiermonnikoog Island 80–1, *81*
Schleswig–Holsteinisches Wattenmeer National Park 92
Schlierbachswald 98, *98*
Schonebrune Palace Gardens 159
Schouwen Island 87
Schwabian Jura >> Schwäbische Alb
Schwäbische Alb 101
Schwäbische–Frankischer Wald 101
Schwarzer Mann 99
Scolt Head 50
Scotland 31–41
Scutari, Lake >> Shkodra, Lake
Seewinkel Area 154, 160–1
Seilles 72
Seine Valley Chalklands 123, *123*
Selçuk 245
Selenter See 92–3
Semois Wetlands, Upper 76, *76*
S'Ena Arrúbia Lake 219
Sept–Îles, Les 120–2, *120*
Serbia 223
Serra da Estrela Natural Park 173, 177, *177*
Serra de Arrábida Natural Park 178
Serranía de Cuenca Reserve 195
Serras de Aire and Candeeiros Natural Park 176

Serre, Montagne de 131
Severn, River 51
Sextener–Dolomiten 209
Shannon Estuary 63
Sharpen Hill *53*
Sheskinmore Lough 56
Shetland Isles 31–2, *32*
Shkodra (Scutari, Skadar), Lake 224, 227; see also Skadarsko Jezero National Park
Sicily 207, 219–21
Siebengebirge Naturpark 99–100
Sierra de Grazalema Natural Park 199, *199*
Sierra del Cadí hunting reserve 190
Sierra España, National Reserve of 197
Sierra Nevada 200, *200*
Silberen 147
Silverdale Area 48
Sinis Peninsula 218–19
Sithonía 231
Sitía 243
Sivá Brada 110
Skadarsko Jezero National Park 224; see also Shkodra, Lake
Skaftafell National Park 2, *2*
Skagen Peninsula 23–4, *23*
Skallingen 26
Skellig Islands 64, *64*
Skellig Michael 64
Skiddaw *30*
Skjern Å, River 27
Skokholm 43, 44
Skomer 43
Skuleskogen National Park 13
Slangebeekbron 71
Sliedrechtse Biesboch 87
Slievanorra 58
Slieve League 58–9
Słonsk Reserve 116
Slovakia 106–7, 108–11, 113
Slovenia 222–3
Slovensky Kras 113
Slowiński National Park 115–16, *116*
Smeerenburg Fjord *3*
Smólikas 232
Snaefellsnes Peninsula 1
Snepkensvijver 69
Snowdon 41
Snowdonia National Park 41–2, *41*
Sologne 126
Solway Firth 40–1
Somiedo, National Reserve of 184
Somme Estuary 123
Somport, Puerto (Col) de 188
Son Bou 203
Sonfjället Group of National Parks 13
Sonsaz National Reserve 192
Sopron Hills 163
Soúnion National Park 237–8
Southwestern Archipelago National Park 21
Spain 183–204
Spárti *239*
Spelunca Gorge 140–1, *140*
Sperchios (Spérkhíos) Delta 235
Spey Valley 36–8, *37*
Spitzbergen *3*, 4, *4*, 41
Spreewald 97
Sreburna Reserve 226
Stabbursdalen National Park 4–5

Stadil Fjord 24–5
Stan Begej, River 170
Stavros Tis Psokhas 252–3
Steinernes Meer Area 157
Steinhuder Meer Naturpark 96
Stellendam 86
Stelvio National Park 208–9
Steps Bridge 54
Stimfalías, Lake 238
Štirovnik 224
Stockholm Area 14
Stora Sjöfallet National Park 12
Store Mosse National Park 15
Strangford Lough 61
Strathy Point and Bay 33
Stromboli 221
Strumpshaw Fen 50
Stubbergard Sø 25
Studland dunes 54
Südeifel Naturpark 99
Súl'ovské Skály 108
Súl'ovské Vrchy 108, 108
Sumava 102, 106, 111–12, 111
Superiore di Mantova, Lake 211
Surtsey 2
Sutherland Flowe Country 34
Sutjeska National Park 223–4
Svalbard >> Spitzbergen
Svartisen 7
Swaledale 48
Sweden 10–16
Swiss Camargue 146
Swiss National Park 152, 208
Switzerland 143–52
Sylt 92
Szatmár–Bereg Plain 169

Tabernas Badlands 200–1
Tablas de Daimiel National Park 196
Tacumshin Lake 65
Taígetos (Taíyetos) Mountains 238–9
Tailles, Plateau des 72–3
Tajo >> Tejo
Tåkern Lake 15
Tara, National Park of 223–4
Tara Gorge 224
Tarn, Gorges du 136
Tarvisio Forest 210
Tatai Öreg-tó 164
Tatra National Parks 118–19, 118
Tatras 114, 115, 118–19, 118; see also Tatra National Parks; Vysoké Tatry
Tatrzanski 119
Teba Gorge 199
Tecino Delta 150–1
Teesdale, Upper 48
Teich Ornithological Park 129
Teign, River 54
Tejo (Tajo), Rio 176, 177, 193
Tejo Estuary 178
Tekke River 254
Tenerife 204, 204
Tenhaagdoornheide 70–1
Tentsmuir Point 40
Terceira 181
Termoncarragh Lake 59

Terschelling Island 80
Tessin Delta >> Tecino Delta
Testa, Capo 217
Teufelshöhle 101
Teut 70–1
Texel 79–80, 80
Texel Gruppe Natural Park 210
Thaya Valley 159
Thethi National Park 227
Thingvallavatn 1
Thingvellir National Park 1
Thornton Force 48
Thunersee 150
Thüringer Wald 91, 100
Tiergarten 159–60
Tihanyi Peninsula 164
Timanfaya National Park 204
Tiroler Ache Reserve 105
Tisza Valley 166–7, 167
Titchwell 50
Tiveden National Park 14–15, 15
Tjornin, Lake 2
Tomorri National Park 227
Topo, Ilhéu do 181
Torcal de Antequera 200, 200
Torneträsk, Lake 10
Toros Mountains 244
Torre del Vinagre 197
Torridon 36
Totternhoe Knolls 52
Tourbières de St Moritz 152
Trebon Basin 112, 112
Tre Cime di Lavaredo 209
Tregaron Bog >> Cors Caron
Trémiti Islands 214
Triglav National Park 210, 222
Trinity Mountains 141
Trogener Klamm 158, 159
Troödos Mountains 250, 251; Foothills 253–4; High 253
Trujillo Area 195–6, 196
Trümmelbach Falls 150
Turkey 244–7
Turnhout–Hasselt Canal 70
Turo de l'Home 193
Turracherhohe area 158

Ubiña, Peña 184
Uists 35
Uluabat Gölü >> Apolyant
Uludağ 246–7, 246
Ulster >> Ireland
Umbra, Forest of 214–15
Undeloh 94
Unst 32
Unteres Odertal National Park 95
Untersberg 157
Untersee 104, 145
Upper Teesdale Nature Reserve 48
Uppsala 14
Uragh Wood 65
Urbion, Sierra de 186–7
Urner See 146
Urwald 159

Vadvetjåkka National Park 10–12

Valais 149
Valbois Ravine 127
Vane Farm 39, 39
Vanil–Noir 147–8
Vanoise National Park 132, 133, 133, 208
Van Voorne Dunes 86
Vara, Pico da 181
Varanger Peninsula 4, 4
Varano, Lake 214
Vauville Dunes 122
Veerse Meer 87
Velebit Mountains 223
Velence, Lake 164–5
Velencei-to >> Velence, Lake
Vel'ká Fatra Mountains 109
Veluwezoom National Park 86
Venezia, Laguna di >> Venice, Gulf of
Venice, Gulf of 211
Vennen 88
Venta, Rio de la 199
Vercors Regional Natural Park 131–2, 132
Verde, Pico 181
Vertes Hills 164
Vessertal 100
Vesuvius 215–16
Vico Lake Nature Reserve 213–14
Vienna 159
Vierwaldstätter See 146
Vignemale 188
Vihorlat 110
Vikos–Aóos National Park 233
Vikos Gorge 233, 233
Villafáfila Area 190–1
Viñamala National Reserve 188
Virelles Lake 66, 73–4, 74
Viroin 74
Visegrád Hills 165
Vistónis, Lake 232
Vitosa National Park 226
Vizzavona Forest 141
Vlieland Island 80
Volkmarsberg 101
Vólvi, Lake 231–2
Vorpommersche Boddenlandschaft National Park 92
Vorsee 104
Vosges du Nord Regional Natural Park 124, 124
Vouga, River 176
Voutenay-sur-Cure 127
Vrana, Lake (Vransko Jezero) 223
Vróndou 235
Vulcano 221
Vysoké Tatry (High Tatras) National Park 107, 109–10

Wadden See (Waddenzee, Wattenmeer) 27–8, 79, 81, 92, 92
Waldviertal Area 159
Wales 41–6
Walney Island 48
Warandeduinen, Les 67
Warmberg–Osterberg Area 96–7
Warsaw 117
Wattenmeer >> Wadden See

Watzmann 105
Weerribben, De 83–4, 83
Weisendorf Ponds 101
Weissenstein 143–4
Welney Wildfowl Refuge 51
Weltenburger Enge 102
Westhoek 67
Westmann Islands 2
Westpunt 81
Westray 33
West–Terschelling 80
Wexford Slobs >> Wexford Wildfowl Reserve
Wexford Wildfowl Reserve 65, 65
Wharfedale 48
Whipsnade Down 52
Whiteford Point 44
White Mountains >> Lévka Óri
White Park Bay 58
White Peak area 49
Whitesands Bay 44
Wicken Fen 51, 51
Wicklow Mountains National Park 63, 63
Widdybank Fell 48
Wieden, De 83–4
Wien >> Vienna
Wienerwald 159–60
Wildalpen–Rothwald Area 159
Windermere 48
Winterton dunes 50
Wistman's Wood 54
Woliński National Park 115
Wollmatinger Ried Reserve 104
Worbarrow Bay 54
Wormerveer Polders 82–3
Wurzacher Ried Reserves 104, 104
Wyre Forest 50–1

Yassi Burnu 254
Ynis–hir 43
Ynyslas 43
Yorkshire Dales National Park 48, 48
Ythan Estuary 38
Yugoslavia 222–4

Žabljak 224
Zahrádky Lakes 107
Zákinthos 240–1, 240
Zandvoort 84
Zannone, Isola 215
Zaragoza region 188
Zegge 69
Zemplén Hills 168
Ziepbeek Valley 71
Zierikzee 87
Zignano, Valle 211
Zingaro 220
Znojmo Area 112
Zóñar, Laguna de 198
Zonhoven 71
Zug, Lake 146
Zugerberg bog area 146
Zugersee >> Zug, Lake
Zuidlardermeer 81
Zwanenwater 81–2, 82
Zwarte Beek 70
Zwin 68, 68, 87

INDEX OF SPECIES

The symbol >> refers to another entry in the index; *p = passim*

Abies cephalonica >> Greek Fir
Abies pinsapo >> Spanish Fir
Acer heldreichii visiani 223
Acer tataricum >> Tartar Maple
Adder (*Vipera berus*) 25, 52, 69, 150, 171
Adder's Tongue Fern (*Ophioglossum vulgatum*) 52, 69
Adenophora liliifolia 166
Adonis Blue (*Lysandra bellargus*) 123, 136, 143
Aesculapian Snake (*Elaphe longissima*) 127, 132, 150, 151, 169, 171
Agama Lizard (Rhodes Dragon; *Agama stellio*) 241
Agile Frog (*Rana dalmatina*) 93, 96, 126, 151, 165, 207, 224, 230
Agrions 84
Alchemilla gircensis 119
Alcon Blue (*Maculinea alcon*) 71, 147, 233
Aleppo Pine (*Pinus halepensis*) 138, 223, 254
Alkanna graeca 236
Allium troodii 253
Almond-eyed Ringlet (*Erebia alberganus*) 185
Alpenrose (*Rhododendron ferrugineum*) 158, 159, 222
Alpine Accentor (*Prunella collaris*) 130, 133, 140, 191, 200, 208, 226, 236
Alpine Aster (*Aster alpinus*) 136, 223
Alpine Bartsia (*Bartsia alpina*) 39
Alpine Bistort (*Polygonum viviparum*) 33
Alpine Chough (*Pyrrhocorax graculus*) 105, 119, 132, 133, 139, 140, 149, 152, 156, 188, 208–11*p*, 226
Alpine Cinquefoil (*Potentilla crantzii*) 39, 41
Alpine Clematis (*Clematis alpina*) 152, 155, 158
Alpine Columbine (*Aquilegia alpina*) 133
Alpine Enchanter's Nightshade (*Circaea alpina*) 47
Alpine Forget-me-not (*Myosotis alpestris*) 39, 48
Alpine Grizzled Skipper (*Pyrgus andromedae*) 189
Alpine Gypsophila (*Gypsophila alpina*) 104
Alpine Longhorn Beetle >> *Rosalia alpina*
Alpine Marmot (*Marmota marmota*) 133, 222

Alpine Meadow-rue (*Thalictrum alpinum*) 38, 58, 60
Alpine Monkshood (*Delphinium montanum*) 148
Alpine Newt (*Triturus alpestris*) 69, 70, 100, 109, 110, 152, 212
Alpine Onion (*Allium victorialis*) 156
Alpine Pasque-flower (*Pulsatilla alpina*) 130, 145
Alpine Poppy (*Papaver burseri*) 105, 148
Alpine Salamander (*Salamandra atra*) 105, 133, 155
Alpine Saw-wort (*Saussurea alpina*) 38, 39, 41, 58
Alpine Sow-thistle (*Cicerbita alpina*) 13, 102, 107, 128
Alpine Squill (*Scilla bifolia*) 99, 126, 214, 247
Alpine Swift (*Apus melba*) 130, 136–8*p*, 141, 199, 216, 224, 234, 237, 242, 245, 254
Alyssoides cretica 243
Alyssum montanum ssp *montanum* 112
American Wigeon (*Anas americana*) 1
Amsinckia intermedia 46
Anatolian Leopard (*Panthera pardus*) 245
Anchusa caespitosa 242
Ancient King (*Saxifraga florulenta*) 139
Anemone apennina 214
Anemone hortensis 139
Anemones 232, 238, 240, 242, 251, 254
Anemone trifolia 211
Angel's Tears (*Narcissus triandrus*) 175, 184, 195
Angular Solomon's Seal (*Polygonatum odoratum*) 74
Anthericum ramosum 110
Antirrhinum charidemi 202
Antirrhinum pulverulentum 195
Ant-lions (*Myrmeleon* spp) 198
Apollo (*Parnassius apollo*) 105, 108–10*p*, 112, 119, 127, 128, 131, 135, 136, 149, 152, 155, 189, 190, 208, 247
Aquatic Warbler (*Acrocephalus paludicola*) 95, 169
Aquilegia aurea 225
Aquilegia kitaibelli 223
Aquilegia ottonis 238
Aquilegia vulgaris ullepitschii 110

Arabis cypria 254
Arabis pieninica 110
Arabis verna 200
Arbutus andrachne >> Eastern Strawberry Tree
Arctic Bellflower (*Campanula uniflora*) 10
Arctic Campion (*Silene wahlbergella*) 10
Arctic Fox (*Alopex lagopus*) 1, 4, 5, 7, 10, 12, 35
Arctic Mouse-ear Chickweed (*Cerastium arcticum*) 6
Arctic Redpoll (*Carduelis hornemanni*) 4
Arctic Rhododendron (*Rhododendron lapponicum*) 10
Arctic Saxifrage (Highland Saxifrage; *Saxifraga rivularis*) 18, 19
Arctic Skua (*Stercorarius parasiticus*) 2, 32, 33
Arctic Tern (*Sterna paradisaea*) 1, 2, 25, 27, 33, 38, 46, 62
Arctic Warbler (*Phylloscopus borealis*) 10
Arenaria humifusa 12
Arisarum proboscideum 216
Armadillidium zenckeri 166
Armeria gaditana 198
Armeria maritima >> Thrift
Armeria pungens 179
Armeria soleirolii 141
Arnica (*Arnica montana*) 85, 97, 98, 102, 131, 136, 146, 158, 209
Arolla Pine (*Pinus cembra*) 147, 171
Arrow-grass (*Triglochin palustris*) 110
Arrowhead (*Sagittaria sagitifolia*) 71, 234
Aruncus sylvestris >> Bearded Spiraea
Ash (*Fraxinus excelsior*) 27, 28, 60, 99, 101, 102, 113, 117, 165, 166, 216, 224
Ashy Cranesbill (*Geranium cinereum*) 188
Asp Viper (*Vipera aspis*) 127, 150, 217
Astragalus siculus 221
Asturcón Horse 185
Audouin's Gull (*Larus audouinii*) 203, 204, 217, 221, 254
Avocet (*Recurvirostra avosetta*) 16, 24–8*p*, 50, 51, 68, 79–81*p*, 83, 87, 91–3*p*, 125, 166, 167, 178, 179, 181, 194, 197, 199, 201, 203, 211, 215, 219, 232, 254
Azores Bullfinch (*Pyrrhula pyrrhula murina*) 181

Azores Buzzard (*Buteo buteo rothschildi*) 181
Azure Hawker (*Aeshna caerulea*) 35, 36
Azure-winged Magpie (*Cyanopica cyana*) 180, 195, 197, 198

Badger (*Meles meles*) 34, 56, 74, 86, 102, 159, 224, 236
Baillon's Crake (*Porzana pusilla*) 125, 126, 179, 237
Baldmoney (Spignel) (*Meum athamanticum*) 73, 127
Balkan Pine (*Pinus leucodermis*) 234
Banded Agrion (*Calopteryx splendens*) 143
Baneberry (*Actaea spicata*) 13, 19
Barbary Ape (*Macaca sylvanus*) 202
Barbary Nut (*Gynandiris sisyrhynchium*) 197, 204
Barbary Partridge (*Alectoris barbara*) 202, 204
Barberry (*Berberis vulgaris*) 71
Barbus prespensis 230
Bark Beetle (*Ips longicollis*) 19
Barnacle Goose (*Branta leucopsis*) 41, 56
Barred Warbler (*Sylvia nisoria*) 16, 94–6*p*, 109, 161, 164
Barrow's Goldeneye (*Bucephala islandica*) 1, 2
Bar-tailed Godwit (*Limosa lapponica*) 79, 178
Bastard Balm (*Melittis melissophyllum*) 123
Bastard Toadflax (*Thesium humifusum*) 108
Bath Asparagus (*Ornithogalum pyrenaicum*) 136
Bavarian Gentian (*Gentiana bavarica*) 112
Bean Goose (*Anser fabalis*) 7, 12, 15, 24, 164, 165
Bear >> Brown Bear
Bearberry (*Arctostaphylos uva–ursi*) 25, 48, 209
Bearded Bellflower (*Campanula barbata*) 158
Bearded Spiraea (*Aruncus sylvestris*) 98
Bearded Tit (Parrotbill) (*Panurus biarmicus*) 15, 50, 51, 81, 83, 86, 95, 103, 196
Bearded Vulture >> Lammergeier
Beaver (*Castor fiber*) 117, 144, 147, 149

263

Bedriaga's Rock Lizard (*Lacerta bedriagae*) 140
Bedriaga's Skink (*Chalcides bedriagai*) 195
Beech (*Fagus sylvatica*) 27, 52, 53, 73, 74, 93, 94, 97–102p, 104, 105, 107–13p, 118, 119, 122, 124, 126, 135–7p, 141, 143–5p, 151, 159, 163–5p, 167, 171, 174, 185, 188, 189, 193, 221, 222, 223, 225, 227, 232–5p, 247
Beech Marten 137, 148, 166, 168, 169, 175, 184, 190, 208, 210, 211, 217, 224
Bee-eater (*Merops apiaster*) 137–40p, 161, 164, 191, 195, 201, 203, 213, 219, 235, 254
Bee Orchid (*Ophrys apifera*) 62, 69, 74, 97, 136, 138, 141, 180, 200, 238, 253
Bellevalia dubia 236
Bellevalia hackelii 179
Bembix rostrata 126
Betula odorata 6
Bewick's Swan (*Cygnus columbianus*) 6, 24, 41, 51, 62, 63
Biarum davisii 243
Bilberry (*Vaccinium myrtillus*) 146, 148, 174
Birch (*Betula* spp) 5–9p, 10, 12–14p, 18, 20, 34, 38, 47, 57, 63, 88, 93, 94, 100, 107, 117, 118, 221
Bird Cherry (*Prunus padus*) 102
Bird's Eye Primrose (*Primula farinosa*) 104, 105, 146
Bird's Nest Orchid (*Neottia nidus-avis*) 100, 214
Biscutella frutescens 199
Bison (*Bison bonasus*) 102, 117, 119
Bittern (*Botaurus stellaris*) 14, 15, 24, 50, 51, 68, 70, 71, 73, 82–4p, 86–8p, 93, 94–6p, 101, 103, 105, 107, 112, 113, 116, 117, 125, 131, 132, 146, 154, 157, 160, 163, 167, 169, 170, 176, 178–81p, 193, 203, 211–14p, 219, 231, 234, 235, 238, 246
Black-bellied Sand Grouse (*Pterocles orientalis*) 179, 188, 190, 191, 195, 197, 201
Blackbird (*Turdus merula*) 181
Black Broom (*Lembotropis nigricans*) 111, 113, 164, 168
Black-eared Wheatear (*Oenanthe hispanica*) 178, 192, 199
Black Francolin (*Francolinus francolinus*) 252, 254
Black Grouse (*Tetrao tetrix*) 26, 36, 48, 52, 69, 73, 81, 99, 100, 102, 107, 133, 148, 151, 171, 209
Black Guillemot (*Cepphus grylle*) 8, 14, 27, 32, 33, 58
Black Kite >> Dark Kite
Black-necked Grebe (*Podiceps nigricollis*) 14, 24, 69, 71, 84, 88, 93, 96, 97, 101, 105, 113, 116, 117, 125, 126, 131, 147, 164, 196

Black Pine (*Pinus nigra*) 221, 233–5p, 253
Black Redstart (*Phoenicurus ochruros*) 199, 237, 238
Black Stork (*Ciconia nigra*) 77, 93, 94, 97, 98, 108, 109, 112, 113, 116, 117, 128, 159, 160, 163, 166, 173, 176, 191, 192, 194, 195, 221, 223, 234, 246
Black-tailed Godwit (*Limosa limosa*) 24–6p, 28, 51, 63, 69, 79, 80, 82, 87, 116, 154, 157, 166, 167
Black Tern (*Chlidonias niger*) 15, 28, 69, 71, 82, 84, 88, 95, 116, 124, 125, 128, 131, 164–6p, 170, 171, 197, 203, 221
Black-throated Diver (*Gavia arctica*) 13, 15, 20, 21
Black Vanilla Orchid (*Nigritella nigra*) 208, 226
Black Vulture (*Aegypius monachus*) 183, 191, 194, 197, 202, 235, 247
Black Wheatear (*Oenanthe leucura*) 176, 199–202p
Black-winged Kite (*Elanus caeruleus*) 195
Black-winged Stilt (*Himantopus himantopus*) 125, 128, 176, 178, 179, 181, 193, 194, 197–9p, 201, 203, 211–13p, 215, 216, 219, 220, 231, 232, 234, 238, 254
Black Woodpecker (*Dryocopus martius*) 21, 27, 29, 70, 73–5p, 77, 93, 96, 98–100p, 102, 105, 117, 131, 148, 157, 161, 168, 184, 190, 208, 209, 214, 217, 247
Bladder Gentian (*Gentiana utriculosa*) 105
Bladder-nut (*Staphylea pinnata*) 113, 147, 168
Bladder Senna (*Colutea arborescens*) 149
Bladderwort (*Utricularia* spp) 34, 59, 63, 69, 88
Bloody Cranesbill (*Geranium sanguineum*) 49, 72, 74
Blue Bugle (*Ajuga genevensis*) 126
Blue Chaffinch (*Fringilla teydea*) 204
Blue-eyed Grass (*Sisyrinchium bermudiana*) 57, 65, 105
Blue Gromwell (*Buglossoides purpurocaerulea*) 99
Blue Hare >> Irish Hare
Blue Rock Thrush (*Monticola solitaris*) 136, 138, 141, 176, 178, 199, 203, 219, 223, 238, 242, 249, 254
Bluethroat (*Luscinia svecica*) 7, 9, 10, 12, 18, 69, 87, 93, 95, 101, 103, 105, 108, 112, 113, 117, 124, 125, 128, 158, 165, 192
Blue-winged Grasshopper >> *Oedipoda caerulescens*
Blyth's Reed Warbler (*Acrocephalus dumetorum*) 21
Bocage's Wall Lizard (*Podarcis bocagei*) 186
Bog Arum (*Calla palustris*) 69, 97
Bog Asphodel (*Narthecium ossifragum*) 44, 57, 59, 63, 73

Bogbean (*Menyanthes trifoliata*) 59
Bog Moss (*Sphagnum* spp) 146
Bog Myrtle (*Myrica gale*) 69
Bog Orchid (*Hammarbya paludosa*) 13, 47, 69, 71, 104
Bog Rosemary (Marsh Andromeda; *Andromeda polifolia*) 44, 59, 63, 71, 94, 128, 146, 157
Bonelli's Eagle (*Hieraaetus fasciatus*) 130, 132, 137, 138, 176, 179, 184, 191, 199, 202, 217, 218, 224, 234, 236, 242, 253
Bonelli's Warbler (*Phylloscopus bonelli*) 105, 149
Booted Eagle (*Hieraaetus pennatus*) 111, 131, 136, 137, 168, 175, 176, 185, 187, 195, 221, 224, 226, 231, 233, 246
Bosnian Pine (*Pinus serbica*) 217, 233
Botrychium lanceolatum 119
Botrychium lunaria >> Moonwort
Bottle-nosed Dolphin (*Tursiops truncatus*) 179
Box (*Buxus sempervirens*) 72, 74
Brachythecium erythrorrhizon 33
Brambling (*Fringilla montifringilla*) 5–7p, 9, 19
Brassica hilarionis 254
Brent Goose (*Branta bernicla*) 4, 57, 61, 64, 80, 124, 125
Brilliant Emerald (*Somatochlora metallica*) 103, 128
Brimstone (*Gonepteryx rhamni*) 103
British Storm Petrel >> Storm Petrel
Broad-billed Sandpiper (*Limicola falcinellus*) 12
Brook Lamprey (*Lampetra planeri*) 70
Brown Argus (*Aricia agestis*) 49
Brown Bear (*Ursus arctos*) 5, 6, 7, 12, 13, 17–19p, 35, 119, 135, 171, 184, 185, 214, 223, 224, 225, 226, 232
Brown Bluebell (*Dipcadi serotina*) 195
Brown Gentian (*Gentiana pannonica*) 112, 119
Brown Hare (*Lepus capensis*) 124, 160, 164, 193
Brown Hawker (*Aeshna grandis*) 60
Brünnich's Guillemot (*Uria lomvia*) 4
Bryophytes 33, 47, 52, 65, 104, 110
Bug Orchid (*Orchis coriophora*) 104, 193, 240
Bullhead (*Cottus gobio*) 70
Bulwer's Petrel (*Bulweria bulwerii*) 181
Bupleurum affine 113
Burnet Rose (*Rosa spinosissima*) 67, 74
Bur-reeds (*Sparganium* spp) 25

Butterfly Iris (*Iris spuria*) 128, 241
Buttonweed (*Cotula coronopiflora*) 180
Buzzards >> Azores Buzzard; Common Buzzard; Honey Buzzard; Long-legged Buzzard; Rough-legged Buzzard

Calandra Lark (*Melanocorypha calandra*) 138, 215, 254
Calypso Orchid (*Calypso bulbosa*) 10, 12
Camberwell Beauty (*Nymphalis antiopa*) 113, 122, 126, 168, 245
Campanula bohemica 109
Campanula carpatica 109, 119
Campanula fenestrellata 223
Campanula hawkinsiana 232
Campanula macrostachya 112
Campanula rupestris 236
Campanula thyrsoides >> Yellow Bellflower
Campanula velebitica 223
Campanula zoysii 159
Camptothecium lutescens 67
Canary (*Serinus canaria*) 174, 183
Canary Pipit (*Anthus berthelotii*) 204
Cannabis (*Cannabis sativa*) 167
Capercaillie (*Tetrao urogallus*) 6, 36, 100, 108, 110, 124, 137, 143, 144, 147, 148, 152, 155, 158, 159, 161, 171, 184, 190, 209, 210, 224
Carabus nitens >> Ground Beetle
Carex bigelowii 58
Carex buxbaumii 84
Carex canescens 71
Carex capillaris 35
Carex elata 166
Carex limosa 71
Carex rupestris 35
Carex vaginata 146
Carnic Lily (*Lilium carniolicum*) 156,159, 222, 224
Carob (*Ceratonia siliqua*) 221, 223
Carpathian Blue Slug 169
Carpathian Crocus (*Crocus carpaticus*) 169
Carpathian Snowbell (*Soldanella carpatica*) 109, 110, 119
Caspian Pond Tortoise (*Mauremys caspica*) 246, 247
Caspian Tern (*Sterna caspia*) 16, 221
Cassiope (*Cassiope tetragona*) 4, 8, 10
Catananche caerulea (Cupidone) 186
Catocala fraxini >> Clifden Nonpareil
Cattle Egret (*Bubulcus ibis*) 138, 178, 180, 219
Cedrus libanii ssp *brevifolia* (Cyprus Cedar) 253
Celtis caucasicus >> Nettle-tree
Centaurea aegiophila 252
Centaurea arguta 204
Centaurea clementei 199
Centaurea kotschyana 119

Centaurea pawlovskii 233
Centaurea retezatensis 171
Centaurea triumfetti 168
Centaurium spicatum 128
Cerambyx cerdo 168
Cetraria islandica 71
Cetti's Warbler (*Cettia cetti*) 68, 122, 140, 190, 212
Cévennes Pasque-flower (*Pulsatilla rubra*) 131, 193
Chaffweed (*Anagallis minima*) 67
Chalkhill Blue (*Lysandra coridon*) 52, 192
Chamaespartium tridentatum 177
Chameleon (*Chamaeleo chamaeleon*) 181, 197, 248
Chamois (*Rupicapra rupicapra*) 104, 105, 110, 119, 124, 133–5p, 139, 143, 145, 148, 149, 152, 155, 161, 163, 171, 184–6p, 188–90p, 208–11p, 222–4p, 226, 227, 233, 235
Chamorchis alpina (Mountain Orchid) 8, 10
Chapman's Ringlet (*Erebia palarica*) 186
Charr (*Salvelinus alpinus*) 1
Chaste Tree (*Vitex agnus-castus*) 204, 232
Chequered Skipper (*Carterocephalus palaemon*) 189
Chestnut (*Castanea sativa*) 125, 135, 139, 147, 151, 163, 175, 195, 211, 221, 231
Chickweed Wintergreen (*Trientalis europaea*) 25, 73, 75, 102, 107
Chinese Water Deer (*Hydropotes inermis*) 52
Chionodoxas 242
Christ's Thorn (*Paliurus spina-christi*) 232
Chukar Partridge (*Alectoris chukar*) 254
Cicendia filiformis >> Slender Yellow Gentian
Cinereous Bunting (*Emberiza cineracea*) 241
Cirl Bunting (*Emberiza cirlus*) 220
Cistanche phelypaea 180, 201
Cistus clusii 214
Cistus crispus 179
Cistus osbeckifolius 204
Cistus palhinhae 179
Citril Finch (*Serinus citrinella*) 140, 141, 145, 149, 155, 188, 242
Cladonia spp >> lichens
Clematis integrifolia 160
Cleopatra (*Gonepteryx cleopatra*) 136, 187, 199, 216, 232, 238, 254
Clifden Nonpareil (*Catocala fraxini*) 122
Clouded Apollo (*Parnassius mnemosyne*) 108, 119, 131, 135, 149, 189
Club-tailed Dragonfly (*Gomphus vulgatissimus*) 51, 143
Clustered Bellflower (*Campanula glomeratus*) 108
Coal Tit (*Parus ater*) 253
Coenagrion mercuriale 44
Colchicum boisseri 237
Colchicum catacuzenium 236

Colchicum cupanii 243
Colchicum triphyllum 193
Collared Flycatcher (*Ficedula albicollis*) 109, 113, 164, 165, 252
Collared Pratincole (*Glareola pratincola*) 178, 180, 181, 194, 231, 235, 252
Columbine (*Aquilegia vulgaris*) 14, 51, 100, 101, 110, 110, 133, 135, 223, 225, 238
Common Buzzard (*Buteo buteo*) 42, 58, 86, 103, 186, 193, 219
Common Chough (Red-billed Chough; *Pyrrhocorax pyrrhocorax*) 149, 176, 191, 217
Common Crane (*Grus grus*) 10, 14, 15, 16, 17, 18, 21, 24, 51, 73, 88, 94, 95, 96, 97, 116, 117, 127, 167, 169, 192, 196, 215, 252, 253
Common Darter (*Sympetrum striolatum*) 60, 100, 234
Common Dormouse (*Muscardinus avellarinus*) 14
Common Eider (*Somateria mollissima*) 1, 8, 14, 16, 26, 27, 33, 35, 38, 40, 46, 58, 81, 210
Common Frog (*Rana temporaria*) 70, 71, 96
Common Hawker (*Aeshna juncea*) 146
Common Juniper (*Juniperus communis*) 20, 33, 36, 38, 48, 58, 72, 74, 84, 94, 195, 247
Common Lizard (*Lacerta vivipara*) 67, 113, 136, 150
Common Newt (*Triturus vulgaris*) 79
Common Oak (*Quercus robur*) 27, 28, 53, 57, 58, 63, 88, 93, 94, 98, 99, 111–13p, 117, 118, 126, 135–7p, 151, 164–6p, 174, 175, 184, 185, 187, 221, 233
Common Primrose (*Primula vulgaris*) 247
Common Rock-rose (*Helianthemum chamaecistus*) 16
Common Sandpiper (*Actitus hypoleucos*) 36, 48, 128
Common Seal (*Phoca vitulina*) 1, 31, 32, 50, 61, 62, 81, 91
Common Shelduck (*Tadorna tadorna*) 38–40, 46, 61–4p, 68, 81, 82, 123, 124
Common Sundew (*Drosera rotundifolia*) 27
Common Swallowtail (*Papilio machaon*) 108, 124, 136, 152
Common Swift (*Apus apus*) 245
Common Tern (*Sterna hirundo*) 1, 21, 27, 38, 46, 62, 92, 103–5p, 124, 217, 223
Common Toad (*Bufo bufo*) 71, 127
Common Tree-frog (*Hyla arborea*) 122, 152, 224
Common Wren (*Troglodytes troglodytes*) 2
Comperia comperiana 241

Convolvulus cantabrica 126
Coot (*Fulica atra*) 27
Coral Necklace (*Illecebrum verticillatum*) 53
Coral-root Orchid (*Corallorhiza trifida*) 5, 40
Corema album 186
Cork Oak (*Quercus suber*) 138, 176, 179, 219
Cormorant (*Phalacrocorax carbo*) 61, 64, 83, 87, 116, 171, 211, 214, 224, 225, 230–2p, 245–7p
Corn Bunting (*Emberiza calandra*) 59, 243, 247
Corncrake (*Crex crex*) 16, 27
Cornelian Cherry (*Cornus mas*) 74, 161
Cornflower (*Centaurea cyanus*) 130, 168
Cornish Heath (*Erica vagans*) 54
Corsican Brook Salamander (*Euproctus montanus*) 141
Corsican Crocus >> *Crocus corsicus*
Corsican Hellebore (*Helleborus argutifolius* ssp *corsicus*) 140
Corsican Nuthatch (*Sitta whiteheadi*) 140, 141
Corsican Pine (*Pinus nigra* ssp *laricio*) 140, 141
Corydalis rutaefolia 253
Cory's Shearwater (*Calonectris diomedea*) 138, 141, 174, 176, 181, 203, 207, 216–18p, 221, 249
Cotton-grass (*Eriophorum* spp) 5, 59, 63, 73, 84, 98, 107, 146, 166
Cottonweed (*Otanthus maritimus*) 138, 238
Cowslip (*Primula veris*) 14, 48, 49, 208
Cow-wheat (*Melampyrum nemorosum*) 98, 161
Coypu (*Myocastor coypus*) 125
Crag Martin (*Hirundo rupestris*) 130, 136, 158, 234, 237, 242
Crambe filifolia 199
Cranberry (*Vaccinium oxycoccus*) 44, 58, 59, 63, 69, 71, 73, 75, 81, 94, 98, 104, 128, 146, 157, 169
Crane >> Common Crane; Demoiselle Crane
Cranesbill 48, 49, 72, 74, 103, 188, 222
Crayfish (*Astacus pallipes*) 163
Creeping Azalea (Trailing Azalea; *Loiseleuria procumbens*) 5, 155
Creeping Bellflower (*Campanula rapunculoides*) 69
Creeping Lady's Tresses (*Goodyera repens*) 36, 148
Crested Lark (*Galerida cristata*) 179, 201
Crested Newt (*Triturus cristatus*) 147, 151
Crested Porcupine (*Hystrix cristata*) 212–14p, 217
Crested Tit (*Parus cristatus*) 21, 36, 37, 129, 131
Cretan Ebony (*Ebenus creticus*) 242

Cretan Goat (*Capra aegagrus*) 242
Cretan Spiny Mouse (*Acomys minous*) 229
Cretzschmar's Bunting (*Emberiza caesia*) 229, 231, 233, 237, 240, 241, 254
Crimson Clover (*Trifolium incarnatum*) 54
Crocus albiflorus >> White Crocus
Crocus asturicus 191
Crocus biflorus 247
Crocus boryi 240
Crocus cambessedesii 202
Crocus cancellatus 237
Crocus carpetanus 175, 191
Crocus corsicus (Corsican Crocus) 140, 141
Crocus cyprius 253
Crocus gargaricus 247
Crocus goulimyii 240
Crocus hartmannianus 253, 254
Crocus heuffelianus 169
Crocus minima 140
Crocus nevadensis 200
Crocus niveus 240
Crocus nudiflorus 185
Crocus pallasii 236
Crocus scepusensis 119
Crocus veluchensis 226, 236
Crocus versicolor 139
Crossbill (*Loxia curvirostra*) 21, 57, 97, 99, 103, 131, 140, 147, 210, 242, 247, 253
Cross Gentian (*Gentiana cruciata*) 112
Crowberry (*Empetrum nigrum*) 25, 73, 82, 98, 186
Crown Anemone (*Anemone coronaria*) 238
Crown Daisy (*Chrysanthemum coronaria*) 243
Crown Vetch (*Coronilla varia*) 126
Cupidone >> *Catananche caerulea*
Curlew (*Numenius arquata*) 49, 59–61p, 64, 69, 79, 80, 82, 84, 104, 112, 128, 136, 138, 146, 161, 166, 167, 169, 179, 188, 192, 195, 197, 203, 210, 213, 219, 231, 235, 254
Cut-leaved Germander (*Teucrium botrys*) 71
Cyclamen 221, 238, 240, 246, 252
Cyclamen balearicum 202
Cyclamen creticum 242, 243
Cyclamen cyprium 253, 254
Cyclamen repandum 140, 215
Cynomorium coccineum 201
Cynthia's Fritillary (*Hypodryas cynthia*) 133
Cypress Spurge (*Euphorbia cyparissias*) 126
Cyprus Bee Orchid >> *Ophrys kotschyii*
Cyprus Butterwort (*Pinguicula crystallina*) 253
Cyprus Cedar >> *Cedrus libanii* ssp *brevifolia*
Cyprus Scops Owl (*Otus scops cypriaca*) 253, 254
Cyprus Warbler (*Sylvia melanothorax*) 252, 254
Cyprus Wheatear (*Oenanthe cypriaca*) 252, 254

Cytinus spp 139
Cytisus austriacus 161
Cytisus purgans 177

Dactylorhiza cordigera 238
Dactylorhiza romana >> Roman Orchid
Daffodils (*Narcissus* spp) 49, 54, 74, 130, 138, 157, 177, 186, 189, 194, 202, 213, 218, 238, 249, 252
Dahl's Whip Snake (*Coluber najadum*) 223
Dalmatian Pelican (*Pelecanus crispus*) 171, 224, 225, 230, 231, 235, 245
Dame's Violet (*Hesperis matronalis*) 168
Damon Blue (*Agrodiaetus damon*) 193
Damselflies 16, 53, 68, 71, 95, 112, 125, 128, 146, 147, 198
Daphne gnidium 179
Daphne rodriguezii 203
Daphne sericea 242
Dark Green Fritillary (*Argynnis aglaja*; *Mesoacidalia aglaja*) 35, 40, 41, 48, 58, 108, 128, 208
Dark Kite (Black Kite; *Milvus migrans*) 98, 103, 123, 128, 135, 143, 145, 190, 195, 202, 219, 238
Dark Red Helleborine (*Epipactis atrorubens*) 33, 35, 48, 97, 98, 104
Darter >> Common Darter; Highland Darter; Ruddy Darter; White-faced Darter
Dartford Warbler (*Sylvia undata*) 53, 138, 203, 221
Deer Grass (*Trichophorum caespitosum*) 146
Deltomerus tatricus 110
Demoiselle Crane (*Anthropoides virgo*) 253
Dense-flowered Orchid (*Neotinea maculata*) 60, 62
Dianthus compactus 119
Dianthus nitidus 108, 109
Dianthus praecox 109, 113
Dianthus superbus 94
Diapensia (*Diapensia lapponica*) 4, 5, 18
Dice Snake (*Natrix tessellata*) 150, 151, 224, 232, 234, 238, 247
Digitalis dubia 203
Digitalis parviflora 187
Dinocras cephalotes 111
Dipcadi serotinum >> Brown Bluebell
Dipper (*Cinclus cinclus*) 46, 51, 52, 98, 137, 141
Dittany (*Origanum dictamnum*) 242
Dodder (*Cuscuta epithymum*) 54
Dolomite Bellflower (*Campanula morettiana*) 209
Dormouse >> Common Dormouse; Edible Dormouse
Dorset Heath (*Erica ciliaris*) 54
Dotterel (*Charadrius morinellus*) 9, 12, 37, 158
Dovre Poppy (*Papaver dahlianum*) 8

Downy Emerald (*Cordulia aenea*) 103, 128
Downy Oak (*Quercus pubescens*) 67, 72, 74, 223, 224
Downy Woundwort (*Stachys germanica*) 111
Draba aizoides >> Yellow Whitlow-grass
Draba dorneri 171
Draba fladnizensis 8
Dragon Arum (*Dracunculus vulgaris*) 234, 241, 243
Dragonflies 1, 15, 16, 35, 37, 44, 50, 51, 53, 54, 56, 60, 65, 68–71p, 73, 76, 84, 88, 94, 95, 97, 100, 101, 103, 104, 107, 112, 117, 124–6p, 128, 130, 131, 135, 137, 138, 140, 143, 145–7p, 149, 150, 163, 164, 167, 171, 195, 198, 210, 212, 232, 234, 237, 238
Dragonmouth (*Horminum pyrenaicum*) 105
Drooping Saxifrage (*Saxifraga cernua*) 39
Duke of Burgundy (*Hamearis lucina*) 48, 49, 52, 98, 123
Dune Helleborine (*Epipactis dunensis*) 41, 49
Dung Beetles (*Scarabeus* spp) 198
Dunlin (*Calidris alpina*) 15, 24, 32–5p, 38, 40, 48, 49, 54, 56, 59, 60, 63, 64
Dupont's Lark (*Chersophilus dupontii*) 188, 191, 193
Dusky Large Blue (*Maculinea nausithous*) 147
Dutchman's Pipes (*Monotropa hypopitys*) 136, 188, 209
Duvalius hungaricus 168
Dwarf Alpenrose (*Rhodothamnus chamaecistus*) 159, 222
Dwarf Birch (*Betula nana*) 5, 107
Dwarf Fan Palm (*Chamaerops humilis*) 203, 220
Dwarf Soapwort (*Saponaria pumilio*) 158

Eagle Owl (*Bubo bubo*) 8, 12, 100, 102, 105, 108–13p, 115, 116, 119, 132, 136–8p, 152, 156–9p, 161, 168, 171, 176, 178, 191–3p, 199, 208–10p, 212, 214, 215, 217, 223, 225, 231, 232, 235, 240
Early Marsh Orchid (*Dactylorhiza incarnata*) 13, 41, 104
Early Purple Orchid (*Orchis mascula*) 60, 108, 189
Early Spider Orchid (*Ophrys sphegodes*) 54, 138, 214, 216, 245
Eastern Festoon (*Zerynthia cerisyi*) 243, 245
Eastern Strawberry Tree (*Arbutus andrachne*) 254
Echinophora spinosa 238, 249
Echinops ruthenicus 166
Echium boisseri 200
Echium gentianoides 204
Echium rubrum 204
Echium wildpretii 204
Edelweiss (*Leontopodium alpinum*) 105, 149, 171, 188, 223

Edible Dormouse (Fat Dormouse; *Glis glis*) 52, 214, 152
Edible Frog (*Rana esculenta*) 69–71p, 96, 103, 126, 127, 135, 246
Edraianthus lovcenicus 224
Egrets 129, 131, 160, 164–7p, 169–71p, 176–80p, 190, 197, 201, 203, 211, 213, 219, 221, 231, 234, 245–8p, 252, 254
Egyptian Mongoose (*Herpestes ichneumon*) 195
Egyptian Vulture (*Neophron percnopterus*) 137, 138, 176, 185, 188, 190, 191, 193–5p, 199, 200, 215, 218, 220, 221, 223, 224, 232–5p, 246, 247
Eider >> Common Eider; King Eider; Steller's Eider
Eleonora's Falcon (*Falco eleonorae*) 138, 202, 203, 207, 219, 221, 241, 243, 245, 252
Elder-flowered Orchid (*Dactylorhiza sambucina*) 16, 131, 136
Elk (*Alces alces*) 5–7p, 9, 10, 12, 13, 17, 18, 21, 117
Emperor Dragonfly (*Anax imperator*) 164, 234
Emperor Moth (*Saturnia pavonia*) 36
English Iris (*Iris xiphioides*) 189
Epipactis microphylla 101
Epipactis muelleri 101
Epipactis troodii 253
Eremias Lizard (*Eremias arguta*) 171
Eresus cannabarinus 165
Erica australis 195
Erica multiflora 249
Erinacea anthyllis 200
Eriophorum russeolum 5
Erodium reichardii 203
Etna Birch 221
Eucalyptus 176, 179
Euphrasia christii 151
European Leaf-toed Gecko 218
European Map (*Araschnia levana*) 101
European Michaelmas Daisy (*Aster amellus*) 152
European Mink (*Mustela lutreola*) 125
Evax rotundata 141
Exaculum pusillum 122

Fagonia cretica 201, 252
False Esparto Grass (*Stipa tenacissima*) 201
False Ringlet (*Coenonympha oedippus*) 154
False Smooth Snake (*Macroprotodon cucullatus*) 202
Fan-tailed Warbler (*Cisticola juncidis*) 123, 140, 179, 190
Fat Dormouse >> Edible Dormouse
Feather Grass >> *Stipa pannonica*
Felwort (*Gentianella amarella*) 52, 148
Fen Orchid (*Lipparis loeslii*) 50, 67, 82, 84, 104, 147, 154

Fen Ragwort (*Senecio paludosus*) 105
Fen Violet (*Viola persicifolia*) 62
Ferruginous Duck (*Aythya nyroca*) 117, 211, 230, 235
Ferula sadleriana 165
Field Cricket (*Gryllus campestris*) 123
Field Eryngo (*Eryngium campestre*) 164
Fieldfare (*Turdus pilaris*) 128
Field Fleawort (*Senecio integrifolius*) 110
Field Gentian (*Gentianella campestris*) 56, 71, 94
Field Maple (*Acer campestre*) 13, 100
Field Mouse-Ear (*Cerastium arvense*) 49
Field Wormwood (*Artemisia campestris*) 99
Fig (*Ficus carica*) 221
Fir 100, 102, 109, 110, 112, 117–19p, 137, 143, 148, 159, 163, 188, 199, 217, 223, 227, 233–8p, 240
Firecrest (*Regulus ignicapillus*) 89, 247
Fire Salamander (*Salamandra salamandra*) 100, 109, 151, 152, 155, 163, 165, 179, 185, 186, 189, 190
Flamingo (Greater Flamingo; *Phoenicopterus ruber*) 137, 181, 194, 197–9p, 201, 202, 219, 221, 253, 254
Flax-leaved St John's Wort (*Hypericum linarifolium*) 54
Flowering Rush (*Butomus umbellatus*) 68, 124, 234
Fly Orchid (*Ophrys insectifera*) 74, 97, 102
Foetid Juniper (*Juniperus foetidissimma*) 253
Four-spotted Chaser (*Libellula quadrimaculata*) 73, 146
Four-spotted Orchid (*Orchis quadripunctata*) 237, 238
Fox Moth (*Macrothylacia rubi*) 35
Fragrant Orchid (*Gymnadenia conopsea*) 13, 58, 93, 104
French Lavender (*Lavendula stoechas*) 175, 179, 194, 195
Fringed Gentian (*Gentianella ciliata*)112
Fringed Sandwort >> Irish Sandwort
Fringed Water-lily (*Nymphoides peltatus*) 125
Fritillaria lusitanica 178
Fritillaria messanensis 224
Frivald's Frog Orchid >> *Pseudorchis frivaldii*
Frog Orchid (*Coeloglossum viride*) 62
Fruit Bat (*Rousettus aegyptiacus*) 252
Fulmar (*Fulmarus glacialis*) 46, 59, 122
Fumana (*Fumana procumbens*) 161
Funeral Cypress (*Cupressus sempervivens*) 254

Gadwall (*Anas strepera*) 39, 81, 196

Galium rotundifolium 103
Gannet (*Sula bassana*) 2, 8, 32, 40, 49, 58, 59,/62, 64, 122
Garganey (*Anas querquedula*) 14, 81, 96, 101, 193, 211, 220, 221, 252
Gavarnie Blue (*Agriades pyrenaicus*) 135, 186
Gavarnie Ringlet (*Erebia gorgone*) 135
Genet (*Genetta genetta*) 125, 135, 137, 175, 178, 184, 197
Genista scorpius 179
Gennaria diphylla 179
Gentiana clusii (Trumpet Gentian) 222
Gentiana frigida 226
Gentiana pannonica >> Brown Gentian
Gentiana symphyandra 223
Gentianella aurea 12
Geranium argenteum >> Silvery Cranesbill
Ghost Orchid (*Epipogium aphyllum*) 5, 10, 12, 102, 148
Giant Fennel (*Ferula communis*) 245, 254
Gibraltar Candytuft (*Iberis gibraltarica*) 202
Gipsywort (*Lycopus europaeus*) 68
Glacier Crowfoot (*Ranunculus glacialis*) 6
Gladiolus 53, 104, 154, 242, 243, 254
Gladiolus imbricatus 109
Gladiolus triphyllus 252
Glandon Blue (*Agriades glandon*) 200
Glasswort (*Salicornia fruticosa*) 201, 231
Glaucous Gull (*Larus hyperboreus*) 2
Globeflower (*Trollius europaeus*) 13, 18, 35, 128, 131, 157, 188
Globe Orchid (*Traunsteinera globosa*) 104
Globe Thistle (*Echinops ritro*) 161, 164, 166
Globularia valentina 193
Globularia vulgaris 16
Glossy Ibis (*Plegadis falcinellus*) 169, 171, 211, 221, 225, 230, 231, 234, 245, 247, 254
Glow-worm (*Lampyris noctiluca*) 136
Goat Moth (*Cossus cossus*) 126
Goldcrest (*Regulus regulus*) 247
Golden Eagle (*Aquila chrysaetos*) 5, 9, 18, 35–8*p*, 105, 109–11*p*, 119, 132, 135–7*p*, 139–41*p*, 148, 149, 152, 155–9*p*, 171, 175, 176, 184, 185, 187–91*p*, 197, 200, 205, 208–11*p*, 214, 217, 218, 220, 221, 222–4*p*, 226, 227, 230, 233, 236, 238, 247
Goldeneye (*Bucephala clangula*) 1, 2, 5, 15, 19, 21, 145, 147
Golden Henbane (*Hyoscamus aureus*) 245
Golden Oak >> *Quercus alnifolia*

Golden Oriole (*Oriolus oriolus*) 20, 69, 85, 89, 117, 123, 126, 128, 131, 136, 138, 139, 159, 161, 164, 179, 191, 195, 197, 219, 254
Golden Plover (*Pluvialis apricaria*) 9, 15, 18, 24, 32–5*p*, 37, 38, 48, 49, 54, 63, 96
Golden Samphire (*Inula crithmoides*) 248
Goldilocks Aster (*Aster linosyris*) 44–5*p*, 149
Goosander (*Mergus merganser*) 5, 13, 14, 20, 21, 25, 27, 93, 146
Goshawk (*Accipiter gentilis*) 84, 86, 102, 130, 136, 137, 141, 145, 155, 158, 184, 187, 192, 194, 218, 219, 225
Grape Hyacinth (*Muscari* spp) 213, 221, 243, 246, 254
Grasshopper Warbler (*Locustella naevia*) 69, 70, 84
Grass Snake (*Natrix natrix*) 69, 150, 151, 234
Grayling (*Hipparchia semele*) 40, 58, 62, 71, 137, 192, 197
Great Banded Grayling (*Brintesia circe*), 137, 192
Great Bustard (*Otis tarda*) 107, 112, 113, 161, 163, 166, 167, 169, 173, 179, 188, 190–2*p*, 195, 197
Great-crested Grebe (*Podiceps cristatus*) 27, 39, 60, 61, 68, 71, 97, 104, 127, 135, 144, 154, 190, 196, 213, 246
Greater Butterfly Orchid (*Platanthera chlorantha*) 167
Greater Butterwort (Large-flowered Butterwort; *Pinguicula grandiflora*) 56, 65, 184
Greater Flamingo >> Flamingo
Greater Horseshoe Bat (*Rhinolophus ferrumequinum*) 176
Greater Spearwort (*Ranunculus lingua*) 68, 103
Greater Spotted Woodpecker (*Dendrocopos major*) 246
Great Grey Owl (*Strix nebulosa*) 6, 18
Great Grey Shrike (*Lanius excubitor*) 86, 128, 179, 201, 203
Great Northern Diver (*Gavia immer*) 1, 2
Great Reed Warbler (*Acrocephalus arundinaceus*) 15, 93, 105, 117, 140, 179, 190, 201, 203, 214, 234
Great Skua (*Stercorarius skua*) 2, 32, 33
Great Snipe (*Gallinago media*) 116
Great Spotted Cuckoo (*Clamator glandarius*) 179, 195
Great Water Dock (*Rumex aquaticus*) 103
Great White Egret (*Egretta alba*) 160, 164–7*p*, 169, 171, 231, 232

Greek Fir (*Abies cephalonica*) 240, 233–8*p*, 240
Greek Fritillary (*Fritillaria graeca*) 238
Greek Maple (*Acer sempervivens*) 223
Greek Saffron Crocus (*Crocus cartwrightianus*) 238
Green-flowered Helleborine (*Epipactis phyllanthes*) 49
Green Hairstreak (*Callophrys rubi*) 44, 51, 63, 157
Green Hellebore (*Helleborus viridis*) 152
Greenish Warbler (*Phylloscopus trochiloides*) 20
Greenland White-fronted Goose (*Anser albifrons flavirostris*) 56, 57, 60, 63, 65
Green Lizard (*Lacerta viridis*) 108, 113, 126, 132, 150, 151, 175, 237, 238
Green Sandpiper (*Tringa ochropus*) 27
Greenshank (*Tringa nebularia*) 21, 33, 34, 36
Green Spleenwort (*Asplenium viride*) 60
Green Tiger Beetle (*Cicendela campestris*) 41
Green Toad (*Bufo viridis*) 224, 253
Green Turtle (*Chelonia mydas*) 247, 252
Green-winged Orchid (*Orchis morio*) 214, 221
Grey-headed Woodpecker (*Picus canus*) 13, 100, 105, 123, 149, 155, 159
Grey Heron (*Ardea cinerea*) 50, 68, 129, 146, 176, 190, 197, 210, 230, 237, 245
Greylag Goose (*Anser anser*) 24, 34, 35, 39, 96, 117
Grey Plover (*Pluvialis squatarola*) 40, 125, 178
Grey Seal (*Halichoerus grypus*) 1, 21, 31–3*p*, 43, 46, 50, 122
Grey-sided Vole (*Clethrionomys rufocanus*) 19
Griffon Vulture (*Gyps fulvus*) 135–7*p*, 156, 176, 185–8*p*, 190, 191, 193–5*p*, 197, 199, 200, 217, 218, 224, 227, 232, 233, 235, 238, 240
Ground Beetle (*Carabus nitens*) 58, 168
Guillemot (*Uria aalgae*) 2, 4, 8, 14, 27, 32, 33, 46, 58, 59, 64, 122,176, 186
Gull-billed Tern (*Gelochelidon nilotica*) 24, 26, 138, 200, 216, 219, 221
Gum Cistus (*Cistus ladanifer*) 179, 195
Gypsophila paniculata 166
Gyrfalcon (*Falco rusticolus*) 1, 2, 9, 12, 13, 18

Haberlea rhodopensis 226
Hairy Alpenrose (*Rhododendron hirsutum*) 158
Hairy Fleabane (*Inula hirta*) 152
Hairy Greenweed (*Genista pilosa*) 54
Hairy Hawker (*Brachytron pratense*) 56, 60, 65, 125, 163

Halimium alyssoides 195
Halimium umbellatum 195
Hampshire Purslane (*Ludwigia palustris*) 53, 135
Harlequin Duck (*Histrionicus histrionicus*) 2
Harlequin Wigeon (*Histrionicus histrionicus*) 1
Harvestmen 222
Hawfinch (*Coccothraustes coccothraustes*) 14, 89, 136
Hawk Owl (*Surnia ulula*) 6, 12, 18
Hazel (*Corylus avellana*) 13, 60, 112, 221
Hazel Grouse (*Bonasa bonasia*) 73, 75, 105, 109, 110, 119, 143, 147, 155, 159, 209; -hen 102, 119, 124, 127, 158, 168, 169
Heath Fritillary (*Mellicta athalia*) 52, 104
Heath Spotted Orchid (*Dactylorhiza maculata*) 69
Heide Schnucken 94
Helianthemum oelandicum 16
Hen Harrier (*Circus cyaneus*) 33, 34, 57, 58, 63, 80, 83, 87, 95, 108, 123, 125, 126, 131, 177, 187, 253
Hepatica (*Hepatica nobilis*) 14, 16, 123, 193, 211
Herb Paris (*Paris quadrifolia*) 108
Hermann's Tortoise (*Testudo hermanni*) 139, 212, 213, 224, 238, 240
Herring Gull (*Larus argentatus*) 249
High Brown Fritillary (*Argynnis adippe*; *Fabriciana adippe*) 48, 128, 143
Highland Darter (*Sympetrum nigrescens*) 35
Highland Saxifrage >> Arctic Saxifrage
Himantoglossum adriaticum 214
Hirundine 201
Hoary Rock-rose (*Helianthemum canum*) 44, 48, 62, 127
Hobby (*Falco subbuteo*) 53, 69, 70, 85, 86, 88, 123, 128, 130, 136, 137, 190, 211, 221
Holly Fern (*Polystichum lonchitis*) 58, 60
Holly-leaved Naiad (*Najas marina*) 50
Holm Oak (*Quercus ilex*) 138, 193, 218, 223
Honey Buzzard (*Pernis apivorus*) 16, 24, 27, 29, 53, 73–5*p*, 77, 84–6*p*, 93, 98, 100, 102, 105, 107, 109, 111, 123, 124, 126, 136, 137, 143–5*p*, 155, 157, 159, 160, 163–5*p*, 168, 169, 171, 187, 192, 202, 209, 211, 212, 214, 217, 221, 223, 224, 232, 233, 235, 246
Hooded Seal (*Cystophora cristata*) 1
Hoopoe (*Upupa epops*) 125, 131, 136, 139, 152, 180, 191, 195, 203, 213, 219, 225, 242, 243, 253
Hop Hornbeam 211, 223, 224

Hornbeam (*Carpinus betulus*) 99, 100, 102, 111, 113, 117, 118, 164, 169, 225, 231, 233

Horned Pansy (*Viola cornuta*) 189

Horseshoe Orchid (*Ophrys ferrum-equinum*) 237, 238, 240, 241

Horseshoe Vetch (*Hippocrepis comosa*) 52, 89, 110

Horvath's Rock Lizard (*Lacerta horvathii*) 207

House Martin (*Delichon urbica*) 93

Hungarian Gentian (*Gentiana hungarica*) 102

Hungarian Glider (*Neptis rivularis*) 159

Hungarian Hawthorn (*Crataegus nigra*) 166

Hungarian Narrow-leaved Ash (*Fraxinus pallisiae*) 166

Hungarian Oak (*Quercus frainetto*) 167, 169

Hungarian Thistle (*Cirsium furiens*) 165

Hutchinsia (*Hornungia petraea*) 104

Hymenoptera 126

Hypericum balearicum 203

Iberian Guillemot (*Uria aalge ibericus*) 186

Iberian Wall Lizard (*Podarcis hispanica*) 186

Iceland Wren >> Common Wren

Icterine Warbler (*Hippolais icterina*) 16, 112

Ilex Hairstreak (*Nordmannia ilicis*) 233

Imperial Eagle (*Aquila heliaca*) 113, 164, 168, 191, 192, 195, 198, 223, 224, 253

Inula brittanica 160

Inula ensifolia 113

Inula montana 176

Iolas Blue (*Iolana iolas*) 193, 195

Ips longicollis >> Bark Beetle

Iris boissieri 175

Irish Hare (Blue Hare; Mountain Hare; *Lepus timidus*) 4, 6, 7, 12, 21, 59, 61, 62, 65

Irish Heath (*Erica erigena*) 60

Irish Lady's Tresses (*Spiranthes romanzoffiana*) 54, 60

Irish Sandwort (Fringed Sandwort; *Arenaria ciliata*) 60

Irish Spurge (*Euphorbia hyberna*) 52, 65

Iris marsica 214

Iris pumila 160, 238

Iris sintenisii 246

Iris spuria >> Butterfly Iris

Iris subbiflora 200

Iris xiphium >> Spanish Iris

Isabelline Wheatear 232

Italian Agile Frog (*Rana latastei*) 207

Italian Wall Lizard (*Podarcis sicula*) 202, 203, 211, 215

Ivory Gull (*Pagophila eburnea*) 4

Ivy-leaved Bellflower (*Wahlenbergia hederacea*) 69

Jackal (*Canis aureus*) 229, 230, 233, 235, 236, 240, 247

Jack Snipe (*Lymnocryptes minimus*) 6,12, 15, 116

Jacob's Ladder (*Polemonium caerulea*) 5, 48, 49

Jankaea heldreichii 235

Janka Lily (*Lilium carniolicum jankae*) 225

Jay (*Garrulus glandarius*) 13, 19, 253

Jersey Tiger (*Euplagia quadripunctaria*) 241

Jovibarba arenaria 109

Juncus stygius 146

Juniper >> Common Juniper; Foetid Juniper; Phoenician Juniper

Jurinea (*Jurinea mollis*) 161

Kentish Glory (*Endromis versicolora*) 37, 38

Kentish Milkwort >> Teesdale Milkwort

Kentish Plover (*Charadrius alexandrinus*) 28, 67, 82, 87, 91, 123, 125, 129, 180, 181, 197, 199, 201, 203, 215, 220

Kermes Oak (*Quercus coccifera*) 231

Kerry Lily (*Simethis planifolia*) 64, 122

Kerry Slug (*Geomalacus maculosus*) 56, 65

King Eider (*Somateria spectabilis*) 4

Kingfisher (*Alcedo atthis*) 70, 71, 74, 88, 94, 98, 101, 103, 105, 112, 140, 147, 149, 157, 163, 166, 176, 190, 191, 211, 214, 230, 234, 238, 246–8p

King-of-the-Alps (*Eritrichium nanum*) 152

Knapweed (*Centaurea* spp) 119, 171, 233

Knot (*Calidris canutus*) 63

Krüper's Nuthatch (*Sitta krueperi*) 241, 245, 247

Labrador Tea (*Ledum palustre*) 6, 98

Lacerta atlantica 204

Lactuca alpina 13

Ladder Snake (*Elaphe scalaris*) 138, 139

Ladybird Spider (*Eresus niger*) 25

Lady Orchid (*Orchis purpurea*) 74, 93, 97, 101, 123, 130, 143, 214

Lady's Bedstraw (*Galium verum*) 169

Lady's Slipper Orchid (*Cypripedium calceolus*) 19, 93, 97, 98, 100, 104, 118, 132, 149, 167, 187, 223

Lamium lovcenicum 224

Lammergeier (Bearded Vulture) (*Gypaetus barbatus*) 135, 139, 140, 156, 186, 188–90p, 211, 224, 227, 232, 233, 242, 247, 252–4p

Lanner Falcon (*Falco biarmicus*) 212, 217, 223, 233, 241

Lapland Bunting (*Calcarius lapponicus*) 10, 18

Lapland Buttercup (*Ranunculus lapponicus*) 18

Lapland (Arctic) Rhododendron (*Rhododendron lapponicum*) 4, 6, 7

Larch (*Larix decidua*) 105, 110, 152, 208, 217

Large Blue (*Maculinea arion*) 112, 147, 190, 193

Large Copper (*Lycaena dispar*) 84, 211

Large-flowered Butterwort >> Greater Butterwort

Large Heath butterfly (*Coenonympha tullia*) 36, 61

Large-leaved Lime (*Tilia platyphyllos*) 13, 74, 96, 98, 100

Large Marsh Grasshopper (*Stethophyma grossum*) 122

Large Marsh Saxifrage (*Saxifraga hirculus*) 19

Large Mediterranean Spurge (*Euphorbia characias*) 139

Large Pasque-flower 223

Large Psammodromus (*Psammodromus algirus*) 194

Large Tortoiseshell (*Nymphalis polychloros*) 113, 124, 168, 245

Large Yellow Gentian (*Gentiana lutea*) 145

Large Yellow Rest-harrow (*Ononis natrix*) 149

Lataste's Viper (*Vipera latasti*) 175, 198, 201

Late Spider Orchid (*Ophrys holoserica exaltata*) 74, 138, 143, 213, 216, 242

Laurel (*Laurus azorica*) 181

Laurel Pigeon (*Columba trocaz*) 174, 204

Lavatera thuringiaca 113, 166, 169

Lavender 49, 68, 139, 175, 179, 194, 195, 201, 202, 254

Lax-flowered Orchid (*Orchis laxiflora*) 124, 135, 211

Leach's Petrel (*Oceanodroma leucorhoa*) 2, 59

Leaf-toed Gecko (*Phyllodactylus europaeus*) 218

Leafy Lousewort (*Pedicularis foliosa*) 188

Least (Lesser) Bur-reed (*Sparganium minimum*) 27, 166

Lesser Bur-reed >> Least Bur-reed

Lesser Bladderwort (*Utricularia minor*) 34, 63

Lesser Butterfly Orchid (*Platanthera bifolia*) 13, 58, 69, 100, 105

Lesser Centaury (*Centaurium pulchellum*) 65

Lesser Clubmoss (*Selaginella selaginoides*) 56, 58

Lesser Grey Shrike (*Lanius minor*) 112, 138, 169, 193, 213

Lesser Horsehoe Bat (*Rhinolophus hipposideros*) 176

Lesser Kestrel (*Falco naumanni*) 176, 180, 188, 196, 199, 223, 227, 242, 252

Lesser Pied Kingfisher (*Ceryle rudis*) 247

Lesser Purple Emperor (*Apatura ilia*) 122, 160

Lesser Spotted Eagle (*Aquila pomarina*) 93, 109–11p, 113, 116, 117, 164, 165, 168, 171, 224

Lesser Twayblade (*Listera cordata*) 52, 58

Lesser Water-plantain (*Baldellia ranunculoides*) 71

Lesser White-fronted Goose (*Anser erythropus*) 5, 12

Leucojum trichophyllum 198

Levant Sparrowhawk (*Accipiter brevipes*) 241, 246

lichens (*Cladonia* spp) 1, 6, 7, 8, 13, 19, 33, 36, 39, 47, 52, 53, 57, 62, 65, 67, 71, 74, 97, 98, 113, 146, 171, 211, 221, 233, 235

Lilford's Wall Lizard (*Podarcis lilfordi*) 203

Lilium carniolicum >> Carnic Lily

Lilium carniolicum jankae >> Janka Lily

Lilium chalcedonicum 235, 240

Lily-of-the-Valley (*Convallaria majalis*) 14, 51, 98, 100, 163

Lily-of-the-Valley Tree (*Clethra arborea*) 174

Lime (*Tilia* spp) 13, 14, 20, 28, 34, 41, 51, 60, 61, 74, 96–8p, 100, 101, 105, 112, 117, 132, 133, 136, 147, 148, 164, 167, 168, 197, 225, 233, 254

Lime Grass (*Elymus farctus*) 26

Limoniastrum monopetalum 194

Limonium insigne 201

Limonium sinuatum 202

Limonium thouinii 202

Linaria platycalyx 199

Linaria thymifolia 129

Lindenia tetraphylla 232

Liquidambar orientalis 247

Lithodora fruticosa 188

Lithodora rosmariniflora 220

Little Auk (*Alle alle*) 4

Little Bittern (*Ixobrychus minutus*) 68, 73, 86, 87, 95, 101, 103, 105, 107, 112, 113, 116, 117, 125, 131, 132, 146, 154, 157, 160, 167, 170, 176, 178–81p, 203, 211–13p, 219, 231, 234, 235, 238, 246

Little Bunting (*Emberiza pusilla*) 5

Little Bustard (*Tetrax tetrax*) 138, 179, 190–2p, 195, 197, 219

Little Crake (*Porzana parva*) 96, 125, 211, 237

Little Egret (*Echium garzetta*) 131, 138, 164, 167, 170, 177, 178, 180, 190, 197, 201, 203, 211, 213, 221, 230–2p, 245–7p, 252, 254

Little Gull (*Larus minutus*) 16, 24

Little Stint (*Calidris minuta*) 4, 40

Little Tern (*Sterna albifrons*) 25, 35, 49, 50, 57, 64, 65, 91, 93, 138, 176, 181, 194, 197, 201, 215, 219, 220, 235

Lizard Orchid (*Himantoglossum hircinum*) 130, 214

Lobaria pulmonaria >> Lungwort

Lobster Moth (*Stauropus fagi*) 123

Loggerhead Turtle (*Caretta caretta*) 207, 218, 229, 241, 247, 252, 254

Long-eared Owl (*Asio otus*) 68, 136

Longhorn Beetle 19, 37, 152, 159, 163, 168

Longhorn Cattle 169

Long-leaved Sundew (*Drosera intermedia*) 94

Long-legged Buzzard (*Buteo rufinus*) 229, 231

Long-spurred Orchid (*Orchis longicornu*) 141

Long-tailed Blue (*Lampides boeticus*) 187, 189, 192

Long-tailed Duck (*Clangula hyemalis*) 2, 7, 14, 15, 62

Long-toed Pigeon (*Columba junoniae*) 204

Lungwort (*Lobaria pulmonaria*) 36, 74, 89, 94

Lusitanian Oak (*Quercus lusitanica*) 176

Lynx (*Felis lynx*) 5, 6, 12, 13, 17, 19, 21, 98, 102, 107, 109, 110, 117, 119, 124, 132, 144, 145, 171, 195, 196, 198, 224, 227

Lythrum virgatum 164, 165

Mackay's Heath (*Erica mackaiana*) 57,60

Madeiran Bilberry (*Vaccinium padifolium*) 174

Madeiran Heather (*Erica arborea*) 174

Madeiran Storm-Petrel (*Oceanodroma castro*) 174, 176

Maidenhair Fern (*Adiantum capillus-veneris*) 211

Mallorcan Midwife Toad (*Alytes muletensis*) 183

Mandrake (*Mandragora officinalis*) 243

Manna Ash (*Fraxinus ornus*) 113

Man Orchid (*Aceras anthropophora*) 74

Manx Shearwater (*Puffinus puffinus*) 2, 35, 58, 64, 203, 216–18p, 249

Map Butterfly (*Araschnia levana*) 101, 124, 126

Marbled Fritillary (*Brenthis daphne*) 187

Marbled Newt (*Triturus marmoratus*) 122, 175, 190, 193, 195

Marbled White (*Melanargia galathea*) 164

Maritime Pine (*Pinus maritima*) 197

Marmora's Warbler (*Sylvia sarda*) 203, 207, 217, 219

Marram Grass (*Ammophila arenaria*) 26

Marsh Andromeda >> Bog Rosemary

Marsh Bilberry (*Vaccinium uliginosum*) 146

Marsh Cinquefoil (*Potentilla palustris*) 81, 103

Marsh Cranesbill (*Geranium palustre*) 103

Marsh Felwort >> Swertia

Marsh Fritillary (*Eurodryas aurinia*) 62, 63

Marsh Frog (*Rana ridibunda*) 96, 104, 144, 165, 180, 193, 196, 234, 247

Marsh Gentian (*Gentiana pneumonanthe*) 54, 69, 71, 80, 81, 112, 146, 147, 154, 166

Marsh Gladiolus (*Gladiolus palustris*) 104, 154

Marsh Harrier (*Circus aeruginosus*), 14, 15, 24–8p, 50, 51, 70, 80–4p, 86–8p, 93, 95–7p, 101, 103, 104, 107, 112, 113, 116, 117, 123, 125–8p, 140, 144, 157, 163–7p, 170, 176, 178, 179, 192–4p, 198, 200, 203, 210–14p, 219, 221, 230, 231, 235, 237, 238, 246, 253

Marsh Helleborine (*Epipactis palustris*) 67, 104, 146, 147

Marsh Orchid (*Dactylorhiza* spp) 27, 32, 33, 41, 43, 50, 62, 80, 82, 103–5p, 146–8p, 159, 163, 238

Marsh Pea (*Lathyrus palustris*) 51, 60, 68

Marsh Pennywort (*Hydrocotyle vulgaris*) 63

Marsh (Bog) St John's Wort (*Hypericum elodes*) 63, 71

Marsh Valerian (*Valeriana dioica*) 68

Marsh Violet (*Viola palustris*) 63, 69

Marsh Warbler (*Acrocephalus palustris*) 16, 148

Martagon Lily (*Lilium martagon*) 98, 101–3p, 105, 128, 143, 156–8p, 190, 193, 208, 223

Masked Shrike (*Lanius nubicus*) 232

May-lily (*Maianthemum bifolium*) 73, 98, 100, 102, 103, 107, 111, 124, 131, 146, 155, 163

Meadow Saffron (*Colchicum autumnale*) 51, 185

Medicago maritima 252

Mediterranean Gull (*Larus melanocephalus*) 231

Mediterranean Snail (*Theba pisana*) 138

Melampyrum nemorosum >> Cow-wheat

Melancholy Thistle (*Cirsium helenioides*) 18, 48

Melodious Warbler (*Hippolais polyglotta*) 203

Menorcan Loosestrife (*Lysimachia minoricensis*) 203

Merendera montana 188, 191

Merlin (*Falco columbarius*) 33, 36, 49, 52, 56–8p, 60, 63, 125, 177

Mezereon (*Daphne mezereum*) 13, 14, 49, 74, 103

Microstylis monophyllos 104

Middle Spotted Woodpecker (*Dendrocopus medius*) 74, 136, 246

Midwife Toad (*Alytes obstetricans*) 122, 126, 175, 183, 195

Military Orchid (Soldier Orchid; *Orchis militaris*) 97, 101, 108, 123, 130, 136, 143, 149

Milk Parsley (*Peucedanum palustre*) 51

Mink (*Mustela vison*) 1, 125

Mirror Orchid (*Ophrys vernixia*) 237, 240, 245

Moehringia lateriflora 6

Mongoose (*Herpestes ichneumon*) 195; Small Indian Mongoose (*H. auropunctatus*) 223

Monkey Orchid (*Orchis simia*) 123, 130, 242, 245

Monk Seal (*Monachus monachus*) 223

Monkshood (*Aconitum napellus*) 102, 143, 145, 148

Montagu's Harrier (*Circus pygargus*) 28, 70, 113, 123–6p, 128, 161, 163, 166, 175, 177, 178, 193, 195, 197, 212, 213, 246, 253

Montandon's Newt (*Triturus montandoni*) 110

Monte Baldo Anemone (*Anemone baldensis*) 148

Montpellier Maple (*Acer monspessulanus*) 224, 233

Montpellier Snake (*Malpolon monspessulanus*) 138, 193, 194

Moon Carrot (*Seseli libanotis*) 127

Moonwort (*Botrychium lunaria*) 40, 119

Moor Frog (*Rana arvalis*) 71, 96, 104

Moorish Gecko (*Tarentola mauritanica*) 199

Moor-king (*Pedicularis sceptrum-carolinae*) 6, 13

Moorland Clouded Yellow (*Colias palaeno*) 73

Morisia monanthos 141

Moroccan Orange-tip (*Anthocharis belia euphenoides*) 199

Moss Campion (*Silene acaulis*) 32, 60

Mossy Saxifrage (*Saxifraga hypnoides*) 41, 49, 72

Moth Mullein (*Verbascum blattaria*) 160

Mouflon (*Ovis musimon*) 85, 94, 97–9p, 118, 139, 168, 197, 207, 217, 218, 222, 253

Mountain Avens (*Dryas octopetala*) 7, 19, 33–5p, 39, 58, 60, 104, 144, 147, 148

Mountain Bladder-fern (*Cystopteris montana*) 39

Mountain Clouded Yellow (*Colchium phicomone*), 133, 135, 189, 190

Mountain Germander (*Teucrium montanum*)113, 164

Mountain Hare >> Irish Hare

Mountain Kidney Vetch (*Anthyllis montana*) 127, 143

Mountain Melick (*Melica nutans*) 51

Mountain Orchid >> *Chamorchis alpina*

Mountain Pine (*Pinus mugo*) 105, 108, 109, 147, 152, 171

Mountain Ringlet (*Erebia epiphron*) 39

Mountain Tassel-flower (*Soldanella montana*) 102

Mount Baldo Anemone >> Monte Baldo Anemone

Mount Cenis Pansy (*Viola cenisia*) 148

Mount Etna Broom (*Genista aetnensis*) 216

Moustached Warbler (*Acrocephalus melanopogon*) 113, 165–7p, 203, 212, 234

Mudwort (*Limosella aquatica*) 122

Muntjac Deer (*Muntiacus reevesi*) 52

Musk Beetle (*Aromia moschata*) 73, 100, 124

Musk Orchid (*Herminium monorchis*) 97

Musk-ox (*Ovibos moschatus*) 4, 8

Mute Swan (*Cygnus olor*) 62

Myricaria (*Myricaria germanica*) 104

Myrtle (*Myrtus communis*) 69, 138, 223

Narcissus asturiensis 177, 184

Narcissus bulbocodium 195

Narcissus bulbocodium nivalis 177

Narcissus-flowered Anemone (*Anemone narcissiflora*) 130

Narcissus nevadensis 200

Narcissus nobilis 184

Narcissus obesus 179

Narcissus rupicola 177, 191, 195

Narcissus serotinus 238, 249

Narcissus stellaris >> Narrow-leaved Daffodil

Narcissus tazetta 219, 221, 249

Narcissus triandrus >> Angel's Tears

Narrow-leaved Daffodil (*Narcissus stellaris*) 157

Narrow-leaved Lungwort (*Pulmonaria longifolia*) 53

Natterjack Toad (*Bufo calamita*) 40, 41, 49, 50, 64, 67, 71, 122, 193

Nebria tatrica 110

Nepeta tuberosa 180

Nettle-tree (*Celtis caucasicus*) 224

Nevada Blue (*Plebicula golgus*) 200

Nevada Grayling (*Pseudochazara hippolyte*) 197

New Forest Cicada (*Cicadetta montana*) 74, 76, 127

Nightingale (*Luscinia megarhynchos*) 16, 21, 27, 67, 146, 195, 242, 245, 253

Nightjar (*Caprimulgus europaeus*) 27, 29, 53, 69–71p, 74, 85, 88, 94, 126, 164, 176, 179

Nigritella nigra >> Black Vanilla Orchid

Nile Soft-shelled Turtle (*Trionyx euphraticus*) 247

Norfolk Hawker (*Aeshna isosceles*) 50, 125, 128, 163, 232

Northern Bedstraw (*Galium boreale*) 110

Northern Birch Mouse (*Sicista betulina*) 8, 14
Northern Buckler Fern (*Dryopteris expansa*) 34
Northern Damselfly (*Coenagrion hastatum*) 27, 95
Northern Eggar (Oak Eggar; *Lasiocampa quercus*) 35, 39, 52
Northern Marsh Orchid (*Dactylorhiza purpurella*) 32, 33, 62
Northern Rock-cress (*Cardaminopsis petraea*) 32, 60
Northern Wolfsbane (*Aconitum septentrionale*) 13
Norway Lemming >> Lemming
Norway Maple (*Acer platanoides*) 117, 147
Norway Spruce (*Picea abies*) 12, 18, 98, 102, 105, 107
Norwegian Mugwort (*Artemisia norvegica*) 8
Norwegian Sandwort (*Arenaria norvegica*) 35
Norwegian Wintergreen (*Pyrola norvegica*) 8, 10
Nose-horned Viper (*Vipera ammodytes*) 240
Nutcracker (*Nucifraga caryocatactes*) 21, 110, 132, 139, 145, 148–52p, 155, 161, 171
Nuthatch (*Sitta europaea*) 140, 141, 226, 237, 238, 245, 247

Oak >> Common Oak; Cork Oak; Downy Oak; Holm Oak; Hungarian Oak; Kermes Oak; Lusitanian Oak; Pedunculate Oak; Pyrenean Oak; *Quercus alnifolia*; Round-leaved Oak; Sessile Oak
Oak Eggar >> Northern Eggar
Ocellated Lizard (*Lacerta lepida*) 139, 198, 201, 211
Ocellated Skink (*Chalcides ocellatus*) 219
Oedipoda caerulescens (Blue-winged Grasshopper) 76
Oenanthe aquatica (Water Dropwort) 163
Old Man's Beard (*Usnea longissima*) 13
Olive (*Olea europaea*) 221, 223
Olm (*Proteus anguinus*) 222
Omphalodes nitida 175
One-flowered Wintergreen (*Moneses uniflora*) 100, 124, 209
One-leaved Butterfly Orchid (*Platanthera obtusata* ssp *oligantha*) 10
Onosma frutescens 236
Onosma tornense 168
Onosma troodii 253
Onosma vaudensis 149
Ophioglossum azoricum 122
Ophrys bertolonii 204
Ophrys cretica 242, 243
Ophrys holoserica exaltata >> Late Spider Orchid
Ophrys kotschyii (Cyprus Bee Orchid) 253, 254
Ophrys lacaitae 221

Ophrys lunulata 220, 221
Ophrys pallida 220
Ophrys reinholdii 240
Orange (*Citrus sinensis*) 137, 199, 221
Orange Lily (*Lilium bulbiferum*) 132, 223
Orange-spotted Emerald (*Oxygaster curtisii*) 125, 128
Orchids 8, 10, 12, 13, 16, 19, 32, 33, 35, 40, 41, 47, 49, 50, 54, 58, 60, 62, 80, 84, 94, 98, 101–5p, 108, 117, 118, 124, 131, 132, 135, 136, 141, 143, 146–9p, 163–5p, 167, 179, 180, 185, 187, 189, 194, 195, 200, 204, 208, 209, 211, 213, 214, 216, 219, 221, 223, 225, 238, 240–3p, 245, 251, 253, 254
Orchis anatolica 241, 243
Orchis brancifortii 220
Orchis italica 216, 221, 242
Orchis morio >> Green-winged Orchid
Orchis patens 211
Orchis pauciflora 242, 243
Orchis prisca 243
Orchis provincialis 138, 221
Orchis sancta 241
Ornithogalum pyramidale 169
Ornithogalum reverchonii 199
Orobanche cypria 253
Orobanche densiflora f. *melitensis* 249
Orphean Warbler (*Sylvia hortensis*) 136, 152, 178
Orsini's Viper (*Vipera ursinii*) 160, 166, 171
Ortolan Bunting (*Emberiza hortulana*) 70, 71, 117, 136, 145, 175, 177, 223, 231, 237
Osprey (*Pandion haliaetus*) 7, 9, 12, 16, 20, 21, 25, 37, 68, 95, 97, 107, 128, 141, 177, 178, 202, 203
Ostrich Fern (*Matteucia struthiopteris*) 6, 18
Otter (*Lutra lutra*) 9, 12, 13, 32–6p, 44, 48, 57, 60, 61, 63, 74, 81, 84, 94, 97, 98, 102, 109, 110, 124, 125, 128, 144, 166, 175, 176, 179, 188, 190, 212, 217, 223, 233
Ovis musimon >> Mouflon
Oxlip (*Primula elatior*) 189, 208
Oxytropis carpatica 110
Oystercatcher (*Haematopus ostralegus*) 33, 40, 41, 64, 68, 81, 129, 201
Oyster Plant (*Mertensia maritima*) 7, 32, 33

Paeonia broteroi 178
Paeonia cambessedesii 202, 203
Paeony (*Paeonia mascula*) 178, 218, 221, 223
Painted Frog (*Discoglossus pictus*) 138, 141, 190, 193–5p, 218
Pale-breasted Brent Goose (*Branta bernicla hrota*) 57
Pale Butterwort (Western Butterwort; *Pinguicula lusitanica*) 33, 34

Pale Pasque-flower (*Pulsatilla patens*) 15
Pallid Harrier (*Circus macrourus*) 253
Pallid Swift (*Apus pallidus*) 141
Palm Dove (*Streptopelia senegalensis*) 245
Pancratium illyricum 218
Papaver radicatum 8
Papaver rhaeticum 209, 210
Papaver rupifragum 199
Parnassius apollo graslini 247
Parrot Crossbill (*Loxia pytyopsittacus*) 21
Parsley Fern (*Cryptogramma crispa*) 52
Parsley Frog (*Pelodytes punctatus*) 200
Pasque-flower (*Pulsatilla vulgaris*) 8, 15, 16, 52, 74, 89, 109, 126, 130, 131, 136, 145, 149, 157, 160, 167, 188, 193, 208
Pastinaca lucida 202
Peak White (*Pontia callidice*) 133, 208
Pearl-bordered Fritillary (*Boloria euphrosyne*) 35, 48, 62
Pedicularis exaltata 119
Pedunculate Oak (*Quercus petraea*) 100
Penduline Tit (*Remiz pendulinus*) 105, 112, 113, 116, 170, 232, 235, 242
Penny Royal (*Mentha pulegium*) 122
Peregrine Falcon (*Falco peregrinus*) 37, 42, 46, 56, 58, 63, 97, 109, 127, 141, 148, 175, 186, 191, 193, 202, 205, 213, 216, 217, 220, 221, 223, 235, 237, 242, 245, 252, 254
Pericallia matronula 127
Periploca laevigata 202, 249
Petromarula pinnata 242
Petteria ramentacea 223
Petty Whin (*Genista anglica*) 71
Pheasant's Eye (*Adonis annua*) 16, 160, 167, 168, 192
Pheasant's Eye Narcissus (*Narcissus poeticus*) 130
Phlomis cypria 254
Phoca hispida saimensis 20
Phoenician Juniper (*Juniperus phoeniceus*) 138
Phyteuma humile 208
Pied Flycatcher (*Ficedula hypoleuca*) 19, 21, 42, 51, 52, 192
Pied Kingfisher (*Ceryle rudis*) 247
Pied Wheatear (*Oenanthe pleschanka*) 253
Pillwort (*Pilularia globulifera*) 53, 88
Pine (*Pinus* spp) 6, 7, 12, 13, 18–20p, 81, 82, 93, 94, 101, 105, 107–9p, 116, 117, 129, 136, 138–41p, 146, 147, 149, 158, 161, 164, 167, 171, 174, 175, 179, 187, 188, 190, 192, 193, 195, 204, 208, 217, 218, 221, 223, 224, 227, 232, 233, 235–8p, 245, 247, 253, 254

Pine Marten (*Martes martes*) 5, 21, 34,36, 56, 65, 84–6p, 100, 102, 125, 152, 159, 168, 169, 197, 212, 213
Pinguicula hirtiflora 232
Pinguicula vallisneriana 197
Pink Butterfly Orchid (*Orchis papilionacea*) 141, 200, 216, 238, 243
Pink Flax (*Linum suffruticosum*) 136, 164
Pink-footed Goose (*Anser brachyrhynchus*) 24, 39, 49
Pintail (*Anas acuta*) 253
Pin-tailed Sandgrouse (*Pterocles alchata*) 138, 179, 192, 195, 197
Pipewort (*Eriocaulon aquaticum*) 60, 65
Plane-leaved Buttercup (*Ranunculus platanifolius*) 107
Platycnemis acutipennis 128
Podarcis filfolensis 249
Polar Bear (*Thalarctos maritimus*) 4
Polar Willow (*Salix polaris*) 18
Polecat (*Mustela putorius*) 44, 62, 74, 81, 84, 85, 152, 161
Polemonium acutiflorum 5, 18
Polygala boisseri 197
Pond Terrapin (*Emys orbicularis*) 125, 128, 138, 212, 232, 242
Pondweeds (*Potamogeton* spp) 15
Pool Frog (*Rana lessonae*) 147
Poplar Hawk Moth (*Laothoe populi*) 35, 57
Porcupine (*Hystrix cristata*) 212–14p, 217, 221
Posidonia oceanica >> Sea-balls
Potentilla hyparctica 12
Potentilla nitida 210
Prasium majus 215
Praying Mantis (*Mantis religiosa*) 76,127, 136–8p, 150, 163, 240
Primula daonensis 208
Primula deorum 226
Primula marginata 139
Primula tyrolensis 209
Provençal Short-tailed Blue (*Everes alcetas*) 130
Provence Blue (*Lysandra hispana*) 130
Provence Orchid (*Orchis provincialis*) 213
Prunella pieninica 110
Pseudorchis frivaldii (Frivald's Frog Orchid) 225
Ptarmigan (*Lagopus mutus*) 1, 2, 5, 9, 18, 34, 37, 38, 105, 132, 133, 147–9p, 152, 155, 188–90p, 208, 209, 222
Pterocephalus porphyranthus 204
Ptilotrichum purpureum 200
Puffin (*Fraterculus arctica*) 2, 8, 32, 33, 46, 56, 58, 59, 64, 122
Pulsatilla grandis 160
Pulsatilla nigricans 160
Pulsatilla rubra >> Cévennes Pasque-flower
Pulsatilla vulgaris gotlandica 16
Purple Crocus (*Crocus purpureus*) 128
Purple Emperor (*Apatura iris*) 75, 122, 124, 160

Purple Gallinule (*Porphyrio porphyrio*) 180, 198, 201, 219
Purple Heron (*Ardeola purpurea*) 83, 84, 101, 103, 112, 113, 117, 124–6*p*, 131, 138, 140, 146, 154, 160, 163, 164, 176, 178–80*p*, 193, 194, 197, 198, 203, 210–12*p*, 219, 230–2*p*, 234, 235, 237, 246, 247, 252–4*p*
Purple Loosestrife (*Lythrum salicaria*) 68, 103, 146, 164
Purple Oxytropis (*Oxytropis halleri*) 33
Purple Sandpiper (*Calidris maritima*) 4, 9, 12
Purple Saxifrage (*Saxifraga oppositifolia*) 13, 35, 38, 39, 41, 58, 60
Putoria calabrica 199
Pygmy Cormorant (*Phalacrocorax pygmeus*) 171, 224, 225, 230–2*p*, 245–7*p*
Pygmy Owl (*Glaucidium passerinum*) 9, 15, 105, 132, 133, 148, 152, 171
Pyramidal Bugle (*Ajuga pyramidalis*) 35, 36
Pyramidal Orchid (*Anacamptis pyramidalis*) 49, 62
Pyrenean Brook Salamander (*Euproctus asper*) 186, 189
Pyrenean Columbine (*Aquilegia pyrenaica*) 135
Pyrenean Desman (*Galemys pyrenaicus*) 135, 137, 185, 186, 190
Pyrenean Fritillary (*Fritillaria pyrenaica*) 137
Pyrenean Honeysuckle (*Lonicera pyrenaica*) 137
Pyrenean Lily (*Lilium pyrenaicum*) 135
Pyrenean Oak (*Quercus pyrenaicus*) 175, 177, 190, 192
Pyrenean Saxifrage (*Saxifraga longifolia*) 186, 188

Quail (*Coturnix coturnix*) 110, 146
Queen-of-the-Alps (*Eryngium alpinum*) 133
Quercus alnifolia (Golden Oak) 254
Quillwort 54, 88

Racoon-dog (*Nyctereutes procyonoides*) 171
Ramonda (*Ramonda myconi*) 135, 188, 189, 193
Ramonda serbica 233
Rampion (*Phyteuma* spp) 73, 98, 185, 208, 209
Rannoch Rush (*Scheuzeria palustris*) 104, 128, 146, 157
Ranunculus cyprius var *cadmicus* 253
Ranunculus gregarius 187
Ranunculus illyricus 223
Ranunculus kykkoensis 253
Ranunculus lapponicus 6
Ranunculus rupestris 200
Ranunculus weyleri 202
Rat-headed Vole (*Microtus oeconomus*) 19
Raven (*Corvus corax*) 5, 39, 42, 56–8*p*, 65, 93, 122, 127, 141, 193, 217, 234, 247, 254

Razorbill (*Alca torda*) 2, 8, 32, 33, 46, 56, 59, 64, 122
Red-backed Shrike (*Lanius collurio*) 16, 70, 71, 73–5*p*, 77, 82, 84, 85, 88, 107, 110, 113, 126, 148, 159, 161, 188, 213
Red-billed Chough >> Common Chough
Red-breasted Flycatcher (*Ficedula parva*) 16, 19, 93, 100, 102, 109, 111, 117, 164, 168, 171, 223
Red-breasted Merganser (*Mergus serrator*) 21, 34, 35
Red-crested Pochard (*Netta rufina*) 104, 105, 113, 131, 138, 140, 144, 145, 154, 164, 180, 192, 194, 196–8*p*, 201, 214, 219
Red Deer (*Cervus elaphus*) 31, 34–6*p*, 38, 52, 56, 60, 65, 73, 85, 86, 97–100*p*, 102, 104, 105, 109, 110, 117, 124, 131, 137, 139, 150, 152, 155, 159, 161, 163, 166, 185, 190, 197, 198, 209, 210, 224, 225, 226, 235
Red-flanked Bluetail (*Tarsiger cyanurus*) 19
Red-footed Falcon (*Falco vespertinus*) 169, 203, 221
Red-fronted Serin (*Serinus pusillus*) 247
Red Grouse (Willow Grouse; *Lagopus lagopus*) 5, 6, 13, 15, 18, 35, 48, 49, 52, 56, 58
Red Helleborine (*Cephelanthera rubra*) 33, 35, 48, 97, 98, 101, 104, 105, 130, 136, 143, 149, 156, 187, 231
Red Kite (*Milvus milvus*) 16, 44, 73–5*p*, 95, 98, 100, 102, 103, 123, 128, 130, 131, 135, 137, 141, 143–5*p*, 175, 188, 192, 212, 217, 220, 221
Red-necked Grebe (*Podiceps grisegena*) 21, 24, 28, 88, 96, 116, 117
Red-necked Nightjar (*Caprimulgus ruficollis*) 176, 179
Red-necked Phalarope (*Phalaropus lobatus*) 2, 9, 32, 59
Redshank (*Tringa totanus*) 6, 35, 41, 48, 56, 57, 59–61*p*, 64, 68, 79–81*p*, 91
Red Squirrel (*Sciurus vulgaris*) 21, 36, 49, 54, 57, 65, 71, 74, 85, 102, 103, 108, 129, 131, 137, 161, 184, 188, 191, 193, 197, 210, 211, 223, 224
Redstart (*Phoenicurus phoenicurus*) 51, 52, 56–8*p*, 63, 102, 126, 141, 199, 237, 238
Red-throated Diver (*Gavia stellata*) 2, 32, 34, 36
Red-throated Pipit (*Anthus cervinus*) 4
Redwing (*Turdus iliacus*) 2, 6, 7, 19, 36
Reed Warbler (*Acrocephalus scirpaceus*) 15, 21, 69, 74, 105, 117, 125, 132, 140, 147, 179, 190, 201, 203, 214, 234

Reindeer (*Rangifer tarandus*) 1, 4–9*p*, 10, 13, 19, 35, 37
Reversed Clover (*Trifolium resupinatum*) 128
Rhodes Dragon >> Agama Lizard
Rhododendron kotschyi 171
Rhododendron ponticum 179
Ringed Plover (*Charadrius hiaticula*) 40, 49, 60, 91
Ringed Seal (*Phoca hispida*) 1, 20
River Beauty (*Epilobium latifolium*) 1
River Warbler (*Locustella fluviatilis*) 21, 105, 112, 116, 117, 160, 166
Rock Bunting (*Emberiza cia*) 137, 149, 168
Rock Dove (*Columba livia*) 58, 141, 199
Rock Jasmines (*Androsace* spp) 105, 130, 149, 152
Rock Nuthatch (*Sitta neumayer*) 226, 237, 238, 247
Rock Partridge (*Alectoris graeca*) 133, 148, 155, 208, 209, 220, 221, 222, 224, 232, 235
Rock Pipit (*Anthus petrosus*) 58
Rock-rose >> Common Rock-rose
Rock Soapwort (*Saponaria ocymoides*) 136
Rock Sparrow (*Petronia petronia*) 137, 141, 176
Rock Speedwell (*Veronica fruticans*) 38, 39
Rock Thrush (*Monticola saxatilis*) 109, 113, 130, 136, 138, 141, 158, 176, 178, 199, 203, 216, 219, 221, 223, 236, 238, 242, 249, 254
Roe Deer (*Capreolus capreolus*) 36, 54, 70, 71, 73, 74, 81, 85, 86, 97, 99, 100, 102, 110, 124, 131, 137, 139, 159, 175, 184, 185, 190, 192, 193, 195, 209, 210, 212, 215, 223, 224, 225, 235
Roller (*Coracias garrulus*) 113, 138, 139, 166, 169, 178, 213, 230, 232, 235, 237, 252, 254
Roman Orchid (*Dactylorhiza romana*) 221
Romulea bulbocodium 221
Ronaldsay Sheep 33
Rosalia alpina (Alpine Longhorn Beetle) 168
Roseate Tern (*Sterna dougallii*) 61, 181
Rouen Pansy (*Viola hispida*) 123
Rough-legged Buzzard (*Buteo lagopus*) 5–7*p*, 9, 10, 12, 16, 18, 19, 81, 95
Round-leaved Oak (*Quercus rotundifolia*) 176
Round-leaved Wintergreen (*Pyrola rotundifolia*) 39, 41, 65
Rowan (*Sorbus aucuparia*) 8, 36, 47, 117
Royal Fern (*Osmunda vulgaris*) 33, 69
Rubus retezaticus 171
Ruddy Darter (*Sympetrum sanguineum*) 60, 103

Ruddy Shelduck (*Tadorna ferruginea*) 253
Ruddy Vole (*Clethrionomys rutilus*) 6
Rue (*Ruta* spp) 35, 38, 58, 60, 68, 76, 147, 163
Rue-leaved Saxifrage (*Saxifraga tridactylites*) 147
Ruff (*Philomachus pugnax*) 16, 24–6*p*, 28, 51, 68, 79, 82, 116, 128, 165, 248
Rufous Bush-Robin (*Cercotrichas galactotes*) 181
Rupicapra rupicapra >> Chamois
Ruppell's Warbler (*Sylvia Rüppelli*) 237, 242, 252
Ruppia drapensis 249
Ruta chalepensis 252

Saimaa Ringed Seal (*Phoca hispida*) 20
Sainfoin (*Onobrychis viciifolia*) 109
St Dabeoc's Heath (*Daboecia cantabrica*) 59
St Patrick's Cabbage (*Saxifraga spathularis*) 65
Saker Falcon (*Falco cherrug*) 111, 160, 164, 165
Salmothymus krkensis 223
Salvia sclareoides 176
Sand Cat's Tail (*Phleum arenaria*) 67
Sand Crocus (*Romulea* spp) 138, 141, 213, 216
Sanderling (*Calidris alba*) 40
Sand Lizard (*Lacerta agilis*) 25, 49, 53, 54, 84, 85, 94, 126, 150, 166
Sand Quillwort (*Isoetes hystrix*) 54
Sandwich Tern (*Sterna sandvicensis*) 25, 26, 38, 50, 57, 60, 62, 92, 122, 124, 129, 194
Saponaria calabrica 233
Sarcocapnos enneaphylla 193, 195
Sardinian Cave Salamander (*Hydromantesgenei*) 218
Sardinian Warbler (*Sylvia melanocephala*) 178, 201, 213, 216, 237, 238, 242
Savi's Warbler (*Locustella luscinioides*) 50, 68, 69, 84, 93, 103, 105, 112, 165, 179, 190, 196
Sawfly Orchid (*Ophrys tenthredinifera*) 236, 238
Saw-sedge (*Cladium mariscus*) 51
Saxifraga biternata 200
Saxifraga marginata 233
Saxifraga moncayensis 187
Saxifraga vandellii 208
Saxifraga vayredana 194
Scabiosa ucranica 223
Scarce Copper (*Heodes virgaureae*) 133, 159
Scarce Swallowtail (*Iphiclides podalirius*) 108, 123, 124, 136, 143, 152, 192, 238, 243, 245
Scarlet Anemone (*Anemone coronaria*) 245
Scarlet Rosefinch (*Carpodacus erythrinus*) 21
Scaup (*Aythya marila*) 40
Schreiber's Green Lizard (*Lacerta schreiberi*) 175
Scilla vincentina 179

Scops Owl (*Otus scops*) 149, 164, 253, 254

Scorpion (*Euscorpius flavi-caudis*) 253

Scorpion Vetch (*Coronilla scorpioides*) 211

Scorzonera purpurea 171

Scotch Argus (*Erebia aethiops*) 109

Scoter (*Melanitta nigra*) 13, 14, 34, 40, 60, 210

Scots Pine (*Pinus sylvestris*) 19, 20, 36, 109, 149, 192, 195

Scottish Asphodel (*Tofieldia pusilla*) 35

Scottish Primrose (*Primula scotica*) 32, 33

Sea Aster (*Aster tripolium*) 81

Sea-balls (*Posidonia oceanica*) 138

Sea Bindweed (*Calystegia soldanella*) 26, 67, 213

Sea-blite (*Suaeda vera*) 201

Sea Campion (*Silene maritima*) 46

Sea Daffodil (*Pancratium maritimum*) 138, 186, 194, 202, 213, 218, 238, 249, 252

Sea Holly (*Eryngium maritimum*) 26, 41, 80, 215, 238, 249

Sea Lavender (*Limonium vulgare*) 49, 201, 202

Sea Medick (*Medicago marina*) 194, 215

Sea Milkwort (*Glaux maritima*) 49

Seaside Centaury (*Centaurium littorale*) 40

Sea Spurge (*Euphorbia paralias*) 41, 67, 238

Sea Squill (*Urginea maritima*) 249

Sea Wormwood (*Artemisia maritima*) 49

Sedges (*Carex* spp) 25, 27

Sedge Warbler (*Acrocephalus schoenbaenus*) 68, 74, 144

Sempervivum hirtum ssp *glabrescens* 108

Senecio nemorensis 107

Senecio rodriguezii 203

Serin (*Serinus serinus*) 144, 237

Serrated Wintergreen (*Orthilia secunda*) 103

Sessile Oak (*Quercus petraea*) 43, 65, 100

Shag (*Phalacrocorax aristotelis*) 64, 122, 176, 186, 203, 217, 223, 254

Sharp-snouted Rock Lizard (*Lacerta oxycephala*) 223

Shearwaters 58, 64, 138, 141, 174, 176, 179, 181, 207, 216–18p, 221, 245, 249

Shelduck >> Common Shelduck; Ruddy Shelduck

Shore Lark (*Eremophila alpestris*) 18, 123, 226, 233, 236, 247

Short-eared Owl (*Asio flammeus*) 28, 33, 50, 68, 95, 161

Short-spurred Fragrant Orchid (*Gymnadenia densiflora*) 93

Short-tailed Blue (*Everes argiades*) 130

Short-toed Eagle (*Circaetus gallicus*) 111, 113, 127, 130, 132, 135–9p, 161, 164, 165, 175–7p, 184, 185, 190, 191, 195, 205, 212–14p, 217, 231, 233, 234, 236–8p, 240, 246

Short-toed Lark (*Calandrella brachydactyla*) 125, 169, 181, 188, 223, 235, 237

Short-toed Treecreeper (*Certhia brachydactyla*) 126, 131, 179, 187, 194, 253

Shoveler (*Anas clypeata*) 39, 61, 63, 68, 82, 135, 196, 197

Shrubby Cinquefoil (*Potentilla fruticosa*) 16, 62

Siberian Iris (*Iris sibirica*) 103–5p, 144, 147, 154, 157

Siberian Jay (*Perisoreus infaustus*) 12, 13, 19

Siberian Tit (*Parus cinctus*) 19, 21

Sika Deer (*Cervus nippon*) 54, 65

Silver Birch (*Betula pendula*) 118

Silver Fir (*Abies alba*) 100, 102, 110, 112, 117–19p, 148, 163, 217

Silver Lime (*Tilia petiolaris*) 225

Silver-Studded Blue (*Plebejus argus*) 71

Silver-washed Fritillary (*Argynnis paphia*) 51, 57, 58, 103, 128, 232

Silvery Argus (*Pseudaricia nicias*) 189

Silvery Cranesbill (*Geranium argenteum*) 222

Six-stamened Waterwort (*Elatine hexandra*) 71

Skomer Vole 43

Slavonian Grebe (*Podiceps auritus*) 2, 14, 21

Slavonian Pasque-flower (*Pulsatilla halleri* ssp *slavica*) 109

Slender-billed Curlew (*Numenius tenuirostris*) 169

Slender-billed Gull (*Larus genei*) 194, 200, 207, 219, 221, 231

Slender Centaury (*Centaurium pulchellum*) 147

Slender Cotton-grass (*Eriophorum gracile*) 84

Slender Yellow Gentian (*Cicendia filiformis*) 54, 74

Small Apollo (*Parnassius phoebus*) 152

Small Blue (*Cupido minimus*) 52

Small Bugloss (*Anchusa arvensis*) 49

Small Indian Mongoose (*Herpestes auropunctatus*) 223

Small-leaved Lime (*Tilia cordata*) 28, 51, 96

Small Mountain Ringlet (*Erebia melampus*) 39

Small Pearl-bordered Fritillary(*Boloria selene*) 35

Small Red Damselfly (*Ceriagrion tenellum*) 44

Small White Orchid (*Pseudorchis albida*) 8, 35, 104, 158, 209

Smooth Rupturewort (*Herniaria glabra*) 54

Smooth Snake (*Coronella austriaca*) 53, 69–71p, 84, 85, 88, 93, 126, 147, 150, 165, 202

Smyrna Kingfisher (*Halcyon smyrnensis*) 247

Smyrnium perfoliatum 164

Snake-eyed Skink (*Ablepharus kitaibelii*) 165, 168

Snake's Head Fritillary (*Fritillaria meleagris*) 143, 169

Snowbells (*Soldanella alpina*) 102, 105, 109, 119, 128, 130, 145, 152, 190

Snow Bunting (*Plectrophenax nivalis*) 1, 2, 4, 9, 10, 18, 123

Snow Buttercup (*Ranunculus nivalis*) 8

Snowdon Lily (*Lloydia serotina*) 41

Snowdrop Windflower (*Anemone sylvestris*) 126

Snow Finch (*Montifringilla nivalis*) 132, 133, 139, 148, 149, 152, 155, 188

Snow Gentian (*Gentiana nivalis*) 39

Snow Vole (*Microtus nivalis*) 105, 152, 155

Snowy Cinquefoil (*Potentilla nivea*) 6

Snowy Owl (*Nyctea scandiaca*) 7, 12

Soldanella carpatica (Carpathian Snowbell) 119

Soldanella hungarica 110

Soldier Orchid >> Military Orchid

Somatochlora alpestris 150

Sombre Tit (*Parus lugubris*) 171, 229, 237

Southern Festoon (*Zerynthia polyxena*) 160, 241

Southern White Admiral (*Limenitis reducta*) 113, 208, 232, 233, 254

Spanish Argus (*Aricia morronensis*) 186, 189, 192

Spanish Chalkhill Blue (*Lysandra albicans*) 192

Spanish Fir (*Abies pinsapo*) 199

Spanish Fritillary (*Eurodryas desfontainii*) 200

Spanish Gatekeeper (*Pyronia bathseba*) 195

Spanish Iris (*Iris xiphium*) 188, 200

Spanish Sparrow (*Passer hispaniolensis*) 141

Sparrowhawk (*Accipiter nisus*) 70, 147, 211, 241, 246

Spectacled Salamander (*Salamandrina terdigitata*) 217

Spectacled Warbler (*Sylvia conspicillata*) 245

Spiders 25

Spignel >> Baldmoney

Spiked Rampion (*Phyteuma spicatum*) 98

Spiked Speedwell (*Veronica spicata*) 16, 122

Spined Loach (*Cobitis taenia*) 70

Spiny-footed Lizard (*Acanthodactylus erythrurus*) 193, 194, 198

Spiny Rest-harrow (*Ononis spinosa*) 169

Spoonbill (*Platalea leucorodia*) 79, 80, 82, 83, 160, 164–7p, 169, 178, 181, 191, 197, 198, 203, 215, 220, 221, 225, 230, 235, 245, 246, 254

Spotless Starling (*Sturnus unicolor*) 141

Spotted Cat's-ear (*Hypochoeris maculata*) 54

Spotted Crake (*Porzana porzana*) 21, 68, 69, 80, 82, 84, 87, 94, 96, 104, 124, 125, 128

Spotted Eagle (*Aquila clanga*) 94, 109–11p, 113, 115–17p, 119, 164, 165, 168, 171, 224, 246

Spotted Redshank (*Tringa erythropus*) 6

Spotted Rockrose (*Tuberaria guttata*) 129

Spring Cinquefoil (*Potentilla tabernaemontani*) 49, 74, 108

Spring Gentian (*Gentiana verna*) 48, 60, 62, 128

Spring Pasque-flower (*Pulsatilla vernalis*) 8

Spring Ringlet (*Erebia epistygne*) 194, 195

Spring Sandwort (*Minuartia verna*) 72

Spring Squill (*Scilla verna*) 33, 58, 62

Spruce (*Picea* spp) 7, 12, 13, 18, 19, 21, 27, 97, 98, 100–2p, 104, 105, 107–10p, 112, 119, 124, 137, 143, 144, 148, 159, 163, 167, 171, 208

Spur-thighed Tortoise (*Testudo graeca*) 198, 224

Spur-winged Plover (*Holopterus spinosus*) 232

Squacco Heron (*Ardeola ralloides*) 131, 138, 164, 170, 221, 232, 234, 235, 246, 252–4p

Squill (*Scilla* spp) 99, 122, 126, 179, 214, 237

Squinancy Wort (*Asperula cynanchica*) 52

Squirting Cucumber (*Ecballium elaterium*) 203

Stag Beetle (*Lucanus cervus*) 126, 163

Star-fruit (*Damasonia alisma*) 128

Starry Saxifrage (*Saxifraga stellaris*) 39

Stauropus fagi >> Lobster Moth

Steller's Eider (*Polysticta stelleri*) 4

Stemless Carline Thistle (*Carlina acaulis*) 145

Stenobothrus curasius 165

Stereocaulon vesuvianum 216

Sternbergia colchiflora 236

Sternbergia lutea 238

Sticky Primrose (*Primula glutinosa*) 208

Stipa jonnis 223

Stipa pannonica (Feather Grass) 118

Stoat (*Mustela ermina*) 56

Stock Dove (*Columba oenas*) 98

Stonechat (*Saxicola torquata*) 53, 60, 70, 71, 88, 94, 110

Stone Curlew (*Burhinus oedic-nemus*) 112, 136, 138, 161, 166, 167, 179, 188, 192, 195, 197, 203, 213, 219, 231, 235, 254

Stoneworts (*Chara* spp) 15

Stork's-bill (*Erodium* spp) 141, 215

Storm Petrel 2, 32, 59, 64, 122, 174, 176, 203, 249

Strawberry Tree (*Arbutus unedo*) 56, 65, 137, 138, 211, 215, 223, 231

Stripe-necked Terrapin (*Mauremys caspica*) 193, 196, 232, 241

Subalpine Warbler (*Sylvia cantillans*) 138, 203, 216

Summer Snowflake (*Leucojum aestivum*) 160

Sundew >> Common Sundew

Suslik (*Spermophilus citellus*) 166, 169

Swallow-wort (*Vincetoxicum hirundinaria*) 71, 108, 126

Swamp Nettle (*Urtica kioviensis*) 166

Sweet Chestnut 151, 175, 195, 211

Swertia (Marsh Felwort; *Swertia perennis*) 119, 148

Sycamore (*Acer pseudopla-tanus*) 99, 100, 111, 118, 145, 155, 159, 167, 224, 233

Sympetrum pedemontanum 150

Syrian Woodpecker (*Dendrocopus syriacus*) 160

Tamarisk (*Tamarix* spp) 104, 128, 201, 231, 246

Tartar (Tatarian) Maple (*Acer tataricum*) 113, 160, 223

Tassel Hyacinth (*Muscari comosum*) 72, 164, 238

Tatarian Maple >> Tartar Maple

Tawny Pipit (*Anthus campestris*) 112, 129, 169, 175, 176, 237

Teal (*Anas crecca*) 61, 135, 197, 198, 201, 252

Teesdale Milkwort (Kentish Milkwort; *Polygala amarella*) 48

Teesdale Sandwort (*Minuartia stricta*) 48

Teesdale Violet (*Viola rupestris*) 48

Teesdaliopsis conferta 184

Temminck's Stint (*Calidris temminckii*) 4, 9, 12

Tengmalm's Owl (*Aegolius funereus*) 6, 9, 15, 19, 73, 97, 98, 100, 102, 105, 108, 109, 112, 130, 132, 152, 158, 159, 190, 209, 235, 247

Tern >> Arctic Tern; Black Tern; Caspian Tern; Common Tern; Gull-billed Tern; Little Tern; Roseate Tern; Sandwich Tern; Whiskered Tern; White-winged Black Tern

Teucrium aroanium 238

Theba pisana >> Mediterranean Snail

Thekla Lark (*Galerida theklae*) 176, 179, 193

Theridium undatum 171

Thlaspi caerulescens ssp *calaminare* 72

Thlaspi goesingense 163

Three-toed Skink (*Chalcides chalcides*) 190, 193

Three-toed Woodpecker (*Picoides tridactylus*) 13, 15, 21, 105, 110, 119, 233

Thrift (*Armeria maritima*) 46, 58, 72, 141, 179, 198

Thrush Nightingale (*Luscinia luscinia*) 16, 21, 27

Thyme Broomrape (*Orobanche alba*) 54

Tongue Orchid (*Serapias lingua*) 184, 185, 195, 238

Toninia caeruleonigricans 211

Toothed Orchid (*Orchis tridentata*) 97, 221

Toothwort (*Lathraea squamaria*) 14

Tortula ruraliformis 67

Touch-me-not Balsam (*Impatiens noli-tangere*) 47

Trachelium caeruleum 197

Trailing Azalea >> Creeping Azalea

Tree Heather (*Erica arborea*) 174, 223

Trifolium durmitoreum 224

Trithemis annulata 195

Trumpet Gentian >> *Gentiana clusii*

Tuberous Bitter-vetch (*Lathyrus tuberosus*) 169

Tufted Duck (*Aythya fuligula*) 39, 68, 104, 128, 145, 147

Tufted Loosestrife (*Lysimachia thyrsiflora*) 82

Tulipa bakeri 242

Tulipa cypria 252

Tulips (*Tulipa* spp) 178, 187, 241, 245

Turban Buttercup (*Ranunculus asiaticus*) 241–3p, 254

Turkish Gecko (*Hemidactylus turcicus*) 223

Turnstone (*Arenaria interpres*) 4

Twinflower (*Linnaea borealis*) 12, 13, 15, 25, 37, 149, 155

Twite (*Carduelis flavirostris*) 33, 34

Two-tailed Pasha (*Charaxes jasius*) 137, 138, 194, 202, 215, 231

Tyrrhenian Painted Frog (*Discoglossus sardus*) 138, 141, 218

Tyrrhenian (Corsican) Swallowtail (*Papilio hospiton*) 218

Tyrrhenian Wall Lizard (*Podarcis tiliguerta*) 141, 219

Umbellate Wintergreen (*Chimaphila umbellata*) 100

Upright Clover (*Trifolium strictum*) 54

Ural Owl (*Strix uralensis*) 12, 111, 113, 119, 171, 223

Usnea longissima >> Old Man's Beard lichen

Valeriana epirota 233

Variegated Monkshood (*Aconitum variegatum*) 148

Vella spinosa 200

Velvet Scoter (*Melanitta fusca*) 14

Verbascum durmitoreum 224

Veronica incana 171

Viola arborescens 179

Viola cazorlensis 197

Viola cheiranthifolia 204

Viola dacica 119

Viola demetria 200

Viola magellensis 232

Viola montcaunica 187

Viola orphanidis 232

Viola palmensis 204

Viola valderia 139

Violet Horned Poppy (*Roemeria hybrida*) 192

Violet Limodore (*Limodora abortiva*) 74, 136, 138, 139, 194, 231

Viper-grass (*Scorzonera humilis*) 85

Viperine Snake (*Natrix maura*) 138, 147, 175, 180, 194, 201

Wall Creeper (*Tichodroma muraria*) 110, 132, 133, 135, 136, 138, 145, 148, 149, 152, 161, 186, 188, 189, 223, 226, 233

Wall-lizard (*Podarcis muralis*) 141, 150, 151, 202–4p, 211, 215

Walrus (*Odobenus rosmarus*) 4

Wart-biter (*Decticus verrucivorus*) 86, 94

Water Buffalo 246

Water Chestnut (*Trapa natans*) 125, 135

Water Dropwort >> *Oenanthe aquatica*

Water Germander (*Teucrium scordium*) 122

Water Lobelia (*Lobelia dortmanna*) 35, 41

Water-milfoil (*Myriophyllum* spp) 15

Water Rail (*Rallus aquaticus*) 60, 70, 71, 74, 82, 105, 122, 135, 146–8p, 160, 211, 235, 238, 248

Water Ringlet (*Erebia pronoe*) 109

Water Saxifrage (*Saxifraga aquatica*) 190

Water-soldier (*Stratiotes aloides*) 50, 84, 171

Water Violet (*Hottonia palustris*) 50, 69, 124

Water Vole (*Arvicola terrestris*) 60, 124, 147, 171, 176

Waxwing (*Bombycilla garrulus*) 6, 18, 19

Western Butterwort >> Pale Butterwort

Western Gorse (*Ulex gallii*) 54

Western Spadefoot Toad (*Pelobates cultripes*) 71, 181, 193, 194, 200

Western Whip Snake (*Coluber viridiflavus*) 126, 150, 219, 248

Wheatear (*Oenanthe oenanthe*) 176, 178, 192, 199–202p, 232, 252–4p

Whimbrel (*Numenius phaeopus*) 4, 18, 32, 34

Whinchat (*Saxicola rubetra*) 81, 104, 105, 146, 163

Whiskered Tern (*Chlidonias hybridus*) 125, 128, 131, 138, 164, 166, 197, 224

White Admiral (*Limenitis camilla*) 51, 103, 113, 208, 232, 233, 254

White-backed Woodpecker (*Dendrocopus leucotos*) 102, 105, 214, 227

White-beaked Sedge (*Rhynchospora alba*) 71

Whitebeam (*Sorbus aria*) 98, 101

White-billed Diver (*Gavia adamsii*) 4

White Crocus (*Crocus albiflorus*) 128

White-faced Darter (*Leucorrhinia dubia*) 36, 73, 94, 95, 146

White-fronted Goose (*Anser albifrons*) 5, 12, 56, 57, 60, 63, 65, 167

White-headed Duck (*Oxyura leucocephala*) 198, 200, 201

White-letter Hairstreak (*Strymonidia w-album*) 122

White Pelican (*Pelecanus onocrotalus*) 171, 230, 231, 245

White Rock-rose (*Helianthemum apenninum*) 108, 123

White Stork (*Ciconia ciconia*) 68, 95, 97, 101, 103, 112, 113, 116, 117, 129, 131, 160, 163, 166, 173, 176, 180, 181, 192, 195, 201, 223, 231, 234, 235, 245–7p, 253

White-tailed Deer (*Odocoileus virginianus*) 21

White-tailed Eagle (*Haliaeetus albicilla*) 1, 5, 8, 17, 18, 21, 27, 35, 83, 93, 95, 97, 107, 115, 116, 127, 164, 166, 169

White Water-lily (*Nymphaea alba*) 44, 71, 88, 97, 125, 170, 178

White-winged Black Tern (*Chlidonias leucopterus*) 170, 171

Whooper Swan (*Cygnus cygnus*) 5, 6, 12, 15, 18, 19, 24, 39, 41, 56, 57, 62, 63

Whorled Sage (*Salvia verticillata; Stachys verticillata*) 160, 169

Whorled Solomon's Seal (*Polygonatum verticillatum*) 98

Wigeon (*Anas penelope*) 1, 39, 51, 63, 64

Wild Asparagus (*Asparagus officinalis*) 65, 122

Wild Boar (*Sus scrofa*) 73, 84–6p, 93, 97, 100, 102, 110, 124, 126, 131, 135, 137, 139, 155, 159, 160, 164, 171, 175, 184, 188–3p, 195, 198, 210–15p, 217, 223, 224, 225, 232, 233, 235, 236, 247

Wildcat (*Felis sylvestris*) 34, 36, 73, 98, 109, 110, 119, 135, 168, 169, 171, 184, 185, 197, 214, 217, 221, 222, 223, 224, 225, 232, 235

Wild Daffodil (*Narcissus pseudonarcissus*) 49, 54, 74

Wild Gladiolus (*Gladiolus illyricus*) 53

Wild Goat 148, 235

Wild Service Tree (*Sorbus torminalis*) 51, 74, 93, 98, 99
Wild Tulip (*Tulipa sylvestris*) 178
Willow Gentian (*Gentiana asclepiadae*) 159
Willow Grouse >> Red Grouse
Wilson's Filmy Fern (*Hymenophyllum wilsonii*) 35, 58
Wintergreens (*Pyrola* spp) 8, 10, 25, 65, 82, 100, 102, 103, 105, 107, 124, 148, 188, 209
Wolf (*Canis lupus*) 6, 7, 18, 19, 107, 109, 110, 117, 119, 175, 177, 184, 185, 191, 214, 217, 223, 224, 225, 227, 230, 232, 233, 235
Wolfsbane (*Aconitum vulpinum*) 13, 145
Wolverine (*Gulo gulo*) 5–7p, 10, 12, 13, 18, 19
Woodchat Shrike (*Lanius senator*) 139, 179, 191, 243, 245
Woodcock Orchid (*Ophrys scolopax*) 130, 237, 245
Wood Cow-wheat (*Melampyrum nemorosum*) 98
Wood Cranesbill (*Geranium sylvaticum*) 48
Wood Lark (*Lullula arborea*) 253
Woodpigeon (*Columba palumbus*) 181
Wood Sandpiper (*Tringa glareola*) 14, 15, 19, 24–8p, 37
Wood Warbler (*Phylloscopus sibilatrix*) 51, 57, 58, 63, 98
Woodwardia radicans 216
Wood White (*Leptidea sinapis*) 56, 57, 62, 63, 65, 98, 123
Woolly Hawkweed (*Hieracium lanatum*) 145
Woolly Inula (*Inula hirta*) 161

Wryneck (*Jynx torquilla*) 21, 100, 123, 126, 161, 171, 213

Xeranthemum annuum 164
Xysticus pini 171

Yellow Anemone (*Anemone ranunculoides*) 128
Yellow Azalea (*Rhododendron luteum*) 241
Yellow Bartsia (*Parentucellia viscosa*) 195
Yellow Bee Orchid (*Ophrys lutea*) 200, 238
Yellow Bellflower (*Campanula thyrsoides*) 159
Yellow Bird's Nest (*Monotropa hypopitys*) 41, 65
Yellow Coris (*Hypericum coris*) 147
Yellow Horned Poppy (*Glaucium flavum*) 249
Yellow Iris (*Iris pseudacorus*) 163

Yellow Marsh Saxifrage (*Saxifraga hirculus*) 5, 19
Yellow Ox-eye (*Buphthalmum salicifolium*) 152
Yellow Pheasant's Eye (*Adonis vernalis*) 16, 160, 167, 168
Yellow Pimpernel (*Lysimachia nemorum*) 63
Yellow Scabious (*Scabiosa ochroleuca*) 109
Yellow Wagtail (*Motacilla flava*) 79
Yellow Water-lily (*Nuphar lutea*) 71, 97, 170
Yellow Whitlow-grass (*Draba aizoides*) 44, 72, 144
Yellow Wood Violet (*Viola biflora*) 98

Zephyr Blue (*Plebejus pylaon*) 193
Zygaena fausta 127